# The Roman Mi

# THE ROMAN MISTRESS

*Ancient and Modern Representations*

Maria Wyke

OXFORD
UNIVERSITY PRESS

OXFORD
UNIVERSITY PRESS

Great Clarendon Street, Oxford OX2 6DP

Oxford University Press is a department of the University of Oxford.
It furthers the University's objective of excellence in research, scholarship,
and education by publishing worldwide in

Oxford New York

Auckland Bangkok Buenos Aires Cape Town Chennai
Dar es Salaam Delhi Hong Kong Istanbul Karachi Kolkata
Kuala Lumpur Madrid Melbourne Mexico City Mumbai Nairobi
São Paulo Shanghai Singapore Taipei Tokyo Toronto

with associated companies in Berlin Ibadan

Oxford is a registered trade mark of Oxford University Press
in the UK and in certain other countries

Published in the United States
by Oxford University Press Inc., New York



First published 2002
First published in paperback 2007



British Library Cataloguing in Publication Data

Wyke, Maria.
The Roman mistress : gender, politics, love poetry, reception / Maria Wyke.
p. cm.
Includes bibliographical references.
1. Love poetry, Latin—History and criticism. 2. Cleopatra, Queen of Egypt, d. 30 B.C.—In literature. 3. Cleopatra, Queen of Egypt, d. 30 B.C.—In motion pictures. 4. Meassalina, Valeria, d. 48.—In motion pictures. 5. Messalina, Valeria, d. 48.—In literature. 6. Man-woman relationships in motion pictures. 7. Man-woman relationships in literature. 8. Feminism and literature—Rome. 9. Feminism and motion pictures. 10. Women and literature—Rome. 11. Women in motion pictures. 12. Sex role in literature. 13. Mistresses—Rome. I. Title.
PA6029.L6 W95 2002
871′.01093543′082—dc21 2001039751

ISBN 978-0-19-815075-6 (Hbk.) 978-0-19-922833-1 (Pbk.)

1 3 5 7 9 10 8 6 4 2

Typeset by SPI Publisher Services, Pondicherry, India
Printed in Great Britain
on acid-free paper by
Biddles Ltd., King's Lynn, Norfolk

# *Acknowledgements*

I would like to thank the following for generously giving permission to reproduce (in various states of revision) papers that have been published previously: *Helios* (Ch. 1); The Roman Society (Ch. 2); The Cambridge Philological Society (Ch. 3); Gerald Duckworth & Co. Ltd (Ch. 4); *Ramus* (Ch. 5); Bristol Classical Press (Ch. 6); Routledge (Chs. 7 and 8). Chapters 1–4 contain only minor editorial changes, including a new introduction for Chapter 4. Throughout these chapters, however, I have attempted to add in the notes (in the form 'see now') reference to the most recent literature that supports or challenges my arguments. Chapters 5 and 6 have been significantly revised and extended to take into account developments in scholarship on Augustan culture up to and including part of 2001. Chapters 7 and 8 revise, collate, and elaborate on a chapter of my book on ancient Rome in film and an article jointly written by myself and Dominic Montserrat on 'Cleomania'. Chapters 9 and 10 are completely new.

I am greatly indebted to John Henderson with whom I had the good fortune to begin my research into representations of the mistress in Augustan love poetry. In recent years, Mathilde Skoie has continued to provide me with opportunities to discuss love poetry and scholarship on it, and generously kept me supplied with new literature in the field. I would also like to thank Margaret Malamud for introducing me to various archives in Washington and New York, and for being such an enthusiastic companion in the study of ancient Rome in modern popular culture, and Dominic Montserrat for our enjoyable discussions of the process of metabiography (that is, in our case, an examination of the process whereby the lives of ancient Egyptians and Romans are represented in modern culture).

Susanna Braund and Stephen Hinds kindly supported my proposal to write this book at a number of stages, while Duncan Kennedy and Amy Richlin offered detailed comments on and criticisms of my original proposal. While I may not always have responded as they wished, I am very grateful for their stimulating suggestions. I was able to complete the larger part of the project as a result of two terms leave in 2000 supported by the Arts and Humanities Research Board and the University of Reading, while the British Academy funded the cost of obtaining illustrations and visiting archives in Rome. I would like to thank Andrew Wallace-Hadrill for the hospitality of the British School at Rome, Maria Pia Malvezzi for the pursuit of Italian permissions and photographs, and Valerie Scott for bibliographic advice. As ever, Ned Comstock of the USC Cinema and Television Library was an invaluable source of material on American popular culture.

Susanne Dixon, Bob Gurval, Mary Hamer, Paul Allen Miller, Pino Pucci, Mathilde Skoie, and Effrosini Spentzou all generously provided me with access to their work prior to publication. Margaret Miles, who invited me to a conference at the University of Urvine on Cleopatra and Egyptomania, kindly allowed me to use material here which will also be published in a joint article with Dominic Montserrat as part of a collected edition of the conference papers.

Finally, I would like to express my gratitude to David Oswell who helped me finish this project by talking about other things.

M.W.

*London*
*April 2001*

# Contents

# *List of Illustrations*

# Introduction

This volume of essays explores the cultural production of modern Italy, Britain, and the United States as well as that of Augustan Rome. It analyses representations of the women of the ancient world in Latin love poetry and British television drama, in Roman historiography and nineteenth-century criminal anthropology, on classical coinage and college websites, as poetic metaphor and in the Hollywood star system. Binding these essays together, as my title suggests, is a central concern with the production, dissemination, and consumption of woman as Roman mistress (and here I include Cleopatra, queen of Egypt, as the infamous mistress of Romans) and with the deployment of the Roman mistress as a site for the display and interrogation of both ancient and modern genders and political systems. Here I set out how these essays (and their relation) contribute to feminist scholarship both on antiquity and the classical tradition.

The elegiac mistress has long occupied a central place in academic debates about the relationship between the lived experience of Roman women and their representation in Latin literature. Unlike the producers of Roman epic, satire, tragedy, or comedy, the authors of Latin elegy frequently focus on a beloved woman as the reason for their existence both as poet and as lover. The first-person male narrator of Propertian love elegy, in particular, demonstrates an anti-domestic, anti-familial obsession for a woman who is not his wife, and by whom he is completely dominated. *Cynthia* stands as the first word of the first poem of the Propertian corpus and names the object of a desire both to love and to write a woman provocatively.

Judith Hallett first placed Propertian elegy at the centre of debates about Roman women and their representation in an article that appeared in 1973 as part of a special issue of the journal *Arethusa* dedicated to women in antiquity. There she argued that Propertian elegy offered a realistic representation of a woman loved for her transgression of traditional Roman prescriptions for femininity and female sexuality and that, by virtue of this critique of conventional Roman womanhood, such poetry carried the appeal of a feminist message. If, in the course of almost thirty years of subsequent scholarship, the feminism of Propertian elegy has been contested, the importance of his poetry to the development of feminist scholarship on Roman women has not (see, for example, the introductions to and contents of *Feminist Theory and the Classics*, eds. Nancy Rabinowitz and Amy Richlin, 1993; *Roman Sexualities*, eds. Judith Hallett and Marilyn Skinner, 1997; *Reading Roman Women* by Susanne Dixon, 2001; and the special issues on elegy of *Helios* in 1998, *Classical World* in 1999, and *Arethusa* in 2000).[1] In this respect, analysis of Propertian love poetry parallels and intersects with that on Catullan, where critics like Marilyn Skinner, Micaela Janan, and William Fitzgerald have disputed claims for a relation between the poetic representation of the beloved mistress Lesbia and her supposed historical inspiration Clodia. Instead they draw attention to Lesbia's depiction in Catullan poetry as an instance of the instability of Roman conceptions of femininity (for she is simultaneously depicted as demonized whore and exalted goddess), to the troubled masculinity of the authorial narra-

[1] Following the emphases of Hallett, the essays on love poetry in this volume focus on the supposedly realistic representations of women in the Propertian corpus and their relation to Augustan society. The elegies of Ovid are considered only where they appear responsive to those of Propertius, and those of Tibullus scarcely feature at all.

tor and its grounding in late republican culture, and to the gendered reception of Catullus both ancient and modern.

My own past analyses of the mistress in Latin elegy which form the first four chapters of *Part 1: Love Poetry* can be contextualized and historicized as part of the gradual development of feminist scholarship on ancient Rome away from an exclusive interest in images of women to a broader concern with issues of gender, the relation between representations of femininity and masculinity, and the inscription of gender onto other discourses of power. During the course of the 1970s and on into the 1980s, attention had been focused on the problem of whether it was possible to retrieve female voices—any trace of real women—from Roman texts that were almost exclusively written by, and skewed towards, the male elite. From the later 1980s, attention turned first to the textuality of Roman women (whether manifested in poetry, oratory, historiography, or material culture) and then to the intersection of their representation with discourses of gender and sexuality and with social and political systems.[2] Thus motivating my first four chapters is a concern to distinguish the mistress of Propertian love poetry from any specific Augustan woman, to demonstrate the textuality of Cynthia even at the level of the beautiful flesh with which she is ascribed, and to argue that her erotic dominance over her lover-poet serves to mark him as morally and politically irresponsible—so enslaved to love as to be incapable of being a proper Augustan citizen or soldier. The perversity of Cynthia serves her author's poetics of delicate versifying and his politics of immorality.

The gender play of Augustan elegy is now well established, as demonstrated in the survey and analysis of feminist scholarship on the genre through the 1990s and on into the twenty-first century that forms my fifth chapter. Critics now regularly recognize that a

[2] For the general shift in feminist scholarship on ancient Rome from the study of images of women to that of gender relations, see esp. Richlin (1992*a*); Rabinowitz and Richlin (1993); Skinner (1993*a*); Greene (1998), pp. xi–xiii; Dixon (2001), ch. 1.

transgressive femininity is deployed in Augustan love poetry in a manner that manifests unease with conventional Roman categories of gender (especially the masculine) and with changes in other hierarchical systems of power that intersect with gender (especially that between patron and client, but also ruler and subject, master and slave, Roman and non-Roman). Roman love poetry invites us to assess its deployment of femininity as a mechanism for the contestation of social and political structures and encourages its readers to problematize woman as both a concept and an identity, especially where it offers extended depictions of the mistress and the matron, the virgin and the madam, in Propertius' fourth poetry-book, as Micaela Janan makes clear in *The Politics of Desire: Propertius IV* (2001).

Both masculinity and femininity are placed in the forefront of Augustan elegy as sites of negotiation and contestation. Elegy interrogates gender but it also constitutes a social technology for gender production. Recent developments in scholarship on Latin literature and Roman gender argue for the interdependence of literature, politics, and gender in Roman culture. While critics like Thomas Habinek (in *The Politics of Latin Literature: Writing, Identity and Empire*, 1998) have argued that literary production at Rome was not a purely aesthetic activity but a practice of power that could enable social, political, and economic activity, others like Maud Gleason (in *Making Men: Sophists and Self-Presentation in Ancient Rome*, 1995) have observed that Roman masculinity was constantly under construction and open to scrutiny in the performance and reception of certain types of cultural production such as rhetorical declamation. It is in such a context, I argue in Chapter 5, that Augustan elegy should be interpreted as itself a practice of power and a performance of gender.

Much recent work on Roman women and representation demonstrates an increasing interest in issues of performance, reading, and reception, recognizing that analysis of how femininity or masculinity is deployed in a text is bound up with the question of how representations of gender are consumed, whether at the point of original performance, during the ancient reading and re-reading of books, in the history of scholarship, modern rereadings, or appropriations and transformations of such representations for medieval through to modern cultural consumption. In *Engendering Rome: Women in Latin Epic* (2000), for example, A. M. Keith explores the social and institutional contexts in which Latin epic was first encountered and interpreted in order to demonstrate its original function as an education for young males into Roman conventions of manliness. She also concludes her discussion with the argument that if scholars wish to map the *full* dynamics of Latin epic's reproduction and interrogation of gender then an important area for future investigation should be its *full* reception history, including the examination of non-institutional, non-elite, non-male responses to its representation of women.

With regard to the genre of love poetry and its ordering of the female, such gender-oriented reception studies have been extended beyond antiquity even to the present. In *Reading Sulpicia: Commentaries 1475 to 1990* (2002), Mathilde Skoie examines responses in the tradition of commentary-writing from the Italian renaissance on to contemporary Germany to the problematic intrusion of a female poet-lover and a feminine subjectivity in the genre of Latin love elegy. She argues that, throughout the centuries, commentators' interpretations of the poems of Sulpicia are products of the intersection between the Latin text and the commentators' own cultural assumptions about gender, sexuality, and 'feminine' writing. Meanwhile, the classical scholars who have edited *Sex and Gender in Medieval and Renaissance Texts: The Latin Tradition* (1997), Barbara Gold, Paul Allen Miller, and Chuck Platter, argue that the ideological values encoded in representations of the feminine and the female body in Latin literature from the fifth to the sixteenth centuries can be better understood in terms of how those texts appropriate and reconfigure the representations of femininity they have inherited from the classical tradition for poetic eroticism.

The second part of *The Roman Mistress* constitutes my own contribution to the new trajectories now developing for the study of Roman women and representation in the area of reception studies outlined above (and, in particular, addresses the concern to trace non-elite and female responses to Roman representations of women). It also continues my own particular concern with the transgressive figure of the Roman mistress and her deployment as a site for the exploration of issues of gender and politics. Here, however, I have chosen to concentrate on the figure of Cleopatra (as the mistress of Romans and described by Propertius himself as the *meretrix regina* or 'whore queen') and that of Messalina (described by Juvenal as the *meretrix Augusta* or 'imperial whore'). I have not included a study of the modern reception of Sulpicia or the mistresses of Augustan elegy, because they have not received anything like the same degree of dissemination or attracted the same kind of high political charge as have Cleopatra and Messalina. In my chapters on Messalina, for example, I note that from the 1870s the empress even came to name and to embody modern female delinquency, such that women's erotic gestures could now be described disapprovingly as 'Messalinian' and her portrait bust be used as a visual index of the physiological deceitfulness of nineteenth-century female criminals.

I begin *Part 2: Reception* with a bridging chapter on the reconfiguration of the Ptolemaic queen Cleopatra in Augustan poetry that looks back to my earlier studies of the mistress in Roman elegy (since Propertius deploys the relationship between Cleopatra and Antony as an historical exemplar for his own characterization as dominated by a mistress) and forward to the following four chapters on the much later reception of Cleopatra and Messalina in the popular cultural production of Italy, the United States, and Great Britain. I here discuss the role of gender and the depiction of a transgressive mistress in the very formation and justification of the Augustan principate, as western civilization is represented as needing virile rescue from the threat of female barbarism.

The remainder of Part 2, following the strategies of analysis I undertook in *Projecting the Past: Ancient Rome, Cinema and History* (1997), explores the popular appropriation of ancient representations of the transgressive *meretrix* to form part of modern technologies for the widespread display and interrogation of modern femininity and female sexuality, and of modern national identities and imperialisms. In my last four chapters, I focus on popular culture, particularly (although not exclusively) on cinema, as popular culture supplies an opportunity for the production of a reception history of the Roman mistress that can document mass, informal, female responses to her representation. Feminist classical scholarship has also borrowed much from the theories of feminist film studies in order to investigate Roman representations of women. Laura Mulvey's analysis of visual pleasure and narrative cinema has been much favoured as a method for engendering Roman literary eroticism in terms of a masculine scopophilic gaze on a feminine subject who has been fetishized and deprived of narrative agency.[3] Similarly, it is from Teresa de Lauretis' explication of cinema as a social technology of gender that Alison Keith and I have borrowed in order to argue for Latin epic and elegy, respectively, as such technologies. Nowhere, however, have classical scholars acknowledged that representations of Roman women themselves form part of cinema's technology of gender or that the gaze on such representations can be far more complex than the Mulvian theoretical model admits.

The final chapters of *The Roman Mistress* survey changes in her popular representation from the nineteenth century through to the late twentieth, as that representation is progressively articulated with concerns over modern women's entry into public and political authority, their development of sexual identities outside marriage and reproduction, the formation of the women's movement, and even of feminist activism itself. One central and important feature of this work on modern Cleopatras and Messalinas is that, with the wide body of evidence available (not just film texts, but also studio publicity and pressbooks, newspaper reviews, articles in fan and women's magazines, interviews with film stars), a study can take

[3] See e.g. Fitzgerald (1995), 146–9; Fredrick (1997); Flaschenriem (1997), 269; Greene (1998), 73–4 and 82, and (1999), 410–11.

place of how identification with these Roman mistresses is solicited by directors and studios and how absorbed by audiences. Performed by modern female film stars, these Roman mistresses are glamourized and commodified. Audiences in the cinema are invited—as women — to neglect the historical narratives that punish Cleopatra and Messalina for their political and sexual transgressions of conventional femininity, to turn on them instead an active consumer gaze, and to purchase associated goods outside the cinema that will shape their own bodies along seemingly ancient contours. Whether as an act of conformity or sedition, we are offered the opportunity to become Roman mistresses ourselves.

# PART 1

# *Love Poetry*

# 1

# Mistress and Metaphor in Augustan Elegy

## WRITTEN AND LIVING WOMEN

A pressing and persistent problem confronts work on the women of ancient Rome: a need to determine the relation between the realities of women's lives and their representation in Latin literature. Several of the volumes on women in antiquity which appeared in the course of the 1980s exposed the methodological problems associated with any study of women in Greek and Roman literary texts.[1] Twenty years later, moreover, the historian Susanne Dixon opens *Reading Roman Women: Sources, Genres and Real Life* (2001) with the admission that she finds herself more sceptical than ever about the possibilities of extracting substantive information about Roman women from the ancient sources.[2] In any study of the relations between Rome's

This chapter is a revised version of an article first published in *Helios* 16.1 (1989), 25–47.

[1] See, for example, the comments of Foley in her preface to *Reflections of Women in Antiquity* (1981), the survey by Fantham (1986), and the articles of Skinner and Culham in *Helios* 13/2 (1986).

[2] I am extremely grateful to Susanne Dixon for providing me with access to the manuscript of her book prior to publication.

written and living women, the heroines of Augustan elegy deserve particular scrutiny because the literary discourse in which they appear purports to be an author's personal confession of love.[3] The texts of Latin love poetry are frequently constructed as first-person, authorial narratives of desire for women who are individuated by name, physique, and temperament. This poetic technique tempts us to suppose that, in some measure, elegy's female subjects reflect the lives of specific Augustan women.

Moreover, Augustan elegy has set an especially seductive trap for historians of women's lives in antiquity. For, written in an autobiographical mode, it appears to confide to its readers a poet's personal confession of love for a woman who is not his wife. Read uncritically, such love poetry has been employed to confirm the existence in Augustan Rome of a whole movement of sophisticated and sexually liberated ladies, as in J. P. V. D. Balsdon's study *Roman Women: Their History and Habits* (1962) and Sarah Pomeroy's *Goddesses, Whores, Wives and Slaves* (1975).[4] Propertius' Cynthia, Tibullus' Delia and Nemesis, at times even Ovid's Corinna, have been extracted from their poetic world to become representative of a cultured society 'où l'émancipation féminine se traduit avant tout par la recherche d'une liberté dans l'amour' (where female emancipation expresses itself above all in the search for erotic freedom).[5] Working from a somewhat different perspective, Ronald Syme suggested a more cautious assessment of the elegiac heroine's place in history. Although proposing that Ovid's poetry has much to offer the historian, Syme did not himself employ the *Amores* as source material for the construction of an Augustan demi-monde. Yet he still set out the general social

[3] Most recently, in the preface to her book on Roman women, Dixon (2001) calls elegy (along with the genres of satire and the novel) an essential if troubling historical source, and devotes a chapter to the analysis of its deceptive strategies of representation.

[4] Balsdon (1962), 191–2 and 226; Pomeroy (1975), 172.

[5] Fau (1978), 103, and cf. Grimal (1963).

conditions in which he saw the mistresses of elegy operating: a post-civil war period that would have witnessed a number of women reduced to a marginal existence through either calamity or a love of pleasure.[6]

In presenting a first-person narrator who is indifferent to marriage and subject to a mistress, Augustan elegy also poses an intriguing question of important literary and social dimensions: if it focuses on a female subject who apparently operates outside the traditional constraints of marriage and motherhood, could it constitute the advocacy of a better place for women in the ancient world? Could Augustan elegy be offering its readers realistic representations of women bound up with a feminist message?[7] This question has generated considerable controversy, as revealed by the initiatory debate between Judith Hallett and Aya Betensky that took place in a special issue of the journal *Arethusa* (1973) dedicated to the study of women in antiquity. The special issue itself formed part of the initiatory debates on women in antiquity instituted by feminist scholarship of the 1970s.[8]

In particular, the corpus of Propertian poems seems to hold out the hope that we may read through its written woman, Cynthia, to a living mistress. Poem 1.3, for example, conjures up before its readers a vision of an autobiographical event. The first-person narrator recalls the night he arrived late and drunk by his mistress's bed. The remembered occasion unfolds through time, from the moment of the lover's arrival to his beloved's awakening. The details of the beloved's sleeping posture, her past cruelty, and her present words of reproach all seem further to authenticate the tale. The portrait of a Cynthia possessed of a beautiful body, a bad temper, and direct

[6] Syme (1978), 200–3.

[7] As now Hallett (1993*a*), 65, reformulating her earlier views on Propertius' poetry in particular.

[8] On which, see now Hallett (1993*a*), 62–5, Miller and Platter (1999*a*), 405, and the discussion in Ch. 5 below.

speech inclines us to believe that she once lived beyond the poetic world as the flesh-and-blood mistress of an Augustan poet.[9]

Even the existence of Cynthia within a literary work appears to be explained away. Poem 1.8 creates the illusion that it constitutes a fragment of a real conversation. The persistent employment of the second-person pronoun, the punctuation of the text by questions and wishes that centre on 'you', turns the poem itself into an event. As we read, Cynthia is being implored to remain at Rome with her poet. Subsequently, we are told that this poetic act of persuasion has been successful:

> hanc ego non auro, non Indis flectere conchis,
> sed potui blandi carminis obsequio.
> sunt igitur Musae, neque amanti tardus Apollo,
> quis ego fretus amo: Cynthia rara mea est! (1.8.39–42)

> [Her I, not with gold, not with Indian pearls, could
> turn, but with a caressing song's compliance.
> There are Muses then, and, for a lover, Apollo is not slow:
> on these I relying love: rare Cynthia is mine!]

Writing poetry, on this account, is only the instrument of an act of courtship. The text itself encourages us to overlook its status as an Augustan poetry-book and to search beyond it for the living mistress it seems to woo.[10]

There are, however, some recognized dangers in responding to Propertian poetry in this way, for other prominent features of Augustan elegy conflict with its apparently autobiographical narrative structure. Not only is elegy's personal confession of passion articulated in a manner which is highly stylized and conventional, but Hellenistic and Roman traditions for erotic writing also contribute clearly to the formation of the world in which the elegiac lover and his mistress move. Once recognized, such discrepancies undermine

[9] For a deconstruction of the apparent realism of poem 1.3, see Wyke (1984) and now Greene (1998), 51–9.

[10] For the theme of poetry as courtship, see further Ch. 2 below.

any attempt to construct a simple relation between elegiac verse and the world in which it was composed.[11] Augustan elegy has therefore been identified as poetic fiction, and the extreme biographical methodology of the nineteenth and early twentieth centuries—the search for close correspondences between the individual characters and events of the text and those of its author and his milieu—has long since been abandoned. Yet neither has the opposite view (that the mistresses of elegy are entirely artificial constructs) proved satisfactory; for, like the Platonic assessment of literary processes, the theory that Latin erotic discourse is modelled on Hellenistic literature, which is itself modelled on Hellenistic life, leaves Augustan poetry and its female subjects at several removes from reality. Most commonly, critics have recognized the presence of considerable artifice in the elegiac texts, yet continued to treat their female figures as belonging to a special category of discourse; a window onto the reality of female lives at Rome. The reader is allowed to move along an unobstructed pathway from woman of fiction to woman of flesh.

An early example of the critical strategies employed to isolate the elegiac mistress from poetic artifice, and to safeguard her status as a living individual, can be found in Jean-Paul Boucher's *Études sur Properce: problèmes d'inspiration et d'art* (1965). There, despite his considerable interest in the impact of Hellenistic literary practices on the Propertian corpus, the author concluded his studies by trying to construct a plausible portrait of a Roman woman out of Cynthia's poetic characteristics. A chapter entitled 'Poésie et vérité' conveniently provided a bridge between formalistic accounts of Propertian poetic techniques and romantic readings of the narrative's heroine. The textual characteristics of a fictive female are disengaged from their context in a poetry-book and reshaped into the detailed portrait of a girlfriend by whom the text was inspired.[12] So constructed, Cynthia is then positioned in the social formation of the Augustan

[11] See e.g. Du Quesnay (1973), 1–2; Veyne (1983), 11–12; Griffin (1985), p. ix.

[12] See esp. Boucher (1965), 468–9.

epoch; the female beloved is read as referring out of the poetic sphere to a specific 'emancipated' woman of the late first century BC. Out of the elegiac text is born the historical reality of a liberated lady.

In the latter part of the twentieth century, other critics have explicitly presented models of the relation between elegiac representations and the realities of women's lives in Rome that they thought capable of accommodating the literariness of elegiac writing while keeping elegy's written women placed firmly on the map of the Augustan world. Poets deal in 'verbal artefacts', according to R. O. A. M. Lyne in *The Latin Love Poets: From Catullus to Horace* (1980, reprinted 1996 and 2000), yet their poetry 'adumbrates', 'embodies', or 'emblazons' life.[13] Love elegy, Jasper Griffin argues in *Latin Poets and Roman Life* (1985, reprinted 1994), is neither an open window affording glimpses of individual Roman lives, nor a mirror offering their clear reflection, but a *picture* of Roman realities over which has been painted a dignifying, idealizing veneer of poetic devices. Poetic artifice can now be readily accommodated to autobiographical narratives, for it simply raises the realities of Roman life to the level of idealized art: Cynthia is a profit-making courtesan over whom the heroines of myth cast a glittering sheen; stylized depictions of female nakedness constitute reflections transposed into poetry of encounters with professionals in Rome.[14] Thus Augustan love poetry has continued to be beset by the romantic theory that it was produced to express its authors' own amatory experiences.

Idioms such as 'adumbrations' or 'transposed reflections' form the ingredients of a critical discourse that no longer treats elegiac poems as accurate, chronological documents of an author's affairs, yet still describes their stylized heroines as somehow concealing specific Augustan girlfriends.[15] Hans-Peter Stahl's contribution to the litera-

[13] Lyne (1980), p. viii and *passim*.

[14] See esp. Griffin (1985), 105, 139, and 110. On Griffin, see now Kennedy (1993), 2–5.

[15] See e.g. Williams (1968), 542.

ture on the Propertian corpus, *Propertius: 'Love' and 'War'. Individual and State under Augustus* (1985), for example, reveals the critical laxity that is often at work. Stahl recognizes that Cynthia possesses 'literary qualities', admits nevertheless that his own work is constructed from a naive standpoint, and leaves it to his readers to draw the line they deem appropriate between Augustan reality and elegiac literariness. Yet the structure of his book does not otherwise assist such an enterprise, for neither recognition nor admission appears until the last footnote of Stahl's fifth chapter, while throughout the main text frequent reference is made to two formative experiences of love and war in Propertius' life—a torturing love for Cynthia and the massacre of Perusia. Readers of Stahl's book are actively directed to look out of the Propertian corpus to the inspiring realities of a woman's love life in Augustan Rome.[16]

Thus the realism of the elegiac texts continues to tempt us. While reading of women who possess some realistic features, we may think that—once we make some allowances for the distortions that a male lover's perspective and a poet's self-conscious literary concerns may impose—we still have an opportunity to reconstruct the lives of some real Augustan mistresses. Controversy arises, however, when we ask exactly what allowances should be made. Is the process of relating women in poetic texts to women in society simply a matter of removing a veneer of poetic devices to disclose the true picture of living women concealed beneath?

It is precisely because readers of Cynthia have encountered such difficulties as these that I propose to explore aspects of the problematic relation between women in texts and women in society by focusing on the Propertian corpus of elegiac poems. My purpose is, first, to survey approaches to the issue of elegiac realism and by placing renewed emphasis on Cynthia as a *written* woman to argue that she should be related not to the love life of her poet but to the 'grammar' of his poetry; second, to demonstrate that the poetic discourse of

[16] On Stahl, see further Wyke (1989*c*) and now Kennedy (1993), 35–7.

which she forms a part is firmly engaged with and shaped by the political, moral, and literary discourses of the Augustan period, and therefore that to deny Cynthia an existence outside poetry is not to deny her a relation to society; and, third, to suggest that a study of elegiac metaphors and their application to elegiac mistresses may provide a fruitful means of reassessing whether Augustan elegy carries the attraction of a feminist message.

## AUGUSTAN GIRLFRIENDS/ELEGIAC WOMEN

The first-person narratives of the elegiac texts and their partial realism entice us. They lead us to suppose that these texts form poetic paintings of reality and their female subjects poetic portraits of real women.[17] Yet realism itself is a quality of a text, not a direct manifestation of a real world. Analysis of textual realism discloses that it is not natural but conventional. To create the aesthetic effect of an open window onto a reality lying just beyond, literary works employ a number of formal strategies that change through time and between discourses.[18]

As early as the 1950s, Archibald Allen drew attention to this disjunction between realism and reality in the production of Augustan elegy. He noted that the realism of the Propertian corpus is partial since, for example, it does not extend to the provision of a convincing chronology for a supposedly extratextual affair. And, focusing on the issue of 'sincerity', Allen argued that the ancient world was capable of drawing a distinction that we should continue to observe, between a poet's art and his life. From Catullus to Apuleius, ancient

[17] See now Kennedy (1993), 1–23, on the centrality to scholarship on elegy of a concern with the relationship between representation and reality, and his analysis of some of the methodological problems attached to explications of that relationship (including my own).

[18] A classic exposition of the disjunction between textual realism and reality, and a detailed exploration of the strategies of nineteenth-century French realist writing, can be found in Barthes' *S/Z* (1975). For the importance of this work, see Hawkes (1977), 106–22.

writers could claim that poetry was distinct from its poet and ancient readers could construe 'sincere' expressions of personal passion as a function of poetic style.[19]

More recently, in *L'Élégie érotique romaine: l'amour, la poésie et l'occident* (1983), Paul Veyne pursued the idea that the *I* of ancient poets belongs to a different order than do later '*Is*' and suggested that *ego* confers a naturalness on elegy that ancient readers would have recognized as spurious. Exploring the quality of *ego* in elegy's narrative, Veyne further argued that the ancient stylistic rules for 'sincerity' observed in the Catullan corpus were scarcely obeyed in Augustan love elegy. Full of traditional poetic conceits, literary games, mannerisms, and inconsistencies, the texts themselves raise doubts about their potential as autobiography.[20]

Both these readings of elegiac first-person narratives warn us to be cautious in equating a stylistic realism with Augustan reality. But what of the particular realist devices used to depict women? Some modern critics have thought, for example, that the elegiac texts do offer sufficient materials from which to sketch the characteristics and habits of their authors' girlfriends or, at the very least, contain scattered details that together make up plausible portraits. From couplets of the Propertian corpus, John Sullivan assembles a physique for Cynthia: 'She had a milk-and-roses complexion. Her long blonde hair was either over-elaborately groomed or else, in less guarded moments, it strayed over her forehead in disarray . . . Those attractive eyes were black. She was tall, with long slim fingers.'[21] Oliver Lyne adds credible psychological characteristics:

> We find a woman of fine artistic accomplishments who is also fond of the lower sympotic pleasures; superstitious, imperious, wilful, fearsome in

[19] Allen (1950*a* and *b*).

[20] Veyne (1983). On Veyne see Wyke (1989*c*), and now Kennedy (1993), 91–100; Miller and Platter (1999*a*), 404; Janan (2001), 7. Cf. now Sharrock (2000) on how Propertian elegy entices its readers to take its elegiac world as real while simultaneously inviting them to see how the perspective of its narrator is undermined.

[21] Sullivan (1976), 80.

temper—but plaintive if she chooses, or feels threatened; pleasurably passionate—again if she chooses. I could go on: Propertius provides a lot of detail, direct and circumstantial. But the point I simply want to make is that the figure who emerges is rounded and credible: a compelling 'courtesan' amateur or professional.[22]

An ancient tradition seems to provide some justification for this process of extracting plausible portraits of Augustan girlfriends out of the features of elegiac poetry-books. Some two centuries after the production of elegy's written women, in *Apologia* 10, Apuleius listed the 'real' names that he claimed lay behind the elegiac labels *Cynthia* and *Delia*. Propertius, we are informed, hid his mistress Hostia behind *Cynthia*, and Tibullus had Plania in mind when he put *Delia* in verse. If we accept these identifications then, however stylized, idealized, or mythicized the elegiac women Cynthia and Delia may be, their titles are to be read as pseudonyms and their textual characteristics as reflections of the features of two extratextual mistresses.[23]

From the outset, however, the difficulty involved in assimilating all the written women of elegy to living, liberated ladies has been clear. Beginning with the ancient tradition that does not offer 'real' names to substitute for *Nemesis* or *Corinna*, the procedure is not uniformly applied. The inappropriateness of attempting to assimilate Ovid's Corinna to a living woman is generally acknowledged, because the text in which she appears easily reads as a playful travesty of earlier love elegy. Many commentators have agreed with the view that Corinna does not have 'un carattere precisamente individuabile ed è priva di autenticità, perché in realtà non esiste' (does not have a precisely recognizable character and is without authenticity, because in reality she does not exist). She constitutes, rather, a generalized figure of the mistress.[24]

[22] Lyne (1980), 62.

[23] For *Cynthia* and *Delia* as pseudonyms, see e.g. Williams (1968), 526–42, and now Newman (1997), 301–4.

[24] Bertini (1983), p. xvi. Cf. e.g. Grimal (1963), 156; Bright (1978), 104; Barsby (1979), 15–16. The question of whether Corinna had an identity independently of the

The Tibullan corpus has been classified as manifestly more 'sincere' than the Ovidian, yet the second Tibullan heroine has likewise aroused suspicion. David Bright offers detailed support for an earlier reading of Nemesis 'as a shadowy background for conventional motifs'.[25] The first Tibullan heroine, Delia, also seems to be entangled in elegy's literary concerns, as the characteristics of Nemesis in Tibullus' second poetry-book are counterbalanced by the characteristics of Delia in the first to produce a poetic polarity. Delia is goddess of Day, Nemesis daughter of Night.[26] Bright states, 'the flexibility of fundamental characteristics and the meaning of the two names, indicates that Delia and Nemesis should be regarded as essentially literary creations.'[27]

In *The Latin Love Poets* (1980, reprinted 1996 and 2000), Oliver Lyne questioned the need for even these concessions to poetic artifice. He found no compelling reason to doubt that Nemesis and Delia were pseudonyms of particular women, and even attempted tentatively to reappropriate Corinna for realism by drawing attention to a physique which John Sullivan had earlier assembled: 'physically she was *candida* with rosy cheeks, tall and dignified . . . with small feet and an abundance of fine closely-curled hair.'[28] The fabric of a poetic text is again turned into a mistress's flesh. Thus despite accounts which foreground the artifice of elegiac poetry and its mistresses, many critics have persisted in reading out from the female subjects of its discourse to specific liberated ladies. Faced with such romantic

elegiac text is insoluble for Du Quesnay (1973), 2–3, and of no literary interest for Sullivan (1961), 522–8. On the fictiveness of Corinna, see also Ch. 4 below and, now, Boyd (1997), 132–64.

[25] Williams (1968), 537.

[26] Bright (1978), 99–123. See now Fineberg (1993) on the female personifications of Age, Punishment, Death, and Night who form part of the narrative transition from bright Delia to dark Nemesis.

[27] Bright (1978), 123.

[28] Lyne (1980), 239–40, argues that 'a reasonable picture does emerge from the poems' of Corinna, and draws attention to, but does not quote, the physique assembled by Sullivan (1961), 524 n. 5. For a living Corinna, cf. Fau (1978), 112, and Green (1982), 22–5. See also the more cautious arguments of McKeown (1987).

readings of Augustan love poetry, we may want to ask whether Propertian realism is anchored any more securely to reality than that of Ovid and Tibullus.

Realist portraits of a mistress do not seem to have so bold an outline, or so persistent a presence, in Propertian poetry as to guarantee for Cynthia a life beyond the elegiac world, because realism is not consistently employed in the corpus and sometimes is challenged or undermined by other narrative devices. Even in Propertius' first poetry-book the apparent confession of an author's love is not everywhere sustained. Poem 1.16, for example, interrupts the realistic use of a first-person narrative. At this point the narrative *I* ceases to be plausible because it is not identifiable with an author and is voiced by a door. Poem 1.20 substitutes for expressions of personal passion the mythic tale of Hercules' tragic love for the boy Hylas. The book closes with the narrator establishing his identity (*qualis*) in terms not of a mistress but of the site of civil war.[29]

The formal strategies that produce for us the sense of an Augustan reality and an extratextual affair are even less prominent or coherent in Propertius' second poetry-book. The *ego* often speaks without such apparently authenticating details as a location, an occasion, or a named addressee. The object of desire is not always specified and sometimes clearly excludes identification with Cynthia. The margins of the book and its core are peopled by patrons and poets or take for their landscape the Greek mountains and brooks of poetic inspiration. At these points, the text's evident concern is not to delineate a mistress but to define its author's poetic practice.[30]

[29] See now Greene (1998), 37–66, and Sharrock (2000) on the strategies deployed even in the *Monobiblos* that challenge or undercut its apparent realism. Cf. Janan (2001), 33–52, on the 'Gallus' poems in particular and their extreme, and disorienting, disjunction.

[30] On the second book's distinctive style, see Veyne (1983), 67 and 71; Papanghelis (1987), 93–7; Ch. 2 below. Cf. now McNamee (1993), who argues that book 2 begins to make explicit the Callimachean poetic concerns expressed implicitly in book 1.

By the third and fourth books a realistically depicted, individuated mistress has ceased to be a narrative focus of Propertian elegy. The third book claims as its inspiration not a girlfriend but another poet. Callimachus has replaced Cynthia as the motivating force for poetic production. The title *Cynthia* appears only as the text looks back at the initial poems of the corpus and draws Cynthia-centred erotic discourse to an apparent close. Far more frequently the first-person authorial narrator speaks of love without specifying a beloved, and poetic eroticism takes on a less personal mode.

In the fourth book there is not even a consistent lover's perspective. Several poems are concerned with new themes, such as the aetiology of *Roma*, rather than the motivations for *amor*. And the narrative *I* fluctuates between a reassuring authorial viewpoint and the implausible voices of a statue, a soldier's wife, and a dead *matrona*. When the more familiar mistress appears, the sequence of poems does not follow a realistic chronology but moves from the stratagems of a dead Cynthia who haunts the underworld (4.7) to those of a living Cynthia who raids a dinner party (4.8).[31]

These inconsistencies and developments in the Propertian mode of incorporating a mistress into elegiac discourse cannot be imputed merely to an author's unhappy experiences in love (to Propertius' progressive disillusionment with a Hostia), for each of the books and their Cynthias seem to be responding to changes in the public world of writing. The general shift from personal confessions of love toward more impersonal histories of Rome may be determined partially by changes in the material processes of patronage in the Augustan era, from the gradual establishment of Maecenas' circle through to the unmediated patronage of the *princeps*,[32] and the particular character of individual poetry-books by the progressive publication of other poetic discourses such as Tibullan elegy, Horatian lyric, and Virgilian

[31] For the narrative techniques of book 4 in particular, see Ch. 3 below and now Janan (2001).

[32] See e.g. Stahl (1985), and now Miller (2001).

epic.[33] But are the individual, realistically depicted Cynthias of the Propertian corpus then immune from such influences?

Literary concerns permeate even the activities and habits of the Cynthias who appear in the first two books. Poem 1.8, for example, implores its Cynthia not to depart for foreign climes and asks: *tu pedibus teneris positas fulcire pruinas, | tu potes insolitas, Cynthia, ferre nives?* (Can you on delicate feet support settled frost? Can you, Cynthia, strange snows endure? 1.8.7–8) The Gallan character of this Cynthia, and the trip from which she is dissuaded, is well known. In Virgil's tenth *Eclogue* attention already had been focused on the laments of the earlier elegiac poet over the absence of another snow-bound elegiac mistress. Propertius caps the Virgilian Gallus, in the field of erotic writing, by contrasting his ultimately loyal Cynthia with the faithless Lycoris. Cynthia's delicate feet both recall and surpass the *teneras plantas* of the wandering Lycoris (*Ecl.* 10.49). Simultaneously, they give her a realizable shape and mark a new place in the Roman tradition for written mistresses.[34]

Similarly, it has been observed that the disturbing narrative techniques of the second book (its discursiveness, parentheses, and abrupt transitions) constitute a response to the publication of Tibullus' first elegiac book.[35] And the process of transforming Propertian elegy in response to another erotic discourse again extends to realist depictions of the elegiac beloved. Poem 2.19 presents a Tibullanized Cynthia, closer in kind to the images of Delia in the countryside than to the first formulation of Cynthia in the *Monobiblos*:

etsi me inuito discedis, Cynthia, Roma,
 laetor quod sine me devia rura coles . . .

[33] See e.g. Hubbard (1974).

[34] For a convenient summary of views on this literary relationship, see Fedeli (1980), 203–5 and 211. Cf. now Newman (1997), 17–53 and Janan (2001), 33–52. For a detailed analysis of how literary concerns are expressed through the Cynthias of books 1 and 2, see Wyke (1984), and now McNamee (1993).

[35] e.g. Hubbard (1974), 57–8, and Lyne (1980), 132.

sola eris et solos spectabis, Cynthia, montis
 et pecus et finis pauperis agricolae. (2.19.1–2, 7–8)

[Even though against my will you leave, Cynthia, Rome,
 I'm glad that without me you'll cultivate wayward fields . . .
Alone you'll be and the lonely mountains, Cynthia, you'll watch
 and the sheep and the borders of the poor farmer.]

Tibullus began his fanciful sketch of a countrified mistress—the guardian (*custos*) of a country estate—with the words *rura colam* (1.5.21). So here *rura coles* begins Cynthia's departure from the generally urban terrain of Propertian discourse. The apparently realistic reference to Cynthia's country visit contains within its terms a challenge to the textual characteristics of a rustic Delia.

The Cynthias of the third and fourth books also disclose the influence of recently published literary works. Book 3 initiates an occasionally playful accommodation of Horatian lyric within erotic elegy. This literary challenge is articulated not only through the enlargement of poetic themes to include social commentary and the elevation of the poet to the rank of priest,[36] but also through the alteration of the elegiac mistress's physique.

The book opens with an erotic twist to the Horatian claim that poetry is an everlasting monument to the poet. For, at 3.2.17–24, Propertian poetry is said to immortalize female beauty (*forma*).[37] The book closes appropriately with the dissolution of that monument to beauty and the threatened construction of one to ugliness:

exclusa inque uicem fastus patiare superbos,
 et quae fecisti facta queraris anus!
has tibi fatalis cecinit mea pagina diras:
 euentum formae disce timere tuae! (3.25.15–18)

[Shut out in turn—may you suffer arrogant contempt,
 and of deeds that you've done may you complain—an old hag!

[36] See e.g. Nethercut (1970), 385–407.

[37] For the comparison with *Odes* 3.30.1–7, see Nethercut (1970), 387, and Fedeli (1985), 90.

These curses deadly for you my page has sung:
the outcome of your beauty learn to fear!]

The threatened transformation of Cynthia on the page from beauty to hag (the dissolution of the familiar elegiac edifice) mirrors similar predictions made about the Horatian Lydia in *Odes* 1.25.9–10.[38]

The two Cynthias of the fourth book take on Homeric rather than Horatian shapes. Although multiple literary influences on the features of these Cynthias may be noted (such as comedy, aetiology, tragedy, epigram, and mime) their pairing takes up the literary challenge recently issued by Virgil. Just as the Virgilian epic narrative conflates an Odyssean and an Iliadic hero in the character of Aeneas, so the Propertian elegiac narrative constructs a Cynthia who becomes first an Iliadic Patroclus returning from the grave (4.7) and then a vengeful Odysseus returning from the war (4.8).

In the last book of the Propertian corpus, the precarious status of realism is put on display. Whole incidents in the lives of a poet and his mistress now reproduce the plots of the Homeric poems, while their details echo passages of the *Aeneid*. In poem 4.7, the first-person authorial narrator recalls the occasion on which he had a vision of his dead mistress. Her reproaches are replete with apparently authenticating incidentals such as a busy red-light district of Rome, worn-down windows, warming cloaks, branded slaves, ex-prostitutes, and wool work. Yet the ghost's arrival and departure, her appearance, and her reproofs sustain persistent links with the heroic world of *Iliad* 23 and the general conventions of epic discourse on visions of the dead. Similarly, in poem 4.8, the first-person narrator recalls the night when Cynthia caught him in the company of other women. The narrative of that night is also littered with apparently authenticating details such as the setting on the Esquiline, local girls, a dwarf, dice, a slave cowering behind a couch, and orders not to stroll in Pompey's portico. Yet Cynthia's sudden return finds her playing the role of an Odysseus to her

[38] Fedeli (1985), 674 and 692–3.

poet's aberrant Penelope. Echoes of *Odyssey* 22 dissolve the poetic edifice of a real Roman event.[39]

When critics attempt to provide a plausible portrait of Cynthia, they must undertake an active process of building a rounded and consistent character out of physical and psychological characteristics that are scattered throughout the corpus and are often fragmentary, sometimes contradictory, and usually entangled in mythological and highly literary lore. Yet the discovery of Gallan, Tibullan, Horatian, and Virgilian Cynthias in the Propertian corpus argues against the helpfulness of this process. The strategies employed in the construction of a realistic mistress appear to change according to the requirements of a poetic project that commences in rivalry with the elegists Gallus and Tibullus and ends in appropriation of the terms of Horatian lyric and Virgilian epic.

It is misleading, therefore, to disengage the textual features of an elegiac mistress from their context in a poetry-book so as to reshape them into the plausible portrait of an Augustan girlfriend, for even the physical features, psychological characteristics, direct speeches, and erotic activities with which Cynthia is provided often seem subject to literary concerns. Thus the realist devices of the Propertian corpus map out only a precarious pathway to the realities of women's lives in Augustan society and often direct us instead toward the features and habits of characters in other Augustan texts.

Yet the repetition of the title *Cynthia* through the course of the Propertian poetry-books may still create the impression of a series of poems about one consistent female figure.[40] Does support remain, then, for a direct link between Cynthia and a Roman woman in the ancient tradition that *Cynthia* operates in elegy as a pseudonym for a living mistress Hostia?

On entry into the Propertian corpus, the epithet *Cynthia* brings with it a history as the marker of a poetic programme. The

[39] For references to the extensive literature on these two poems, see Papanghelis (1987), 145–98 and Chs. 3 and 5 below. See now Janan (2001), 100–27.

[40] Cf. Veyne (1983) on *Delia*.

Hellenistic poet Callimachus had linked Mount Cynthus on Delos with Apollo as the mouthpiece of a poetic creed. That association was reproduced in Virgil's sixth *Eclogue* where the god directing Virgilian discourse away from epic material was given the cult title *Cynthius*.[41] The Propertian text itself draws attention to that history at, for example, the close of the second book where Callimachus, Virgil, Cynthius, and Cynthia are all associated with writing-styles. First Callimachean elegy is suggested as a suitable model for poetic production (2.34.31–2) then, in a direct address to Virgil, *Cynthius* is employed as the epithet of a god with whose artistry the works of Virgil are explicitly compared: *tale facis carmen docta testudine quale* | *Cynthius impositis temperat articulis* (Such song you make, on the learned lyre, as | Cynthius with applied fingers controls, 2.34.79–80). Finally, a reference to *Cynthia* closes the poem and its catalogue of the male authors and female subjects of earlier Latin love poetry: *Cynthia quin etiam uersu laudata Properti*—| *hos inter si me ponere Fama uolet* (Cynthia also praised in verse of Propertius—| if among these men Fame shall wish to place me, 2.34.93–4).

The alignment within a single poem of Callimachus, Virgil, Cynthius, and Cynthia constructs for Propertian elegy and its elegiac mistress a literary ancestry. The title *Cynthia* may be read as a term in the statement of a poetics, as a proper name for the erotic embodiment of a particular poetic creed. In a corpus of poems that frequently voices a preference for elegiac over epic styles of writing, that uses a critical discourse inherited from Callimachus and developed in Virgil's *Eclogues*, the title *Cynthia* contributes significantly to the expression of literary concerns.[42]

The name of the elegiac mistress does not offer us a route out of a literary world to the realities of women's lives at Rome. Yet, as with her other apparently plausible features, her name is inextricably

[41] See Clausen (1976), 245–7, and Boyancé (1956), 172–5.

[42] See Wimmel (1960). For the intimate association of Cynthia and Callimachus in the Propertian corpus, see also Wyke (1984), Ch. 2 below, and now McNamee (1993).

entangled in issues of poetic practice. Any attempt to read through the name *Cynthia* to a living mistress, therefore, overlooks its place in the 'grammar' of elegiac poetry where *Propertius* and *Cynthia* do not perform the same semantic operations. In the language of elegy, a poet generates a different range and level of connotation than his mistress.

The issue of the elegiac mistress's social status further elucidates the peculiar role women play in the poetic language of Augustan love poetry; for, when attempts have been made to reconstruct a real girl-friend out of Cynthia's features, no clear clues have been found in the poems to the social status of a living mistress, and conclusions have ranged from adulterous Roman wife to foreign prostitute, or the evident textual ambiguities have been read as reflections of the fluidity of social status to be expected within an Augustan demi-monde.[43]

In Propertius 2.7, for example, the narrator describes his mistress as having rejoiced at the removal of a law that would have separated the lovers. He declares that he prefers death to marriage:

> nam citius paterer caput hoc discedere collo
> quam possem nuptae perdere more faces,
> aut ego transirem tua limina clausa maritus,
> respiciens udis prodita luminibus. (2.7.7–10)

> [For faster would I suffer this head and neck to part
> than be able at a bride's humour to squander torches,
> or myself a husband pass your shut doors,
> looking back at their betrayal with moist eyes.][44]

And he rejects his civic duty to produce children who would then participate in Augustus Caesar's wars: *unde mihi Parthis natos praebere triumphis? | nullus de nostro sanguine miles erit* (From what cause for Parthian triumphs to offer my sons? | None from my blood will be a

[43] Respectively, Williams (1968), 529–35; Cairns (1972), 156–7; Griffin (1985), 27–8.

[44] The interpretation of verse 8 is open to much dispute. See now Gale (1997) on 2.7, who reads the poem as highly ambiguous or ironic, and cf. Miller (2001), sec. 4.

soldier, 2.7.13–14). Here, if nowhere else in Augustan elegy, we might expect to find a clearly defined social status allocated to the elegiac mistress, because, at this point in the elegiac corpus, the text seems to be directly challenging legal constraints on sexual behaviour.

Nevertheless, even when the elegiac narrative takes as its central focus a legislative issue, no clear social position is allocated to Cynthia. We learn instead that men and women play different semantic roles in this poetic discourse. The female is employed in the text only as a means to defining the male. Her social status is not clearly defined because the dominating perspective is that of the male narrator. What matters is his social and political position as an elite male citizen who, in having a mistress (however indifferent she may be), refuses to be a *maritus* or the father of *milites*.[45]

What this analysis of elegiac realism seems to reveal is that the notion of *concealment* (the idea that the stylized heroines of elegy somehow conceal the identities of specific Augustan girlfriends) is not a helpful term in critical discourse on elegiac women. Perhaps Apuleius' identification of Cynthia with a Hostia is suspect, since it forms part of a theatrical self-defence and should be read in the light of a long-standing interest in biographical speculation. (We do not now accept, for example, Apuleius' identification of Corydon with Virgil or of Alexis with a slave boy of Pollio.)[46] But the point is that, whether or not a Hostia existed who was associated with Propertius, the Cynthia of our text is part of no simple act of concealment.[47]

[45] See esp. Veyne (1983), who argues that it is sufficient for elegy's purposes to locate its *ego* 'chez les marginales' and cf. Conte (1989), 445. See now Konstan (1994), 150–9, who notes that in the elegiac tradition the beloved is neither a *virgo* awaiting a legitimate marriage nor a *matrona* running the marital household, and 'is thus located outside the patrilineal structure that constitutes the status and the horizons of a proper Roman girl' (p. 157). Cf. Myers (1996), 4–6, who adds that the beloved is neither *virgo*, nor *matrona*, nor easily purchasable *meretrix*.

[46] See e.g. Fairweather (1974), 232–6.

[47] See now Kennedy (1993), 83–100 for a detailed discussion of scholarship's concern with the problem of identifying names in the elegiac texts with real people.

While the combination of realist techniques and parodic strategies in the Ovidian corpus is generally thought to deny Corinna any reality, the realist strategies of the Propertian corpus have been isolated from other narrative techniques and left largely unexplored in order to secure for Cynthia an existence outside the text in which we meet her. I have argued, however, that even the realist devices of Propertian elegy can disclose the unreality of elegiac mistresses. Cynthia too is a poetic fiction: a woman in a text, whose physique, temperament, name, and status are all subject to the idiom of that text. So, as part of a poetic language of love, Cynthia should not be related to the love life of her poet but to the 'grammar' of his poetry.[48]

The Propertian elegiac narrative does not, then, celebrate a Hostia, but creates a fictive female whose minimally defined status as mistress, physical characteristics, and name are all determined by the grammar of the erotic discourse in which she appears. The employment of terms like 'pseudonym' in modern critical discourse overlooks the positive act of creation involved in the depiction of elegy's mistresses.[49] Therefore, when reading Augustan elegy, it seems most appropriate to talk not of pseudonyms and poeticized girlfriends but of poetic or elegiac women.

## METAPHORS

So the bond between elegiac women and particular Augustan girlfriends has proved to be very fragile. The realistic features of elegy's heroines seem to owe a greater debt to poetic programmes than to the realities of female forms. But if we deny to Cynthia an existence outside poetry, are we also denying her any relation to society? If elegiac narratives are concerned with fictive females, how do women

[48] Now see further Gold (1993*a*), 87–8, and (1993*b*), 291–2; McNamee (1993); Kennedy (1993); Flaschenriem (1997).

[49] Bright (1978), 103–4.

enter their discourse? What relation might still hold between women in Augustan society and women in its poetic texts? And what function could a realistically depicted yet fictive mistress serve in elegy's aesthetics?

One possible approach to some of these questions has already been suggested, as I have argued that the characteristics of elegiac women are determined by the general idioms of the elegiac discourse of which they form a part, and that Cynthia should be read as firmly shaped by the Propertian poetic project. Yet elegiac discourses and poetic projects are, in turn, firmly engaged with and shaped by the political, moral, and aesthetic discourses of the Augustan period. And so it is through the relation of elegiac narratives to all the other cultural discourses of the specific period in which they were produced that we can at last see a more secure fit between women in elegiac texts and women in Augustan society.

The general idioms peculiar to elegiac writing have been as intriguing to the reader as the specific attributes provided for women at various points in the elegiac corpus, for they seem to be offering a challenging new role for the female, a poetic break away from the traditional duties of marriage and motherhood.

First of all, features of the elegiac vocabulary seem to overturn the traditional Roman discourses of sexuality. In the poetic texts the elegiac hero is frequently portrayed as sexually loyal while his mistress is not.[50] The Propertian lover protests: *tu mihi sola places: placeam tibi, Cynthia, solus* (You alone please me: may I alone please you, Cynthia, 2.7.19). He desires as the wording on his epitaph: *unius hic quondam seruus amoris erat* (Of a single love this man once was the slave, 2.13.36). Now this elegiac expectation of eternal male faithfulness, according to one analysis, 'spurns the double standard characterizing Roman male–female relationships' because, traditionally, extramar-

[50] For male faithfulness in the elegiac corpus, see Lilja (1965), 172–86, and Lyne (1980), 65–7.

ital sex was tolerated for husbands while their wives were legally required to uphold the principle of *fides marita*.[51] It was the ideal of a woman's faithfulness to one man that was most frequently expressed on Roman epitaphs and, furthermore, it was expressed in the same terms as the elegiac ideal: *solo contenta marito, uno contenta marito* (content with her husband alone; content with but one husband).[52]

Another feature commonly cited as a central structuring principle of elegiac desire, and as crucial evidence for an elegiac transformation of traditional sexual roles, is the application of the *seruitium amoris* metaphor to a heterosexual liaison.[53] A parallel for the topos of the lover-as-enslaver can be found in Hellenistic erotic writing, but Augustan elegy's casting of the female in the dominant sexual role seems to work against the operations of other Roman sexual discourses. The Propertian narrator asks: *quid mirare, meam si uersat femina uitam | et trahit addictum sub sua iura uirum?* (Why are you astonished if a woman drives my life | and drags, bound beneath her own laws, a man? 3.11.1–2).[54]

The male narrator is portrayed as enslaved, the female narrative subject as his enslaver. The Tibullan lover, for example, says farewell to his freedom: *hic mihi seruitium uideo dominamque paratam: | iam mihi, libertas illa paterna, uale* (Here for me I see slavery and a mistress at the ready: | now from me, that fathers' freedom, adieu, 2.4.1–2). Thus the control of household slaves, a woman's version of the economic status of a *dominus*, has been transformed figuratively into the erotic condition of control over sexual slaves. The sexual domain of the

[51] Hallett (1973), 111. On the double sexual standard for Roman husbands and wives, see now Dixon (1992), 88; Edwards (1993), 49–53; Williams (1999), 47–56.

[52] *Carm. Epigr.* 455 and 643.5, for which see Williams (1958), 23–5. See now Treggiari (1991), 229–319, and Dixon (1992), 88–90.

[53] For erotic *seruitium* in the elegiac corpus, see Lilja (1965), 76–89; Copley (1947), 285–300; Lyne (1979), 117–30; Conte (1989), 443–4. See now McCarthy (1998); Fitzgerald (2000), 72–7.

[54] For further discussion of Prop. 3.11, see Ch. 6 below.

elegiac *domina* contrasts with that traditionally prescribed for Roman *matronae*, namely keeping house and working wool.[55]

A third significant feature of this poetic discourse is the declaration that the pursuit of love and poetry is a worthy alternative to more traditional equestrian careers. This elegiac declaration is best known in its formulation as the *militia amoris* metaphor.[56] The elegiac hero is portrayed as already enlisted in a kind of military service, battling with love or his beloved. The Propertian narrator receives the following instructions:

> at tu finge elegos, fallax opus: haec tua castra!—
> scribat ut exemplo cetera turba tuo.
> militiam Veneris blandis patiere sub armis,
> et Veneris pueris utilis hostis eris.
> nam tibi uictrices quascumque labore parasti,
> eludit palmas una puella tuas. (4.1.135–40)

> [But you, devise elegies, a tricky task: this is your camp!—
> That they, the remaining crowd, write at your example.
> The warfare of Venus you'll endure under alluring weapons
> and to Venus's boys a profitable enemy you'll be.
> Because for you whatever Victorias your effort's procured,
> escapes your awards one girl.]

Similarly an Ovidian poem entirely dedicated to the exploration of the metaphor of *militia* begins *militat omnis amans, et habet sua castra Cupido* (Every lover soldiers, and Cupid has his own barracks, *Am.* 1.9.1).

Augustan elegy represents its hero as faithful to his usually disloyal mistress, and as engaged metaphorically in either sexual servitude or erotic battles. Yet the unconventional sexual role bestowed,

[55] Hallett (1973), 103, contrasts the epitaph of Claudia (*ILS* 8403): *domum serauit, lanam fecit*. See now Gold (1993*b*), 288–9, who notes that the term *domina* (unlike *dominus*) effectively constrains the powers of the elegiac mistress to the domestic and the sexual.

[56] For erotic *militia* in the elegiac corpus, see Lilja (1965), 64–6; Lyne (1980), 67–78; Conte (1989), 444–5. See now Gale (1997), 78–85; Davis (1999), 438–42.

through poetic metaphor, on the elegiac male seems to implicate the elegiac female in equally unconventional behaviour: he slights the responsibilities of being citizen and soldier, while she operates outside the conventional roles of wife and mother. So, if specific features of the elegiac mistresses do not seem to reflect the realities of particular women's lives, might not the general idioms employed about them nevertheless reflect general conditions for the female in Augustan society? Is the elegiac woman unconventional because there are now some unconventional women in the world?

Once again, the elegiac texts tempt us: if, as Georg Luck has argued, 'the woman's role in the Roman society of the first century BC explains to a large extent the unique character of the love poetry of that period',[57] then elegy would be invested with a social dimension of substantial interest to the student of women in antiquity. The mistresses stylized in elegy might then constitute poetic representatives of a whole movement of sexually liberated ladies and may be read as 'symbolic of the new freedom for women in Rome's social life in the first century BC'.[58] To establish such a connection between elegiac mistresses and Augustan women it is first necessary to find parallel portraits of the female outside the poetic sphere. If external evidence can be found for the gradual emergence of a breed of 'emancipated' women, then it might be possible to argue that such women *provoked* elegiac production.

Sallust's description of an unconventional Sempronia provides the most frequently cited historical parallel for the elegiac heroines:

> litteris Graecis et Latinis docta, psallere, saltare elegantius quam necesse est probae, multa alia, quae instrumenta luxuriae sunt. Sed ei cariora semper omnia quam decus atque pudicitia fuit . . . lubido sic accensa ut saepius peteret uiros quam peteretur. (*Cat.* 25.2–4)

[57] Luck (1974), 15.

[58] King (1976), 70. On the social dimensions of elegy, see further Ch. 5 below.

[Well educated in Greek and Latin literature, she had greater skill in lyre-playing and dancing than there is any need for a respectable woman to acquire, besides many other accomplishments such as minister to dissipation. There was nothing that she set a smaller value on than seemliness and chastity . . . Her passions were so ardent that she more often made advances to men than they did to her.][59]

Similarly, the Clodia Metelli who appears in Cicero's forensic speech *pro Caelio* is often adduced as an example of the kind of emancipated woman with whom Roman poets fell in love in the first century BC and about whom (thus inspired) they composed erotic verse. The early identification of Clodia Metelli with Catullus' *Lesbia* seems to strengthen such a link between living and written women and to bind the habits of a late republican noble woman (as evidenced by Cicero's *pro Caelio*) to poetic depictions of a mistress in the Catullan corpus.[60]

However, the process of matching love poetry's heroines with a new breed of 'emancipated' women raises methodological problems. Sallust's Sempronia and Cicero's Clodia have often been employed as evidence for the phenomenon of the New Woman (as elegy's historical twin is sometimes called).[61] Yet it is important to observe that, even outside the poetic sphere, our principal evidence for the lives of ancient women is still on the level of representations, not realities. We encounter not real women, but representations shaped by the conventions of wall paintings, tombstones, and, most frequently, literary texts. Any comparison between elegiac women and emancipated ladies tends, therefore, to be a comparison between two forms of discourse about the female.[62]

[59] The translation is that of Lefkowitz and Fant (1982), 205. For Sempronia's use as part of the social backdrop for elegiac production, see Lyne (1980), 14, and King (1976), 70 and n. 7. See now Newman (1997), 280–1.

[60] See e.g. Lyne (1980), 8–18, and Griffin (1985), 15–28. Wiseman (1985), 15–53, uses Clodia extensively as an example of women of high society in Catullus' time while, more cautiously, identifying Lesbia only with a member of Clodia Metelli's family—probably a sister (136–7).

[61] Balsdon (1962), 45.

[62] See now Edwards (1993), esp. pp. 34–62, where she argues that the adulteresses to be found in Roman moralizing discourses should be read as resonant metaphors for

Sempronia and Clodia are both to be found in literary texts. And as written women, they are (like their elegiac sisters) no accurate reflection of particular female lives. Sallust's Sempronia is written into a particular form of literary discourse, for, in the context of his historical monograph, she is structured as a female counterpart to Catiline. Her features also belong to a larger historiographic tradition in which the decline of Roman *uirtus* and the rise of *luxuria* are commonly associated with aberrant female sexuality. Sempronia's qualities contradict the norms for a *matrona*. She is whorish because a whore embodies moral degeneracy and thus discredits the Catilinarian conspiracy.[63] Clodia is also written into a text. The villainous features of this prosecution witness are put together from the stock characteristics of the comic *meretrix* and the tragic Medea. Cicero's Clodia is a *proterua meretrix procaxque* (*pro Cael.* 49) because sexual promiscuity was a long-standing topos in the invective tradition against women. As part of a forensic discourse, the sexually active woman is designed to sway a jury. The rapaciousness of this supposedly injured party turns the young, male defendant into a victim and her sexual guilt thus underscores his innocence.[64]

When attempting to reconstruct the lives of ancient women from textual materials, some critics have drawn upon a kind of hierarchy of discourses graded according to their usefulness as evidence. Marilyn Skinner, for example, argues that Cicero's letters offer a less tendentious version of Clodia Metelli than does his oratory. And the Clodia she recuperates from that source is one concerned not with sexual debauchery, but with the political activities of her brother and

social and political disorder, but not necessarily as matching the behaviours of specific people. Cf. Dixon (2001), esp. chs. 2 and 5.

[63] Paul (1966), 92; Boyd (1987); and now Dixon (2001), chs. 2 and 9. For this use of the aberrant female in Roman discourses of moral and political disorder, see now Edwards (1993), esp. p. 43, and Dixon (2001), chs. 2, 5, and 9. Cf. Chs. 6 and 9 below on Roman representations of Cleopatra and Messalina respectively.

[64] Lefkowitz (1981), 32–40, and Skinner (1983), 275–6. Wiseman (1985), 15 recognizes the need for caution in reading Cicero's portrait of Clodia Metelli, but still sees no reason to doubt its accuracy (p. 30). See now Edwards (1993), 46; Fitzgerald (1995), 21–2; Dixon (2001), chs. 3 and 9.

husband and with property management.[65] Perhaps this picture of a wealthy, public woman is a better guide to the new opportunities of the first century BC, but it is not the picture of female behaviour that Augustan elegy paints. The term *domina* could identify a woman of property, an owner of household slaves. Within the discourse of Augustan elegy, however, it takes on an erotic (not an economic) significance. The female subject that the poetic narrative constructs is not an independent woman of property but one dependent on men for gifts: *Cynthia non sequitur fascis nec curat honores,* | *semper amatorum ponderat una sinus* (Cynthia doesn't pursue power or care for glory, | always her lovers' pockets only she weighs, 2.16.11–12). Augustan elegy, then, does not seem to be a response to the lives of particular emancipated women, but another manifestation of a particular patterning of female sexuality to be found in the cultural discourses of Rome.

Rome was essentially a patriarchal society sustained by a familial ideology. The basic Roman social unit was the *familia* whose head was the father (*pater*): 'a woman, even if legally independent, socially and politically had no function in Roman society in the way that a man, as actual or potential head of a *familia*, did.'[66] Using the Ciceronian Clodia as her starting-point, Mary Lefkowitz has documented the prevalence of this way of structuring femininity in antiquity. Praise or blame of women, Lefkowitz argues, is customarily articulated with reference to their biological role, assigned according to their conformity with male norms for female behaviour. The good woman is lauded for her chastity, her fertility, her loyalty to her husband, and her selfless concern for others. The bad woman is constantly vilified for her faithlessness, her inattentiveness to household duties, and her selfish disregard for others.[67] In the conceptual framework of Roman society, female sexuality takes on positive value only when ordered in terms that will be socially effective for patriarchy, that is in the

65 Skinner (1983).

66 Gardner (1986), 77; Dixon (1988), 13–40. See now Dixon (1992).

67 Lefkowitz (1981), 32–40. Cf. now Dixon (2001), chs. 5 and 9.

satisfactory performance of marital and reproductive duties. Sexually unrestrained women are marginalized. Displaced from a central position in cultural categories, they are associated with social and political disruption.[68] A notable example of this politically charged polarization of women into the chaste and the depraved occurs at the beginning of the principate: 'In the propaganda which represented Octavian's war with Antony as a crusade, it was convenient to depict [Octavia] as a deeply wronged woman, the chaste Roman foil of the voluptuous foreigner Cleopatra.'[69]

This patterning of discourses about the female can be grounded in history. A figure like Sempronia was not articulated in Roman texts before the middle of the second century BC, after Rome's rise to empire (and its consequent wealth and Hellenization) had brought with it significant social and cultural change.[70] From this period there began a proliferation of moral discourses associating female sexual misconduct with social and political disorder. And by the first century BC marriage, adultery, procreation, and childlessness were appearing regularly as subjects for concern in the texts of writers such as Cicero, Sallust, Horace, and Livy, interlocked with anxieties about the collapse of traditional Roman society and the outbreak of civil war.[71]

So persuasive have these discourses on the female been that they have often been taken for truth. Many of the histories on which elegy's commentators once relied for reconstructions of Rome's New Woman invested their accounts of changes in women's social position with elements of moral turpitude transferred wholesale

[68] Richlin (1983); Dixon (1988). See now Edwards (1993), esp. 35–6; Skinner (1997), 9–11; McGinn (1998), esp. 17; Hemelrijk (1998), 7–21; Williams (1999), 113–15; Dixon (2001), chs. 3, 5, and 9; below Chs. 6 (on Cleopatra) and 9 (on Messalina).

[69] Balsdon (1952), 69, and see further Ch. 6 below.

[70] I am indebted to Elizabeth Rawson for this observation.

[71] See e.g. Richlin (1981), 379–404; Dixon (1988), 92–7. Cf. now Treggiari (1991), 211–15; Dixon (1992), 119–23 and (2001), chs. 3 and 5; Edwards (1993), 42–7 and 93–7; McGinn (1998), 78–9.

from the writings of the Roman moralists. For example, the first edition of *The Cambridge Ancient History* claimed that 'by the last century of the Republic, females had in practice obtained their independence, and nothing but social convention and a sense of responsibility barred the way to a dangerous exploitation of their privilege'.[72] Similarly, Balsdon's *Roman Women* stated emphatically: 'Women emancipated themselves. They acquired liberty, then with the late Republic and the Empire they enjoyed unrestrained licence.'[73] Thus in the ready association of liberty with licence, the strictures of Roman moralists were turned into the realities of republican lives.[74]

One particular form of discourse about female sexuality had considerable and significant currency during the period in which elegiac eroticism was produced. From 18 BC on, legislation began to appear that criminalized adultery and offered inducements to marry and reproduce.[75] However, the production of elegy's female figures cannot be read as a direct poetic protest against this social legislation, although it appears to be the subject of one Propertian poem:

> gauisa est certe sublatam Cynthia legem,
> qua quondam edicta flemus uterque diu,
> ni nos diuideret. (2.7.1–3)

> [She was delighted for sure at the law's removal—Cynthia—
> over whose publication once we both cried long,
> in case it should part us.]

Since the tradition of erotic writing to which the Propertian Cynthia belongs stretched back at least as far as the Gallan corpus, the earliest examples of the elegiac mistress considerably predate the legisla-

[72] Last (1934), 440.
[73] Balsdon (1952), 14–15.
[74] Cf. Gardner (1986), 261. See now Edwards (1993), 35–6; Dixon (2001), chs. 1, 5, and 9.
[75] For the details of the Augustan legislation, see Last (1934), 441–56; Brunt (1971), 558–66; Dixon (1988), 84–6. See now Treggiari (1991), 60–80 and 277–98; Dixon (1992), 78–81; McGinn (1998), 70–104 and 140–215.

tion.[76] Yet the appearance of the Augustan domestic legislation from 18 BC does demonstrate that the discourses about female sexuality with which elegy was already engaged were now being institutionalized: female sexual practice was now enshrined in law as a problematic issue with which the whole state should be concerned.[77]

Augustan elegy and its mistresses constitute, therefore, a response to, and a part of, a multiplication of discourses about the female that occurred in the late republic and early empire. Similarly, in his first volume on the history of sexuality, Michel Foucault demonstrates that, when 'population' emerged as an economic and political problem in the eighteenth century, 'between the state and the individual, sex became an issue, and a public issue no less: a whole web of discourses, special knowledges, analyses, and injunctions settled upon it'.[78] In the first century BC, at a time when female sexuality was seen as a highly problematic and public concern, the poetic depiction of the elegiac hero's subjection to a mistress would have carried a wide range of social and political connotations. And the elegiac mistress, in particular, would have brought to her poetic discourse a considerable potential as metaphor for danger and social disruption.

A brief outline of the operations of realism and of metaphor in Augustan elegy discloses that elegy's mistresses do not enter literary language reflecting the realities of women's lives at Rome. An examination of their characteristics reveals that they are fictive females engaged with at least two broad (but not necessarily distinct) categories of discourse. Shaped by developments in the production of

[76] Badian (1985), 82–98, doubts that even by the time Propertius' second book was published any attempt had yet been made to introduce the legislation concerning marriage. Cf. now Gale (1997), 89–90, and Miller (2001), sec. 4. For the relation between Augustan elegy and the moral legislation, see also Wallace-Hadrill (1985), 180–4. Cf. now Sharrock (1994), esp. 113, and Davis (1999), 435 and 444–9.

[77] See now Edwards (1993), 34–62 and Galinsky (1996), 128–40. Contrast Habinek (1997), who argues that Ovid's *Amores* and *Ars Amatoria* record the invention of sexuality as a discrete topic of discussion, now disembedded from other socio-political relations.

[78] Foucault (1981), 26.

literary texts and in the social construction of female sexuality, they possess potential as metaphors for both poetic projects and political order.

The second of these two categories will be further explored in the remainder of this chapter; for it is the range of connotations that the elegiac mistress gains as a result of her association with the erotic metaphors of *seruitium* and *militia* (rather than those arising from her identification with the Muse and the practice of writing elegy) that may most intrigue the student of women in antiquity.[79] Amy Richlin argues that on entry into a variety of Rome's poetic and prose genres (such as invective and satire) the ordering of female sexuality is determined by the central narrative viewpoint which is that of a sexually active, adult male.[80] So, in depicting their hero as subject to and in the service of a sexually unrestrained mistress, do the elegiac texts offer any challenging new role for the female, or for the male alone?

Some critics have made much of the boldness of appropriating the term *laus* for the erotic sphere and *fides* for male sexual behaviour, but their descriptions of such strategies are seriously misleading. The Propertian narrator declares: *laus in amore mori: laus altera, si datur uno | posse frui: fruar o solus amore meo!* (Glorious in love to die: glorious again, if granted one love | to enjoy: o may I enjoy alone my love!, 2.1.47–8). Both Judith Hallett and Margaret Hubbard, for example, frequently refer to such material as involving a bold reversal or inversion of sex roles—the elegiac hero sheds male public virtues and takes on the female domestic virtue of sexual loyalty.[81] Such terminology suggests, erroneously, that in elegiac poetry the female subject gains a position of social responsibility at the same time as it is removed from the male.

It is not the concern of elegiac poetry to upgrade the position of women, only to portray the male narrator as alienated from positions

[79] For the elegiac mistress as a metaphor for her author's poetics, see further Veyne (1983) and Chs. 2–5 below.

[80] Richlin (1983).

[81] Hallett (1973) and Hubbard (1974).

of power and to differentiate him from other, socially responsible male types. For example, in the same poem of Propertius' second book, the narrator's erotic battles are contrasted with the activities of the *nauita*, the *arator*, the *miles*, and the *pastor*, without any reference to a female partner:

> nauita de uentis, de tauris narrat arator,
>     enumerat miles uulnera, pastor ouis;
> nos contra angusto uersantes proelia lecto:
>     qua pote quisque, in ea conterat arte diem. (2.1.43–6)

> [The sailor tells of winds, of bulls the farmer,
>     numbers the soldier wounds, the shepherd sheep;
> we instead turning battles on a narrow bed:
>     in what each can, in that art let him wear down the day.]

Similarly, in book 1 the Propertian lover expresses, in the abstract terms of an erotic militancy, his difference from the soldier Tullus (1.6.19–36).

Furthermore, the elegiac texts take little interest in elaborating their metaphors in terms of female power but explore, rather, the concept of male dependency. The elegiac mistress may possess a camp in which her lover parades (Prop. 2.7.15–16) or choose her lovers as a general chooses his soldiers (*Am.* 1.9.5–6), but generally elegiac metaphors are concerned with male servitude not female mastery, and with male military service not female generalship. In *Amores* 1.2 it is Cupid who leads a triumphal procession of captive lovers, not the Ovidian mistress, and in *Amores* 1.9 it is the equation *miles / amans* not *domina / dux* that receives the fullest treatment.[82]

The metaphors of *seruitium* and *militia amoris* thus disclose the ideological repercussions for a man of association with a realistically

[82] See now Greene (1998) against Hallett's reading of elegy as empowering women. Greene argues instead that the use of the *militia* metaphor connects conquest in war with the male lover's violent desire to overcome his hard mistress, while the *seruitium* metaphor operates as both an erotic ruse (designed to sway the beloved) and as an aesthetic pose (designed to gain a poetic reputation). See further Ch. 5 below.

depicted mistress. In a society that depended on a slave mode of production, and in which citizenship carried the obligation of military service, these two metaphors define the elegiac male as socially irresponsible. As a slave to love, he is precluded from participating in the customary occupations of male citizens. As a soldier of love, he is not available to fight military campaigns.

The heterodoxy of the elegiac portrayal of love, therefore, lies in the absence of a political or social role for the male narrator, not in any attempt to provide or demand a new social role for the female subject. The temporary alignment with a sexually unrestrained mistress that Augustan elegy depicts does not bestow on the female a new, challenging role but alienates the male from his traditional responsibilities. The elegiac poets exploit the traditional methods of ordering female sexuality (that locate the sexually unrestrained and therefore socially ineffective female at the margins of society) in order to portray their first-person heroes as displaced from a central position in the social categories of Augustan Rome. And, moreover, they evaluate that displacement in conventional terms. At the beginning of the second book of the *Amores*, the poet is introduced as *ille ego nequitiae Naso poeta meae* (I, Naso, that poet of my own depravity, 2.1.2), and in the Propertian corpus the lover and poet of Cynthia is also associated with the scandal of *nequitia* ('vice' or 'depravity', 1.6.26 and 2.24.6). Thus, the poetic depiction of subjection to a mistress is aligned, in a conventional moral framework, with depravity.

Finally, despite claims of eternal devotion, none of the elegiac poets maintain this pose consistently or indefinitely. At the end of the third book, the Propertian lover repudiates his heroine and describes himself as restored to Good Sense (*Mens Bona*). At the end of his first book, the Tibullan hero finds himself dragged off to war. And, toward the end of the *Amores*, the appearance of a *coniunx* on the elegiac scene disrupts the dramatic pretence that the narrator is a romantic lover involved in an obsessive and exclusive relationship.[83]

[83] Cf. Butrica (1982), 87.

The purpose of this chapter has been to suggest that, when looking at the relations between women in Augustan elegy and women in Augustan society, we should not describe the literary image of a mistress as a kind of poetic painting whose surface we can remove to reveal a real Roman woman hidden underneath. Instead, an exploration of the idioms of realism and metaphor has demonstrated that elegiac mistresses are inextricably entangled in, and shaped by, a whole range of discourses that bestow on them a potential as metaphors for the poetic projects and political interests of their authors.

This analysis is designed only as the starting-point for a critical study of elegy's heroines and their constructive power as metaphors for poetic and political concerns. Yet already one aspect of this analysis may seem unsatisfactory or unsatisfying, for it seems to offer no adequate place for living Augustan women in the production of elegiac poetry. Further questions immediately confront us. How did women read or even write such male-oriented verse? Would a female reader in Augustan Rome be drawn into the male narrative perspective? And how did a female writer, such as Sulpicia, construct her *ego* and its male beloved? In such a context, would the erotic metaphors of *seruitium* and *militia* be appropriate or have the same range of connotative power?[84]

[84] On these questions, see further Ch. 5 below.

# 2

# Written Women: Propertius' *scripta puella* (2.10–13)

### CONSTRUCTING A REAL CYNTHIA

The narrative organisation of Propertius' first poetry-book seems to encourage a practice of reading the characters and events of his love elegy as real. The predominantly autobiographical mode allows the reader to equate the lover of the text with the author Propertius. Direct addresses to a beloved Cynthia who is allocated physical and psychological characteristics suggest that the narrative's female subject has a life outside the text as Propertius' mistress. The illusion of a real world populated by real individuals is then sustained by various other formal mechanisms such as the regular deployment of addresses to the historically verifiable figure of Tullus or occasional references to the landscape of Baiae, Umbria, and Rome. Having established a recognizable setting, the book seems even to account for its own existence as literary discourse with the claim that composi-

This chapter is a revised version of an article first published in *JRS* 77 (1987), 47–61.

tion is a method of courtship. Writing is subsumed within, and subordinated to, an erotic scheme: Propertius writes to woo a woman.

Not all the poems in the first book have narrators who seem identifiable with a love-lorn author. Some do not have a beloved Cynthia as their subject. Several have been found to contain elements of literary polemic, including a Callimachean advocacy of elegy over other writing-practices.[1] Yet, as noted in Chapter 1, poetic devices for the production of realism have operated so successfully that their technique has often been taken for truth: the *Monobiblos* has become 'the supreme example of "subjective love-elegy" for modern scholars, and so persuasively has Propertius handled the conventional amatory topics that most have taken the staging for reality'.[2] Poem 1.3 (the most favoured poem for analysis from this most favoured book) opens with an artful series of mythological parallels for the sleeping Cynthia and closes with Cynthia now awake and remonstrating with her late-returned lover. The unusual and exceptionally realistic strategy of ascribing direct speech to elegy's female subject seems to end events with a mistress speaking for herself. So the poem has been described as a little drama in which we learn how the author's mythic idealization of his beloved as a Sleeping Beauty was once shattered by the *reality* of her wakeful reproaches;[3] the lover's illusion of a peaceful Cynthia is destroyed by an encounter with the *real-life*, abusive woman.[4] Thus for many critics faced with a poem presenting elegy's heroine as a physical and active presence that breathes, sleeps,

[1] As, for example, Fedeli (1981), 227–42, and Wyke (1984). See now McNamee (1993), who argues that the Callimachean poetic concerns highlighted in book 2 are evident also in book 1, but are not formally announced there, and cf. Newman (1997), 190–212. See also Greene (1998), 37–66, Keith (1999), 54–6, and Sharrock (2000) on the strategies of book 1 that work to subvert its realism.

[2] Ross (1975), 110. For such misunderstandings of Augustan elegy, cf. Veyne (1983), 10, and see Ch. 1 above.

[3] Lyne (1980), 114–20. Cf. Griffin (1985), 52–3.

[4] Stahl (1985), 75. For this frequent use of the words *real* and *reality* about poem 1.3, cf. e.g. Curran (1966), 187–207. Contrast now Greene (1998), 51–9, on the poem's *literariness*.

wakes, and even speaks, the written woman lives beyond the poetic world as a flesh-and-blood Augustan girlfriend.

The romantic view that Propertian love-elegy is a sincere expression of its author's feelings and a realistic representation of an Augustan girlfriend is clearly facilitated by poems in which narrative realism predominates. Realist strategies, however, are not so prominent in Propertius' second poetry-book. There the virtual absence of historically documented or even named addressees, the frequent shifts between second- and third-person reference, and the general lack of a well-defined occasion for enunciation prohibit for the reader any easy transition from the text to an extra-textual reality. Now, even for the romantic critic Lyne, Propertius 'no longer creates the illusion of himself uttering on an occasion outside literature, in life'.[5] The substitution of interior for dramatic monologue leaves the male subject (the elegiac man) without a realistically constructed world in which to act. The female subject (the elegiac woman) is less frequently articulated as a physical entity with an assumed existence outside the text; her title is less frequently employed as if it had the force of a pseudonym. Cynthia is often 'only a shadowy presence'.[6]

Furthermore, as the poetic mechanisms for the production of realism are curtailed, so references to Cynthia's function in literary discourse increase. Hence the beloved's capacity to captivate begins the first book of Propertian elegies, but the next opens with a consideration of her role in the practice of writing. The elegiac man is now explicitly both lover and writer, the elegiac woman both beloved and narrative material. In the first poem of the new book a Sleeping Beauty is the starting-point for poetic production: *seu cum poscentis somnum declinat ocellos, | inuenio causas mille poeta nouas* (or if eyes begging for sleep she lowers, | I find a thousand novel reasons to be a poet, 2.1.11–12). Similarly, at the second book's close, *Cynthia quin etiam uersu laudata Properti* (and Cynthia also praised in the verse of Propertius, 2.34.93) is the subject matter which locates the elegiac poet in a Roman tradition for producers of female repre-

[5] Lyne (1980), 125. [6] Richardson (1977), 15.

sentations. Thus, in poems that frame her second formulation, Cynthia is depicted as matter for poetic composition not as a woman to be wooed through writing.

Since the text no longer encourages a reading of its subjects as flesh-and-blood lovers nor seems to subordinate elegiac writing to an erotic courtship, constructing a real Cynthia out of the characteristics of the second book is a much more difficult enterprise. It is no coincidence, for example, that at least one romantic account of the Propertian corpus has devoted less space to book 2 than to the *Monobiblos*, although it is twice the size of the first book. Oliver Lyne's *The Latin Love Poets* (1980, reprinted 1996 and 2000) favours a practice of reading even the second Cynthia as real, because it highlights only those techniques of the second book which most closely match the realist strategies of the first.[7]

Similarly, in order to safeguard her status as a living Augustan girlfriend, critics have often insulated the second Cynthia from issues of poetic production that the text now raises prominently. The second book is framed by the naming of Callimachus, by extensive borrowings from the Callimachean polemic in favour of writing elegy, and by references to the elegiac woman as Propertius' poetic material.[8] This explicit association of Cynthia with Callimachus might suggest that Cynthia herself is a subject in the Callimachean tradition. Yet the outer margins of an Augustan poetry-book are not unexpected places to find the expression of such literary concerns. For the most notable and well-documented structural principle of Callimachean poetry is the framing device, often a prologue and epilogue concerned with the text's status as poetic discourse and its place in the literary tradition.[9] Since Callimachus is explicitly invoked only in those poems

[7] Lyne (1980), 140, justifies the brevity of his survey of books 3 and 4 on the grounds that they are no longer Cynthia-centred, but does not remark on the discrepancy between his accounts of books 1 and 2. Cf. the priority given to the *Monobiblos* over book 2 in Stahl (1985).

[8] See Wimmel (1960); Boucher (1965), 168; Juhnke (1971), 107.

[9] See Dawson (1950), 1–168; Clayman (1976), 29–35; Parsons (1977), 1–50; Thomas (1983), 92–113. For Callimachus and the Augustan poetry-book, see *Arethusa* 13 (1980), *passim*.

which frame Propertius' second book, it has been possible to claim that Callimachean material is here employed only in passing, to support the author's preference for elegy over epic.[10] An inner core of poems then remains relatively undisturbed by issues of Alexandrian artifice or Callimachean apologetics, and is still read as representing the vicissitudes of a poet's affair with the living Cynthia: Cynthia and Callimachus are kept apart.

Thus, despite his considerable interest in the impact of Hellenistic literary practices on Augustan elegy, Jean-Paul Boucher concluded *Études sur Properce* (1965) with a chapter that attempted to construct a plausible portrait of a specific Roman out of the elegiac woman's textual characteristics.[11] In the following decade, John Sullivan entitled the third chapter of his book on Propertius 'Cynthia Prima Fuit' and the fourth chapter 'Roman Callimachus'. In the latter he rejected sincerity as a meaningless romantic criterion of literary value and examined the Augustan author's Alexandrian heritage. Yet in the former he called for a reassertion of the primacy of life in critical methods, and supported Apuleius' identification of Cynthia as a pseudonym for one Hostia.[12]

Yet Cynthia and Callimachus are inseparable for, as Walter Wimmel's history of 'die apologetische Form' has established by means of a line-by-line commentary, Callimachus' polemic in favour of the elegiac writing-style is extensively deployed and remodelled not only in the opening and closing poems of Propertius' second book but also within the book's more realist core, in poem 2.10.[13] And, at the same time as 2.10 parades a poetics, it describes the production of epic as dependent on the completion of elegy's heroine—*bella canam, quando scripta puella mea est* (wars I shall sing, since my girl has been written, 2.10.8). It is therefore the narrative strategies of

[10] Boucher (1965), 166–7. Cf. Lyne (1980), 147.

[11] For such attempts to construct a physique for Cynthia out of her poetic features, see also Chs. 1 above and 4 below.

[12] Sullivan (1976).

[13] Wimmel (1960).

2.10 that I propose to examine in the course of this chapter precisely because, in the pursuit of a 'real' Cynthia, such strategies are frequently overlooked or understated. Against the view that 2.10 once opened a new book of the corpus, I shall argue that the poem forms part of a group integrated with the second book, a group that breaks away significantly from the devices of realism, and instead associates Cynthia so intimately with the practice of writing elegy as to undermine her identity independently of that practice. From an analysis of Propertius' *scripta puella* it will emerge that to read Cynthia as a pseudonym is to misread or disregard the narrative organization of the second book and its deployment of Cynthia as the embodiment of a Callimachean poetics.

## 2.10: THE *SCRIPTA PUELLA*

The terrain mapped out at the opening and close of 2.10 marks the changed narrative mode.[14] For the first time in the Propertian corpus the reader is presented with the topography of a particular literary tradition:

> Sed tempus lustrare aliis Helicona choreis,
> et campum Haemonio iam dare tempus equo . . .
> nondum etiam Ascraeos norunt mea carmina fontis,
> sed modo Permessi flumine lauit Amor. (2.10.1–2 and 25–6)

> [But it's time to traverse, with other dances, Helicon,
> and the field to the Haemonian horse now it's time to give . . .
> not even yet the Ascraean springs do my songs know,
> but only in Permessus' stream has Love bathed them.]

After Hesiod had set his Muses on Mount Helicon in Boeotia at the beginning of the *Theogony*, it became a general literary practice nurtured by Callimachus' *Aetia* to evoke Hesiod (and the particular tradition of writing with which he was associated) by reference to

[14] On 2.10, see now Newman (1997), 216–19.

the topography of that area. So *Helicona*, *Ascraeos . . . fontis* and *Permessi flumine* all chart a Hesiodic practice of writing. The elegiac world changes locale. From the landscape of Italy (with such markers of realistically constructed space as the Rome, Baiae, and Umbria of the *Monobiblos*), it is transplanted to the landscape of language itself. The strategically placed references to a geography of poetic inspiration indicate that the intervening narrative has broken away from the devices of realism and is now overtly concerned with its own status as discourse.

The figures who formerly peopled a realistically shaped elegiac world also change to suit their new habitat:

> aetas prima canat Ueneres, extrema tumultus:
> bella canam, quando scripta puella mea est.
> nunc uolo subducto grauior procedere uultu,
> nunc aliam citharam me mea Musa docet. (2.10.7–10)

> [Let early life sing Venuses, late insurrections:
> wars I shall sing, since my girl has been written.
> Now I wish with detached expression to advance more soberly,
> Now a different lyre my Muse teaches me.]

The elegiac man is not portrayed as a lover compelled to express his love in verse. Instead his role is solely that of poet; a master of discourse who himself chooses between modes of poetic composition, and can contemplate the termination of amatory elegy (2.10.8). So, when it is argued that the narrator's life should fall into two parts, the stages named (*Ueneres* and *tumultus*) constitute not occupations such as lover and soldier, but subjects for elegiac and epic writing-styles. Likewise, the transition between modes of composition (from *Ueneres* to *tumultus*) involves not a change of heart for a lover, but a different facial expression for a poet (2.10.9–10); another guise to articulate another literary practice.[15] The substitution of *bella* for a *puella* requires not a change of life-style, but of poetic performance.

[15] See now Keith (1999), 53–4.

Correspondingly, the elegiac woman is not portrayed as a beloved receiving or inspiring poetry, but as a narrative subject to be continued or abandoned. The role assigned to elegy's *puella* in 2.10 is that of a fiction which may be finished (2.10.8). The subordinate clause *quando scripta puella mea est* has been variously translated as, for example, 'now that I have set forth all my mistress' charms', 'since I have done with writing of my love', 'da die Geliebte ganz beschrieben ist', or 'since writing about my mistress is done'.[16] Yet each of these translations restricts unjustifiably the possible meanings of *scribere puellam*. When describing the process of literary composition, *scribere* more often takes as its direct object a word which signifies some aspect of language than one which signifies a person. The *Oxford Latin Dictionary* cites a few instances where the activity of writing poetry about someone is rendered by *scribere* with a personal object: Horace *Odes* 1.6.13–14 begins with an apparent forecast to Agrippa that *scriberis Vario fortis et hostium* | *uictor* (you shall be written about by Varius as of enemies a brave | conqueror), and goes on to ask *quis Martem . . .* | *digne scripserit?* (who about Mars . . . has written worthily?); Martial 5.53 begins *Colchida quid scribis, quid scribis, amice, Thyesten?* (about Colchis why do you write, why do you write, friend, about Thyestes?). However in the prologue to Terence's *Eunuchus*, for example, *currentem seruom scribere* (to write a running slave, v. 36) parallels *bonas matronas facere* (to construct good wives, v. 37) as a means of describing the activity of creating characters. Some ambiguity may therefore reside in the construction *scripta puella mea est*, which consequently could be rendered 'my girl has been written' as well as 'my girl has been described'. By such techniques as the addition of 'charms', or the employment of 'beschreiben' rather than 'schreiben', commentators have limited the possible senses of the clause and thus safeguarded the elegiac woman's status always as flesh and blood, never as fiction.[17]

[16] Respectively, Butler (1976), 93; Camps (1967), 109; Luck (1964), 79; Stahl (1985), 157.

[17] The use of *scribere* elsewhere in the Propertian corpus supports the argument for ambiguity here. *Scribitur et uestris Cynthia corticibus* at 1.18.22 gives Cynthia

Yet the parallelism the text evinces at this point between hexameter and pentameter verse demonstrates that the *puella* is to be read here not as a living girlfriend to whom the author has dedicated his life, but as a female fiction that can be discarded. For, in each of the verses 7 and 8, the two mutually exclusive discourses of elegy and epic are assigned a chronological relation. In the first they are signified respectively by *Ueneres* and *tumultus*, in the second (chiastically) by *bella* and *puella*. Since *canere Ueneres* and *scribere puellam* describe the same activity, the juxtaposition of *Ueneres* and *puella* signals their comparable function as signifiers of a form of fiction. The arena of literary eroticism is here circumscribed both by an indefinite plurality of *Ueneres* and by a single, unindividuated *puella*.

The substitution of Helicon and a written woman for Cynthia and Rome, at this point in the corpus, marks a departure from the strategies of realism. The landscape of language provides a setting in which the poet alone acts, and the only event envisaged is his choice of subject matter for poetic production: either *bella* or a *puella*. But the choice which is articulated in 2.10 between the production of epic and elegiac verse and the ultimate withdrawal from epic (with which the poem closes) are set in both a literary and a political context. The epic opus partially undertaken and then postponed has as its subject the supreme signifier of both literary and political orthodoxy, Augustus:

> surge, anime, ex humili; iam, carmina, sumite uires;
>   Pierides, magni nunc erit oris opus.
> iam negat Euphrates equitem post terga tueri
>   Parthorum et Crassos se tenuisse dolet:
> India quin, Auguste, tuo dat colla triumpho,
>   et domus intactae te tremit Arabiae;
> et si qua extremis tellus se subtrahit oris,
>   sentiat illa tuas postmodo capta manus!

momentarily the status of a word not a woman, while the parallelism of *unde . . . scribantur amores* with *unde meus ueniat liber* at 2.1.1–2 marks *amores* there as amatory writings.

haec ego castra sequar; uates tua castra canendo
  magnus ero: seruent hunc mihi fata diem!
at caput in magnis ubi non est tangere signis,
  ponitur haec imos ante corona pedes;
sic nos nunc, inopes laudis conscendere carmen,
  pauperibus sacris uilia tura damus. (2.10.11–24)

[Arise, mind, from the low; now, songs, take up strength;
  Pierides, a great voice now will be needed.
Now Euphrates refuses to protect from behind the rider
  of the Parthians and, that it kept the Crassi, laments:
even India, Augustus, to your triumph gives its neck,
  And the home of untouched Arabia shudders before you;
and whatever land to the furtherest shores withdraws,
  let it, captive, then feel your hand!
This camp I shall pursue; a bard mighty by singing your camp
  I shall become: fate reserve for me this day!
But when the head of great statues it's not possible to reach,
  the garland is placed before their lowest feet,
so now, unfit to climb the song of praise,
  in a pauper's sacrifice, we offer cheap incense.]

The new name *Augustus* appears rarely in the elegiac corpus but is used here in a direct address.[18] It is also embedded in the grandiose language of eastern conquest and enclosed by poetic markers of the shift in stylistic level that the enunciation *Auguste* requires: a departure *ex humili* and a replacement of the *poeta* by a *uates*.[19]

Yet, significantly, the name also establishes a narrative time for the poem after 27 BC, a period that saw the birth of the principate and the consolidation of Augustus' political powers.[20] Walter Wimmel had found, in the prologues to Virgil's third book of *Georgics* and Horace's

[18] See Syme (1978), 183.

[19] For the elevated diction of 2.10.11–20, see Nethercut (1972), 81–2.

[20] A period around 25 BC is offered as a more specific date by some commentators, such as Nethercut (1972), 79–80, and Stahl (1985), 346 n. 42, and now Lyne (1998), 24. For a more cautious approach to the poetic depiction of campaigns, see Syme (1978).

second book of *Satires*, literary precursors and parallels for the movement of 2.10: from a playful promise to write about Octavian, the poets retreat to an apology for a temporary incapacity to do so.[21] But he did not observe the difference in political significance with which such statements of literary intent are imbued when set in their differing historical contexts. The promise made in the *Georgics* and the advice offered by Trebatius in the *Satires* to write about Octavian were both publicized almost immediately after the victory at Actium and, although not acted upon then, were subsequently fulfilled in some measure by the composition of the *Aeneid* and the *Odes*. A promise withdrawn at a later stage, therefore, assigns a literary and political unorthodoxy to the Propertian love elegy that is to displace the patriotic poem temporarily proposed in 2.10. *Amor* not *Auguste* is the last, lingering word of the poem.[22]

The last couplet (quoted above) supplements the Propertian poetics of unorthodoxy. For it maps out the terrain on which Virgil had constructed a literary initiation for the elegiac poet Gallus. One particular spot, *Permessi flumine*, is marked out for Propertian elegy within the larger map of Hesiodic literary discourses in order to differentiate his literary eroticism from the more broadly based narrative modes of his precursor. The detention of the Propertian *carmina* at the foot of Helicon contrasts with the Gallan ascent in *Eclogue* 6 to the composition of an aetiology for the Grynean Grove.[23] Furthermore, the retreat by the Propertian narrator from a desire *fortis memorare ad proelia turmas* (to relate troops brave for combat, 2.10.3) parallels the Virgilian withdrawal at *Eclogue* 6.3 from the production of verse on kings and battles. The Augustan elegist postpones

[21] Wimmel (1960), 193–202.

[22] For 2.10 as a statement of political unorthodoxy, cf. Hubbard (1974), 102–3 and 114; Nethercut (1972), 79–94; King (1980), 78. Contrast Alfonsi (1979), 53, and Stahl (1985), 155–62.

[23] See Rothstein (1966), 283–5; Enk (1962), 153 and 166–7. Cf. Wimmel (1960), 193–202, and Coleman (1977), 195–6; and now Newman (1997), 46–8, and Lyne (1998), 25–8.

indefinitely the literary development of both Gallus and the later Virgil, and aligns his work with the poetic voice of a politically pessimistic, pre-Actium era.[24] The final retreat back to erotic verse, the return from *bella* to a *scripta puella*, marks the Cynthia of the surrounding poems as an unorthodox way of writing. For 2.10 reveals that, as long as Cynthia is being written, a poem on Augustus is being eternally deferred.

Cynthia's association with a practice of writing has not, however, gone entirely unobserved. Godo Lieberg, for example, noted that during the course of the elegiac corpus the Propertian *puella* is clearly provided with three different relations to poetic production: 'Cynthia ist zugleich Quelle, Gegenstand und Ziel der elegischen Dichtung' (Cynthia is simultaneously the inspiration, subject-matter, and addressee of elegiac poetry).[25] Yet critics who recognize and highlight this poetic device have centred only on the two relations of the *puella* to literary production that do not appear to deny her an extratextual status. Presented as an instigator (*Quelle*) or addressee (*Ziel*) of a writing-practice, Cynthia may still be read as existing outside its confines. So, despite his identification of three separate roles for Cynthia in relation to poetic composition, Lieberg centred only on that of *Quelle*. The project of his article 'Die Muse des Properz und seine Dichterweihe' was to demonstrate that in the elegiac text the *puella* was presented as a Muse, and that it was to establish this identification that the title *Cynthia* had been adopted.[26] This narrowed perspective enabled Lieberg to state categorically at the beginning of his article that *Cynthia* was a pseudonym for a living woman whose real name was Hostia.[27] For, as a Muse, the elegiac woman is presumed to be external and prior to the poetry she inspires.

W. Stroh also drew attention to points in the Propertian corpus where Cynthia was linked with the composition of poetry, but he too

[24] Hubbard (1974), 114; Williams (1980), 222–3; Stahl (1985), 159–60. For the relation of Propertian elegy to the Augustan regime, see further Chs. 3, 5, and 6 below.

[25] Lieberg (1963), 269.

[26] Lieberg (1963), 118.

[27] Lieberg (1963), 116.

confined his analysis only to one manner of articulating that relation. His objective was to establish the fundamental contribution of the *Nützlichkeitstopik* (the theme of poetry's sexual utility) to the construction of elegiac discourse, and for that reason he favoured a reading of Cynthia as *Ziel* (as the recipient of a literary courtship). He began his case with the claim that poem 1.8 gives a practical demonstration of elegy as courtship poetry.[28] Faced with the differing textual characteristics of the second Cynthia, Stroh then constructed a more elaborate reading of poem 2.1 as indirect courtship, with the elegiac woman (despite her presentation in the third person) still acting as the living recipient of poetry-books through which she is wooed.[29]

Yet poem 2.10 does not readily fit these observations. Here it is no longer the presence or absence of love for a specific woman that is said to govern Propertian discourse, but the poet's own inspiration made concrete and personified as *mea Musa* or *Amor*. Responsibility for the rejection of amatory elegy is assigned to a Muse (2.10.10) who is provided with the conventional paraphernalia of classical poetic composition—one particular musical instrument, one set of divine instructions. After the production of Augustus' *res gestae* has been defined as a poetic project for the future, at the close of 2.10 responsibility for the resumption of amatory elegy is not assigned to an elegiac woman. Poem 2.10 ends not with a woman of flesh and blood calling back her lover-poet, but with the abstract term *Amor* confining Propertian *carmina* to the lower reaches of the Hesiodic landscape of literary language. Nowhere in this poem is the *puella* Muse.[30]

If Propertian elegy's heroine is not *Quelle*, neither is she *Ziel*. The poem is not structured as an erotic event, an act of communication

[28] Stroh (1971), 9–53, and see Ch. 1 above.

[29] Stroh (1971), 54–64. For King (1980), 61–84 and (1981), 169–84, the elegiac woman must also be well educated in order to appreciate the learned, Callimachean nature of her lover's poetry.

[30] Contrast Lieberg (1963), 265. To sustain a role for Cynthia as Muse in 2.10, he was obliged to reintroduce her as a *Kreatur Amors*.

with or persuasion of a living mistress. For the only addressee envisaged (the ostensible first reader) is not a woman to be wooed but Augustus, the patron of letters. The narrative trajectory is from a male writer to a male reader, in which *bella* and a *puella* (wars and a mistress) simply demarcate the boundaries between modes of poetic discourse.

That the project of 2.10 is to establish an unorthodox position for Propertian elegy within a Hesiodic literary tradition has been well documented, but the role of the elegiac woman in this polemic has been overlooked or misunderstood. In poem 2.10 the *puella* has no life outside the Propertian writing-practice: she is neither *Quelle* nor *Ziel*, neither Propertius' inspiration nor his courted literary critic.[31] At this point in the corpus no physical or psychological characteristics are ascribed to elegy's female subject; instead the single reference to a *scripta puella* deliberately acknowledges her status as a particular form of literary language, a poetic *Gegenstand*.[32] Here elegy's mistress is unorthodox political fiction, perennially opposed to the topics of patriotic poetry.

## 2.11 AND 12: FICTION AND FLESH

After the literary concerns of poem 2.10, and its uncomfortable disclosure that elegy's *puella* is a form of poetic production, the narrative strategies of poems 2.11 and 2.12 seem to restore to her the status of a living, rather than a written, woman. A few of the devices of realism now re-enter the text. First of all, poem 2.11 adopts a narrative format especially favoured in the *Monobiblos*—a dramatic monologue addressed directly and consistently to a beloved. A patterned deployment of personal and possessive pronouns in the second person singular reconstructs for the reader the possibility

[31] These are the only two relations to poetic production the *puella* is allowed by Stahl (1985), 172.

[32] Cf. now, on the *Cynthia lecta* of 2.24.2, Gold (1993*b*), 290–2, and Fear (2000), 228–9.

of a transition from the text to an extratextual recipient: as if 2.11 were a fragment of conversation with a living, listening mistress. Secondly, poem 2.11 opens with the *puella* no longer presented as the direct object of the practice of writing. The narrator shifts his description of elegiac discourse from *scripta puella mea est* to *scribant de te* (2.11.1). A syntactical retreat is made from the elegiac woman's earlier, more intimate union with the activity of writing. Finally, elegy's female subject is once again associated with physical and mental attributes. In 2.11 she is threatened with a denial of her standing as a well-educated mistress (*docta puella*, 2.11.6); in 2.12 she is endowed with a physique (*caput et digitos et lumina nigra*, 2.12.23) and a delicate gait (*molliter ire pedes*, 2.12.24).

Yet, within the constraints of their slightly more dramatic articulation, poems 2.11 and 2.12 together repeat the movement of 2.10, from rejection to renewal of literary eroticism. In 2.11 the narrator appears to be telling a listening mistress that he has rejected her as the subject of his poetry, while in 2.12 Love has never left his heart, and the Propertian writing-practice is once again defined as the delineation of a woman's physical attributes. The repetition of rejection followed by renewal establishes a parallelism between 2.10 and the pair 2.11–12 which encourages the reader to recognize that the latter reproduce and rewrite the concerns of the former. Together 2.11–12 comprise another statement of renewed literary intent.[33]

The emphatic position of *scribant* as the first word of 2.11 shows that this poem too has writing as its primary concern. The addition of *de te alii* broadens that concern into a second rejection of erotic writing. Furthermore, the shape and subject matter of 2.11 set its rejected *puella* within Hellenistic poetic conventions:

> scribant de te alii uel sis ignota licebit:
>     laudet, qui sterili semina ponit humo.
> omnia, crede mihi, tecum uno munera lecto

[33] For the interrelation of poems in the Propertian corpus (including the pairing of 2.11 and 2.12), see Ites (1908).

auferet extremi funeris atra dies;
et tua transibit contemnens ossa uiator,
nec dicet 'Cinis hic docta puella fuit'. (2.11)

[About you others can write or you can be unknown:
He may praise you, who puts seed in barren ground.
All (believe me) the gifts and you, on one couch,
the black day of the final funeral shall carry off;
and your bones the disdainful traveller will pass by,
and not say 'This ash was a clever girl.']

The unusual brevity of the poem fits oddly in the Propertian papyrus roll. Its physical shape and format (its patterned six lines) signal its source in an earlier literary form, the Hellenistic epigram.[34] And the enunciation of literary issues within the structure of a sepulchral epigram finds parallels in a number of poems in the Greek Anthology.[35]

Thus two conflicting narrative modes appear to be operating in poem 2.11. Despite the reintroduction of a few realist techniques, the text clearly follows a conventional pattern in setting out the rejection that precedes poetic renewal. The literariness of the discourse in which the *puella* is now encountered distances the reader from whatever realistic image for the elegiac woman poem 2.11 additionally constructs.

Furthermore, the actual characteristics with which elegy's female figure is here endowed can readily be shown to assist a statement of literary intent. Thus the proposed termination of erotic writing is articulated in the form of an epitaph. The *puella* begins the poem as an apparently living individual directly addressed by the narrator, but ends as bones and ash. At 2.11's close the grammatical immediacy of a direct address to a mistress has been retracted, and the *puella* is

[34] Although two of the MSS attach 2.11 to the previous poem, the consensus of Propertian criticism reads the six lines as a separate epigram. Boucher (1965), 354, notes that in the Propertian corpus epigrammatic poems occur elsewhere only at the ends of books.

[35] Two such poems are attributed to Callimachus (*AP* 7.415 and 525), and one is concerned with Callimachus' *Aetia* (*AP* 7.42). See King (1980), 79.

referred to in the third person, and the past tense, within the reported speech of a traveller contemptuously passing her grave. No longer to be written by Propertius, she has undertaken a grammatical withdrawal, a retreat from the reader. The cessation of a particular practice of writing will deprive the Propertian mistress of her existence and place her in the past precisely because she is herself a part of that practice, its narrative material.[36] Similarly, it is in the act of being written by others that the *puella* will be denied a characterization as *docta*. The learning of the elegiac mistress is dependent on her production by Propertius. Yet learning is an attribute of texts or their producers in Augustan avowals of Alexandrian *doctrina*.[37] So a *puella* who is *docta* possesses a characteristic of erudite poetry, and a rejection of such poetry necessitates the denial of that characteristic.[38]

The *puella* is rejected as a subject for elegiac discourse in 2.11, yet at the end of 2.12 reappears as the poet's elegiac material. The brief depiction of a fleshly mistress with which poem 2.12 closes is, however, immediately preceded by (and interwoven with) a lengthier and recognizably literary depiction of a *puer*. The attribution of physical characteristics to Amor, with which 2.12 begins, sets the poem in a Hellenistic fictive tradition for the personification of love:

> quicumque ille fuit, puerum qui pinxit Amorem,
>   nonne putas miras hunc habuisse manus?
> is primum uidit sine sensu uiuere amantis,
>   et leuibus curis magna perire bona.
> idem non frustra uentosas addidit alas,
>   fecit et humano corde uolare deum:
> scilicet alterna quoniam iactamur in unda,

[36] Compare now Flaschenriem (1997) on the regular appearance of death in declarations of the Propertian poetic project, such as 1.7, 2.1, 2.13, 3.1, and 3.16.

[37] For *doctus* as a term in the Augustan literary-critical vocabulary, see Fedeli (1985), 620, on *docte Menandre* in Prop. 3.21.28.

[38] See Veyne (1983), 73, for this play on *doctus* and the Propertian game of treating his literary creation as a well-lettered girl. Cf. now Habinek (1998), 128–9, who notes that Cynthia's *doctrina* relates only to her poet's literary advancement, it prompts only *his* poetic activity.

nostraque non ullis permanet aura locis.
et merito hamatis manus est armata sagittis,
et pharetra ex umero Cnosia utroque iacet:
ante ferit quoniam tuti quam cernimus hostem,
nec quisquam ex illo uulnere sanus abit. (2.12.1–12)

[Whoever he was, who painted Love a boy,
don't you think he had amazing hands?
He first saw that without sense lovers live,
And in slight cares lose great riches.
He also without error added wings of wind,
And made him a god who flies from the human heart:
Since of course on alternate waves we are tossed,
And our breeze does not stay on any spot.
And justly with barbed arrows his hand is equipped,
and from each shoulder a Cnosian quiver hangs:
since he strikes us secure before we discern our enemy,
nor does anyone from that wound walk away unharmed.]

Attention has been drawn to precursors and parallels for the delineation of Amor as a boy possessed of wings and arrows (*puer* 1–4; *alae* 5–8; *sagittae* 9–12). Hellenistic epigram and school exercises in rhetoric have been provided as models for the enunciation in 2.12 of the iconography of Love.[39] The poem also locates itself within a Hellenistic literary eroticism by such poetic markers as the reproduction of Greek words and sounds (*pharetra* and *Cnosia*).[40]

Furthermore, the subsequent revision of the iconography of Amor (the removal of its wings from the *puerilis imago*) counterpoints with poetic renewal the rejection of erotic writing expressed in 2.11:

in me tela manent, manet et puerilis imago:
sed certe pennas perdidit ille suas;

[39] See e.g. Rothstein (1966), 286–9; Enk (1962), 169–79; Camps (1967), 112; Cairns (1972), 75; Quinn (1963), 170–1.

[40] The reproduction of Greek sound effects has been observed on a larger scale in the Hylas narrative of 1.20 by Curran (1964), 281–93.

euolat heu nostro quoniam de pectore nusquam,
  assiduusque meo sanguine bella gerit. (2.12.13–16)

[In me his darts remain, remains also his boyish image:
  but certainly his feathers he has lost;
since he never flies, alas, from out of our heart,
  and constantly with my blood wages war.]

Paintings not infrequently provide parallels for Propertius' mythological material,[41] but on this occasion paintings are a poem's explicit concern. 2.12 thus contrasts conventional depictions of Amor with one more suited to the narrator of elegiac love. And, in adapting the pictorial representation of Amor to match the requirements of his poetic narrative, Propertius even plays with a technique found also in the visual arts. In the wall-paintings that survive from Pompeii and Herculaneum, for example, the iconography of Amor sometimes varies to suit the details of the mythic tale depicted: a painting of Ariadne's abandonment by Theseus portrays a tearful Eros holding a limp bow and deprived of his arrows, in order to signify love's betrayal (Fig. 2.1).[42] Similarly the illustration of a wingless, tenacious love-god sketched in poem 2.12 signifies a Propertian poetics ceaselessly concerned with love.

So here the image of a wingless *puer* who never leaves the poor poet's heart acts as a signifier of a renewed poetic practice in the same way as the Amor who washed Propertius' poems in the waters of Permessus at 2.10.26. And just like Ovid's Cupid who steals a foot in order to form a pentameter verse in *Amores* 1.1, so Propertius' Amor humorously plays a troublesome tutelary divinity to the practice of writing love elegies: the tenacity attributed to this disabled form of the love-god playfully demonstrates the impossibility of love elegy's rejection.

[41] See e.g. Boucher (1965), 263–7, and Lyne (1980), 83–6.

[42] For a description, see Barré (1861), 129, and Helbig (1868), 256 n. 1223. See now Fredrick (1995) on the immense popularity of 'Ariadne abandoned' in Roman erotic painting. Such visual representations have been thought to lie behind the description of Ariadne in Prop. 1.3.1–2, see e.g. Whitaker (1983), 91–2.

FIG. 2.1 Ariadne abandoned by Theseus. Drawing after a Pompeian wall-painting.

Thus, at both stages in poem 2.12, the *puer* is clearly either a traditional or an innovative representation of Love in art: the able love-god is shaped according to a conventional, Hellenistic iconography; the disabled love-god marks a new and renewed erotic discourse. But what of the *puella* who is suddenly pictured at the close of the poem? Does the sketch of her physique offer instead a glimpse of a living woman's anatomy?

quid tibi iucundum est siccis habitare medullis?
  si pudor est, alio traice tela tua!

intactos isto satius temptare ueneno:
  non ego, sed tenuis uapulat umbra mea.
quam si perdideris, quis erit qui talia cantet,
  (haec mea Musa leuis gloria magna tua est),
qui caput et digitos et lumina nigra puellae
  et canat ut soleant molliter ire pedes? (2.12.17–24)

[What pleasure is there for you to dwell in dried-out marrow?
  If you've any shame, transfer your darts elsewhere!
The untouched it's more satisfying to assail with that poison,
  not I, but my slender shadow is being beaten.
If you destroy it, who will there be to celebrate such things,
  (this my slight Muse is your great glory),
who a girl's head and fingers and black eyes
  to sing and how her feet are wont to move softly?]

To sustain Cynthia's apparent status as a woman of flesh and blood, it is necessary to read 2.12's *puella* differently from its *puer*, to read the poem's female physique as belonging not to a polemical fiction but to a real figure. Yet the text itself clearly signals that the physical attributes of the *puella* parallel, in a different medium, the iconography of the *puer*. The poem opens with attention focused on one male producer of erotic artistry, the painter (vv. 1–6). It closes with another such producer, the poet (vv. 21–4). The two composers of erotic artefacts, the painter and the poet, are then linked by the deployment of identical epithets to describe facets of their modes of composition: the *leuibus* and *magna* of line 4 reappear as the *leuis* and *magna* of line 22. So poem 2.12 offers twin portraits of a painted boy (*pingere Amorem*) and a sung girl (*canere puellam*), and the cohesion of these two sketches encourages the reader to observe that the transition from *puer* to *puella* is one from a visual to a verbal work of erotic art.

Both modes of representation, visual and verbal, then demarcate the arena for erotic discourse. Poem 2.12 moves from a work of paint to that of a pen, and the polemical function of the head, fingers, and dark eyes of the elegiac mistress is demonstrated by their position alongside, and in opposition to, the attributes of the winged boy-warrior of traditional artistic eroticism. So it is sufficient for the polemical purposes of this poem to provide only the slightest sketch of the physique that forms elegy's subject matter: *caput et digitos et lumina nigra puellae* (v. 23). The only adjective that qualifies this brief catalogue of female physical features locates the Propertian *puella* within a literary tradition for female beauty.[43] In addition, substantial space is allocated not to the elegiac woman's body but to her motion: *ut soleant molliter ire pedes* (v. 24). Significantly, the phrase employed can equally well describe metrical movement, the rhythm of elegiac feet. For, elsewhere in the corpus, the process of producing characteristically Propertian verse is defined as *mollem componere versum* (to compose soft verse, 1.7.19), while in an Horatian satire the refining of Lucilius' poetry is said to involve *uersiculos . . . magis factos et euntis | mollius* (little verses . . . better made and moving | more softly, *Sat.* 1.10.58–9). The elegiac woman's walk may also delineate metrical motion precisely because her body may be read as the anatomy of an elegiac text.[44]

Thus the restoration of flesh to the elegiac mistress is shown, by its juxtaposition with the embodying of elegiac Love, to subserve the poetics of amatory renewal. The wingless *puer* signals the perseverance of Propertian erotic poetry. That poetry is then additionally, and more specifically, signified by the return of a rhythmical *puella*. She is not to be read as *Quelle* because another source of poetic inspiration is already provided by *mea Musa* (v. 22). Neither is she *Ziel* because a recipient of poetry has already been identified (although left unindividuated) by the second person address *putas* (v. 2). Once again the Propertian mistress is the subject of poetic production and her features, however realistically constructed, are shaped to suit the expression of a rejection or a renewal of that production. So poem

[43] Richardson (1977), 247, compares Cat. 43.2 and Horace, *Odes* 1.32.11. See further Ch. 4 below.

[44] Cf. *Amores* 3.1.8, where the personification Elegia is provided with unequal feet to match the unevenness of elegiac verse. For this use of the female body to shape a poetics, see Ch. 4 below.

2.11 sketches a female figure dramatically in order that her bones and ash may mark the Propertian practice of erotic writing as apparently defunct. The renewal of that practice, to which poem 2.12 gives voice, then requires the restoration of flesh to the bones of the elegiac mistress, the return of a head, and fingers, and black eyes.

## 2.13: STUPEFIAT CYNTHIA

The beginning of poem 2.13 still evinces the same poetic concerns as the earlier poems:

> non tot Achaemeniis armatur †etrusca† sagittis,
>   spicula quot nostro pectore fixit Amor.
> hic me tam gracilis uetuit contemnere Musas,
>   iussit et Ascraeum sic habitare nemus,
> non ut Pieriae quercus mea uerba sequantur,
>   aut possim Ismaria ducere ualle feras,
> sed magis ut nostro stupefiat Cynthia uersu:
>   tunc ego sim Inachio notior arte Lino. (2.13.1–8)

> [Not with so many Achaemenid arrows is { } armed,
>   as the darts Love has thrust in my heart.
> He forbade me to disdain such slight Muses,
>   and ordered me thus to dwell in the Ascraean grove,
> not that Pierian oaks might follow after my words,
>   nor that I could lead from the Ismarian vale wild beasts,
> but rather that by my verse Cynthia might be stunned:
>   then I, in skill, might be more famous than Inachian Linus.]

The initial description of Amor as a warrior armed with arrows that pierce the poet's heart (vv. 1–2) links poem 2.13 with the renewal of eroticism expressed in the preceding poem through the quivered but wingless love-god. The subsequent description of Amor as a poetic mentor commanding the poet to dwell on Hesiodic terrain in a particular fashion (vv. 3–8) links 2.13 with the retreat from patriotic poetry expressed in 2.10 through the love-god who launders Propertian verse in particular Hesiodic waters. Yet, at the same time, 2.13 completes the reconstruction of a fleshly woman out of the female fiction which first emerged in 2.10, because the title *Cynthia* now returns to the text and is employed dramatically as if it were the pseudonym for an extratextual, living recipient of poetic production. Once again the reader appears to be offered a glimpse of a real woman only for her to be overshadowed by literary concerns.

Moreover, when Cynthia re-enters the text as a woman to be wooed through writing, the discourse in which she is encountered is placed within a specifically Hellenistic tradition: Amor plays the part of a Callimachean Apollo guiding his protégé towards a poetic form within the Hesiodic tradition Callimachus had favoured;[45] the Linus who is said to be surpassable in artistic fame also figures in the *Aetia* and a Virgilian version of Callimachus' polemics.[46] Although this conjunction of Cynthia's dramatic presentation with the statement of a Callimachean aesthetics calls for an analysis of the interrelation between Cynthia and Callimachus, nonetheless the intimacy imposed by such a strategy has not been sufficiently or adequately explored.

Support for the eighteenth-century subdivision of poem 2.13 would seem to assist the physical separation of Cynthia from Callimachus within the Propertian corpus. For, although 2.13 begins with a brief third-person reference to a Cynthia swamped by issues of poetic production, at verse 17 the elegiac mistress makes an abrupt grammatical advance to the forefront of the text that is accompanied by the fading of explicit references to fiction. A shift to a direct second-person address is initiated, and a relationship is now posited for Cynthia not with Propertian poetic writing but with the poet's envisaged death. Because of these more comfortable narrative strategies, acceptance of a division of the poem at verse 17 would seem to safeguard a living mistress from the earlier encroachment of poetic processes, and to keep Cynthia and Callimachus apart.[47]

[45] See Wilkinson (1966), 142. See now Newman (1997), 323–5.

[46] *Aetia* fr. 1.27; Virgil *Ecl.* 6.67. See King (1980), 83.

[47] See e.g. Lyne (1980), 137, where he refers to 2.13b and thus accepts without comment the subdivision attributed to Broekhuyzen in Barber (1960).

But the *puella* may not be so easily extricated from discourse in which a Propertian version of Callimachus' poetics is enunciated. Not only have many commentators on the text of 2.13 argued cogently for its unity,[48] but several have sustained their arguments with the observation that, despite the change of subject and addressee at verse 17, Cynthia continues to be entangled (although not so outspokenly) with Callimachean imagery.[49] For example, the elegiac mistress is ordered to provide her poet with a tomb of Callimachean proportions:

deinde, ubi suppositus cinerem me fecerit ardor,
 accipiat Manis paruula testa meos,
et sit in exiguo laurus super addita busto,
 quae tegat exstincti funeris umbra locum. (2.13.31–4)

[Then, when the heat underneath has made ash of me,
 let a tiny urn welcome my spirit,
and over the small tomb let a laurel-tree be superimposed,
 whose shade might cover the site of the quenched funeral.]

*Paruula* and *exiguo* attribute to the poet's funeral arrangements the delicacy Callimachus had recommended for the production of poetry.[50]

Even where writing is the poem's explicit concern, it is through the attributes of a realistically constructed, listening mistress that a poetic position for Propertius is articulated:

non ego sum formae tantum mirator honestae,
 nec si qua illustris femina iactat auos:
me iuuet in gremio doctae legisse puellae,
 auribus et puris scripta probasse mea.
haec ubi contigerint, populi confusa ualeto
 fabula: nam domina iudice tutus ero. (2.13.9–14)

[48] As Rothstein (1966), 289–90; Enk (1962), 179; Camps (1967), 115.

[49] As Wimmel (1960), 41 n. 1; Wilkinson (1966), 141–4; Ross (1975), 34–5; King (1980), 84; Williams (1980), 125–8.

[50] Wilkinson (1966), 143.

[I am not so much an admirer of a distinguished appearance,
nor if any woman boasts illustrious ancestors:
let me be pleased to have read in the lap of a clever girl,
and on pure ears to have tested my writings.
Once these things have happened, goodbye the public's mixed-up
talk: for, with a mistress as judge, I shall be secure.]

Characteristics of Callimachean poetry (*docta* and *puris*) are ascribed to the cherished *puella* who can thus express dramatically her author's Callimachean contempt for grandiosity (vv. 9–10) and common opinion (vv. 13–14).[51]

If in poem 2.13, then, Cynthia is *everywhere* associated with Callimachus, can she still retain a status as an independent agent, as a living woman? In order to resolve the apparent enigma of a real woman's presentation in such unrealistic discourse as Callimachean diatribe, heavy reliance has been placed on the avowed claim that elegy's purpose should be to render Cynthia stunned (v. 7). For now the pervasive operation of Callimachean polemic in the Propertian text can be safely disclosed, since an extratextual, intelligent girlfriend is retained to read it. Thus, according to one critic, the second section of 2.13 'exercises on Cynthia—or rather seeks to exercise—the type of influence that the poet claims in the first section his poetry aims at: it serves a practical purpose in his love-affair with Cynthia'.[52] And, according to another, the whole of 2.13 'serves as a courting poem flattering the mistress as a *docta puella* and demonstrating in action how a poet can appeal to a woman in Callimachean-type elegy'.[53]

The text of 2.13, however, does not encourage such literal readings of *ut nostro stupefiat Cynthia uersu*. Firstly, in this account of the processes that govern Propertian literary production it is Amor, not a mistress, who defines the arena for poetic discourse.

[51] As Wilkinson (1966), 142–3. Cf. Habinek (1998), 129–30, on Cynthia's erudition redounding only to her creator's credit.

[52] Williams (1980), 128.

[53] King (1980), 84.

Grammatically *stupefiat Cynthia* is subordinate to, and subsequent on, an instruction to dwell in a particular landscape of language. So stunning Cynthia is an aspect of writing Hesiodic verse. Secondly, verses 3–8 (and, therefore, their stunned Cynthia) form part of a Propertian polemic clearly signalled by the reproduction of the terminology and the terrain for poetic texts mapped out in *Eclogue* 6. The Virgilian Gallus was led up Mount Helicon to effect a change from erotic elegy to poetry about nature, the production of which was associated with the activity of *rigidas deducere montibus ornos* (leading stiff ash-trees down from the mountains, 6.71). So, in the Propertian poem, the spellbinding of *quercus* (v. 5) and *feras* (v. 6) functions as a means of identifying Gallan elegy. And against it the spellbinding of Cynthia (v. 7) is then ranged. As in poem 2.10, the literary task Amor sets Propertius in 2.13 (*sic habitare nemus . . . ut nostro stupefiat Cynthia uersu*) serves to differentiate this poet's continuously amatory elegy from the diversified elegy of Virgil's Gallus.[54] Syntax reinforces the differentiation between the roles of *quercus*, *feras*, and Cynthia in identifying poetic processes: *non ut* (v. 5) balances *sed magis ut* (v. 7) as introducing comparable but opposed aspects of Amor's literary instructions. Within a Hesiodic tradition for writing, the rejected Gallan practice is defined as the activity of attracting *natura*, the Propertian as the activity of attracting a *puella*.

Thirdly, neither of the terms of Amor's command to write in a particular way (*stupefiat* and *Cynthia*) assists the reader in looking out from the text to a mistress courted in Augustan Rome. For each term constrains the elegiac woman within the landscape of literary language mapped out in the *Eclogues* and, therefore, contributes constructively to the statement of a Propertian poetics. Already in the *Eclogues* themselves the verb *stupefacere* had been employed precisely to describe the apparently magical effects of poetry on nature. Introducing the songs of the shepherds Damon and Alphesiboeus in *Eclogue* 8, the narrator had added *quorum stupefactae carmine lynces* (by

[54] See D'Anna (1981), 288–9.

whose song lynxes were spellbound, 8.3).[55] The spellbinding of Cynthia is expressed in the same vocabulary as the spellbinding of *natura* but, since the activity of attracting wild beasts and trees demarcates in the Propertian corpus a rejected form of Hesiodic discourse, *stupefiat Cynthia* becomes an analogous yet opposed form of poetic production.

At this point the text even encourages the reader to interpret the title *Cynthia* as a key Callimachean term in Propertian poetics, a term that establishes a unique literary terrain for its author's discourse. For the word appears as the last in a list of adjectival forms derived from Greek names for mountains, each of which was variously associated with and signalled literary production; *Pieriae* (v. 5), *Ismaria* (v. 6), *Cynthia* (v. 7). Mount Pierus in Thessaly was associated with poetic processes at the beginning of Hesiod's *Works and Days* and in his *Theogony*. The tradition is continued in *Eclogue* 6 where the Muses are called *Pierides* (*Ecl.* 6.13). Mount Ismarus in Thrace was said to be an abode of Orpheus, a connection that again is highlighted in Propertius' topographical model *Eclogue* 6: *Ismarus Orphea* (*Ecl.* 6.30). Finally Mount Cynthus on Delos was linked with Apollo as tutelary divinity to the Callimachean writing-style, and that association too is reproduced in *Eclogue* 6 where the god who directs Virgilian discourse is given the cult title *Cynthius* (*Ecl.* 6.3).[56]

So the adjectival forms of place-names that precede the *Cynthia* of verse 7 draw attention to the word as itself marking a literary terrain. Similarly, the parallelism between the ends of the hexameter and pentameter of the couplet in which it appears (*Cynthia uersu* and *arte Lino*) continues to help identify Cynthia as a polemical signifier of fiction. For, in *Eclogue* 6, Linus acted as the god who conducted Gallus up the hierarchical mountain of poetic production, while Cynthius imposed limitations on the Virgilian narrator of that poetic progress.

55 The parallel is observed by Enk (1962), 182, and Hanslik (1979), 57.

56 For the employment of *Cynthius* as a key Callimachean term by Virgil, see Clausen (1976), 245–7 and (1987), 3; for *Cynthia* as a subsequent development, see Boyancé (1956), 172–5, and Ch. 1 above.

Thus it is through the enunciation of the title *Cynthia* itself that Propertius here, as in 2.10, aligns his work with the early Virgilian and neo-Callimachean practice of writing.

The correspondence and opposition that the text itself establishes between the *Cynthia* of verse 7 and the *Pieriae quercus* and *Ismaria . . . ualle feras* of the preceding couplet do not, therefore, justify the practice of most commentators who are only prepared to translate *natura*, not a *puella*, into literary terms. While verses 5–6 are read symbolically as references to modes of Hesiodic poetry, the next line is still read literally as a reference to a real woman. Yet the close correspondence between these lines requires either that *quercus* and *feras* also be read as living recipients of poetic texts or that Cynthia too be decoded as a signifier of fiction. The reader is not actively encouraged to construct out of the terms *stupefiat* and *Cynthia* a real woman who reads and is moved by Callimachean verse. Each of the terms and their position in poem 2.13 disclose that the spellbinding of a mistress itself categorizes Propertian poetry as Callimachean.

## CYNTHIA, CALLIMACHUS, AND CAESAR

Poems 2.10–13 thus form a group that re-establishes an allegiance to a politically unorthodox, Callimachean poetic practice.[57] Each of the poems then associates the Propertian mistress so intimately with that practice as to undermine her identity apart from it. From the translation of the mistress into the terms of literary production in 2.10, the text gradually moves back to the reinstatement of realism as a narrative mode. And since the features with which Cynthia is realistically shaped in the three later poems clearly subserve the statement of a renewed Callimachean aesthetics, those features only help to confirm the initial account of elegy's beloved as a *scripta puella*—a female fiction.

57 The *Zusammenhang* of 2.10–13 was observed by Ites (1908), 26–7, and accepted as part of his schema for book 2 by Juhnke (1971), 104 and 112.

When some of the polemical strategies of this group have been noted, however, they have not been allowed to disturb readings of the more comfortably realist narratives by which the group is surrounded. For poems 2.10–13 have often been displaced by critics from their position in book 2. Margaret Hubbard's book *Propertius* (1974), for example, allocates one chapter to each of Propertius' four books and the issues that arise from their examination. The second chapter considers the concept of the poetic unit and its implications for the subdivision of book 2, the third the role of Callimachus and politics in the composition of book 3. The transference of her account of 2.1, 2.10, and 2.34 from the chapter 'Some Problems of Unity' to 'The Quest for Callimachus' then effectively dislocates those poems from their place within the second book and enables them to be read as contributing only to the interpretation of the third.

In particular, the thesis originally put forward by Karl Lachmann, and later supported by O. Skutsch, that 2.10 once began another book of the Propertian corpus has encouraged critics to deny the poem a place within the heart of book 2.[58] Lachmann found the reference to *tres . . . libelli* at 2.13.25 disturbing, unless it could be relocated within an original third book. The apparent advocacy of patriotic poetry in 2.10 he then considered the appropriate prologue to the rediscovered work.[59] However, the reference to three books in a second may simply suggest that there existed a long-term plan (however generally conceived) for the poetic organization of events into three books, an acknowledgement of which may be disturbing because it diminishes the possible contribution an affair with a real woman could make to the sequence of events the books artfully describe.[60] Nor is a sequence of rejection and then renewal of love

[58] My purpose here will not be to argue a full case for the unity of book 2, but to offer reasons for the place of poems 2.10–13 *within* the book.

[59] Lachmann (1816), pp. xxi–xxii, and cf. Skutsch (1975), 229–33. See now Lyne (1998), who concedes that 2.10–13 are interrelated, but considers 2.10–11 to have concluded the original second book of poems, and 2.12–15 to have begun the third.

[60] The existence of such a long-term plan does not necessitate the simultaneous publication of all three volumes, as was suggested by Williams (1968), 480–95.

elegy a sufficient criterion for the relocation of poems 2.10–12 at the opening of another book. As Walter Wimmel argued, the appearance of poetic apologetics in Horace's *Odes* at 1.6, 2.12, and 4.2, and in the Propertian corpus at 3.3 and 3.9, demonstrates that they need not function as a prologue or *Bucheinleitung*.[61] Furthermore, a similar sequence of renunciation and renewal can be found embedded within another second book of amatory elegies, at *Amores* 2.9, a poem that also specifically recalls Propertius 2.12 in its address to personified Love (a Cupid to Propertius' Amor). The parallel position of *Amores* 2.9 within Ovid's revised edition and its specific reminiscences of Propertius 2.12 suggest that the Propertian poems of rejection and renewal were read by Ovid as incorporated *within* a second Propertian poetry-book, rather than placed at the margins of a third.[62]

Even the text of 2.10 itself, despite its break away from the techniques of realism, establishes a close relation between the poem and those that it immediately follows in book 2. In the first verse, the words *sed tempus* and *iam* 'demand imperiously that something should precede them'.[63] *Haemonio . . . equo*, in the second verse, recalls both the *Haemoniis . . . equis* of 2.8.38 and the story of Haemon and Antigone to which the earlier poem refers.

So poems 2.10–13 are not only interrelated, they are also integrated with the rest of book 2; the polemical statement about poetic choices which they contain should not be read as an autonomous motif having nothing to do with the erotic realities apparently expressed elsewhere in the second book. Their focus on Cynthia as a poetic fiction, whose features are shaped to suit an avowal of political unorthodoxy, suggests that realism is not equivalent to reality nor a realistically constructed beloved equivalent to a real woman. And,

[61] Wimmel (1960), 193 and 188 n. 1.

[62] The revised three-book edition of the *Amores* has also been compared for its similarly lengthy middle book by Nethercut (1980), 94–109.

[63] Hutchinson (1984), 100. See now Gale (1997), 87, who notes that 2.4 to 2.13 constitute a cycle of poems bound together by their concern with erotic rivalry, renunciation, and renewal.

occurring within the heart of the second book, this suggestion obstructs and interrupts any attempt to construct a real mistress out of the textual characteristics of the second Cynthia. Thus even the narrative organization of the second poetry-book, far from facilitating a practice of reading Cynthia as real, favours a reading of her as a unique form of writing—as the embodiment of a Roman Callimacheanism and as the continuous displacement of poetry about Augustus Caesar.

# 3

# The Elegiac Woman at Rome: Propertius Book 4

How do women enter the discourse of Augustan love poetry and become elegiac? Studies of the representation of women in antiquity generally suggest that women enter its literatures doubly determined. Broadly speaking, literary representations of the female are determined both at the level of culture and at the level of genre: that is to say, by the range of cultural codes and institutions that order the female in a particular society and by the conventions that surround a particular practice of writing.[1] Having largely focused in the previous chapter on consideration of generic determinants (the configuration of Cynthia in the Propertian corpus as a distinctive poetics of Roman Callimacheanism), I propose in this chapter to explore further the place of the elegiac woman in the literary landscape of Augustan Rome through an examination of the *interplay* of her generic and cultural determinants.

This chapter is a revised version of an article first published in *PCPS* 213 (1987), 153–78.

[1] See e.g. Foley (1981) and now Dixon (2001).

Among the Augustan elegists themselves the practice of writing elegies is so closely identified with one particular type of woman that when the genres of Elegy and Tragedy are personified, they are clearly differentiated as respectively mistress and matron.[2] The most familiar elegiac woman is, therefore, the mistress: the Propertian Cynthia, the Tibullan Delia and Nemesis, the Ovidian Corinna. Yet the figure of the mistress is by no means the exclusive shape which the elegiac woman takes. So, in order to encompass within a single analysis the broad spectrum of female types which the elegiac woman embraces (and better to define the role of the mistress in the elegiac ordering of femininity), I propose to focus on that book of the elegiac corpus which displays the greatest diversity of female subjects: namely the fourth book of the Propertian oeuvre in which we find not just a mistress, but also a wife, a vestal virgin, a witch, and a mother.[3]

Perhaps the first questions we should ask about the fourth book of Propertian elegies are: how are we to account for this diversity? and what relation do these female figures have to the Cynthia who no longer holds centre stage? At least one critic has attempted to put the familiar figure of the mistress back into the centre of the fourth book's fictive world, by arguing that new figures appear only to be contrasted unfavourably with her. Then, surrounded by apparently more conventional female types, the Propertian Cynthia is read as triumphing over more orthodox assessments of a woman's worth.[4] Such a reading of the relations between the fourth book's female subjects seems, however, highly unsatisfactory. For the elegiac mistress Cynthia is not an interpretative key, a narrative pivot, of the fourth or even the third Propertian poetry-books.

Already the third book of the Propertian corpus presents as its starting-point and inspiration not an elegiac mistress but the Hellenistic poets Callimachus and Philitas, and it only employs the title

[2] See further Ch. 4 below.
[3] See now Janan (2001).
[4] Hallett (1973), 103–24.

*Cynthia* towards its close in poetic declarations of erotic desertion or dismissal. Within that narrative framework, the third book broadens the range of Propertian elegy and extends the compass of its elegiac woman beyond a subjugating Cynthia to include, for example, a loving wife abandoned at Rome by her campaigning husband (3.12). A single narrative viewpoint steadies apparent fluctuations between public and private, personal and political, themes that the expanded poetic range engenders. However, the first-person, authorial narrator speaks now not as Cynthia's lover in particular but simply as a lover, or even a spokesman for other lovers, at Rome. The key to this poetry-book, it is generally recognized, lies not in the amatory idioms of love for Cynthia, but in the publication of Horace's first three books of *Odes*. The third book of the Propertian corpus does not pivot round Cynthia, but around Callimachus and Horace, offering a playful and an appropriately elegiac response to the postures of recent lyric verse.[5]

Similarly, the elegiac mistress does not provide a key to the diversity of styles and female subjects that the last book of the Propertian corpus incorporates. The first poem of the first book appears to evoke the beginning of an affair, the last poems of the third book to draw that affair to a close. Poem 1.1 begins Cynthia's role as the dominant subject of elegiac discourse, poems 3.24 and 25 seem to conclude it. A cycle of allusions signalling a narrative progression from erotic madness to celibate wisdom shapes the first three books into a poetic unit, and effectively marks off any subsequent book of elegies as a significant departure from what was once Cynthia-centred discourse.[6]

Appearing some years after the earlier sequence of three books, and rendered additionally distinct by the greater length of its elegies, the fourth book begins with an announcement of new themes: rites,

[5] For these characteristics of book 3, see e.g. Solmsen (1948), 105–9; Hubbard (1974), 68–115; Putnam (1980). Cf. Ch. 1 above.

[6] Williams (1968), 480–95; Barsby (1974), 128–37; Putnam (1980), 108–10.

festivals, and the ancient names of places (*sacra diesque canam et cognomina prisca locorum*, 4.1.69). This announcement suggests that the boundaries of Propertian elegy will be extended even beyond those drawn in book 3. For now Rome, and specifically its presentation in Virgil *Aeneid* 8, are taken as the starting-point for renewed poetic production. Callimachus continues to be claimed as advocate of elegiac over epic writing-practices, and as model for linguistic delicacy and polish, but now he is also appropriated to signal not the further writings of a love poet but the writing of Rome itself. An authorial narrator suggests that this next book of elegies will commemorate the city not in Ennian epic but in a Romanized version of Callimachean aetiology: a genre able to accommodate comfortably the narratives of Rome's history and Caesar's weaponry that poem 4.1 appears to initiate but which the earlier Propertian poetry-books generally eschewed, deferred, or even condemned.

However, this is not the only announcement of a poetics with which the fourth book begins, for poem 4.1 has a bipartite structure. A second speaker, the astrologer Horos, intervenes just as the authorial narrator is setting out the ambitious goals (the construction of an elegiac counterpart to Virgilian Rome) towards which his race-horse of poetry must labour (*has meus ad metas sudet oportet equus*, v. 70). Answering the earlier account of Rome's glorious Trojan origins with more tragic perspectives on Roman warfare and Troy's fall, and offering in its place an idiosyncratic reminder of the poet's previous career as a love elegist, Horos demands a return to the familiar amatory idioms of the earliest books—to poems about servitude under a single mistress.

Women feature predominantly in the second section of the opening poem, forming part of the advocacy of stylistic moderation and the qualification of the earlier account of Rome's glorious history. A mother's grief for the loss of her sons in battle undercuts the earlier depiction of Rome's grandeur (vv. 89–98), the slaughter of a young girl and the rape of a prophetess interpose a more critical view of the Trojan war (vv. 109–18), and the familiar figure of the mistress appears as part of an erotic military service with which Horos believes the poet would be better occupied (vv. 135–40). We might therefore anticipate that in the fourth Propertian book female subjects will be more likely to implement the second rather than the first section of the opening poetic programme.

So the novel, bipartite design of the first poem offers two conflicting programmes for the fourth book, but because the authorial narrator offers no response to the interventions of the second, it is not immediately clear which (if either) form of elegiac writing will now be undertaken.[7] The poems that follow fluctuate between the two poles of aetiological and amatory elegy established by the initial, dramatic clash between poetic programmes. Yet, whereas a narrative thread of eroticism binds together the disparate materials of the third book, no overarching authorial voice, no unifying lover's perspective, appears to bind together the poems of the fourth book. In book 3, for example, the battle of Actium enters Propertian elegy as part of the lover-poet's explanation of his erotic servitude (3.11), and is enclosed by poems that offer the elegiac lover's views on the occasion of his beloved's birthday (3.10) and on a husband's desertion of his loyal wife (3.12).[8] In book 4, however, Actium now enters elegiac discourse in the absence of any immediate amatory context, as part of a priestly poet's aetion of Apollo's Palatine temple (4.6). And even the poems that surround it are dominated not by the voice of an authorial lover, but by the voices of a madam (4.5) and a mistress (4.7).[9]

[7] On the new characteristics of the fourth book and its two poetic programmes, see Camps (1965), 1–6; Pillinger (1969); Van Sickle (1974); Hubbard (1974), 116–56; Macleod (1976); Miller (1982); Stahl (1985), 248–305. See now Newman (1997), 265–75 and Janan (2001) esp. 15 and 102–3, where she engenders the book's bipolar poetics as masculine and feminine.

[8] Putnam (1980).

[9] Nethercut (1983), 1849–50, explores the similarities, rather than the differences, between the narrative fluctuations of books 3 and 4. On Propertius' Actium poems, see further Ch. 6 below.

Faced with a book where the unifying viewpoint of a lover is not threaded through its disparate poems, where an authorial lover scarcely appears as a central character even in the amatory elegies, and which begins with an unresolved conflict between the poetics of *Roma* and *amor*, there is no justification for reading Cynthia and Cynthia-centred eroticism as still dominating its discourse.

How, then, can we account for the diversity of the fourth book and the range of its female forms? So apparent is the heterogeneity of this book that it has been thought to constitute a posthumous work which an editor patched together out of the unpublished poems of the late Propertius.[10] Less drastically, the book has been thought to comprise fragments of an unfinished collection of Roman aetia which Propertius subsequently padded out with miscellaneous amatory pieces and published with a suitably hybrid introduction.[11] Particularly since the 1950s, however, the body of scholarship attesting to the essential cohesiveness of the fourth book has steadily grown. Many critics argue that its diversity does not constitute an unfortunate afterthought but, rather, its central dynamic—its poetic project. The bipartite structure of poem 4.1 then establishes the interchange between aetiological and amatory themes as a poetic principle operative in the rhythm of an elegiac poetry-book. Superficially, the subsequent elegies leading up to, and including, poem 4.6 alternate between the aetiological (2, 4, 6) and amatory (3, 5) categories, while those leading up to the last poem form amatory (7, 8) and aetiological (9, 10) pairs. Yet cross-references and overlaps abound between the poems located in these supposedly rigid classifications, until the book closes with a poem (4.11) that seems to belong simultaneously to neither and to both categories. Such studies suggest strongly that the last book of the Propertian corpus forms a coherent whole, that it sets out a poetics

[10] Fedeli (1965), pp. xxii and xxx, for example, appears to concur with Postgate's original view that book 4 is a posthumous work.

[11] See e.g. Hubbard (1974), 116–18, following Dieterich.

of polarity with which its subsequent poems and, therefore, its female subjects are constantly engaged.[12]

Poem 4.2 also offers lessons on how to read the fourth book's diverse female figures. Here a new first-person narrator, the statue Vertumnus, tells us that he contains his own many shapes in one body (*meas tot in uno corpore formas*, v. 1) and that whatever shape he becomes, whether man or woman, he is still *decorus* (v. 22). In a number of ways, the text itself encourages its readers to interpret the statue's declarations as yet another programme for, and justification of, the diversity of book 4. For example, the changeful yet singular statue may act as symbol of a changeful yet unified Propertian book because several of the *shapes* into which Vertumnus boasts that he can turn also form past and present *subjects* of Propertian poetry. The Iacchus (or Bacchus) and Apollo which Vertumnus becomes (vv. 31–2) feature together as inspirers of Propertian verse towards the beginning of the third book (3.2.9), and are hymned respectively in poems 3.17 and 4.6. More significantly, the very first transformation for which Vertumnus playfully professes a capacity recalls the characteristics of the elegiac mistress Cynthia and the amatory idioms of the earliest Propertian poetry-books (1.2.1–6, 2.1.1–16), since, surprisingly for a bronze statue, he can become a soft girl in Coan silks (*indue me Cois, fiam non dura puella*, v. 23).

Identifiable in places with forms of Propertian discourse, associated explicitly with the poem in which it gains a voice (v. 57), described as a finely crafted work of art (vv. 59–64), this statue's proclamation of its tasteful transformations may thus be read as an instrument for the expression of a new, playful poetics of metamorphosis: *opportuna mea est cunctis natura figuris: | in quamcumque uoles uerte, decorus ero* (fit for all shapes is my nature: | into whichever one

[12] The history of claims for book 4's cohesiveness is conveniently set out by Nethercut (1968); cf. Hutchinson (1984), 100–3. See now DeBrohun (1994), 42–4, and O'Neill (2000), 259–60.

you want, turn me, I'll be comely, vv. 21–2).[13] By the time we reach poem 4.3, where we find the first-person narrator has been transformed again into a young bride, it becomes clear that the range of women who speak in the fourth book also forms part of the Propertian poetic project. They contribute to an innovatory, bipolar poetics, a programme comprising surprising and sometimes playful transformations of narrative voice and a range of elegiac tones that oscillates between the aetiological and the amatory, the public and the private, the grand and the sorrowful.

## ARETHUSA

The first poem of the book to place a woman on Propertius' elegiac map of Rome is structured as if it were in fact a woman's work. For, in its entirety, poem 4.3 presents itself as a love letter composed at Rome by a female, rather than a male, lover. And in keeping with the poetic project of diversification, the new elegiac narrator Arethusa does not even speak as a mistress but as a wife.[14]

Earlier Propertian poetry-books were written predominantly in an autobiographical mode that appeared to confide to readers a poet's confession of love for a woman who was not his wife. The male authorial narrator preferred death to marriage (2.7.7–12).[15] His beloved Cynthia was depicted as transcending the simple categories of wife and mistress (2.6.41–2) and was even cast occasionally in the role of a new kind of meretricious Lucretia who spins when abandoned by her lover (3.6.15–18).[16] However, the new elegiac narrator Arethusa declares that all love is great, but that found in manifest

[13] As Marquis (1974); Pinotti (1983). See now DeBrohun (1994), Newman (1997), 275–7; Lindheim (1998*b*); O'Neill (2000); Janan (2001), esp. 14–15; Ch. 5 below. DeBrohun argues that, in fact, the Hercules of 4.9 constitutes a more appropriate embodiment of the clashing styles of book 4 than Vertumnus.

[14] On 4.3, see now Janan (2001), 53–69.

[15] For Propertius' poetic treatment of marriage generally, see Lilja (1965), 230–9.

[16] As Fedeli (1985), 213, and cf. Prop. 1.3.41.

marriage is greater still (*omnis amor magnus, sed aperto in coniuge maior*, 4.3.49). She also restores to herself, as faithful wife, the rightful role of a loyal matronal Lucretia who spins war-time's wool while awaiting her husband's return (*castrensia pensa laboro*, v. 33).[17] Wool-working is now associated familiarly with the chastity of a *matrona* not, paradoxically, with the enforced continence of a *meretrix*. In poem 4.3, the elegiac woman as loyal wife appears to match an ideal of Roman womanhood evoked throughout the Augustan age in many epitaphs and even, according to Suetonius, in the household of the *princeps* himself.[18] So the common elegiac idiom of a lover's slavery to his beloved is replaced in poem 4.3 by the less provocative picture of a husband's conquest of his wife: Arethusa recalls her sexual surrender on her wedding-night when she gave up to her husband's rough pressure her vanquished arms (*cum rudis urgenti bracchia uicta dedi*, v. 12).[19]

The elegiac narrator Arethusa is also distinguished from the narrative first-person, the 'I', of earlier Propertian poems by her loyalty to her soldier-husband. In Propertius' first book the male elegiac narrator declines an invitation to leave Rome with the soldier Tullus and describes himself as already occupied in the military service of love (1.6.29–30). In subsequent books the metaphor of *militia amoris* continues to be employed as a means for rejecting warfare and the composition of epic poems on military themes: it is in his girlfriend's camp that the lover parades (2.7.15–16) and it is with her that he fights his battles (3.5.1–2).[20] In the third book, the narrative first-person expresses surprise that Postumus was able to abandon his wife Galla in the pursuit of Augustan standards, associates the

[17] See Maltby (1981). See now Janan (2001), 62–4.

[18] Suet. *Div. Aug.* 64. See Williams (1958), 21 n. 20; Purcell (1986), 94; and now Janan (2001), 63. Cf. Ogilvie (1965), 222, on Livy's wool-working Lucretia; Dee (1974), 88, on Propertius' Arethusa. On the ideal Roman *matrona*, see now Treggiari (1991), 229–319.

[19] Cf. Dee (1974), 83.

[20] For the elegiac metaphor of *militia amoris*, see Baker (1968) and Murgatroyd (1975). See now Gale (1997), 78–95; Davis (1999), 438–42; above, Ch. 1.

despoiling of Parthia with greed, and expresses the wish that all those who prefer weapons to bed may perish (3.12.1–6). Arethusa, however, studies maps of the terrain her husband Lycotas will cover in his campaigns and longs to join him in camp (vv. 35–48): she wants to become loyal luggage in his military expeditions (*militiae sarcina fida tuae*, v. 48). So, in keeping with the grandiose plans expressed at the beginning of the fourth book, Arethusa's letter seems to change the old poetic idioms and to enlarge even further the dimensions of the Propertian practice of elegiac writing.

The adoption of such a female voice in the Propertian corpus also seems to reinstate the conventional opposition between male and female spheres of activity that epic poetry had exploited and earlier Propertian poems had undermined. The topography of epic generally places women within the city and men outside on the battlefield: in the *Iliad*, the gates of Troy separate the women's world of spinning and weaving inside from the men's world of war outside.[21] Yet in the erotic discourse of the earlier Propertian poems that separation of male from female was subverted by the position of the authorial *amator*. In book 3, for example, the male lover-poet stays within the gates of Rome encouraging the soldiers of Augustus to depart, or observing their return from the vantage point of his mistress' embrace (3.4). The model for male behaviour which the third book holds up is not a Hector who leaves the city to engage in battle, but the unheroic Paris who wages war only in Helen's lap (3.8.29–32). Now, in poem 4.3, it is only the woman who stays within the city, the man fulfils the role the state requires of him: at war, abroad, implementing Augustus' frontier policy.[22]

However, there is still a fundamental generic difference between epic narratives and this new elegiac account of male and female roles.

[21] See Arthur (1981) and Perkell (1981). For Greek tragedy's alignment of the sexes inside and outside the house, cf. Zeitlin (1978). On the gendering of Roman epic, see now Keith (2000).

[22] Dee (1974), 81–2, notes the oppositions in poem 4.3 between Rome/abroad, domestic/military, female/male.

Composed in the form of a woman's letter sent from Rome to a soldier-husband abroad, poem 4.3 locates Arethusa at the centre of the elegiac world and warfare on its periphery. The elegiac poem does follow general epic practice when it places the woman at home and the man away at war: in *Aeneid* 8 (the conversion of which into elegy had been the initial poetic programme of Propertius' fourth book) men march away from Evander's little city while their mothers watch fearfully from the walls.[23] Unlike *Aeneid* 8, however, the city walls are the limits of the elegiac world and the poem's structure does not permit it to narrate directly the deeds of Lycotas on campaign. The elegiac letter stays within a woman's world at Rome where any engagement in battles to maintain the frontiers of the Roman empire is a distressing mark of absence.[24]

If a lyric narrative of Augustan campaigns is compared with this elegiac treatment, it further demonstrates how the strategy of producing a wife's letter permits Propertius to fulfil a part of the programme of the fourth poetry-book (to look beyond the earlier more private limits of erotic elegy to public Roman themes), and yet to draw back from more grandiose possibilities. Traditionally it was the thanksgiving of a faithful wife, rather than the spectatorship of a disinterested elegiac lover, that signalled the soldier's return, the achievement of victory and peace. So, in Horace *Odes* 3.14.5–10, a chaste Livia (who rejoices in a single husband) is encouraged to offer sacrifice and to join a procession of women giving thanks for the safe return of Augustus from his victories in Spain. Similarly, the elegiac poem 4.3 does not close with a male narrator promising to applaud an army's return whilst disengaging himself from its activities, but with a female narrator praying for a triumph for her husband as a result of Parthian conquests and declaring that, with an inscription,

[23] The comparison with *Aeneid* 8.583–93 is made by Little (1982), 303.

[24] Cf. now Spentzou (forthcoming) on Ovid's *Heroides*. She argues that such feminine love letters subvert the elevated genres of epic and tragedy by their double compression as both elegies and epistles. They produce indirect narratives of nostalgia or anticipation that are short, fragmentary, introverted, domestic, and unstable.

she will dedicate his weapons in gratitude at the gate through which her man safely returns (*armaque cum tulero portae uotiua Capenae, | subscribam SALVO GRATA PVELLA VIRO*, vv. 71–2).

Although approximately parallel roles are provided for Livia and for Arethusa, nonetheless there are again significant generic differences between the lyric and the elegiac perspectives, generated by the narrative strategy of a woman's letter. The ode places Augustus' military prowess in a public context by beginning with the unique vocative *o plebs* and, in his role as public bard rather than sympotic poet, the Horatian narrator declares the occasion of Augustus' return to be a joyful one for him.[25] The elegiac poem, when shaped as a wife's private letter, finds no place for authorial comments on military matters, for public addresses, or even for Augustus, because this first-person narrator is concerned exclusively with the activities of a single soldier in whom she expresses an amatory interest.

The elegiac letter thus transforms elements of the ideology of woman into the literary effects required by the conventions of the genre and the project of a Propertian poetry-book. The process whereby the faithful wife who waits for her soldier-husband's return is transformed into an elegiac woman, and the implications of that process for readings of Propertian poetry, can be elucidated if two Augustan versions of the loyal Lucretia are compared. In Augustan historiography, in Livy's prose account of Rome's beginnings, Lucretia spins at home while her husband besieges Ardea. The depiction of her *pudicitia* operates as a moral foil to the depravity of her assailant. The violation of her chastity is then presented as precipitating the fall of the kings, and thus opens up a pathway to the political freedom of the early republic. For that purpose it is sufficient to depict Lucretia briefly, spinning within the house.[26] When, however, Lucretia later enters the discourse of Ovid's *Fasti*, and becomes an elegiac woman

[25] Fraenkel (1957), 288–91, however, discloses more ominous tones in the sympotic last stanzas.

[26] Livy 1.57–9. On which, see Ogilvie (1965), 218–20; and now Janan (2001), 62–4, and Dixon (2001), Ch. 4.

(2.741–60), her conduct as she awaits her husband's return is described in more detail and she takes on some new features that parallel and recall those of the Propertian Arethusa. She inquires after the battle that occupies her husband, but calls the besieged city *improba* for keeping him away. He is rash to risk his life in war, while it is she (not her soldier) who is 'dying' of despair. Thus, on entry into an elegiac genre, the woman's perspective is enlarged and, in her loneliness at home, warfare becomes not a glorious but a sorrowful matter.

The account of militarism which the elegiac Lucretia thus provides leads to the devaluing of her soldier-husband's activities. Similarly, as another faithful wife left at home while her husband is away at war, the first-person narrator (the female elegiac 'I') of the Propertian poem 4.3 also gives voice to a devaluation of war. As poem 4.3 progresses, warfare is increasingly associated with the erotic and subordinated to amatory concerns that recall the idioms of earlier elegiac poems. The absence of the soldier-husband, which war necessitates, occasions an outburst against the inventor of war (vv. 19–22) such as had already issued from the mouth of the male lover, forced to abandon his beloved and leave for war, in earlier Tibullan elegy.[27] The soldier, from his loving wife's viewpoint, has delicate arms (*teneros . . . lacertos*, v. 23) and unwarlike hands (*imbellis . . . manus*, v. 24) just like the delicate mistresses of earlier love poetry.[28] Here war wounds are mistaken for, or preferred to, the marks of sexual encounters with other women (vv. 25–8). In earlier elegiac eroticism, however, the marks of sexual encounters had demonstrated the metaphoric militancy of love.[29] At home, in Rome, uniforms are woven rather than worn (v. 33) and weapons are kissed rather than

[27] Tib. 1.10.1–6, and cf. Tib. 1.3.1–56. For the relation of this outburst, and Arethusa's subsequent complaints, to the topoi of elegiac erotic writing, see Dee (1974).

[28] Compare the *teneros lacertos* of Lycotas, for example, with Cynthia's *pedibus teneris* (1.8.7). As now Janan (2001), 58–9. Janan also demonstrates that even Lycotas' battles appear from Arethusa's perspective as forms of erotic contest (64–5).

[29] As in Prop. 3.8.

carried (*osculor arma tua*, v. 30). Arethusa learns about Augustan campaigns and the geography of the Roman empire ultimately only to ascertain when Lycotas will be coming home (vv. 35–40). Finally, at the close of the poem, Arethusa's prayer that her husband will return and obtain a triumph is grammatically dependent on her one stipulation that he preserve unspoiled the contract of her marriage-bed (*incorrupta mei conserua foedera lecti! | hac ego te sola lege redisse uelim*, vv. 69–70).

In earlier Propertian elegy, the narrative of an attachment to a mistress differentiated the lover-poet from the soldier and, presented as an engagement in erotic warfare, aided the rejection of militarism and epic poems on military themes. In poem 4.3, instead of the old elegiac metaphor of the soldiery of love undertaken by the male narrator, we find the female narrator's love of the soldier: not so much *militia amoris* as *amor militis*. The effect, however, is similar. The ideological alignment of the loyal wife with the domestic can be utilized to glorify or to denigrate war. In Arethusa's letter, where war is observed exclusively from the domestic setting, eroticism still holds greater value than militancy.

So, while Arethusa constitutes a new female narrator in the Propertian corpus, she is nonetheless provided with some of the attitudes of the earlier authorial narrator.[30] And she is even provided with some of his attributes, for when she presents herself as a lonely lover enduring bitter nights of separation (vv. 29–32), she takes on the condition of the *exclusus amator* of the very first Propertian poem, who had endured bitter nights when shut out by Cynthia (1.1.33).[31] Therefore, in the very first transformation which follows on from the many shapes of Vertumnus, Propertius takes on the character of the faithful wife Arethusa and she, paradoxically, takes on the character of the earlier Propertian narrator.

[30] Lilja (1965), 234–5, observes that in 4.3 marriage is depicted in the same colours as elegiac affairs.

[31] See Dee (1974), 87, and Fedeli (1985), 127, and cf. Prop. 4.3.31–2 with the restlessness of the Ovidian lover in *Am.* 1.2.2.

Yet this transformation does not lead us right back into the world of the earlier books. In poem 3.12, war had already been presented as entailing the perversion of Roman marriage and the desolation of the abandoned wife, but there the reader was offered an apparently authorial viewpoint: a poet's critique of military matters.[32] In the fourth book, the narrative device of a single elegiac epistle not only comfortably accommodates the limitations of elegiac interest in military matters, it also precludes any close identification of the first-person narrative voice with the viewpoint of an elegiac poet.

The employment of Greek names for the husband, the wife, and even the wife's dog, does not encourage any easy identification of the scenario envisaged in the letter with particular events at Rome to which the poet Propertius might have been privy. Some critics do read Arethusa and Lycotas as pseudonyms and look elsewhere in the corpus for the Roman characters which these names are thought to disguise,[33] but the name *Arethusa* is itself highly appropriate for a narrator of the fourth book's changeful poetics. Just like the immediately preceding narrator (the god Vertumnus), the nymph Arethusa possesses her own story of metamorphosis: from woman into fountain. Moreover, in Virgil's *Eclogues* she had been employed as a symbol of a writing-practice that introduced the elegist Gallus into a pastoral landscape. Heading a pastoral poem that narrated an elegiac lover's complaints about his absent mistress, Arethusa had already been associated with the amatory idioms of elegiac writing.[34]

The elegiac epistle, the freestanding fictional love letter in verse, appears itself to be a new genre in Latin literature.[35] So Arethusa

[32] See e.g. Little (1982), 301–3.

[33] Rothstein (1966), 229, took Lycotas to be a translation of the Latin name Lupercus found at Prop. 4.1.93, and was supported by Grimal (1953), 8. Fedeli (1985), 119, thought a connection with the Postumus of 3.12 more probable.

[34] Putnam (1970), 344–5. Hubbard (1974), 142–5, notes that the Greek names probably have pastoral connotations: Lycotas reappears as a defender of rural values in Calp. Sic. *Ecl.* 7.

[35] Jacobson (1974), 319–48. See now Spentzou (forthcoming).

writes a letter because an elegiac epistle suits the innovatory approach of a Roman Callimachus interested in new practices of elegiac writing.[36] Furthermore, in a letter, the first person is not presented directly: we are not asked to imagine an Arethusa addressing her Lycotas face-to-face. Instead, through explicit references to the physical processes of writing and reading, we encounter a woman who has been written into an elegiac letter and who asks to be read (vv. 1–6).[37] In poem 4.3, therefore, Propertius is not expressing sympathetically a particular woman's reaction to loneliness so much as taking on a cultural classification of woman and shaping it to suit the generic limitations and the poetic designs of his fourth book of elegies.[38] And, significantly, the very first woman he brings into his reconceived elegiacs is explicitly constructed as a distinctive form of writing.

## TARPEIA

The next poem to place a woman in the centre of the elegiac map of Rome also seems to position its discourse ambiguously between grand ambitions to commemorate the city and the stylistic limitations subsequently recommended in the bipartite poetics of the fourth book.[39]

The elegiac Arethusa constituted a significant departure from the female figure of early Propertian discourse (the beloved Cynthia), but the elegiac Tarpeia is even further removed from the mistress of

[36] As Pillinger (1969), 174–8; Miller (1982), 380–1.

[37] Cf., on Ovid's *Heroides*, Henderson (1986) and most recently Spentzou (forthcoming).

[38] For the social and political significance of this Propertian play with the feminine, see further Ch. 5 below and now Janan (2001), 53–69. Janan argues that Arethusa's point of view constitutes a feminine scepticism towards *romanitas* that discloses how military expansionism paradoxically corrupts Roman masculinity and marital relations, and turns Rome into a desert.

[39] See now O'Neill (1995); Newman (1997), 362–8; Miller and Platter (1999*b*); Janan (2001), 70–84.

previous books. For, unlike Arethusa, Tarpeia has a public role and plays an important part in the history of the city. By recounting the legend of the vestal virgin who betrayed Rome's citadel on the very anniversary of the city's birth, poem 4.4 seems to take up the initial ambitious proposal of the fourth book: to match Virgilian Rome with an elegiac counterpart. Thus the poem even opens in a grand Ennian manner and proceeds to expound on themes already envisaged in the topographical survey with which the whole book began: the Tarpeian hill on which father Jupiter dwells (v. 7), the feast-day celebrating the foundation of Rome (vv. 19–20), and the role of the Sabine king Tatius in forming the three tribes of the Roman race (vv. 29–32).[40]

Explaining the origin of an old name for the Capitoline hill is an appropriate task for the poet who began his fourth book with the aetiology of Rome, promised to sing the ancient names of places, and explicitly declared himself to be the Roman Callimachus, the elegiac narrator of origins.[41] Furthermore, since poem 4.4 takes as its subject a site which was pointed out to Virgil's epic hero in *Aeneid* 8,[42] the poem also follows up the initial implicit proposal of Propertius in this book to bring Virgilian epic within elegy's terms. As the Virgilian Evander once showed to Aeneas the dwelling place of Jupiter on the Tarpeian hill, so Propertius tells his readers how the hill got its name from Tarpeia's betrayal of it. And in his role as public poet, as the poet of Rome's destiny, the narrator of 4.4 makes it clear right from the start that his elegiac version of the Tarpeia legend still makes of her a detestable traitress.[43] This particular elegiac lover, we are told, is an evil girl (*mala . . . puella*, v. 17).

Undisturbed by the focus in the poem on an act of betrayal (rather than a moment of triumph) in Rome's history, those few modern critics who read the fourth book as giving literary consecration to

[40] Boyd (1984), 85.
[41] For the Callimachean character of poem 4.4, see Miller (1982), 371–85.
[42] As noted by Fedeli (1985), 137.
[43] Wellesley (1969), 96, and cf. Boyd (1984), 86.

and a poetic justification of Augustus' acts, have observed that the Caesars claimed descent from the Sabine king. Accordingly, they read the narrative of Tarpeia's treachery as a commemoration of Rome and Augustus because her treachery led ultimately to the happy union of the Sabine and Roman peoples.[44] Since, however, literary meaning is constructed for Propertian poems through the process of establishing a similarity and difference in relation to other texts, a comparison of the elegiac Tarpeia with the Tarpeia of Augustan historiography proves instructive. The elegiac Tarpeia expresses the belief that she has the capacity to release forces engaged in battle (vv. 59–62). In Livy's version of events, though, it is the abducted Sabine women who actually part the hostile forces, who plead with their Sabine brothers and their Roman husbands to agree terms and make a single state out of two peoples. Livy tells Tarpeia's story briefly and baldly, and the story serves only to explain how the Sabine soldiers gained access to the citadel. It is the Sabine women, not Tarpeia, who bring this episode in Romulus' reign to a glorious close, and not before Romulus' prowess in battle has been described in glowing epic colours (1.9–13).[45]

To enter the poetic discourse of Propertius' fourth book and become an elegiac woman, Tarpeia's story is rewritten. Roman legend now takes on elegiac tones. Tarpeia's treachery constitutes a Roman version of a myth common in the Graeco-Roman world: a girl, usually the daughter of the king, betrays her besieged city either for gold or for love of the besieger.[46] The Tarpeia of Livy's narrative betrays Rome for gold, and the motive of greed for gold is the accepted version of events in Roman historiography. The elegiac Tarpeia, however, betrays Rome out of desire for the opposing general.[47] In articulating her dilemma, her choice between civic duty and love, between the city and her beloved, the Propertian Tarpeia places

[44] e.g. Grimal (1953), 25–8; Baker (1968), 342–4; Pinotti (1974), 21–7. See now Janan (2001), 70.

[45] Ogilvie (1965), 64–78.

[46] Pinotti (1974), 18. Cf. Hollis (1970), 34.

[47] Ogilvie (1965), 74–5. Cf. Pinotti (1974), 18–19.

herself in the tradition of Greek heroines torn between such rival claims: she declares that she understands the choice made by a Scylla or an Ariadne (vv. 39–42). In this way, the text itself brings to its readers' attention the elegiac Tarpeia's debt to earlier Hellenistic forms of erotic writing: Callimachus may have written about Scylla in the *Aetia*;[48] several heroines of this type appear in the writings of Parthenius.[49] Since Plutarch cites an undated version of the Tarpeia legend composed in Greek elegiacs in which she betrays the citadel to Gauls out of love for their leader, it is not clear whether Propertius is the originator of Tarpeia's romantic dimensions, but what is clear is that the elegiac Tarpeia is shaped according to Alexandrian conventions.[50]

Once again a fundamental generic difference between forms of written women is disclosed. Composed according to Hellenistic conventions, poem 4.4 places Tarpeia at the centre of the elegiac world and warfare on its periphery. Narrative of action is compressed, direct speech is extended. Thus considerable space (almost half the elegiac poem) is dedicated to the female subject's point of view. The battles between Roman and Sabine, the prowess of Romulus that figured in Livy's connected narrative, have no part to play in such verse. Propertian elegy is discontinuous and fragmentary:[51] the limits of an aetiological poem are Tarpeia's punishment and the allocation of her name to the Capitoline hill.

Similarly, there is no place in the poetic discourse of poem 4.4 for the theme of successful reconciliation, the union of two peoples for the greater glory of Rome. In the conceptual framework—the familial ideology—of Roman society, the female is structured as both nec-

[48] Hollis (1970), 32.

[49] Pinotti (1974), *passim*. Adrian Hollis suggested to me that a specific model for the Tarpeia narrative may lie in the tale told in Ap. Rhod. fr. 12 (Powell) to which the elegist might have had access via Parthenius' *Narr. Amat.* 21.

[50] Hubbard (1974), 119–20, and Brenk (1979), 166–74.

[51] Grimal (1953), 35.

essary to its continuity and as disruptive of it: women are conceived to be subject to conflicting allegiances.[52] On the mythic plane, such an ambivalent position is expressed as either a force for disruption or for reconciliation. Thus, in Roman legend and Augustan historiography, the abducted Sabine women bring together two races by reconciling their fathers and their husbands.[53] Tarpeia, however, is the other side of the dichotomy. She is the woman whose desire for a husband leads to the betrayal of her fatherland: *prodiderat portaeque fidem patriamque iacentem,* | *nubendique petit, quem uelit, ipsa diem* (she had betrayed both the trust of the gate and her fallen fatherland, | she herself asks for the wedding-day she wants, vv. 87–8). The dowry of this would-be bride is Rome surrendered (*dos . . . prodita Roma*, v. 56). The elegiac narrative not only focuses on woman as agent of disruption, it also underlines the perversity of Tarpeia's deed when it retains the Varronian tradition that made of Tarpeia a vestal virgin.[54] Historically, sexual activity on the part of a vestal might be linked with a crisis in the state.[55] The flame she was required to tend symbolized the survival of Rome, yet in the Propertian poem that flame has been extinguished (vv. 45–6).

A similar differentiation between women as agents of political disruption or reconciliation can be seen to operate in the epic narrative of the *Aeneid*. The book that is dominated by the figure of Dido opens with the hope that from union with Aeneas will arise a great kingdom (4.47–9), but closes with a curse requiring that there be not peace but endless war between their two peoples (4.622–9).[56] As an agent of political disruption, the elegiac Tarpeia is portrayed in a manner

[52] See now Dixon (1992), 142 and Skinner (1997), 9–11.

[53] See now Janan (2001), 75–6.

[54] Varro *LL* 5.41. Cf. Ogilvie (1965), 74–5.

[55] Beard (1980), 16. See now Janan (2001), 76.

[56] See now Keith (2000), esp. 68–9. Cf. Janan (2001), 76–8, who extends the parallel beyond Dido to the Bacchant and the Amazon as figuring the problematic feminine respectively within and outside the state.

that recalls Dido's predicament: both are torn between civic duty and love. Several verbal echoes then reinforce the bond between these two female figures.[57]

Yet, although Tarpeia is provided with a role which parallels approximately that of Dido, there are also significant differences between the elegiac and epic narratives generated by the limitations of aetiological poetry. Dido is a central character only for the space of the *Aeneid*'s fourth book. The conventions of epic require that attention be returned to the hero Aeneas and his mission to found the Roman race. Later in the epic we briefly meet Lavinia, the agent of political reconciliation. Initiating the second half of the *Aeneid*, an oracle discloses that Lavinia's union with a foreigner will breed a Latin race so potent as to achieve worldwide dominion (7.45–106).[58] The Propertian action, however, is completed by the death of Tarpeia. Effectively the elegy does not look forward beyond the bounds of the *Aeneid*'s fourth book, and thus a redefinition of the Propertian poetics seems to have been reached: now it is not so much Virgilian *Roma* as Virgilian *amor* with which the elegiac poem takes issue.

Once again contemporary ideologies of woman are seen to be transformed into the effects required by the conventions of a particular form of writing and by the project of a particular literary discourse, for the production of an elegiac Tarpeia places poem 4.4 ambiguously between the two conflicting proposals for elegiac writing set out in the first poem of the fourth book. Although the initial section of the opening poem surveys Jupiter's dwelling place, the celebrations of Rome's foundations, and the role of the Sabines in the formation of the Roman people, through its elegiac Tarpeia poem 4.4 focuses on the capture of Jupiter's home and the betrayal of the Roman people on the very day that they celebrate their city's birth. The elegiac Tarpeia, therefore, does not quite correspond to the ini-

[57] See Warden (1978), 177–87.

[58] See now Keith (2000), 49–50 and 73–4.

tial topics of the first programmatic poem: Virgilian *Roma*, the weaponry of Caesar, and the victorious arms of Troy reborn (4.1.46–7). Nor, however, does elegiac Tarpeia quite fit the subsequent commands to write about the military service of love, the erotic victories and defeats of a lover-poet (4.1.135–40). Like Arethusa, however, the vestal virgin does bring an erotic interest to military matters.[59] Weapons, for example, when carried by a male beloved take on a beauty associated in earlier poems with the features of a mistress (*et formosa oculis arma Sabina meis*, v. 32). When Tarpeia expresses a desire for Tatius' horse to carry her love into military camps (*meos in castra reponet amores*, v. 37), she thus discloses the manner in which the elegiac woman implements a requirement of the fourth book. The application of eroticism to military matters, the softening of weapons that Tarpeia describes as her goal (*mollire arma*, v. 62), fulfils the poetic command to engage with the apparent polarities of *arma* and *amor*.[60]

## ACANTHIS AND CYNTHIA

In the past, readings of the women of Propertian elegy frequently rested on methodological inconsistency. Elegy's mistress and elegy's madam were not objects of the same critical procedure. In the case of elegy's mistress, critics often recognized the literariness of the language in which she was shaped while nevertheless exploring ways to bring her out of the elegiac world and put her on the map of Augustan Rome. Then, no matter how artificial the erotic discourse in which she appeared, no matter how often that discourse openly declared its debt to earlier traditions of erotic writing, the written

[59] See now Janan (2001), 80, who notes that Tarpeia's admiration extends beyond Tatius to his weapons, his horse, his army, and their arms.

[60] See now Janan (2001), 70–84, who looks beyond questions of poetics to argue that the Tarpeia of 4.4 gives voice to a feminine desire that collapses the binary and hierarchical oppositions of conventional Roman thought, including those of Man/Woman and Roman/non-Roman.

Cynthia was still read as somehow disclosing the realities of a specific woman's life in Rome. Many critics operating in the Anglo-American tradition of classical scholarship thus read the elegiac mistress as at least a reflection transposed into poetry (or a verbal painting) of an elegiac poet's Augustan girlfriend.[61] The elegiac madam, however, has always been subjected to a much closer critical scrutiny. And scarcely any attempt has been made to associate Acanthis, the old witch of Propertius' fourth book, with a specific living woman, even though the authorial narrator presents himself as a participant in the events of poem 4.5: he reports the advice Acanthis gave a young girl and curses her for the suffering it brought him.

It is, therefore, not the least bit contentious to suggest that this particular elegiac woman is a female fiction: a literary construct whose advice, whose alcoholism, whose magical powers, and even whose withered skin, are all products of cultural and generic conventions for writing. Nor is it particularly contentious to suggest that here the elegiac text even draws attention to its literary debts and the unreality of the events it purports to relate. Thus, it is agreed, the advice of Acanthis is framed by authorial curses familiar from Alexandrian epigram. The Propertian madam then hints at her own literary origin when she offers as an example of exemplary behaviour a pricey tart from Menandrian comedy: *sed potius mundi Thais pretiosa Menandri, | cum ferit astutos comica moecha Getas* (but rather elegant Menander's pricey Thais, | when the comic whore tricks the cunning Geta, vv. 41–4). Two Tibullan poems (1.5 and 2.6) provide precursors for this transfer of comedy's bawd into elegiac narrative. And, finally, since the occasion of the madam's advice is left unclear, the impression is created not of a particular person but of a generalized figure: the madam of the comic stage has been brought again into an elegiac poem.[62] But why does she appear here for the first time in the Propertian corpus?[63]

61 For criticism of this reading, see esp. Veyne (1983). Cf. above, Chs. 1 and 2.

62 Courtney (1969); Puccioni (1979); Hubbard (1974), 137–42; Barsby (1979), 90–107.

63 On the madam of Prop. 4.5, see now Myers (1996); O'Neill (1998) and (1999); Janan (2001), 85–99.

At the level of Roman cultural conventions, acceptable female sexuality is constrained within the institutions of marriage and motherhood. As neither wife nor mother, the old, unmarried, and childless woman then operates as a sign of the socially unacceptable, the entirely alien female. Displaced from a central position in cultural evaluations of the 'good' woman, the old spinster is associated with social disruption.[64] Thus, on entering the discourse of comedy, she may take on the dramatic role of a madam: the figure who attempts to subvert the values associated with marriage, who attempts to persuade a mistress not to demonstrate the sexual loyalty of a wife. In Plautus' *Mostellaria*, for example, the young man curses the white-haired maid when he overhears her advising his mistress against devotion to a single lover (190–202).[65]

When the madam of the comic stage is then brought into the discourse of the Tibullan corpus, her arts are accordingly opposed to the interests of the elegiac lover-poet. Erotic teaching is remodelled to suit the requirements of the genre. The madam appears briefly only to be cursed, and her role as teacher of the erotic arts is now usurped by the elegiac male who professes opposing principles.[66] Thus, in the early books of the Propertian corpus, it is the authorial narrator who always plays the role of erotic expert, who places the joys of a single mutual love above any comic bawd's advocacy of worldly riches and multiple lovers, and who expresses a belief that it is not money but the power of his song which will win over his beloved.[67]

It therefore comes as a considerable surprise when a poem of Propertius' fourth book returns to the techniques of comedy by giving centre stage to the erotic advice of the withered madam Acanthis, while confining the lover's curses to the opening and closing sections of the elegiac narrative. Just as the elegiac Tarpeia's shameful tomb does not quite fulfil the initial proposal of book 4 to build an elegiac

[64] Richlin (1983), 109–16 and (1984).

[65] See now Rosivach (1998).

[66] On the Tibullan poems, see now Lee-Stecum (1998), 156–79 and (2000), 196–9.

[67] Wheeler (1910*a* and *b*) and (1911).

counterpart to the glories of Virgilian Rome, so the advice of the elegiac Acanthis does not quite fulfil the subsequent demand to return to the familiar amatory idiom of loyal erotic servitude. By transforming the comic madam into the elegiac *lena* who dominates poem 4.5, the poetic text instead takes on yet another narrative voice that casts to one side, and undercuts, the old Propertian fiction of the loyal lover-poet who (by means of his elegiac poetry) courts a beautiful, listening mistress.

When the elegiac Acanthis holds the stage and delivers her disquisition on the art of gaining lovers, the break with earlier Propertian erotic discourse (the departure from the stance of the Propertian narrator, the male 'I' of previous books) is clearly marked. In the second poem of the *Monobiblos*, the male narrator (the lover-poet) had questioned the value of adornment and the wearing of Coan silks in particular (1.2.1–6). So when Acanthis now advises that a girl select as lovers only the moneyed soldier, sailor, or slave, but not the poet who brings verses rather than silk dresses (vv. 49–58), she not only inverts the authorial teachings contained in the first Propertian poetry-book, but even singles out one particular passage on which to pour her scorn.[68] If the text is not interpolated at this point, Acanthis even quotes the offending couplet and thus underlines a recurring strategy of the fourth book—namely to challenge and change the erotic discourse of earlier books through the adoption of new, especially female, narrative voices.[69]

Furthermore, the elegiac madam not only challenges the stance of the earlier lover-poet, she also represents (within the requirements of erotic writing) the polar opposite of the elegiac mistress. Invectives against the old woman attribute to her perversions of a mis-

[68] Wheeler (above) catalogues the differences between the *praecepta* of Acanthis and those of the earlier male narrator. See now Myers (1996); O'Neill (1998); Janan (2001), 85–99.

[69] As Veyne (1983), 74, but, for the rejection of vv. 55–6 from the text of Prop. 4.5, see Heyworth (1986), 209–10. See further Ch. 5 below and Janan (2001), 28–9 and 89.

tress's features. While the mistress inspires a catalogue of conventional beauty, the old woman compels a catalogue of conventional ugliness.[70] Thus, at the close of Propertius' third book, a farewell to the mistress Cynthia as subject of elegiac writing was effected through the denial of beauty and the prediction of the arrival of ugliness (3.24–5): mistress is transformed into hag. It is therefore entirely in keeping with the poetics of the fourth book that the familiar elegiac mistress is relegated to an insignificant spot in the landscape of poem 4.5, and that in the foreground should be placed an old, wrinkled witch.[71]

Yet, if the third book bid farewell to Cynthia as the subject of elegiac writing, why then does she reappear in the seventh and eighth poems of the fourth book? Written in the authorial first-person, poems 4.7 and 4.8 purport to be autobiographical narratives of the poet's liaison with his mistress, but the appearance of these two poems in the fourth book, and their juxtaposition, raises considerable difficulties for any readers who might still wish to take their few realist techniques for reality. At the end of the third book Cynthia was dismissed as material for Propertian poems. In poem 4.7 she comes back, but only as a ghost in a burnt dress. The narrator recalls how, after her death, Cynthia seemed to appear to him in a dream and speak through withered lips. And, in words which he reports directly, her ghost declares that she had been true to him till death. In the very next poem, however, Cynthia suddenly reappears alive and well and utterly faithless. Now the narrator tells the story of what happened tonight on the Esquiline: Cynthia returned from a jaunt on the Appian way to break up a party he had arranged in her absence and to restore her authority over him. We may well wonder

70 See e.g. Richlin (1984), 69–72.

71 See now Janan (2001), esp. 94–6. Janan argues that 4.5 not only challenges the erotic creed expressed in the first three books of Propertius, but also comprehensively interrogates the flawed structure of Roman sexual relations. Acanthis insists that, within the conventional dynamics of desire, Woman is only a series of masks donned to complement Man.

how Cynthia manages to be so lively, if she is dead in the previous poem.[72]

The elegiac mistress and her depiction in earlier books has exercised such charm over readers of the Propertian corpus that, in the past, many felt able to declare her reality while nevertheless admitting the unreality of the elegiac madam. Those who read the Propertian corpus as poetic autobiography were then compelled to offer solutions to the problem that the conjunction of poems 4.7 and 4.8 posed for them. So poem 4.8 was extracted from its apparently problematic position in the fourth book and then dated safely before Cynthia's dismissal. Similarly, readers were advised either that Cynthia was not *literally* dead at the time poem 4.7 was composed (that 'death' is just a means of satirizing the affair) or, alternatively, that Cynthia was not *actually* alive at the time poem 4.8 was composed (that 'tonight' is just poetic licence—a means of giving dramatic immediacy to the recollection of old experiences).[73] However, the problem does not arise at all when it is recognized that the elegiac mistress is as much a fiction as the elegiac madam, that even Cynthia is a literary construct whose life or death, whose loyalty or faithlessness, whose beauty or ugliness, are all determined by cultural conventions and poetic programmes. And at this point in the Propertian corpus, the text itself seems especially to encourage that recognition.

Cynthia's return to the elegiac world has already been heralded in the first poem of the fourth book, when the astrologer Horos qualifies the initial, ambitious schemes for elegiac writing by commanding a return to the older amatory idioms. Nevertheless, why should her return be delayed until halfway through the book? Significantly, the sequence of poems 4.6 and 4.7 seems to come closest to fulfilling the conflicting requirements of the initial poem: an aetion which concerns itself with the Palatine temple of Apollo, which takes as its

[72] See now Janan (2001), 100 and 114–15.

[73] For comment on such views, see Dee (1978) and Warden (1980), 78–81.

theme the reputation of Augustus, and which describes (however curiously) Apollo's contribution to the victory at Actium, clearly constructs a grand elegiac monument to Virgil's *Aeneid* 8;[74] while Cynthia's retrospective account of the elegiac love-affair draws on many themes of Propertius' early books, and recalls in particular poem 1.3 where once before she had been provided with direct speech in which to call attention to her loyalty and her lover's negligence.[75] Thus within the architecture of the last book, Cynthia's reinstatement as a practice of writing seems to occur not because an author's love for his mistress has been rekindled, but because his poetics of polarity now requires it.

The close relationship between poems 4.7 and 4.8 further demonstrates that even the elegiac mistress of the fourth book is shaped to suit its bipolar poetics, and that even the two Cynthia-centred poems engage with the interplay of the aetiological and amatory, epic and elegy, *arma* and *amor*.[76] After the Cynthia-centred erotic discourse of poem 4.7, poem 4.8 begins with a grand antiquarian exposition of Juno's fertility rites at Lanuvium, as if to continue the superficial, yet regular, alternation between aetiological and amatory elegies that has proved to be a poetic principle operating up to this point in the fourth book, but then it becomes largely concerned with the comic antics of a vengeful mistress. Now, therefore, the dynamic of the fourth book changes *within* rather than between poems.[77] And it is Cynthia herself who bridges any apparent divide between these two levels of elegiac discourse, for her headlong ride down the Appian way even appears to match local depictions of the cult's patron goddess.[78]

Moreover, poems 4.7 and 4.8 incorporate into their elegiac narratives material from a wide variety of genres whose interplay both

[74] On Prop. 4.6, see e.g. Pillinger (1969), 189–99, and Ch. 6 below.

[75] As Warden (1980), 72. See now Flaschenriem (1998) and Janan (2001), 100–4 and 107, who describes 4.6 and 7 as the double centre of the fourth book.

[76] For the close relation between 4.7 and 4.8, see now Janan (2001), 114.

[77] As now Janan (2001), esp. 115–16.

[78] Hubbard (1974), 115, and Warden (1980), 150. See now Janan (2001), 126.

disturbs any surface semblance of reality and challenges the apparent polarity between *arma* and *amor* with which the fourth book began. The two poems that momentarily restore the mistress to her old place at the centre of the elegiac map of Rome, like the earlier poems depicting various elegiac women, also position their poetic discourse ambiguously between the new ambitions and the old restrictions of the book's bipolar programme.

If poems 4.7 and 4.8 together observe an unrealistic narrative sequence in which a dead Cynthia is immediately followed by a living Cynthia, it is because the fourth book pairs an elegiac *Iliad* with an elegiac *Odyssey*. Several studies have detailed the ways in which the two Cynthias of the fourth book are shaped as elegiac counterparts of Homeric heroes. Echoes of *Iliad* 23 at strategic points in the narrative of poem 4.7 establish a parallel for Cynthia's ghost in the Homeric Patroclus who appears to Achilles in a dream and complains of his companion's forgetfulness. Echoes of *Odyssey* 22 in poem 4.8 establish a parallel for the vengeful Cynthia in the Homeric Odysseus who returns home to rout the suitors and be reunited with Penelope. So, in pursuit of the programme of a Roman Callimachus (the production of an elegiac counterpart to epic), poem 4.8 stands in relation to poem 4.7 as *Odyssey* to *Iliad*.[79]

Paradoxically then, it is the Cynthia-centred pair of poems that take on the greatest literary challenge set by Virgil: to produce Roman poetic counterparts for whole Homeric episodes. And, as we might anticipate, there are fundamental and humorous generic differences between those epic narratives and the apparent transformation of the elegiac mistress into both Homeric and Virgilian hero. For example, although the ghostly Cynthia of poem 4.7 returns from the underworld to demand a fitting burial in the manner of the Homeric Patroclus, the circumstances in which she claims to have been pre-

[79] Evans (1971); Currie (1973); Muecke (1974); Hubbard (1974), 149–56; Allison (1980); Warden (1980), 13–61; Dalzell (1980), 33–5. Cf. Ch. 1 above, and see now Newman (1997), 326–30 and 358–62.

cipitated there bear all the hallmarks of a comic plot, complete with poisonings, rivals, and the threatened torture of cunning slaves.[80] Fittingly, it is as a result of domestic and erotic dispute (not public and heroic battle) that the elegiac mistress has died. Similarly, although the triumphant Cynthia of poem 4.8 returns home in the manner of the Homeric Odysseus to overcome and cast out those who would usurp her rightful place, she returns not from years of trials on land and sea but from a day's amorous outing, and arrives to confront not the court of a king but a gathering of courtesans, dwarves, and drunks quite suited to the comic stage. The language of militarism, of epic triumphs and cities sacked, is here applied to domestic brawls and bedroom battles.[81]

The close of poem 4.8, in particular, demonstrates the often playful manner in which the Cynthia-centred poems fulfil the fourth book's poetic project. The lover's final capitulation to his vengeful mistress unites within a single line the poetic themes that the first poem had polarized: *respondi, et toto soluimus arma toro* (I responded, and over the whole couch we discharged weapons, v. 88). However, the conjunction of *arma / toro* and the words *respondi* and *soluimus arma* bring into play obscene possibilities, given that the Latin language abounds in military metaphors for sexual acts.[82] Here, as befits the employment of an elegiac mistress to effect the reconciliation of two apparently disparate poetics, the conjunction of *arma* and *toro* carries with it the humorous undertones of a poetic discourse on *militia mentulae*.

The poem that follows 4.8 also tells the story of a hero's arrival at Rome, and clearly complements the narrative strategies of the preceding poem. In poem 4.8 the *elegiac* mistress Cynthia is provided with incongruous *epic* attributes, while in poem 4.9 the *epic* (and notably Virgilian) hero Hercules is provided with incongruous

[80] See now Janan (2001), 105–8, on the poem's disparities of tone.

[81] In addition to the above, see Dee (1974) and McKeown (1979), 74–8. For the comic tone of 4.8, see now Janan (2001), 114.

[82] See Adams (1982), 14–21 and 145–59, and now Janan (2001), 116 and 126–7.

*elegiac* attributes. He has dressed himself up as a soft girl (like elegy's mistresses) and has begged for entry into a woman's domain (like elegy's excluded lovers).[83] Such generic incongruities suit the narrative of a poet who plays the role of an ever-changing Vertumnus, while their evident patterning casts serious doubts on the authenticity of the elegiac mistress. The patterned interplay of *arma* and *amor* which the sequence 4.6–9 effects (both within and between poems) locates 4.7 and 4.8 squarely within the architecture of the fourth book and thus denies a realistic chronology to Cynthia. The narrative strategies of the fourth book reveal that elegy's mistress as well as elegy's madam is a female fiction shaped to suit a poetic programme. And thus, to balance the critique of early Propertian elegy delivered by the dying Acanthis on one side of the central Actium poem, the dead Cynthia on the other demands that all Cynthia-centred verse be immediately burned (4.7.77–8).[84]

## CORNELIA

What then of the last woman to be placed on Propertius' elegiac map of Rome? At this point in the narrative of the fourth book, we might think it both safe and appropriate to match the text's elegiac woman closely with the realities of a specific individual's life in Augustan society. For poem 4.11 concerns itself with the conduct of Cornelia, the stepdaughter of Augustus, who died in 16 BC, and no attempt is made to disguise the historical identity of the woman who is the poem's subject. For a moment, the pathway between written and living woman seems comfortably clear of obstacles such as cultural

[83] Anderson (1964); Warden (1982). See now DeBrohun (1994); Janan (1998) and (2001), 128–45; Lindheim (1998*a*).

[84] See further Ch. 5 below and Janan (2001), 100–13. Janan argues that both Cynthia's shabby death and her ghostly accusations of neglect challenge readers to reconsider with scepticism Propertius' poetry and the totality of the genre (given the male lover-poet's claims of fidelity, devotion, and servitude, and his demand that the beloved refuse monetary considerations).

codes, generic conventions, or poetic programmes. Consequently, poem 4.11 has been read by at least one critic not as a cornerstone in the architecture of a poetry-book, but as one of two commissioned works around which a number of disparate poetic pieces have been loosely clustered. The elegiac Cornelia then becomes an isolatable tribute (whether warm or cool) to a patron's wife.[85]

However, unlike the earlier Propertian elegy on the death of Marcellus (3.18), poem 4.11 does not have the structure of an authorial comment on an untimely death in the family of Augustus. Set in a Virgilian underworld, recalling the tragedy of a Euripidean heroine, and presented in its entirety as Cornelia's own words to the judges of the dead, the poem does not encourage an easy transition from text to extratextual realities. Continuing the innovatory character of the fourth book, and the treatment of female subjects that such innovation requires, the elegiac Cornelia's account of her life plays with a number of literary forms.[86] When she begins by addressing her husband from the grave, the poem simultaneously recalls the structure of monumental epigrams (in which the dead person is envisaged as speaking from the tomb) and casts the weeping husband in the role of elegy's excluded lover. When the poem adopts the structure of Roman funeral orations and court defences, the Propertian Cornelia is also found to be speaking in Virgil's underworld. And when the text reproduces the conventional pattern of consolations, it also takes on the tragic dimensions of the farewell to her husband delivered by the Euripidean Alcestis.[87] The literariness of the elegy's language, the artificiality of its structure, and the debt it owes to a range of generic conventions for writing about the dead, together set up a considerable distance between the elegiac Cornelia and the realities of a woman's life and death in Augustan Rome. Like Vertumnus, and

[85] Hubbard (1974), 116–18. On 4.11, see now Newman (1997), 330–7, and Janan (2001), 146–63.

[86] Pillinger (1969), 174–8.

[87] In addition to the commentators, see Curran (1968); Paduano (1968); Hubbard (1974), 145–9; Warden (1980), 103. See now Janan (2001), 147–8 and 158–62.

like Arethusa (the first elegiac woman of the fourth book), the Propertian Cornelia is clearly articulated as a work of art, a form of writing undertaken by a poet that fulfils and now finally completes the ambiguous, bipartite programme of a poetry-book.

First of all, this elegiac woman is given a voice at a significant position in the architecture of the fourth book. The sequence of poems 4.7–10 (two poems centred on Cynthia, two on the cults of gods) raises no expectations as to the character of the final poem. The juxtaposition of a poem on the *arma* of past Roman commanders (4.10) with one where Roman commanders figure only as the relations of the female narrator (4.11) might suggest that the last poem will focus predominantly on *amor*. Whether imagined as sustaining a pyramid or a panel structure, however, the first, central, and last poems provide a framework for the Propertian narrative by, for example, marking the only three points where the name *Caesar* appears.[88] Thus, befitting the organizational role of the last poem, the naming of the *princeps*, and the articulation of grand themes at strategic points in the fourth book, the last elegiac woman is very far removed from the figure of the mistress, the main female subject of previous books. Elsewhere in Augustan elegy, the figure of the matron is even opposed to the figure of the mistress as the appropriate subject for an elegiac poet: when Ovid describes an encounter with two styles of writing embodied in female form, the accepted elegiac genre is characterized as a *meretrix*, the rejected genre as a *matrona*.[89] Nonetheless, in the last poem of Propertius' innovatory fourth book, the subject of elegiac writing is precisely a Roman matron: a daughter, a wife, a mother, and a member of the patrician aristocracy.

In Roman society, membership of a *familia*, marriage, and motherhood order the female in socially effective terms, so that positive evaluations of woman centre on her as daughter, sister, wife, and

[88] Nethercut (1968). Cf. Grimal (1953).

[89] See further Ch. 4 below.

mother.[90] But when poem 4.11 reproduces these entirely conventional categories and evaluations of the character of a good woman, it also distinguishes the new and final female narrator from the unorthodox male lover (the narrative 'I') of previous books. Now the female narrator Cornelia estimates her worth partly by the military victories of her male ancestors (vv. 29–30), while the earlier authorial narrator had considered ancestral triumphs of little importance compared to the joys of lording it over girls at dinner-parties (2.34.55–8). Now, too, the Propertian Cornelia estimates her worth by her fidelity to a single husband, and gives voice to the ideal of Roman womanhood when she asks for the expression *uni nupta* to be engraved on her tombstone (v. 36).[91] Earlier in the corpus, the male lover had appropriated such conventional phrases to declare sexual loyalty to a single mistress and, therefore, an ideological unorthodoxy (2.7.19 and 2.13.35–6).[92] The last narrator of the fourth book also claims honour for her fertility, her production of three children (vv. 61–70), while the earlier authorial narrator had explicitly rejected his civic duty to have children and thereby assist the state in the provision of a new generation of soldiers (2.7.13–14).[93] Thus the Propertian Cornelia's survey of a good woman's life restores the values of loyalty, constancy, and chastity to their traditional context—that of marriage rather than the elegiac love affair.

The introduction of the ideology of the good woman into the elegiac text thus facilitates the project of the opening sequence of the first poem: the extension of the dimensions of elegiac writing and the departure from earlier elegiac practice into grander themes. Since

[90] See e.g. Gardner (1986); Dixon (1988); and Hallett (1984), esp. 53–4 on Cornelia in Prop. 4.11 specifically. See now Treggiari (1991), 243–9; Skinner (1997), 9–11; Hemelrijk (1998), 10–13.

[91] On Cornelia's declarations of chastity and their intersection with expressions of Roman military success, see now Janan (2001), 154–6.

[92] Williams (1958), 23–5; Hallett (1973), 111. See also Chs. 1 above and 5 below.

[93] For Cornelia's implied reference to the provisions of the Augustan marriage legislation that rewarded mothers of three children, see now Janan (2001), 159–60.

that ideology organizes the female according to her relations with the male, it also permits poem 4.11 to close book 4 with themes that match its opening. It permits the good Cornelia as daughter, sister, wife, and mother of public figures to detail the military achievements of Rome's past and to address Rome directly as witness to her rectitude.[94] It even permits the fourth book to close with Augustus in the character of a god (vv. 57–60).

So a new subject position is adopted that changes the old amatory idioms, and challenges the old poetic fictions of the unorthodox elegiac lover and his amoral mistress. Furthermore, the last elegiac woman of the Propertian corpus is also the furthest removed from the figure of the mistress. As abandoned wife, the elegiac Arethusa constituted a departure from the beloved mistress Cynthia. As a desirous vestal virgin, Tarpeia set the elegiac discourse in which she was shaped even further away from the personal erotic themes of earlier poems. But the idiom of *amor militis* (the erotic perspective imposed upon military matters) nevertheless lent the representations of Arethusa and Tarpeia the colour of earlier, more personalized male passions. The elegiac Cornelia never speaks in such terms.[95]

It is not just the initial, grand themes of the book that poem 4.11 balances and complements. The central poem of the fourth book effected an abrupt transition from public to private, martial to sympotic, poetic roles by utilizing a recognized polarity in the attributes of the god of poetry Apollo.[96] The first poem effected a dramatic conflict between public and private poetic roles by juxtaposing (through distinct narrators) two apparently conflicting poetic creeds, although both were extracted from the polemics of Callimachus.[97] The last poem, however, exploits aspects of the cultural coding of the *matrona*, and Graeco-Roman conventions for writing about the dead, to redefine conflicts between the public and the

[94] As Hutchinson (1984), 102.

[95] Lilja (1965), 233–7, makes comparable observations on the difference between the portraits of Arethusa and Cornelia.

[96] Pillinger (1969), 189–99.

[97] Van Sickle (1974), 121–2.

private, the glorious and the sorrowful, in the practice of poetic production.

The Roman *matrona* is herself located ambiguously between domestic and political, public and private space.[98] So a poem which is presented as her own words allows only the partial intrusion of warfare and civic responsibility onto the elegiac map of Rome. Through the elegiac Cornelia a generic difference between the epic style of writing and the Propertian practice continues to be expressed. An epic narrative would have concerned itself directly with the military prowess and magisterial careers of Cornelia's male relatives. Instead the terminology of male civic responsibility is incorporated into the sphere of the female. For the elegiac Cornelia's speech shapes her as orator, magistrate, and triumphant general.[99]

Similarly, brought into an elegiac depiction of untimely death, the ideological alignment of the *matrona* with the private (as well as the public) facilitates the revision of the *Aeneid* in elegy and permits the exclusion of its heroic colouring. For the elegiac Cornelia is set in an infernal landscape that forms only a fragment of the underworld in the continuous narrative of Virgil's sixth book. As a woman's speech awaiting sentence before the judges of the dead, poem 4.11 is frozen both in time and in place. There cannot be a progression to Elysium, to the Virgilian disquisition on the joys of rebirth and the survey of Rome's great heroes.[100] The god Caesar remains forever in tears, forever mourning the loss of a companion worthy of his daughter (vv. 59–60).

Finally, on becoming an elegiac woman, the *matrona* Cornelia gains features that associate her paradoxically with the *meretrix* Cynthia. Poem 4.11 is a recognized companion piece to poem 4.7. Both comprise speeches delivered by a woman from beyond the grave, who declares her devotion to one man, classifies herself among the

[98] See Purcell (1986) for the anomalous movement of Livia right out into the public sphere, and cf. the comments in Ch. 6 below on both Livia and Octavia.

[99] Curran (1968), 134–5.

[100] Cf. Curran (1968), 136. See now Janan (2001), 162–3.

great women of myth or history, and delivers instructions on the care of her household now that she is dead.[101] Thus, not least when it suggests parallels between a *matrona* and a *meretrix*, the final poem of the fourth book succeeds where the first had failed in amalgamating the simple categories of public and private, martial and amatory, styles of elegiac writing.

The last poem of the corpus teaches yet another important lesson on how to read the elegiac woman. For if the female appears everywhere organized in relation to the male, if Cornelia's daughter is said to be a token or symbol of her father's public career (v. 67), then the elegiac woman is also a token or symbol of her author's practice of writing. And when the last poem of the last book of the Propertian corpus ends with a woman waiting for a response from her judges, it ends also with an author waiting for a response from his auditors or readers.[102]

[101] See esp. Lange (1979), and now Janan (2001), 85–6, 100, and 105. Janan also connects the poem to 4.5 on Acanthis as a triad concerned with 'the return of the dead'.

[102] For the elegiac poet's adoption of a feminine position in relation to his audience, see further Ch. 5 below. See now Janan (2001), 162–3 who argues that the poem's deferral of judgement on Cornelia allows the account of her obedience to the protocols of Roman matronal life to be read simultaneously as either sublime self-sacrifice or meaningless waste.

# 4

# Reading Female Flesh: Ovid *Amores* 3.1

The Propertian lover-poet itemizes the physical attractions of his mistress in poem 2.3 at the same time as he declares that it was her skills in dancing, singing, and poetic composition that captivated him more:

> Nec me tam facies, quamuis sit candida, cepit
> (lilia non domina sint magis alba mea;
> ut Maeotica nix minio si certet Hibero,
> utque rosae puro lacte natant folia),
> nec de more comae per leuia colla fluentes,
> non oculi, geminae, sidera nostra, faces,
> nec si qua Arabio lucet bombyce puella
> (non sum de nihilo blandus amator ego) . . . (2.3.9–16)

> [It's not so much the face, although radiant, that captivated me
> (lilies could not be whiter than my mistress;

This chapter is a revised version of an article first published in *History as Text* (1989) edited by Averil Cameron, and is reproduced by permission of the publishers, Gerald Duckworth and Co. Ltd.

just as if Maeotian snow with Iberian vermilion contended,
  and just as on pure milk rose petals swim),
nor hair habitually over a smooth neck flowing,
  not eyes, twin torches (our stars),
nor if the girl glitters at all in Arabian silk
  (I am not a lover who flatters without cause) . . .]

In order to materialize as an elegiac mistress, the female body is here fragmented into parts (face, hair, eyes) and metamorphosed into a catalogue of inhuman or inanimate metaphors (lilies, snow, vermilion, milk, rose petals, torches, stars). Reified in the extreme, woman enters the elegiac text with a body constructed for her by the poet that is in no way her own.[1]

The process of gathering such brief physical descriptions from their scattered locations in the Propertian corpus in order to assemble out of them a credible and singular portrait of an Augustan girlfriend has been essential to the project of romantic scholars. Yet the conventionality, textuality, and aesthetic ambitions of western love poetry's female flesh have long been recognized even within the tradition of that poetry's production. In the world of fourteenth-century Petrarchan love poetry (following that of Augustan elegy) woman dominates and man adores the codified perfection of her beauty. Yet later writers in the erotic tradition regularly parodied and undercut the conceits of such Petrarchan desire for golden hair, ivory hands, ebony eyes, rosy cheeks, lily-white skin, coral lips, or breasts like globes of alabaster.[2]

In the preface to *Le berger extravagant* (1627), for example, Charles Sorel expressly declared his intention to entomb the absurdities of poetry (in this case, the amatory world of the Italian pastoral).[3] The hero of his French novel (much like a romantic critic in the extreme) has read too many pastorals and taken them for truth. Having taken

[1] I borrow here for Propertian elegy the analysis by Flynn (1997) of the fragmented female body that can be found in medieval Latin lyrics.

[2] See e.g. Forster (1969), 1–60, and Stapleton (1996).

[3] Whitfield (1963), 37.

to the way of life of the fictional shepherd they depict, the hero's unhealthy illusion is first flattered and then shattered by his friends. In the second book, the deluded hero commissions a visual portrait of his beloved Charite (just as Petrarch had represented himself in his sonnets commissioning a portrait of Laura)[4] but the outcome is most disturbing, as the engraving of beautiful Charite which accompanies Sorel's text vividly reveals (Fig. 4.1). For the painter

> had in this business acted a piece of ingenious knavery; observing what the Shepherd had told him of the beauty of his Mistress, and imitating the extravagant descriptions of the Poets, he had painted a Face, which instead of being of a flesh-colour, was of a complexion white as snow. There were two branches of Coral at the opening of the Mouth; and upon each Cheek a Lilly and a Rose, crossing one another: where there should have been Eyes, there was neither white nor apple, but two Suns sending forth beams, among which were observed certain flames and darts . . . And to add perfection to the work, the Hair floted about all this in divers manners: some of it was made like Chains of Gold; other-some twisted, and made like networks; and in many places there hanged lines, with hooks ready baited.[5]

Taken literally, the metaphors of Petrarchan love delineate not a living mistress but the beautiful monstrosity that is erotic poetry.

Within the confines of this chapter, I shall argue that, as in Sorel's anti-Petrarchist novel, Ovid *Amores* 3.1 constitutes a point in the tradition of western love poetry where an amatory text itself signals demonstrably and humorously that such poetry's female flesh can bear a reading as fiction.[6] Like the painting described in Sorel's novel, *Amores* 3.1 is 'a piece of ingenious knavery' that picks up on and deconstructs the anatomy of the elegiac mistress that had been

[4] On which see Miller (1997), 144–5.

[5] I quote from the translation of the French by John Davies, *The Extravagant Shepherd. The Anti-Romance. Or, the History of the Shepherd Lysis* (London: Thomas Heath, 1653), 25. I am most grateful to David Constantine for having originally drawn my attention to this image and its implications for the female body in erotic poetry.

[6] Cf. Stapleton (1996) on Ovid's *Amores* as a model for such later subversions of conventional love poetry as Shakespeare's sonnets.

Fig. 4.1 La belle Charite. Engraving to illustrate Charles Sorel's novel *Le berger extravagant* (1627).

supplied in the earlier elegies of Propertius and Tibullus. And like the anti-romantic novel itself, *Amores* 3.1 is designed to mock and entomb the absurdity of reading amatory poetry as real. A close reading of *Amores* 3.1 can thus provide clues to the operations of female representation elsewhere in Augustan elegy, and (I shall argue further) teaches an important lesson in why and how we should read Cynthia, Delia, Nemesis, and Corinna as textual bodies bearing both poetic and political meanings.

## FEMALE FLESH AS POETICS

The scene of *Amores* 3.1 is set in the vicinity of a cave. The narrator (as poet) recalls his encounter there with two writing-practices in female form: Elegia and Tragoedia. He describes their appearance and comportment and a debate in which each woman advocates her own mode of poetic production, denigrating or dismissing the other. Eventually the narrator adopts Elegia (however temporarily) as his Muse. Thus the third and final book of Ovid's *Amores* gets under way.[7]

The manner in which Ovid has here depicted female flesh (as if poetic genres were proud possessors of a human anatomy) has been cited by a romantic critic as an example of how poets' encounters with naked prostitutes at Rome are raised to the level of art by the application of a thin brushstroke of mythology or allegory: 'the picture of a Roman man about town, running an eye over the girls on offer in some louche establishment' is often visible beneath a dignifying veneer of appropriate poetic devices.[8] Others have read the female flesh with which Elegia is endowed rather differently: 3.1 has readily been accepted by some commentators as depicting not a pros-

[7] The question of what relationship holds between the first and second editions of the *Amores* does not have a substantial bearing on my readings of 3.1. Cameron (1968) argues that the second edition constitutes little more than a shortened version of the first. See now Boyd (1997), 136 and 142–7, who argues cogently that the second edition is packaged as a complete 'story' of the poet's conversion to, and control over, amatory elegy.

[8] Griffin (1985), 105.

titute but an elegiac poetics. The poem is one of a whole series scattered throughout the corpus of Augustan elegy that map out a debate over styles of writing. On this occasion, however, the terrain is not Helicon's slopes, but female physiques.[9] It is worth dwelling for a moment on the second of these approaches to *Amores* 3.1, since critics are so rarely prepared to read female flesh as poetic fiction. Clearly that practice is acceptable here because the flesh is labelled 'Elegy'.

*Amores* 3.1 is viewed as principally concerned with a stylistic contrast first expounded in the polemical works of Callimachus as an opposition, in poetic practices, between the *lepton* (fine) and the *pachu* (fat). The Latin literary-critical terminology for this *Stilkampf* was then established in neoteric poetry, further developed in Virgil's *Eclogues*, and frequently deployed in the Propertian corpus.[10] In the context of 3.1, the advocacy of Fine Poetry is constructed round the dramatic device of a contest between two women but, entitled Elegia and Tragoedia, these women have only a precarious signification as individuals, so that a catalogue of their physical features functions more importantly as a catalogue of stylistic practices. The attributes of poetic genres are made flesh, and women are displayed as choices of generic style for males, as Sir Joshua Reynolds understood when he borrowed from this poem (among other sources) to depict the actor David Garrick choosing between Tragedy and Comedy.[11] Critics have noted that in this famous painting, exhibited at the Society of Artists in 1762, Comedy is depicted in the style of Correggio and Tragedy in the style of Guido Reni, establishing a stylistic opposition that works to highlight the directions in which both the actor and the painter were torn: between types of dramatic performance in the

[9] See esp. Schrijvers (1976). Cf. Reitzenstein (1935); Wimmel (1960), 295–7; Berman (1975), 14–20.

[10] See Wimmel (1960), *passim*. On the Propertian corpus, cf. Quadlbauer (1968) and (1970), and Chs. 2 and 3 above.

[11] E. J. Kenney's suggestion of *Amores* 3.1 as a source for the painting is discussed by Postle (1995), 25.

FIG. 4.2 Garrick between Tragedy and Comedy. E. Fisher, after original exhibited in 1762 by Sir Joshua Reynolds.

case of Garrick, and types of portraiture (intimate or heroic) in the case of Reynolds himself (Fig. 4.2).[12]

In the case of *Amores* 3.1, every aspect of Ovid's women (their shape, comportment, and speech) is constructed in accordance with a Callimachean apologetics, and everywhere the reader is required to unite these women with issues of poetic production: 'The point throughout depends on the simple device of treating these two personifications as human beings and at the same time as poetic genres.'[13] Thus even the cave before which the women come to play out their struggle for an author (whose sylvan setting Reynolds recalls in his painting) reproduces the topography of the poetic programme

[12] See e.g. Wendorf (1996), 147–51, and Postle (1995), 20–32.
[13] Lee (1962), 169. Cf. Bertini (1983), 227.

with which Propertius introduced *his* third poetry-book. From the outset, Ovid's poem demands comparison in particular with Propertian poetic production.[14]

The narrator describes the first woman's approach:

> uenit odoratos Elegia nexa capillos,
>   et, puto, pes illi longior alter erat.
> forma decens, uestis tenuissima, uultus amantis,
>   et pedibus uitium causa decoris erat. (vv. 7–10)

> [She came—Elegy—her scented curls bound up,
>   and, I suspect, one foot longer than the other:
> well-formed, finely dressed, a lover's look,
>   imperfect movement occasioning elegance.]

Elegia is endowed with the body of the elegiac mistress: 'Mademoiselle Elégie ressemble à tout point à la bien-aimée chantée par les poètes élégiaques' (Miss Elegy resembles in every detail the beloved sung by the elegiac poets).[15] The hairstyle, outline, dress, and expression catalogued in the hexameter verses 7 and 9 all reproduce attributes ascribed elsewhere to elegy's beloveds. When Cynthia first makes a physical appearance in the Propertian corpus, her hair is elaborately styled and perfumed, her dress is of fine Coan silk, and she possesses an ornamented *forma* (1.2.1–8).[16] The affinity between Elegia and the elegiac mistress is disclosed, moreover, by the reappearance of Elegia's attributes in the two poems directly following *Amores* 3.1, where physical features are assembled for an Ovidian *puella*: her look is full of erotic promise (2.2.83), her dress is delicate (2.2.36), her body defined by *forma* and *decens* (3.3.7–8).

To the attributes of a beauty, however, the pentameter verses 8 and 10 attach an incongruous limp. Accustomed to the physical characteristics usually allotted to the elegiac beloved, a reader would

[14] See Berman (1975), 15–16 and Morgan (1977), 17–18.

[15] Schrijvers (1976), 415.

[16] In the first poem of the *Monobiblos*, nothing is ascribed to the name *Cynthia* except a pair of eyes and the capacity to captivate.

expect this *puella* to possess feet which were snowy-white or slight: a reminder arrives at *Amores* 3.3.7 (*pes erat exiguus—pedis est artissima forma*). In this poem, however, the elegiac woman's body has been awkwardly reshaped to serve poetic concerns. Now entitled Elegia and supplied with elegiac feet to match the unevenness of elegiac verse, this comic representation of a female form has 'un caractère nettement fictif' (a completely fictive character).[17] In particular, the allocation to this woman of unequal feet demonstrates that here at least a female body has been shaped to suit an elegiac poetic programme, because physically they constitute a defect (*uitium*), stylistically an asset (*decor*).

In the pentameter verses *pes* signals ambiguously both human and metrical feet, but some critics have observed that such ambiguities are also generated by the language of the hexameter verses. So *forma* and *tenuissima* are recognized to be as applicable to a collection of words as they are to a woman. Guy Lee, for example, retains the ambiguity of these terms with translations such as 'she had style'.[18] The delicacy which *tenuissima* suggests is read as qualifying the clothing of a Callimachean discourse, since *tenuis* is a well-documented signifier of the writing-style which Callimachus had designated *lepton*.[19]

The vocabulary in which Elegia is formulated as flesh is thus allowed to point to her as being also a way of speaking, a mode of poetic composition. Yet, elsewhere, part of that vocabulary delineates the elegiac mistress. So *Amores* 3.1 invites its readers to ask the question whether other love elegies also present the female body in ambiguous terms. In the second poem of the *Monobiblos* for example, where Propertius first sets out the features of his elegiac mistress, she too possesses clothing that is *tenuis*, and a body defined by *forma*. The

[17] Schrijvers (1976), 416.

[18] Lee (1968), 119.

[19] Bertini (1983), 227; Lee (1962), 169. On *tenuis*, see also Quadlbauer (1968), 95–6; Fedeli (1985), 54 and 59.

Propertian *puella* is charged with an excessive use of ornament in a poem whose style is paradoxically ornate and whose central theme has been identified as artifice itself.[20] Since there is every reason to suppose that—as the subject of Propertian art—the female form is an appropriate site for the expression of artistic concerns, what theoretical justification is there for depriving Cynthia of literary-critical possibilities, when they are welcomed for Elegia?[21]

Thus, in *Amores* 3.1 the flesh of the elegiac mistress is reproduced and recalled in the hexameter verses 7 and 9. In the pentameters (vv. 8 and 10) it is provided additionally with unequal feet. The comic incongruity reveals that here the beloved's body has been placed openly at the service of poetic concerns. Since the elegiac metre requires that the stylistic asset of foot-shortening be put into practice precisely at the two moments when Elegia's physical defect is being pronounced, at least at this point in the elegiac corpus the body of a woman may be read uncontentiously as the anatomy of a text.

Tragoedia has now arrived in hot pursuit:

> uenit et ingenti uiolenta Tragoedia passu:
> fronte comae torua, palla iacebat humi;
> laeua manus sceptrum late regale mouebat,
> Lydius alta pedum uincla cothurnus erat. (vv. 11–14)

> [She came too in grand strides—impassioned Tragedy:
> braids draping a darksome brow, her gown the earth,
> left hand wielding wide the princely sceptre,
> a Lydian boot her foot's high prop.]

The second party to the *Stilkampf* is not the recipient of the favourable stylistic appraisal suggested earlier by *decens* and *tenuissima*, but once again the attributes of a writing-practice are fleshed out and a female figure constructed to suit a Callimachean polemic.

[20] See, for instance, Curran (1975).

[21] Curran (1975), for example, distinguishes the 'real' woman of Prop. 1.2.1–8 from the artist's creation which he claims the remainder of that poem is advocating.

As symbols of a Graeco-Roman tragic tradition, *palla*, *sceptrum*, and *cothurnus* have already made an appearance in *Amores* 2.18.15–16.[22] There they were associated with the narrator (as producer of tragic discourse). Here they are associated with a narrative practice personified. Thus *uiolenta* is suggestive of both human behaviour and dramatic technique.[23] In every way, Tragoedia is shaped to compare and contrast with Elegia. While Elegia's limp mimics the movement of elegiac couplets, Tragoedia's enormous stride embodies the grandeur of the tragic metres. Similarly her hairstyle (*fronte comae torua*) characterizes the diction of a dignified writing-style.[24] As with the features of Comedy and Tragedy in the painting by Reynolds, female flesh and its paraphernalia evidently operate here as a means of differentiating one genre from another. If, however, Tragoedia dramatizes the *pachu*, then the body of the elegiac mistress has entered the Ovidian narrative here because it is a manifestation of the *lepton*.

After Tragoedia has advocated her own production in terms which are both moralistic and appropriately passionate, the narrator next recalls her comportment and that of her rival for an author's attentions:[25]

hactenus, et mouit pictis innixa cothurnis
densum caesarie terque quaterque caput.
altera, si memini, limis subrisit ocellis;
fallor, an in dextra myrtea uirga fuit? (vv. 31–4)

[Thus far, and propped on her ornamented boots she bowed
three times and four her thick-fleeced head.
The other (if I remember) stole a peek and giggled—
am I wrong, or in her right hand was there a myrtle twig?]

[22] See Brandt (1963), ad loc., and cf. Reitzenstein (1935), 83.

[23] Cf. Brandt (1963), on *Am.* 3.1.11.

[24] For the tragic tone of *torua*, cf. Pacuvius *Trag.* 36 and 37, and Accius *Trag.* 223.

[25] Schrijvers (1976), 417–21, offers a detailed account of the speech as incorporating a parody of tragic diction.

Each woman is attired with an emblem of poetic practice (*cothurnis* and the *myrtea uirga*), and each behaves in a manner appropriate to her own literary production. Tragoedia nods majestically like an Homeric Zeus. Elegia flirts in the manner of the elegiac mistress at the races in *Amores* 3.2.83: *risit et argutis quiddam promisit ocellis*. Diction matches behaviour as a means of differentiating levels of discourse: *caesarie* is a highly poetic word, in Ovid's work found otherwise only in hexameter verse; *limis* does not usually belong in literary language.[26] Thus two opposed poetic traditions are demarcated by the two different ways in which these fictive females move.

So far, in this reading of *Amores* 3.1, attention has been drawn to the poem as a narrative of conflicting literary interests in which female forms have been shaped to suit a poetic purpose. The body of the elegiac mistress then enters such a discourse as a device to signify one particular practice of writing. A similar strategy is in operation when, in the course of her plea for production, Elegia mentions Corinna and the ease with which her pupil learned to slip through front doors (vv. 43–52). For in the general context of that speech (vv. 35–60), Corinna functions demonstrably as a signifier of erotic (specifically Ovidian) discourse and, therefore, may be read as representative of elegiac fictions. Firstly, the doors through which Corinna once stole have already been identified as among the props of elegy's producers rather than as an obstacle facing Augustan lovers (vv. 35–42) and, secondly, the woman who taught Corinna is subsequently identified wholly as text (vv. 53–8).

In the first part of her speech Elegia concedes *non ego contulerim sublimia carmina nostris: | obruit exiguas regia uestra fores* (I would not set towering poetry beside my own; | your palace eclipses tiny doorways, vv. 39–40). The contrast between palace entrances and house doors is set within another opposition: Tragoedia is accused of being

[26] Brandt (1963), on *Am.* 3.1.33; Reitzenstein (1935), 83–4; Schrijvers (1976), 421.

perpetually *grauis* (v. 36), while Elegia boldly confesses that she is *leuis* (v. 41). The signification of the *grauis/leuis* opposition is drawn away from the level of female dispositions and towards the level of writing-styles by frequent references in the course of the passage to poetic production: compare *carmina* here (v. 39), with *uerbis* (v. 35), *numeris* (v. 37), and *uersibus* (v. 38). Furthermore, the reader will recognize the *grauis/leuis* opposition within which the respective doorways are described as the terminology of a Callimachean polemic already so used in *Amores* 1.1. There weapons were to be narrated *graui numero* (v. 1), but beloveds (either boy or girl) *numeris leuioribus* (v. 19). Thus the doors are positioned in a literary-critical framework signalled in vv. 39–40 by *sublimia* and *exiguas*.[27] The word *sublimia* is of particular interest. Its etymology is obscure, but the possibility of its derivation from *sub limen* immediately connects it as a stylistic evaluation with the subsequent discussion of doors. In such a context, *regia* and *fores* signify majestic and modest arenas of discourse respectively, as do allusions to streams of Helicon elsewhere.[28] So, since the royal palace constitutes the scenic backdrop for a tragic performance with no status independently of a tragic text, the house door becomes merely a property employed in elegy's amatory production.

In the last part of her speech, Elegia offers three examples of how she has suffered for love (vv. 53–8). The personification is continued through the use of active verbs such as *non uerita* (v. 54) and *memini* (v. 55), but the circumstances suffered (being pinned to a door, hidden in the folds of a dress, or submerged in water as an unwelcome birthday present) are appropriate for a tablet of wax, ludicrous for a woman. In each case, a comic mismatch between *puella* and love poem arises in which Elegia's status as text is paramount.[29] The first

[27] For the array of literary-critical terms, cf. Lee (1962), 169–70; Schrijvers (1976), 422.

[28] See e.g. Virgil *Ecl.* 6 and Prop. 2.10, and the discussion of them in Ch. 2 above.

[29] As Brandt (1963), on *Am.* 3.1.57: 'hat nun das Mädchen weiter nichts als ein liebesgedicht bekommen'.

of these examples, after all, identifies her clearly as a literary practice, a poetical scroll, because she is *legi* (v. 54). Thus Elegia is first presented in *Amores* 3.1 as a living woman of flesh (although even that flesh is incongruously elegiac in its structure) but, by the poem's close, the woman of flesh has been playfully reshaped into a work of elegiac art.

The centrepiece of Elegia's speech, vv. 43–52, recalls both her own success as a *magistra amoris* and her prize pupil Corinna but, as we have seen, this teacher is also a poetic text and her speech an avowal of a Callimachean poetics. So Corinna and the *custos* she has deceived constitute past samples of the writing-practice Elegia advocates and stand in opposition to the *facta uirorum* (v. 25) for which Tragoedia has just now called. Both the demeanour and the circumstances of the elegiac mistress are fashioned in order to signal past poems of the elegiac corpus. Firstly, memories of her *tunica uelata soluta* (v. 51) recall Corinna's negligent appearance at *Amores* 1.5.9 (*tunica uelata recincta*). Thus, in a poem which puts female flesh on the poetic genre Elegy, physical features ascribed elsewhere to the elegiac mistress (most notably the first detailed depictions of both Cynthia and Corinna) are constantly recalled. Secondly, the elegiac beloved's past circumstances are so articulated as to survey the elegiacs of Tibullus. For Elegia claims to have provided Corinna with the sort of protection offered by Venus in Tibullus 1.2,[30] and sets the scene for that claim by reproducing terms that featured prominently in the first and last poems of that Tibullan poetry-book (namely *rusticus* from Tibullus 1.1.8 and *lasciuus Amor* from Tibullus 1.10.57). Similarly, Elegia's ability to render a *ianua laxa* (v. 46) recalls poems by all three Augustan elegists. Centred on the mistress's closed door, these poems include Tibullus 1.2, Propertius 1.16, Ovid *Amores* 1.6 and 2.19. Thus Corinna and her front door are constructed to recall an array of elegiac poems and function as signifiers of a poetic tradition opposed to the tragic narration of kings and palace entrances.

[30] As Reitzenstein (1935), 84.

Finally, to conclude the narrative of *Amores* 3.1 and introduce a third book of love-elegies, the adoption of Elegia as a practice of writing is recounted (vv. 61–70). Now her attractions are described solely in terms of poetic production and a Callimachean poetics, for she is said to grant *nostro uicturum nomen amori* (v. 65). Elegiac composition is chosen not as the result of a pressing, romantic commitment to a mistress, but out of a desire for lasting fame. In *Epigr.* 7(9) Pfeiffer, Callimachus had already suggested that, since Theaetetus followed a clear poetic path towards the composition of epigrams rather than tragedies, Greece would forever sing his skill.

The theme of great glory arising, paradoxically, out of slight poetry features frequently in Latin literature descended from the Callimachean tradition.[31] Consequently, as a recipient of lasting acclaim, the Ovidian *amor* may be read as equivalent to a Callimachean *sophiê* or skill: love is literary eroticism and its artful composition. Thus, by the close of *Amores* 3.1, the encounter between two female figures has been clearly identified as a contest between styles of writing, and love is understood to be a poetic activity. The only respect in which Ovid has veered from the clear path of Callimachus' poetics is in his suggestion that he has some interest in, and will shortly embark upon, tragic composition. The elegiac mistress (as the embodiment of Callimachus' *lepton*) is only temporarily the poet's practice for, at some point, Ovid does produce a tragedy—the now lost *Medea*. Reynolds borrows this conceit too for his painting of Garrick's choice of performance styles: Garrick is posed glancing backwards at Tragedy with an apologetic expression. Like Ovid, the actor appears to be promising Tragedy that he won't be gone for long.[32]

*Amores* 3.1 provides poetic genres with female flesh in order to dramatize a Callimachean opposition between poetic practices. However, Corinna (along with her front door) enters the debate as an example of elegiac composition in the requisite Callimachean

[31] See e.g. Quadlbauer (1968), 96–7 on Prop. 3.1.9.

[32] As Postle (1995), 25, on Kenney's Ovidian reading of the painting.

manner and, throughout the poem, the attributes and activities of the elegiac mistress are recalled and subsumed under personified Elegy. The text sets up a series of witty mismatches between what is appropriate to the depiction of an elegiac *puella* and to the description of an elegiac poem: supplied now with elegiac feet and subjected to a variety of indignities, the body of the elegiac mistress has become a site for the humorous expression of Callimachean concerns.[33]

## FEMALE FLESH AS POLITICS

*Amores* 3.1 is not concerned exclusively, however, with issues of poetic practice and their articulation through representations of the female form. The account it provides of the narrator's choice between the relative attractions of Elegia and Tragoedia travesties the structure of another famous choice between female forms—namely the allegorical presentation of Hercules' choice between Aretê (Virtue) and Kakia (Vice) first expounded by the sophist Prodicus, transmitted in Xenophon's *Memorabilia* 2.1.21–34, and then widely and repeatedly imitated in western literature and art. In Sebastian Brant's enormously popular late fifteenth-century German morality tale *Narrenschiff* (The Ship of Fools, 1494), for example, the fools who do not heed the right road in life are briefly contrasted with the Prodicean Hercules who makes the correct choice of Wisdom over Joy, Virtue over vain Delight. The woodcut that accompanies this chapter of Brant's illustrates well his description of Wisdom as a pale, hard, sour, and joyless woman in contrast to the physical attractions of Delight (Fig. 4.3).[34]

[33] Cf. now Keith (1999) on the literary-critical terminology inherited from Callimachus (and mediated by Roman rhetorical theory) in which the body of the poet-lover is described in Augustan elegy.

[34] Zeydel (1944) conveniently provides a description and English translation of Brant's work. Panofsky (1930) and Galinsky (1972) discuss chapter 107 (and its dependency on both Xenophon and Ovid) in the context of their accounts of the choice of Hercules in western literature and art.

FIG. 4.3 The choice of Hercules. Woodcut illustrating 1497 edition of *Narrenschiff* by Sebastian Brant.

A few commentators on Ovid's *Amores* 3.1 have observed the correspondence between the narrator's choice and that of Hercules,[35] but its implications for reading elegy's female forms as playful signifiers of a moral or political position have not been fully explored. Only P. H. Schrijvers noted briefly that moral arguments are employed in *Amores* 3.1 and that the allocation of victory to Elegia involves 'la réévaluation des valeurs' (the re-evaluation of values),[36]

[35] Reitzenstein (1935), 81–2; Brandt (1963), on *Am.* 3.1.11; Schrijvers (1976), esp. 407–13.

[36] Schrijvers (1976), 422.

but the article in which these valuable points were made appeared as part of a Festschrift for J. C. Kamerbeek and was therefore concerned primarily with issues centring on the practice of tragedy.

The narrative strategy of positioning the conflict between Elegia and Tragoedia in a direct line of descent from that between Aretê and Kakia discloses an important structural function of female flesh as signifier of male political and moral practices. The recollection and comic debasement of the earlier moral allegory assigns the Ovidian narrator the role of a latter-day Roman Hercules deciding not just between writing-styles, but between life-styles, and it is through the shape, comportment, and speech of the poem's two female constructs that conflicting moral and political ideologies are articulated and appraised.

In their appearance, their attire, and their pose, Elegia and Tragoedia are clearly differentiated as respectively *meretrix* and *matrona*. As matron, Tragoedia is clothed in the concealing garments of a respectable Roman wife (*palla iacebat humi*, v. 12), and adopts highly dignified gestures (vv. 31–2).[37] As mistress, Elegia is provided with both a sexually provocative dress (*uestis tenuissima*, v. 9) and expression (v. 9 and v. 33). Yet the earlier, allegorical account of divergent modes of conduct had also been expressed in terms of a choice between *meretrix* and *matrona*, and later manifestations of Hercules' choice followed suit.[38] According to Xenophon's account, Hercules had been faced with a choice between Aretê as a woman wearing a modest look and the purity of white or Kakia as a woman wearing a brazen expression and a dress that revealed all (*Mem.* 2.1.22), while the fifteenth-century illustration of the event hides the body of stern Wisdom in floor-length garments and discloses all but the genitalia of smiling Joy.

In the features and in the dress of the Ovidian women, a counterpart for Elegia is to be found in Kakia, and for Tragoedia in Aretê. By

[37] Schrijvers (1976), 416–17.

[38] As e.g. Gigon (1956), 64. See now Kuntz (1994).

reproducing the features of female forms that are employed elsewhere to typify codes of conduct, the Ovidian text identifies its female figures also as such types: in *Amores* 3.1, Tragoedia functions as an Augustan embodiment of Virtue and Elegia as an embodiment of Vice. The victory of Elegia as Vice, the preference for a *meretrix* over a *matrona*, then constitutes a witty and provocative re-writing of the mythic parable in which Hercules chooses Virtue.[39]

It is not just through female physiques that an ideologically provocative position is established for the narrator of *Amores* 3.1. Moral and political concerns are to the forefront of Tragoedia's plea for authorship. Before advocating herself as a practice of writing, Tragoedia condemns her opponent:

> nequitiam uinosa tuam conuiuia narrant,
> narrant in multas compita secta uias.
> saepe aliquis digito uatem designat euntem
> atque ait 'hic, hic est, quem ferus urit Amor'.
> fabula, nec sentis, tota iactaris in Vrbe,
> dum tua praeterito facta pudore refers. (vv. 17–22)

> [Your depravity tipsy parties tell,
> crossroads tell it—split into many streets.
> Often someone with his finger points out the passing bard
> and says 'That's him, that's the one cruel Love burns!'
> You're talk, you don't realize, spread round the whole city,
> while you report your own acts, shame abandoned.]

The context of this passage and its central reference to a *uatem* and *Amor* (rather than to a lover and his girlfriend) identify it as an assault on erotic elegy, although that assault is expressed in terms of an author's actions and is enclosed by the terminology of moral conduct—namely *nequitiam* (v. 17) and *pudore* (v. 22). As an Augustan matron and embodiment of Virtue, Tragoedia gives voice to the

[39] The same has been said for the painting by Reynolds who was known to have read a version of Hercules' choice in the works of Lord Shaftesbury. See Postle (1995), 21–3.

values of the establishment and interprets the production of elegy as vice, for matrons would be expected to regret the passing of *pudor* and to denigrate the sexual licence that *nequitia* suggests. The practitioner of poetic eroticism is portrayed as isolated from the rest of the community at Rome and labelled as morally corrupt. Tragoedia thus ascribes to Augustan elegy an unorthodoxy boldly proclaimed by its authors elsewhere: the poet was introduced at the beginning of a second book of *Amores* as *ille ego nequitiae Naso poeta meae* (2.1.2)[40] and in the Propertian poem 2.24 (which *Amores* 3.1 here recalls) the scandal of *nequitia* is said to accrue to the creator of poems on Cynthia.[41] Once again, at this point in the corpus of Augustan elegy, its unorthodox nature is to be understood through the agency of a female form.

Tragoedia continues her case by commanding her immediate production:

> tempus erat thyrso pulsum grauiore moueri;
>   cessatum satis est: incipe maius opus.
> materia premis ingenium; cane facta uirorum:
>   'haec animo' dices 'area digna meo est'.
> quod tenerae cantent lusit tua Musa puellae,
>   primaque per numeros acta iuuenta suos.
> nunc habeam per te Romana Tragoedia nomen:
>   implebit leges spiritus iste meas. (vv. 23–30)

> [Time, propelled by the weightier wand, to be moved—
>   there's been ample idleness. Undertake a greater task.
> Your material suppresses talent; celebrate the feats of heroes:
>   'this arena', you'll say, 'suits my spirit'.
> Ditties for delicate girls to sing your Muse has played,
>   first youth driven by its proper rhythms.
> Now, through you, let Roman Tragedy win fame;
>   your energy will satisfy my demands.]

40 Cf. Brandt (1963), on *Am.* 3.1.17.

41 The language of 3.1.17–22 recalls that of Prop. 2.24.1–8 where *urere*, *fabula*, *tota urbs*, and *pudor* are also to be found.

Tragoedia offers not only the allurement of a grander writing-style but, following the mythic parable of Hercules, the attractions of work and social responsibility. According to Prodicus' tale, there are no thoughts of war or business in the pursuit of Kakia (Xen. *Mem.* 2.1.24). Similarly, in *Amores* 3.1, the rival of Elegia/Kakia describes elegy's pursuit as unemployment, or an act of idleness; used of poetic eroticism *cessare* suggests that it involves the absence of any adequate political or social role for its author. Elegy is associated with girls, delicacy, adolescence, and play; tragedy with men, deeds, and dignity. Tragoedia concludes her speech by describing the result of her practice in the community: from elegy there arises gossip at Rome, but from tragedy glory. *Romana* marks the different positions tragedy and elegy hold in relation to the state, for drama may be read as a national genre (a state institution) while erotic elegy is often associated with the history of struggles against Roman militarism. Thus the *Amores* as a whole is rounded off by the location of its narrator within the Paelignian (rather than the Roman) race, and then that race is recorded as having fought against Roman oppression during the Social Wars (*cum timuit socias anxia Roma manus*, 3.15.10). Propertius too had closed a collection of elegiac poems by linking its author's birthplace with civil war and a period *cum Romana suos egit discordia ciuis* (when Roman discord drove her own citizens, 1.22.5).

While Tragoedia thus takes on the part of Aretê in denying moral or social responsibility to the authorship of elegy, Elegia cleverly appropriates the vocabulary of Virtue to express a different ideological position for her narrator. In Prodicus' parable, Aretê talks to Hercules about the necessity of suffering to achieve the good life awarded by the gods (Xen. *Mem.* 2.1.28), a suffering that manifests itself in the fifteenth-century woodcut as thorn bushes and a dark night sky around Wisdom (in contrast to the flowers and sunlight surrounding Joy). In the Ovidian poem, Elegia redefines what is to be thought of as the good achieved through *ponos* for the world of erotic discourses;[42] the end of some rather ludicrous ordeals becomes sexual access (vv. 43–58).

In *Amores* 3.1, therefore, Aretê and Kakia have been reproduced in the flesh and speech of Tragoedia and Elegia respectively. The written women of this elegy are also to be read as signifiers of moral and political ideologies. However, in allowing his narrator to be won over by the attractions of the *meretrix*, rather than the *matrona*, Ovid has radically rewritten the mythic parable (as Reynolds will much later).[43] Pursuit of Virtue is still depicted here as a hard task—the Ovidian *labor aeternus* of writing tragedies (v. 68) parallels the Prodican long, hard road to Aretê,[44] but the glory that was once its reward is no longer Virtue's to bestow. According to Prodicus, the friends of Virtue are not forgotten and dishonoured, but remembered and celebrated (Xen. *Mem.* 2.1.33). In the morally perverse world of literary eroticism it is the awkward figure of limping Elegia/Vice who bestows on her poets everlasting fame (*nostro uicturum nomen amori*, v. 65) and not the swift death which, in the fifteenth-century woodcut, is envisaged as Delight's hidden companion.

The female forms Elegia and Tragoedia have clearly been constructed to suit a playful Ovidian narrative of moral and political difference, but the extent of the political unorthodoxy which the choice of Elegia articulates is best understood in the historical context of elegy's production as an ideological discourse. For the presentation of an Augustan 'Hercules' choosing Vice rather than Virtue, a *meretrix* rather than a *matrona*, actively conflicts with the contemporary, institutionalized role of Hercules as symbol of the Roman state and its *princeps*. In Roman culture, as Karl Galinsky has observed, Hercules had become idealized as the perfect embodiment of Stoic virtue and was so closely conjoined with Augustus as

42 Cf. Schrijvers (1976), 422.

43 See now Boyd (1997), 197–200, on Ovid's divergence from the Prodican tale.

44 Schrijvers (1976), 424.

'to be considered an Augustan symbol'.[45] Both through Augustus' own efforts (such as in timing his triple triumph of 29 BC to coincide with the official festival of Hercules on 13 August) and through such notable literary representations as those in Virgil's *Aeneid*, Hercules became a symbol of political orthodoxy, of the hegemony of the Augustan state in the post-Actium period.[46] Thus comic debasements of the Hercules mythology, such as the conversion of hero into clumsy suitor in Propertius 4.9 and in *Heroides* 9, are read as narrative strategies for the expression of anti-Augustan sentiment.[47] Here, in *Amores* 3.1, when faced with the same dilemma as Hercules in the shape of *meretrix* or *matrona*, the elegiac narrator rejects the expected response institutionalized in myth and opts for a female form openly dissociated from social and political responsibility.

Through the flippant association of Ovid's female forms Elegia and Tragoedia with the mythic parable of Kakia and Aretê, *Amores* 3.1 signals that its written women articulate a political, as well as a poetic, heterodoxy for their narrator. Here women enter elegy's fictive world to formulate an amusing manifesto of both literary and political difference, and their bodies are clearly shaped to suit that manifesto. In particular, the asymmetric body with which Elegia is endowed functions as a signifier both of a Callimachean poetics (the advocacy of what is *lepton*) and an anti-Augustan politics (the advocacy of *nequitia*). Since, however, Elegia's body has already been identified in all respects (except its unequal feet) with the body assigned elsewhere to the elegiac mistress, the question immediately arises as to whether Elegia's narrative function in *Amores* 3.1 has any implications for the function of the mistress elsewhere in the corpus of Augustan love-poetry.

[45] Galinsky (1972), 153.

[46] Galinsky (1972), 126–66. See now Galinsky (1996), 222–4.

[47] On Prop. 4.9, see Anderson (1964), 11, and Pillinger (1969), 189; and now DeBrohun (1994), Lindheim (1998*a*), and Janan (1998) and (2001), 128–45. On *Heroides* 9, see Galinsky (1972), 153–60.

THE ELEGIAC MISTRESS

It is not possible, in fact, to confine a reading of female flesh as political fiction to *Amores* 3.1 and thereby safeguard the identification of elegy's female subjects with specific individuals living in Augustan Rome. For, at the same time as *Amores* 3.1 incorporates many features of the elegiac *puella*, it encourages its readers to look both outwards to other modes of representing the female form and backwards at the role of the *puella* in articulating elegy's poetic and political concerns.

The narrative structure of *Amores* 3.1 locates its female figures firmly in a tradition for representing women that stretches back to Prodicus' parable and on beyond Ovidian elegy. Although the story of *Hercules in Biuio* has been represented in numerous and diverse ways in the accounts of philosophers, poets, and painters,[48] the allocation of attributes to the female embodiments of man's moral or political choices falls into a set pattern: the features of Ovid's Elegia and the elegiac beloved she recalls are thus also those commonly possessed by such figures as *Kakia*, *Hêdonê*, *Tyrannis*, *Pseudodoxia*, *Adulatio*, or *Voluptas*.[49] In his epic poem on the second Punic War, Silius Italicus (especially close to Ovid in the chronology of representations of Hercules' choice) presents P. Cornelius Scipio with a dilemma. He structures his account to match the mythic dilemma of Hercules by depicting a contest for the soldier's allegiance between the divine figures *Voluptas* and *Virtus*. The physiques of his goddesses closely resemble those of Elegy and Tragedy:

> alter Achaemenium spirabat uertice odorem,
> ambrosias diffusa comas et ueste refulgens,
> ostrum qua fuluo Tyrium suffuderat auro;
> fronte decor quaesitus acu, lasciuaque crebras
> ancipiti motu iaciebant lumina flammas.
> alterius dispar habitus: frons hirta nec umquam
> composita mutata coma; stans uultus, et ore

[48] See esp. Panofsky (1930).

[49] See the catalogue constructed by Alpers (1912), 51–8.

incessuque uiro proprior laetique pudoris,
celsa humeros niueae fulgebat stamine pallae. (*Punica* 15.23–31)

[One from her crown breathed Persian scent,
spilling her ambrosial curls, and brilliant in a dress
Tyrian purple had traced with rosy gold;
elegance on her brow acquired with a pin, her desirous eyes
darted left and right repeated flames.
Far different the other's look: a shaggy brow never by
styled hair altered, a firm gaze,
both face and pace nearer to a man's and joyfully modest;
towering, her shoulders gleamed with thread of snowy robe.]

From Ovid's Elegy, *Voluptas* has inherited scented hair, expensive clothes, and a provocative look. From Tragedy, *Virtus* has inherited a mannish stride, dishevelled hair, a stern expression, and matronly gown.[50] The same grouping of physical features, the same *meretrix/matrona* dichotomy for female flesh, is to be found in Silius' hexameters as in Ovid's elegiacs because those features bring with them a whole constellation of cultural values through which to articulate the moral and political choices men face. The *meretrix* figure again acts as a signifier of social irresponsibility and idleness, the *matrona* of state duties and military pursuits. It is because everywhere such female types may have ideological repercussions that Silius is able to deploy the same *meretrix/matrona* dichotomy in order to dramatize Scipio's Stoic pursuit of a command in Spain.[51]

The employment of such archetypes for female flesh has not of course been confined to variations on the theme of *Hercules in Biuio*.[52] The opposition between Innocent and Seductress has subsequently played a crucial role in shaping the Christian Church's models for

50 The list is that of Bruere (1959), 240–2.

51 For Scipio as built in the image of the Stoic Hercules, see Bassett (1966).

52 See now McGinn (1998), esp. 147–71 and 208–9, who argues that the distinction between *matrona* or *mater familias* and *meretrix* was deeply rooted in Roman ideas about social status and sexual morality. The Augustan legislation of 18 BC then gave legal force to what was before a social and moral contrast.

female behaviour (the Virgin Mary and Eve)[53] while, for instance, 'the two most common types of women in film noir are the exciting, childless whores, or the boring, potentially childbearing sweethearts'.[54] For images of women, and the values attached to them, arise out of both the social relation between the sexes and concepts of gender in a given culture. In patriarchal cultures, the central measurement of women, the way women enter cultural forms, is through sexuality. Patriarchy's familial ideology then associates the sexually unrestrained, childless woman with social disruption and locates her on the margins of society. Marriage and motherhood, being concerned with the ordering of female sexuality in terms which will be socially effective for patriarchy, restore women to a central position, while still withholding full economic or political power.[55] In the case of the theme *Hercules in Biuio*, women enter cultural discourse to define male moral and political choices and their physiques are shaped accordingly and appropriately labelled *meretrix* or *matrona*.

Thus the similarities between the *meretrix* figures of Prodicus' tale, Ovid's elegies, and Silius' epic demonstrate that the flesh of the elegiac mistress has a history beyond the physical features of any Augustan girlfriend and belongs, rather, to an archetypal dichotomy whore/matron through which is expressed male political and moral

[53] See e.g. Warner (1976).

[54] Harvey (1980), 25. On the cultural polarization of Woman into either demonized whore or exalted goddess as used to depict conflicting facets of Latin love poetry's beloved, see now Janan (1994), esp. 71. She uses this polarization specifically to compare Catullus' Lesbia in poems 11 and 51. Cf. Greene (1998), 62–6, on the duality of Propertius' Cynthia, and 80–1 on Ovid's Corinna. Fredrick (1997) also argues that the elegiac mistress oscillates between a representation as virgin and as whore.

[55] See e.g. Berger (1972); Lipshitz (1978); Kaplan (1980). For the prevalence of this mode of structuring femininity in antiquity, see Lefkowitz (1981) and Dixon (1988); and now Edwards (1993), 34–62, Skinner (1997), 9–11, McGinn (1998), esp. 17, and Dixon (2001), chs. 3 and 5. See also Ch. 3 above on the women of Propertius book 4, and Chs. 6 and 9 below on Roman constructions of (respectively) Cleopatra and Messalina.

conflicts. It is the silks and scents, the coiffure, and the provocative look borrowed from the elegiac mistress that link Elegia with symbols of pleasure and the absence of virtue. Silius' *Voluptas* owes more to the features of an elegiac *puella* than to a personification of elegiac poetry since only the evident attributes of writing-styles have been carefully avoided in his version; elegy's limp, tragedy's boots.

Ovid's Elegia identifies her component parts as belonging to a pervasive tradition in which female flesh functions as a signifier of male ideological positions. In her flimsy dresses and adorned to lure lovers (Prop. 1.2, 1.15.1–8), the elegiac mistress is differentiated from the Roman *matrona* who wears the long gown of respectability (Tib. 1.6.67–8) and is said to have no place in elegiac discourse (*Ars Amat.* 1.31–2). Not the narrator's wife, she is a *meretrix* in the broadest sense of the word: a symbol of *nequitia* and the absence of *pudor* (Prop. 2.24.1–8). Thus by claiming to be entrapped by an unrestrained female sexuality, by the figure of 'une irrégulière',[56] the writers of elegiac poetry are able to portray themselves as abandoning traditional social responsibilities: not soldier, lawyer, or politician, but poet of love (*Am.* 1.15).

There is a second, pressing reason why it is not possible to view the function of female flesh in *Amores* 3.1 as unique to this particular point in the corpus of Augustan love-poetry, but necessary instead to view the poem as having important implications for reading the flesh of the elegiac mistress elsewhere. As a narrative openly expressing poetic concerns (the rejection of a higher form of writing in favour of elegy), *Amores* 3.1 belongs to a group of Augustan elegies ultimately indebted to the rejection of epic that Callimachus had expressed in the elegiacs of the *Aetia*. Often to be found at the opening or close of poetry-books, these poems have been grouped together under various headings, such as the *recusatio* or the *apologetischen Form*.[57] Poem 3.1 cannot easily be isolated from other such programmatic poems within the *Amores* since they have been read as offering a unifying

[56] Veyne (1983), 15.

[57] See esp. Wimmel (1960).

movement to the collection, from an initial acceptance of elegy to its ultimate rejection.[58]

In particular, references within *Amores* 3.1 to a pressing demand for tragic composition bind it tightly to an earlier *recusatio*:

> sceptra tamen sumpsi curaque tragoedia nostra
> creuit, et huic operi quamlibet aptus eram:
> risit Amor pallamque meam pictosque cothurnos
> sceptraque priuata tam cito sumpta manu;
> hinc quoque me dominae numen deduxit iniquae,
> deque cothurnato uate triumphat Amor. (2.18.13–18)

> [Still I seized sceptres, and tragedy, thanks to my pains,
> grew. But, however suited I was to this labour,
> Love laughed at my gown and ornamented boots
> and the sceptres so quickly seized by a humble hand.
> From this also a cruel lady's sway fetched me back,
> and over a booted bard triumphs Love.]

In this version of the *apologetischen Form*,[59] it is the narrator who plays Tragoedia's role as advocate of a grander writing-style. Here the symbols of tragic discourse (the sceptre, the gown, and the painted boots) adorn the figure of a poet not a personified genre.[60] The narrator is already equipped with the regalia Tragoedia offers him at *Amores* 3.1.63.

If it is the narrator who plays Tragoedia's role, it is *Amor* and a *domina* who play Elegia's and orchestrate the retreat from the production of tragedy. It is also *Amor* and a *puella* who orchestrate a retreat from epic earlier in the poem, as *quoque* recalls:

> nos, Macer, ignaua Veneris cessamus in umbra,
> et tener ausuros grandia frangit Amor.
> saepe meae 'tandem' dixi 'discede' puellae:
> in gremio sedit protinus illa meo;

58 Du Quesnay (1973), 5–6.

59 See Wimmel (1960), 305–6; Morgan (1977), 15–17; Fedeli (1980), 186.

60 As Brandt (1963), on *Am.* 2.18.15 and 3.1.11.

saepe 'pudet' dixi: lacrimis uix ilia retentis
'me miseram, iam te' dixit 'amare pudet?'
implicuitque suos circum mea colla lacertos
et, quae me perdunt, oscula mille dedit.
uincor, et ingenium sumptis reuocatur ab armis,
resque domi gestas et mea bella cano. (2.18.3–12)

[I idle, Macer, in Venus' lazy shade
and delicate Love shatters my grandiose ventures.
'At last', I've often said to my girl, 'leave':
she's sat on my lap immediately.
'I'm ashamed', I've often said: with tears scarcely checked
'poor me', she's said, 'are you ashamed to love already?'
She's wrapped her arms around my neck
and kisses that kill me, she's given a thousand.
I'm beaten: my talent is recalled from the armour it seized,
I celebrate domestic action and my personal battles.]

Just as Elegia lures the poet away from tragedy with a lover's look and a provocative smile, so an elegiac mistress lures him away from epic with an erotic embrace.

This *puella*, however, is only as relevant to the real life of a love poet as armour to an epic poet or painted boots and a sceptre to a tragedian. In *Amores* 2.18 weapons, stage properties, and a girl function as material symbols of poetic production in a *Stilkampf* where elegy always gains ultimate ascendancy.[61] Thus elegy is humorously identified as already incorporating elements of epic when military metaphors are applied to erotic activity (vv. 11–12):[62] overpowered by a woman (*uincor*), a poet must summon his talent back from the front (*reuocatur ab armis*) and write instead militant elegies on bedroom battles (*resque domi gestas et mea bella*). Similarly, the contrast between *tener* and *grandia* with which the epic poet Macer is confronted recalls the stylistic contrast between *lepton* and *pachu* set out

[61] For *arma* as a symbol of epic, see Fedeli (1985), 57–8. For the actor's costume of gown and boots as a symbol of tragedy, see Brandt (1963), on *Am.* 2.18.5.

[62] As Quadlbauer (1968), 94 n. 5.

in the *Aetia*. Yet the elegiac *puella* is also implicated in the victory of delicacy, since her physical prevention of epic composition (vv. 5–12) enacts and elaborates the destruction by delicate *Amor* of a poet's ambitious schemes (v. 4). So, in submitting to the attractions of an elegiac mistress, the narrator also embraces an embodiment of Callimachus' *lepton*.

Positioned at the opening of a third book of erotic elegies, *Amores* 3.1 also invites comparison with the introduction to the second book of the collection. Following the pattern for the *apologetischen Form*, *Amores* 2.1 rejects a higher form of poetic discourse in favour of elegiacs.[63] The poet first declares that he had ventured on the production of a Gigantomachy (vv. 11–16). As material symbols of such an exalted practice, the Ovidian narrator is depicted playfully clutching clouds, a thunderbolt and, most irreverently, Jupiter himself (*in manibus nimbos et cum Ioue fulmen habebam*, v. 15). The poet confesses that he then dropped poor Jupiter and his thunderbolt to resume the production of elegiacs (vv. 17–22). Once again it is a Callimachean poetics that is expressed through such a bizarre evocation: Jupiter's thunderbolt marks the 'thundering' style which Callimachus had opposed to his own in *Aetia* fr. 120,[64] while production of elegies which are *leuis* (v. 21) obeys the Callimachean call for *leptotês*.[65] But what instigates the retreat into Callimachean elegiacs? As in *Amores* 2.18, epic composition is disrupted by the elegiac mistress who this time slams her front door (*clausit amica fores: ego eum Iove fulmen omisi*, v. 17). Just as Elegia institutes the third book of the *Amores*, so an elegiac *puella* institutes the second.

Thus, within the *Amores*, a succession of humorous programmatic poems deploys female forms to articulate a Callimachean apologetics. Elegia opens book 3 playing the role already undertaken by the elegiac mistress in the second, and the association between personi-

[63] See Wimmel (1960), 303–5; Morgan (1977), 12–14; Giangrande (1981), 33–40. See now Boyd (1997), 191–4, and Keith (1999), 51–2.

[64] Cf. Innes (1979), 166–7.

[65] Giangrande (1981), 38.

fication and realistically constructed beloved is sustained by a reduplication of physical features. The ungainly figure of asymmetric Elegia then challenges any romantic reading of the elegiac mistress because it incorporates many of her attributes, and replays her part in the elegiac narrative, at the same time as it embodies political and poetic concerns. It is, moreover, her reproduction of the elegiac figure of the *meretrix* that enables Elegia to symbolize an anti-establishment politics while, in symbolizing a Callimachean poetics, Elegia plays with the beloved's function in earlier versions of the *apologetischen Form*.

So the physique of the Ovidian *puella* appears to be as much a travesty of love elegy's conventions as the text in which she figures. The series of programmatic poems that culminate in *Amores* 3.1 first ridicule and then decode elegy's own romantic convention that love poets begin to write because they are in love, that a frustrating passion for a woman who exists outside the confines of the text instigates its production, that her physical features are beautiful beyond compare. Comic circumstances surround the renewal of elegiac composition in *Amores* 2.1 (a girl's door slams, the poet drops Jupiter in surprise), and in *Amores* 2.18 the poet is forced to abandon his ambitious schemes when pinned down by a girl in his lap. As the last poem in the series to institute elegiacs through a female form, *Amores* 3.1 even abandons realism and, by providing its *puella* additionally with a limp and the title 'Elegy', reduces the romantic convention to an amusing conceit that finally exposes elegy's female subjects as fictions.[66]

## CYNTHIA REVISITED

*Amores* 3.1 recalls the earlier fictive practices of Tibullus and Propertius, belongs to a cycle of *Apologien* that extends back beyond the

[66] See now Keith (1994), who analyses the *puellae* in some of the non-programmatic poems of the *Amores* in terms of the relationship between their 'style' and the aesthetic principles of elegy.

Ovidian corpus, and is even set in the landscape of Propertius' programmatic poetry. The poetic text, therefore, encourages its readers to locate it squarely within the corpus of Augustan elegy, and to associate it with a particular pattern of narrative strategies deployed throughout the *Amores* to probe Propertian erotic discourse. Does the poem's playful warning (that elegiac *puellae* are simply textual bodies) then apply even to Cynthia?

Critics recognize that the narrative of the *Amores* is constructed within the framework of a general critical strategy they variously describe as a burlesque of elegiac conventions, a *reductio ad absurdum* of elegiac practices, a breaking of elegy's rules, a parody of Propertian poetry, a demystification of elegy's romanticism and its fiction of male erotic enslavement to one dominating mistress.[67] Ovid is seen to be decoding the romantic and realistic practice of writing associated most notably with the Propertian corpus. In this way, the strategy of recalling earlier Propertian poems has been called one of the most significant aspects of the *Amores*, and the programmatic poems identified as important stages in its execution.[68]

As an example of this process, the first poem of *Amores* 1 reveals a rich seam of 'demystification'. There the first logical step is taken to construct a literary eroticism: the adoption of the elegiac metre. The poet was planning to write epic in solemn hexameters, when Cupid stole a foot from the second line and thus converted the poetry into elegiacs. At this point the narrator is not yet in love. He does not make the declaration of love for a specific woman that his audience might expect from a poet continuing the tradition established in Augustan elegy by Gallus, Tibullus, and Propertius (*nec mihi materia est numeris leuioribus apta*, 1.1.19). The role of poet is given priority

[67] See e.g. Otis (1938); Du Quesnay (1973); Lyne (1980), 239–87; Davis (1981); Conte (1989), 449–56. See now Greene (1998), 67–113, and O'Neill (1999).

[68] Respectively Du Quesnay (1973), 6, and Morgan (1977), 7–26. See now Boyd (1997), 1–18. While Boyd concedes that the *Amores* reverse the illusion of sincerity central to the poetry of Propertius and Tibullus, she does not consider that reversal to be the overriding concern of the Ovidian poems.

over that of lover and the Ovidian narrator expresses his metrical (rather than emotional) concerns. The poem demands comparison with the beginning of Propertius' *Monobiblos*.[69] There the narrator makes no such overt reference to poetic preferences: Cynthia is the cause of his being in love. The reader understands that the *Monobiblos* has been written in an autobiographical mode and that, at least on the narrative's surface, the Cynthia of the text is to be read as if a real woman. Ovid's poem, however, by drawing attention to the creative process, warns that realism is merely a property of the text. By describing the poet's mastery over his own material, Ovid exposes the conventions of elegiac romanticism and the fictionality of its mistress.[70] Similarly, the programmatic poems of Ovid's second book have been thought to imply a playful criticism of Propertian arguments in favour of elegiac production that were addressed to the epic poet Ponticus in poems 7 and 9 of the *Monobiblos*.[71]

If *Amores* 3.1 is not commonly read as forming part of this general Ovidian strategy to expose realism's romantic conventions, it is precisely because here elegy's realistic representation of female flesh undergoes demystification and exposure as a poetic convention. The crooked contours of Elegia (the *puella* as a practice of writing) mark the culmination of a series of three programmatic poems (2.1, 2.18, 3.1) that first burlesque and then decipher the realistically constructed Propertian *puella* and her part in the expression of poetic and political concerns.

Furthermore, the sequence of poems makes its own operations manifest by commencing with an account of how a mistress's antics thwarted the composition of a grand Gigantomachy (2.1.11–16). This isolated reference in the *Amores* to a failed Gigantomachy, its position in the first poem of a second book, its language and line

[69] As e.g. Gross (1975–6), 153–4. See now Keith (1992), and Boyd (1997), 136–8 and 147–9.

[70] Cf. now Greene (1998), 68–73 on *Amores* 1.3.

[71] Morgan (1977), 12–17, and Du Quesnay (1973), 25–7.

structure, are all designed to recall the Gigantomachy rejected by Propertius in favour of elegiac composition in the introduction to his own second book (2.1.17–20).[72] The first poem in Ovid's series indicates clearly that, on this occasion, the physique of the Propertian *puella* has been taken as starting-point for the process of demystification. For, among all the programmatic poems of the Propertian corpus, it is 2.1 that employs the body of the elegiac mistress most openly and most extensively to trace its author's poetic and political heterodoxy:[73]

siue illam Cois fulgentem incedere ⟨cogis⟩,
  hac totum e Coa ueste uolumen erit;
seu uidi ad frontem sparsos errare capillos,
  gaudet laudatis ire superba comis;
siue lyrae carmen digitis percussit eburnis,
  miramur, facilis ut premat arte manus;
seu cum poscentis somnum declinat ocellos,
  inuenio causas mille poeta nouas;
seu nuda erepto mecum luctatur amictu,
  tum uero longas condimus Iliadas;
seu quidquid fecit siue est quodcumque locuta,
  maxima de nihilo nascitur historia. (2.1.5–16)

[If gleaming in Coan silks you make her go,
  of that Coan dress the whole book will be composed;
or if on her brow I have seen scattered curls stray,
  she delights to walk with pride in praised hair;
or if the lyre's song with ivory fingers she's struck,
  we wonder at the quick hands she presses with skill;
or when she lowers eyes that desire sleep,
  I discover causes, a thousand new ones for a poet;
or if naked she grapple with me, her robe stripped off,
  surely then we construct lengthy Iliads;

[72] Cf. Morgan (1977), 16, and see now the remarks of Boyd (1997), 197.

[73] Cf. now Keith (1999), 52–3 on the analogous use of the poet-lover's body in 2.1 to describe a Callimachean corpus.

or whatever she's done, or whatever she's said,
from nothing the grandest history is born.]

The context makes it clear that this *puella*, who instigates a second book of love elegies, forms part of a serious polemic on literary and political choices. The first line of the poem introduces the elegiac mistress as the answer to a literary question that concerns only the narrator and his readership (*quaeritis, unde mihi totiens scribantur amores*, 2.1.1). After her appearance, Callimachus is called upon openly as a model for the production of alternatives to the epic writing-style (vv. 39–42), and the subject of Cynthia is presented as occupying the space of an unorthodox account of the birth of the Augustan state: the unwritten poem on Caesar's *bellaque resque* that a *puella* replaces locates Actium in a catalogue of bloody civil wars (vv. 25–34). Poetic and political concerns thus enclose and inform a serious and realistic depiction of the second book's heroine.[74]

The series of *Apologien* that culminates in *Amores* 3.1 has led its readers back to this earlier Propertian poem. With the playful warning offered by Elegia in mind, a re-reading of the Propertian *puella* here underscores some disturbing features of the text that jeopardize even the status of Cynthia as a living Augustan girlfriend and declare the textuality of her body. Firstly, Cynthia's attributes and activities (which are said to precede and excite elegiac production) are already set in a tradition for erotic writing before they become the material of Propertian fiction. For a beloved's appearance and skills, her sleep, and erotic battles, are far more frequently the themes of Hellenistic erotic epigrams than the love elegies of the Propertian corpus.[75] Even Cynthia's clothing assists the identification of elegiac *puella*

[74] On the overt Callimachean polemic of vv. 17–46, see Wimmel (1960), 13–43, but contrast now Fredrick (1997), who finds Callimachean polemic here undercut by epic parody. Cf. Greene (2000) and Miller (2001), sec. 3. For the unorthodox perspective on Roman history in vv. 25–34, see Galinsky (1969), 81–2; Hubbard (1974), 100–2; Putnam (1976), 121–3; Nethercut (1983), 1839–40; and now Miller (2001), sec. 3.

[75] Boucher (1965), 210–11.

with elegiac practice, since *Cous* is used elsewhere in the Propertian corpus to signal the Hellenistic poet Philitas. Just as Elegia is adorned in a Callimachean delicacy, so Cynthia is decked in the poetic discourse of Philitas.[76] Cynthia's attributes and activities are implicated yet further in a Callimachean apologetics: as inspirer of poetic *causas* the elegiac mistress becomes the key to a new version of Callimachus' *Aetia*, one that looks into the origins of a mistress's behaviour, rather than the workings of myth and ritual. This Propertian *Aetia* is then set against the higher genres of epic and history through the agency of a female form. The erotic struggles of Propertius' *puella* match the battles of Homeric heroes, and accounts of her every word and deed surpass all previous histories (vv. 11–16).[77] At the very moment that the elegiac mistress is realistically and physically depicted as existing prior to elegiac discourse, a rejection of higher forms of writing in favour of a Callimachean practice takes place through her agency.

Secondly, the vocabulary in which Cynthia is formulated as a creator of art also points to her as being an artistic creation. Momentarily Cynthia's physique is said to be manufactured out of ivory (v. 9), suggesting a *puella* who is herself an artform rather than an instigator of art.[78] Since, however, the epithet is transferred from a musical instrument to its player, and is not incongruous with the features of a beauty, the Propertian attribution of ivory fingers is far less disturbing than the Ovidian attribution of unequal feet.

Finally, the entire depiction of elegy's female subject is enclosed by two terms that undermine even further Cynthia's superficial status as a woman who exists prior to the production of an elegiac text. Precisely because it does not give the beloved her expected independence, many commentators have queried the MS tradition's *cogis*

[76] Cf. now Miller (2001), sec. 3.

[77] King (1980), 63, and cf. Wiggers (1976–7), 336. See now Greene (2000) on the comparable construction of the male lover in Prop. 2.1 as a kind of epic hero.

[78] Cf. Wiggers (1976–7), 335.

(you make her, v. 5);[79] while *de nihilo* (from nothing, v. 16) suggests that the history of a mistress is being composed that has no firm basis in reality. Thus even a Propertian poem itself argues against the attribution of an independent identity to its female subject and for her status (even at the level of her flesh) as political and poetic polemic. Nor is it the only Propertian poem to do so.

It is precisely from the material of poems such as 2.2 (as well as 2.3 quoted at the opening of this chapter) that critics have built a living partner—an intelligent blonde—for its author Propertius, since 2.2 overtly describes the power of a look to restore its narrator to his occupation as lover. Yet the poem which immediately precedes it presents elegiac poetry (and, therefore, the *entire* second book) as an alternative to epic—an erotic *Aetia*—when it calls openly on Callimachus as a model for Fine Poetry. So the same critics who have read the text of 2.2 transparently in order to construct a fleshly mistress for Propertius have also conceded the presence in the poem of literary concerns: the poem has been interpreted as an immediate demonstration of the claim of Propertius, in 2.1, to his Callimachean heritage, while a real woman is retained to read her own conversion into a Callimachean literary practice. That poetic practice is observed at work in the physical shape of the poem (its epigrammatic brevity), its esoteric narrative style, and its revision of epic motifs. Even the figurative presentation of Cynthia in 2.2.6–14 (her comparison with Juno, Pallas, Ischomache, and Brimo, and her victory in a recast judgment of Paris) is read as a manifestation of a Callimachean writing-practice: the revision of epic material in slight poetry, the delineation of Cynthia in epic proportions.[80]

Not all of the poem can be thus decoded, however, if the notion is still to be sustained that Cynthia is the pseudonym of an extratextual addressee. After all, if Cynthia is to signify a woman of flesh she must be provided with some. So there occurs a noticeable silence, an absence of comment, on the point in the poem where the elegiac

[79] See e.g. Camps (1967), 66, for the substiution of *uidi*.

[80] King (1981).

mistress is provided with physical properties: *fulua coma est longaeque manus, et maxima toto | corpore* (tawny hair, and long hands, and vast entirely in body, vv. 5–6). What justification is there for thus preserving by omission a referentiality for these lines? Can they be said to sketch the unique physical characteristics of one Augustan woman?

The documented popularity of the Junoesque blonde in classical literature suggests rather that Propertius has assembled here a selection from a repertoire of archetypal features for the female beauties of fiction. For example, the catalogue of feminine physical assets possessed and absent in Catullus 86 and 43 respectively provides an obvious parallel for the features of this Propertian woman.[81] Moreover, since the Homeric poems, tall stature (*megethos*) had been a characteristic of literary representations of the ideal woman and yellow hair (*xanthotês*) a set feature of the beauty in the Greek novel.[82] A reading of the list of feminine qualities which occur at 2.2.5–6 as detached from the physique of any one Roman woman is aided by the syntax of the passage and the narrative mode adopted for the poem as a whole. A dative of the (human) possessor is provided neither for *fulua coma* nor *longaeque manus*, and *maxima* has no immediate noun to qualify. The whole may therefore be considered as loosely attached to the impersonal *facies* with which the poem opens and closes. The qualities of a body are allotted to an abstract Look, not to an individuated and realistically constructed mistress.

If the textual characteristics of Cynthia do not amount to the unique features of an Augustan girlfriend, could they have been chosen to suit the poetic context (the narration of a Callimachean literary practice), as a reading of *Amores* 3.1 has suggested? Interesting parallels for the delineation of Cynthia at 2.2.5–6 may be found outside the realms of erotic discourse, in the literary construction of the warrior (the epic man). The adjective *fuluus* signals the area for com-

[81] Quinn (1963), 66–73. See also Richlin (1983), who argues that a prescribed list of ideal female features can readily be compiled from Roman epic, lyric, and elegy (pp. 32–3 and 44–56 in the 1992 edn. of her book on Roman sexuality and aggression).

[82] Lilja (1978), 123–4 and 128–9.

parison, for yellow hair is far more frequently identified by *flauus* in the discourses of Roman fictive eroticism. *Fuluus*, however, is employed in the *Aeneid* as an epithet of ferocious animals (such as the eagle or the lion) or of ferocious warriors. At *Aeneid* 10.562, for example, the bravery of Aeneas is matched by the resistance of his opponents: *fortemque Numam fuluumque Camertem*. The other physical properties with which the elegiac mistress is provided evoke particularly the large-limbed Homeric warrior. The more delicate build customarily devised for the female Beauty would be more readily suggested by the application of *longus* to fingers rather than the whole hand. The transference allows a parallel to be drawn from an attribute of the epic man: the Homeric *cheiri pacheiêi*, the *manu magna* or *dextra ingenti* of the Virgilian *bellator*.[83] Similarly, the tall stature of the ideal beloved is often signified by *longa* in erotic poetry. The wording here, however, compares with the description at *Aeneid* 11.690–1 of two opponents worthy of Camilla's military prowess: *Orsilochum et Buten, duo maxima Teucrum | corpora*.

It appears then that at 2.2.5–6 a selection has been made from among the standard features of the female Beauty that produces a sketch of an elegiac woman in epic proportions. But, in the previous poem, Propertius had illustrated his obedience to the Callimachean call for *leptotês* by emphasizing that his erotic *Aetia* would incorporate and thus subvert epic material: *Iliads* would be transformed into elegiac narratives of erotic battles (2.1.11–14). Book 2 takes as its project a paradoxical version of the Callimachean polemic: the revision of epic in elegy.[84] Poem 2.2 then contributes to that project by presenting a woman of epic proportions in a short poem, incorporating into poetry which is *kata lepton* the *megalê gynê* opposed to it and rejected by Callimachus in the preface to the *Aetia* (fr. 11–12).[85] Thus

[83] Virgil *Aen*. 5.241 and 11.556.

[84] See King (1981).

[85] I am grateful to Professor Kenney for this suggestion. See now Kennedy (1993), 31–3, Greene (2000), and Miller (2001), sec. 3, on the characterization of the beloved elsewhere as *dura*. They argue that such an attribute breaks down the boundaries between elegy and epic, and turns the beloved into an adversary worthy of her elegiac 'hero'.

even the flesh of Cynthia is moulded to fit a poetic purpose. Furthermore, a political (as well as a poetic) context is supplied for this project in 2.1. That poem contains not just one, but two tables of contents for the second book; one erotic (vv. 5–16) and one political (vv. 17–38), of which the first is formulated as substitute for the second, a sexual instead of a military *historia* (vv. 13–16). Cynthia replaces Caesar as the subject of poetic discourse. One anti-epic speaks for another.

The flesh with which the elegiac mistress is endowed in Propertius 2.2 is moulded to suit the politics and poetics of its author: Cynthia's body is built out of the bones buried at Perugia and yet signifies a style of writing that is *lepton*. A brief study of some of Cynthia's textual characteristics thus demonstrates again that useful lessons are to be learned from reading *Amores* 3.1. The awkward figure of Elegia operates in a direct line of descent from the massively proportioned Cynthia of Propertius' second book. Her title, her limp, and her comic plight all contribute to a humorous demystification of elegy's female flesh and its exposure as everywhere a site for the expression of poetic and political concerns.

Like the painting described and illustrated in the anti-romantic novel that demonstrates ingeniously the absurdities latent in Petrarch's codification of his beloved's beauty, Ovid *Amores* 3.1 discloses that the Propertian beloved is a textual body clothed in ideological and aesthetic ambitions. Ovid's *Amores* also suggest that clues to such a reading of elegy's female flesh are already there in the Propertian corpus, just as they were considered to be in the love poetry of Petrarch. Even contemporary readers of Petrarch's Laura identified her with the ambitions of his poetry; we should do no less for Propertius' Cynthia.[86]

[86] On this reading of Laura, see e.g. Miller (1997), and Stapleton (1996), 115–32. See now McNamee (1993) for such a reading of Cynthia's attributes in the *Monobiblos*, and Keith (1994) for a comparable analysis of the *puellae* to be found elsewhere in Ovid's *Amores*.

# 5

# Taking the Woman's Part: Gender and Scholarship on Love Elegy

When a woman writes herself into the genre of Roman love elegy she appears to break the recognized conventions for its production, according to which woman is generally the mistress over whom the male *ego* has erotic and poetic mastery, the passive object of erotic desire not its active subject, the written not the writer. In discussing the elegiac poetry composed by Sulpicia, one means by which critics have expressed her extraordinary achievement has been to engender Roman love elegy. For Nick Lowe, Sulpicia's unique intervention was to compose poetry on the subject of her own erotic experience in 'an obstinately male genre'. For Amy Richlin, Sulpicia breached a double barrier, both the 'male job' of writing and the 'male genre' of elegy. With reference to Sulpicia, in my opening chapter I also labelled Augustan elegy as 'male-oriented verse' that constructs a

This chapter is a substantially revised and extended version of an article first published in *Ramus* 23 (1994), 110–28.

'male narrative perspective'.[1] It is obviously the case that, with the notable exception of Sulpicia, the biological sex of all the authors of Roman elegy is male. In this final chapter on love elegy, however, I argue that the genre is not unequivocally masculine, and that to engender elegy unproblematically as male fails to do justice to the genre's crucial play with Roman categories of gender.[2] Over the course of the preceding chapters, I have developed the argument that the elegiac mistress (the Propertian Cynthia just as much as the Ovidian Corinna, or the Tibullan Delia and Nemesis) is a textual body that incarnates her author's aesthetic and ideological ambitions. The poetics of Callimacheanism and the politics of immorality shape the elegiac stage and the players who perform on it. Here, paying much closer attention to the politics of erotic discourse, I pursue the argument that elegy also interrogates Roman culture's constructions of masculinity and femininity (through its very own figures of the dominating mistress and her enslaved *amator*).

This exploration of gender play in Augustan love elegy also doubles as a journey through many of the debates and developments in the Anglo-American feminist criticism of the genre that was initiated almost thirty years ago by Judith Hallett, who then presented a tempting depiction of Propertian elegy's mode of attention to women as a form of 'counter-cultural feminism'.[3] The first part of my title, therefore, is meant to designate the several respects in which I propose to approach the gender play of the elegiac genre here (concentrating, as did Hallett, on the Propertian corpus). 'Taking the woman's part' refers both to aspects of the practice of elegiac production in Augustan Rome and to some strands in the interpretation of that literary production by the Anglo-American academic community over the last few decades. Augustan elegy can be said to 'take the woman's part' in its central construction of a

[1] Lowe (1988), 193; Richlin (1992*b*); Ch. 1 above.

[2] Already, in 1989, Mary-Kay Gamel argued that Ovid's *Amores* contained an extensive examination of questions of gender. Cf. Gold (1993*a*) for such claims in relation to the Propertian corpus.

[3] Hallett (1973).

female object for erotic discourse (the elegiac mistress) and in its attribution of traditionally feminine characteristics to its male narrator (the elegiac *amator*). Modern scholarship on Roman elegy can be said to 'take the woman's part' when it brings the genre's lovers and their beloveds into the broader investigation of ancient representations of women and the mechanisms of gender construction in ancient societies.

## WOMANUFACTURE[4]

There appear to be good grounds on which to support the claim that Roman love elegy is an obstinately male genre into which Sulpicia made a remarkable intrusion. In contrast to the sexual symmetries David Konstan observes in the genre of the novel, there is no parity between the male lover-poet (the narrating *ego*) and the female beloved (the narrated *puella*) in the erotic discourse of Propertius, Tibullus, and Ovid. Elegiac erotic relations are formulated as between a lover and his beloved, not as between two mutual lovers.[5] In the elegiac texts as a rule, the mistress is the object rather than the subject of passion and constituted as a means to define the uniqueness of her male narrator (as both enslaved lover and Callimachean poet). With the exception of Propertius' fourth book of elegies and Ovid's *Heroides*, these love poems almost constantly give centre stage to a male narrator's description of his frustrated desire for a silent or absent mistress and to his advocacy of this form of erotic writing. Elegiac desire is sometimes described without reference to a specified *puella*, and dramatized as a lesson to other men in the pain of erotic suffering or the pleasures of composing verse in a genre that is not epic. The female beloved is assigned scarcely any subjectivity or individuating features, and those she has correspond to the requirements of the narrator's discourse of frustrated love and elegiac production.

[4] I take as my heading here the title of an article by Alison Sharrock (1991*a*).

[5] Konstan (1994), 159; Sharrock (1994), 27–8.

In Augustan elegy, then, desire is generally male and the female beloved elusive.[6] On the level of erotics (within the male lover's rhetoric of desire), the elegiac *ego* manifests little curiosity about the female object of his amatory courtship. As Paul Veyne puts it for the rhetoric of Propertius' relationship to his elegiac mistress Cynthia:

> This poetry devoted to a woman is really quite egocentric. The poet speaks almost exclusively of the actions, passions, sorrows, and words of Ego, who talks only about himself. We are not lacking for his opinions on women or makeup, but what we learn of Cynthia comes down to two things: on the one hand, she has every possible attraction, including incompatible ones, and seems made to fulfill one's every wish; on the other, she makes her poet suffer.[7]

The elegiac narrative of erotic seduction is painfully self-absorbed. Its idioms also serve the interests of the amorous narrator. In *The Arts of Love: Five Studies in the Discourse of Roman Love Elegy* (1993), Duncan Kennedy cites Augustan elegy's regular projection onto the beloved of a cruel self-image as an example of how the discourse of love generally operates to turn the beloved into an object which the lover can then attempt to control. He places the erotic elegies of Propertius, Tibullus, and Ovid within the general systematization of 'a lover's discourse' set out by Roland Barthes, according to which 'the beloved's autonomy of feeling or action becomes in a lover's discourse of secondary importance to the motives or actions attributed to him or her by the lover, to the extent that the beloved is depersonalized and becomes an object'.[8] If onto the beloved Cynthia of Propertius 1.1 is projected the self-image of hard-heartedness (the *domina* who is *dura*), she can only reject that identity through submission to her lover. 'The lover's discourse emerges as an inces-

[6] See esp. Greene (1998) on elegy's erotics of *male* desire. Cf. Flaschenriem (1997) and Connolly (2000) for the lover-poet's elusive beloved.

[7] Veyne (1988), 136. On the variance of Cynthia's character, cf. Gold (1993*b*), 291–3, and Janan (2001), 35, 119, and 121–2.

[8] Kennedy (1993), 70.

sant attempt to control, to mould, to construct for the beloved an identity (as "object") that she will accept or reject in the same way, by "giving" herself to the lover.'[9] Similarly, the lover-poet's construction of himself as a distressed *exclusus amator* has been interpreted as a rhetorical strategy by which he cajoles his beloved figuratively into unlocking the door to her house, her body, her heart.[10]

Even elegy's apparently provocative metaphor of erotic slavery can be understood in these discursive terms. In *The Erotics of Domination: Male Desire and the Mistress in Latin Love Poetry* (1998), Ellen Greene argues that the first-person narrator's adoption of an apparently servile position towards his beloved operates as a seducer's strategy of manipulation. The poet-lover must boast a range of servile manners first to overcome his mistress's resistance and then to keep her. The elegiac mistress is thus, paradoxically, rendered compliant precisely by her lover's display of servility's total loyalty, dedication, vulnerability, and obedience.[11] However, it is important to note (as does Parshia Lee-Stecum in his book on Tibullus) that in the elegiac world the process of exchanging erotic enslavement for sexual conquest tends ultimately to failure, and the lover-poet is generally figured as powerless to persuade.[12]

The erotic failings of elegy's male lover-poet are, of course, the poetic successes of the genre's authors.[13] In tandem with explorations of the elegiac mistress's subservience to the erotics of her male narrator, critics have observed how she is also subservient to her authors' poetics. Two central themes of Augustan elegy are love and poetry. A common elegiac trope involves the identification of loving and writing, being loved and being read: as the first word of

[9] Kennedy (1993), 74.

[10] Lindheim (1998*a*).

[11] See Greene (1998), esp. 63, and (1999); McCarthy (1998); Fitzgerald (2000), 73–5; Miller (2001), sec. 3.

[12] Lee-Stecum (1998), 292 and 294–5.

[13] As Lee-Stecum (1998) also notes. See further the discussion below of impotence as one of Augustan elegy's defining characteristics.

Propertius' first elegiac collection, in the most commonly adduced example, *Cynthia* names both the elegiac beloved and the elegiac book.[14] Following through this trope (in the direction from love to writing, from beloved to book), I have argued in the preceding chapters that, in the case of the Propertian Cynthia, her name, physical features, and psychological characteristics shaped a woman who should not be read as external to the elegiac text, but as its embodiment. Even Cynthia's apparently rebellious and uncontrollable attributes reveal her to be a written woman (a *scripta puella*, 2.10.8). She is the subject-matter of a Callimachean poetic practice, her author's creation, and a commodity of exchange between the Augustan elegist and the literary market-place.[15]

Twin themes then of Augustan elegy are love and poetry. The romantic interpretations of the genre advocated in past years by critics such as Oliver Lyne and Jasper Griffin sought to acknowledge the poetics of elegy at the same time as they subordinated poetry to love as the instrument of love's expression. For such critics elegy's *puella* enjoys an existence independently of the texts in which she appears, and revealed through her stylized representation in verse are the features of an Augustan girlfriend over whom her lover-poet can exercise no control.[16] They thus tend to overlook the male narrator's stratagems for erotic seduction, and instead reiterate his point of view, inscribing it within their romantic readings of individual poems.[17] In the latter part of the twentieth century, other critics developed a more formalist counter-orthodoxy that privileged the elegiac poet's meta-literary self-consciousness or 'textual self-fashioning' over romantic speculation on his erotic

[14] The trope is discussed by Veyne (1988); Kennedy (1993), 46–63; Sharrock (1994), 21–86.

[15] As Gold (1993*a*), 88–9, and (1993*b*), 291–3; McNamee (1993); Greene (1998), 37–66; McCarthy (1998).

[16] Lyne (1980, repr. 1996 and 2000); Griffin (1985, repr. 1994). See above Ch. 1.

[17] As Greene (1998), p. xii, following Ancona (1989) on traditional criticism of Horatian love poetry. Cf. Fitzgerald (1995) on Catullan criticism.

biography.[18] The genre's erotics could be translated into the poetics of an Augustan Callimacheanism although, in its most extreme versions, such a reading strategy might appear to leave Augustan elegy without social, political, or even emotional content.[19] However, when criticism of elegy recognizes the figural reciprocity of poetry and sex, it becomes more attentive to the genre's *gendered* system of enunciation, both in terms of how the elegiac lover 'speaks' his beloved and the poet his fiction of a mistress.[20]

Recognizing the interplay of elegy's erotics and poetics helps point readers towards what Alison Sharrock has termed elegy's process of 'womanufacture'. The myth of Pygmalion, and his beloved statue which comes to life, acts as a useful reminder of the asymmetrical and gendered relations that are at work when woman is constructed in and through male literature and art.[21] According to Alison Sharrock, the Ovidian representation of the myth of Pygmalion in *Metamorphoses* 10.243–97 also acts specifically as a reflection on and disclosure of the eroto-artistic relationship between the lover-poet and his mistress in Latin love elegy. Both Pygmalion and the elegiac *ego* have total mastery over their beloved creations. Noting the many allusions in the Ovidian narrative back to Propertius 1.2 and 1.3 in particular, Sharrock argues that the story of the artist who constructed and desired his own artistic creation operates as a paradigm for the story of male elegiac composition. By rendering explicit the identification of love and artistic composition, beloved and artistic creation, the Pygmalion narrative exposes the gendered power rela-

[18] On this postmodern development in Latin literary criticism generally, see Hinds (1998), esp. 89–90. My own early emphases on Cynthia's Callimacheanism are indebted to such approaches.

[19] As Fowler (2000), 20–9, points out in relation to formalist readings of Catullus 51. Cf. Sharrock (1995), 179 n. 60.

[20] On the figural reciprocity of poetry and sex see, e.g. Kennedy (1993), 46–63; Sharrock (1994); Oliensis (1995); Hinds (1998), 10–16; McCoskey (1999), 29–33; Fear (2000); Lee-Stecum (2000). See further the discussion below of how elegy is figuratively sexualized and engendered.

[21] Sharrock (1991*b*), 181.

tions in elegy's erotic discourse. This artist/lover models, sculpts, shapes, and gives life to his erotic object. He manufactures woman as desired art-object. When Ovid rereads the elegiac processes of male erotic desire and poetic creativity, the sheer power of the male over his mistress is rendered totally exposed.[22]

It is not simply that Ovid points to the power of the elegiac poet over his textual fantasy of courtship, as if an erotics of abjection were always purely a metaphor for a dominating poetics of Callimacheanism. He also demonstrates through the metaphor of sculpture the power of the elegiac lover over his beloved. The sculptor's manufacture of and gaze on his creation recalls and unmasks the mechanics of the lover's gaze on his sleeping beloved in Propertius 1.3—the very poem so admired by romantic critics. There the lover's gaze on sleeping Cynthia casts her as its passive, malleable object. The beloved is rendered most desirable when devoid of voice and agency, when she appears to reflect back her observer's desires, when she is no more than the male fantasy of a statue that breathes.[23]

But if, in these terms, Roman elegy is an obstinately male genre that evinces a pattern of male discursive control over the female object of both his erotics and his poetics, then, according to Phyllis Culham, the texts of Propertius, Tibullus, and Ovid scarcely deserve the further scrutiny of feminist scholars of antiquity. For to give primacy in the feminist critical project to such male-authored texts would be, in Culham's view, to deny women's experience of and in ancient societies.[24] If Augustan love elegy is labelled unequivocally as a male genre, much of the preceding analysis of the elegiac corpus would seem to be locked into the earliest formulations of the feminist critical project designated by Elaine Showalter as 'feminist critique'. The feminist critique undertaken by writers such as Kate

[22] Sharrock (1991*b*), and cf. Greene (1999) on *Am.* 1.7. For the Ovidian technique of exposing the elegiac *puella* as a particular mode of male discourse, see also Ch. 4 above.

[23] Greene (1998), 51–9, on which see O'Neill (2000), 271–2. For the importance of Prop. 1.3 to romantic criticism, see Chs. 1 and 2 above.

[24] Culham (1990). *Contra* see, most recently, Dixon (2001), preface.

Millett in the early 1970s was largely concerned with revisionary readings of the literary representations of women in canonic male-authored texts. Since such an approach appeared to Showalter to require of feminist scholars that they merely catalogue female stereotypes and the dreary record of women's oppression as the passive objects of male literary production, the practice was much maligned and, for more recent cultures, replaced by 'gynocritics' or the study of female-authored texts where women appear as active agents of literary production, as writers not the written, and as producers rather than consumers of textual meaning.[25] In the case of Roman love elegy, such a move from feminist critique to gynocritics has been available to critics if attention is transferred from the elegies of Propertius, Tibullus, and Ovid to those of Sulpicia. Thus some of the late-twentieth-century studies of the Sulpician elegies can be placed in the larger context of attempts by feminist scholars to map the female consciousness of antiquity.[26]

If, then, the myth of Pygmalion and his living statue acts as a paradigm for the elegiac *ego*'s discursive mastery over his beloved mistress, the intervention of the poet Sulpicia into elegy's system of enunciation marks an extraordinary break from the genre's gendered conventions. Here a *puella*, rather than being silenced, actively speaks her own desire and, rather than being written, writes herself into Augustan love poetry.[27] The female narrator of the six poems conventionally assigned to Sulpician authorship (and preserved in the manuscripts of the Tibullan corpus) appropriates many of the discursive strategies employed by the male *ego* in the poems of Propertius,

[25] For Showalter's terms 'feminist critique' and 'gynocritics', see e.g. Greene and Kahn (1985); Todd (1988); Robbins (2000).

[26] The applicability of Showalter's terms to the development of feminist criticism of the elegiac corpus is discussed by Gold (1993*a*) and, following her, Greene (1998), pp. xi–xii. On these trends in feminist criticism of classical literature more generally, see Richlin (1992*a*); Rabinowitz and Richlin (1993); Dixon (2001), ch. 2.

[27] My general observations on the Sulpician elegies are indebted to the following analyses: Hallett (1989); Santirocco (1979); Hinds (1987); Roessel (1990); Lowe (1992); Parker (1994); Keith (1997); Hemelrijk (1998), 229–32; Flaschenriem (1999); Skoie (2000) and (2002).

Tibullus, and Ovid.[28] This lover-poet, like the others, renders the beloved subservient to her elegiac narrative of largely frustrated love and poetic composition. *Ego* speaks about herself and, in the first of her poems, describes her love for an unspecified 'him' (*illum*, 3.13.3) or 'my man' (*meus*, 3.13.8) as a useful subject for the conversation of others. In all six Sulpician poems, the male beloved for whom the lover-poet expresses desire possesses few individuating features and no speaking voice. This elegiac eroticism conforms to the pattern of love's discourse whereby the beloved is deprived of autonomous feeling and has projected onto him a self-image of hard-heartedness (*securus*, 3.16.1; *lento pectore* 3.17.6) which he can only reject through acquiescence to his lover. Similarly, following the elegiac trope of identifying love and poetry, writing-tablets (*tabellis*, 3.13.7) signify both erotic messages to a beloved and book-publication; the beloved's name, *Cerinthus* (3.14.2; 3.17.1), the honey-sweetness of both a lover and a poem. Thus the lover-poet of the Sulpician corpus, like the other narrating *egos* of elegy, manifests a discursive mastery over the object of both her erotics and her poetics.

Yet, as critics have demonstrated, this lover-poet is highly sensitive to the disturbance the presence of a female *ego* creates in elegy. For a female *ego*, much of what the other elegiac narrators say on the subject of warfare, politics, patronage, the rejection of public life, and the preference for elegy over epic, is irrelevant or unavailable for enunciation. Instead the writings of Sulpicia frequently address their very constitution as a double violation of ancient social conventions, conventions which dictated that a respectable women remain silent in the public domain of poetic production and that she accept the administration of her sexual behaviour by her male relatives.[29] The

[28] Parker (1994) argues that to 3.13–18 should be added 3.9 and 11 as poems by Sulpicia. See, *contra*, Holzberg (1999), who offers a radical reconsideration of all these poems as part of a single-authored collection by a male poet posing as the young Tibullus.

[29] As Hallett (1989), 71; Lowe (1988), 204; Keith (1997), 301; Hemelrijk (1998), 238–40. Cf. Winkler (1990), 163, on the writings of Sappho, and Habinek (1998), 122–36, more generally on the silencing of educated Roman women.

Sulpician poems respond to this dilemma by naming the narrating poet explicitly as also an amorous *puella* (3.14.3; 3.15.1; 3.17.1) and an aristocratic *filia* (3.16.4).[30]

In the birthday poem 3.14, for example, the narrator adopts at one and the same time the position of the Tibullan lover-poet threatened with departure from the city at the command of Messalla and the position of the Tibullan beloved unsuited to country life. Thus this *puella*-poet simultaneously recalls both subject and object of Tibullan love poetry's discourse.[31] As narrating poet she may control the self-image of her male beloved, but as *puella* her own self-image is defined and limited by her familial dependency on her relative Messalla (3.14) and her father Servius (3.16). The contorted sub-subordinations of the Sulpician poems' syntax, where they refer to *fama* as both moral and poetic reputation in the opening poem 3.13, match the contortions required of an aristocratic Roman woman who writes of love.[32] At the same time, the narrator's expression of unease as to whether she should have covered (*texisse*) rather than disrobed (*nudasse*) her love (*amor*) figures her struggle for full poetic and erotic selfhood in sartorial terms, terms that are elsewhere applied to the proprieties of a respectable Roman woman's sexual and linguistic behaviour.[33] Thus the *puella*-poet of the Sulpician corpus both controls, and struggles not to be controlled by, the gendered requirements of Roman love and writing.

The entry of a female *ego* into the elegiac genre clearly involves a disturbance of its discursive fields but, in highlighting Sulpicia's intervention, the question remains whether the genre as practised by Propertius, Tibullus, and Ovid should be described as unequivocally male. I would argue, instead, that the Sulpician play with gender in the elegiac genre, the narrator's adoption of multiple masculine and

[30] As Hemelrijk (1998), 237–8.

[31] See esp. Hallett (1989), 70–1.

[32] Santirocco (1979), 235; Lowe (1988); Hemelrijk (1998), 238–40; Flaschenriem (1999).

[33] As Keith (1997), 301, and Flaschenriem (1999).

feminine subject positions, is not unparalleled elsewhere in the corpus of elegiac poems, and that it is precisely elegy's pervasive occupation with the question of gender categories that makes the genre readily available for appropriation and transformation by a woman writer.

## GYNESIS[34]

If one mode of criticism of the elegiac corpus has focused attention on the elegiac *ego*'s discursive mastery over his elegiac mistress, and a second has transferred attention to an examination of Sulpicia's intervention in the genre and her resistance to that discursive mastery, a third mode returns attention to the male-authored elegiac texts but explores them as intriguing manifestations of a *destabilization* of the conventional gender categories that operated in Augustan Rome. It is by now well-established and thoroughly documented that Roman sexual relations (one of Augustan elegy's central themes) were discursively constructed as both a hierarchical relation of power and as heavily gendered.[35] Sex is constituted as penetration of one body by another. Participants are polarized as insertive or receptive, dominant or submissive, and engendered accordingly as masculine or feminine,

in such a way that it becomes meaningful for a Roman author to speak of a man who submits to the passive role in intercourse with another man by the phrase *muliebria pati* (Sallust, *Catiline* 13.3), to undergo the woman's role. Within this scheme, the situation so frequently depicted in Roman elegy, a man subdued and enslaved by love for a woman represented as playing the dominant role in the relationship, enacts an inversion of these conventional gender stereotypes.[36]

[34] I take as my heading here the term that Barbara Gold borrows from Alice Jardine in order to identify the discursive strategies of the Propertian play with gender categories. See Gold (1993*a*).

[35] The literature on Roman sexuality is now extensive. See e.g. Richlin (1983) and (1992*a*); Edwards (1993); Skinner (1993*a*), 110–12, and (1996); Hallett and Skinner (1997); Williams (1999).

[36] Kennedy (1993), 30–1. Cf. Edwards (1993), 65 n. 4; Greene (1998), pp. xi–xiii, and (2000), 241–2; Lee-Stecum (1998), 286–8. Kennedy, it should be noted,

This strand of interpretation of Augustan elegy was initiated by Judith Hallett in the 1970s, when she catalogued the respects in which she saw the elegists (and Propertius in particular) as inverting conventional sex roles in their poetry. She concluded that Latin love elegy's application of a whole range of traditionally feminine characteristics to the male lover-poet, as well as the central focus in the Propertian corpus on a masterful *puella*, constituted an ancient form of feminism.[37] In the 1990s, Barbara Gold borrowed the concept of gynesis from Alice Jardine to analyse the Propertian corpus, more circumspectly, as putting into discourse 'woman' or the 'feminine' as problematic.[38] Collating the observations made within the interpretative techniques of this mode of gender criticism, Propertian love elegy hardly seems to qualify as the product of an obstinately male genre.

There are a number of significant respects in which the male lover-poet of Propertian elegy is acknowledged as undergoing the woman's role, taking the woman's part, or putting himself into play as the feminine.[39] At numerous points in the corpus, the Propertian *ego* clearly draws on female mythic models for an erotic identity in relation to his dominating mistress. He becomes (in 1.11) the faithful wife Andromache expressing total devotion to Cynthia's Hector, or (in 4.8) a stay-at-home Penelope obedient to the commands of Cynthia's returning Odysseus;[40] while, as justification for his erotic submissiveness, he offers (in 3.11) the mythic example of the supposedly hypermasculine Hercules, who had himself taken up the servile role (and even the costume and domestic occupations) of

describes this type of gender criticism of elegy in the context of remarking upon its apparently essentializing processes of thought, whereby the terms 'sexuality' and 'gender' are employed as if they transcend history.

37 Hallett (1973); (1989), 65; (1990), 193; (1993*a*), 62–6, and (1993*b*), 344–5.

38 Gold (1993*a*).

39 See esp. Skinner (1993*a*) for Catullan love poetry as a precursor of the Propertian in this respect. Cf. Janan (1994), esp. 2; Greene (1998), 1–17.

40 On the Propertian play with female mythic models, see further Flaschenriem (1998), 52–3, on 1.15.

woman to the dominating queen Omphale.[41] Furthermore, frequently in the Propertian corpus (most notably in 2.7 and 2.13), the male lover-poet is portrayed as sexually loyal while his mistress is not, yet traditionally it was Roman wives not their husbands who were legally required to uphold the principle of marital fidelity.[42]

Central to this unorthodox erotic system, to the male lover's usurpation of the woman's part in the depiction of his sexual relations, is the conception of the Propertian *ego* as slave to his mistress. In poem 1.9, for example, the man who enters into elegiac love is defined as one who loses freedom of speech (*libera uerba*, 2), who becomes prostrate and suppliant (*iaces supplexque*, 3), and who must learn to endure a woman who commands (*iura*, 3), governs (*imperat*, 4) and tames (*domet*, 6) her lovers.[43] Given that Roman sexual relations were constituted in terms of activity and passivity, of domination and subordination, of superiority and inferiority, engendered as masculine and feminine, and aligned with the relationships of master and slave, the persistent Propertian strategy of casting the male lover in a submissive, servile role in relation to his obdurate mistress disturbs the gendered protocols of Roman sexuality. The male *ego* enacts the role of a faithful, submissive, subordinate woman.

In the Propertian corpus, moreover, it is not only the narrating *ego* who takes on feminine characteristics but also the genre of elegy itself.[44] Within the Propertian avowal of a Callimachean poetic programme, the disdained genre of epic is identified as hard (*durus*), the desired genre of elegy as soft (*mollis*). In contrast to the rigidity that defines epic production, the elegiac poet is said to produce soft verse (*mollem . . . uersum*, 1.7.19), and a soft book (*mollis . . . liber*, 2.1.2), to wear the soft garland of a Callimachean poet (*mollia . . . serta*,

[41] See Lindheim (1998*a*), 61–2.

[42] See also Ch. 1 above. In her reading of the disputed *nuptae . . . more* of Prop. 2.7.8, Gale (1997), 88, argues that here, in relation to Cynthia, Propertius seems to play the role of both wife and bride.

[43] On the metaphor of *seruitium amoris*, see also Ch. 1 above.

[44] Kennedy (1993), 31–3 and 58–9; Sharrock (1991*b*), 173.

3.1.19), and to walk on the soft terrain that signals a Callimachean poetic practice (*molli . . . Heliconis in umbra*, 3.3.1; *mollia . . . prata*, 3.3.18). Yet the quality of *mollitia* or softness is so closely aligned in Roman discursive systems with the feminine that the term was claimed to be derived from *mulier* or 'woman'.[45] Propertian elegy claims for itself the realm of the feminine as inspiration (*Quelle*), subject-matter (*Gegenstand*), and readership (*Ziel*)[46] and as a set of characteristics with which to align its male *ego* but, in designating elegiac production as *mollis*, the Propertian narrator also claims the realm of the feminine even as the very texture of his verse.[47]

Is Propertian elegy then an obstinately feminine genre? Given that it centres on the theme of a dominating mistress, and ascribes feminine attributes both to its male *ego* and his poetic practice, could its gender play even be labelled an Augustan form of feminism, as Judith Hallett argued in her ground-breaking article of the 1970s?

In the dynamics of moralizing rhetoric during the Roman republic, the concept of morality was deployed to define entry into membership of the elite, and attacks on the immorality of its members effectively questioned their position in structures of social and political power. For men, the appearance of marital propriety and responsibility for a family worked to legitimate their role as true citizens of the *res publica* and as rightful governors of empire. Public charges of sexual immorality (given its association with potential anomalies of gender and power) were an especially privileged means for denigrating otherness of class, ethnicity, or political agenda.[48] Thus one strategy for shoring up the political authority of Octavian in the decade between Philippi and Actium was to associate other political

[45] Isid. *Orig*. 10.179, for which see Sharrock (1991*b*), 173.

[46] See Ch. 2 above for a discussion of the terms employed by Godo Lieberg to describe the Propertian *puella*'s relations to poetic production.

[47] For the female anatomy of the elegiac genre, see Ch. 4 above on the figure of Elegia in *Amores* 3.1.

[48] See esp. Edwards (1993); Hallett and Skinner (1997), esp. 11–12, Galinsky (1996), 128–40.

leaders with a failure to control their own sexual behaviour and that of their female dependants. The very establishment of the principate became articulated with a man's proper performance of his marital and familial duties. Civil war was troped as a battle between the sexes during the Perusine campaign of 41–40 BC. As a participant, Fulvia was figured as an aberrant woman who ruled her husband Antony and could only be tamed by Octavian's truely phallic power. By the time of the battle of Actium in 31 BC, gender had effectively become nationalized. Enslaved by his passion for Cleopatra, Antony had now become entrapped by feminine and feminizing Egypt. Only Octavian could save Rome for masculinity.[49] After Actium, the legitimacy of Augustus' authority continued to be interlocked with questions of moral probity. His wife Livia and his sister Octavia were frequently honoured and displayed as models of compliance with traditional strictures on women's conjugal and parental behaviour.[50] The politics of immorality (the perceived threat posed to the Augustan order by unregulated sexuality) became even more evident in 18 BC, when the regime's legislation against adultery legally enhanced the long-established Roman distinction between the respectable *matrona* and the disreputable *meretrix*. Adulteresses from among the elite were to be deprived of their social privileges and degraded to the class of professional prostitutes. The most severe penalties for adultery closely resembled those for treason.[51]

In relation to such a discursive system, elegiac indifference to marriage and reproduction, its descriptions of male sexual submission to a wilful mistress, and its depictions of an erotic leisure that precludes civic responsibility, all carry a considerable charge. If critical attention is then transferred from the male *ego* of amatory elegy to his beloved mistress, the gender play of the genre may appear to

[49] As Janan (1998), 67; Williams (1999), 135–7; Keith (2000), 78–81. See further Ch. 6 below.

[50] See e.g. Dixon (1988), 74–84; Keith (2000), 78–81; Ch. 6 below.

[51] Edwards (1993), esp. 61–2; McGinn (1998), 140–215, esp. 208–9; Williams (1999), 113–15.

offer a challenging new role for Roman women. For the unconventional sexual and social role bestowed on the soft elegiac *ego* may seem to implicate his hard elegiac mistress in equally unconventional behaviour: he slights the duties of being a citizen and soldier of the Augustan *patria* in favour of being a faithful lover and slave to his *puella*, while she slights the conventional roles of dependent wife and mother in favour of being an independent, sexually unrestrained, and dominating mistress.

On the level of politics (in the conventional sense of states and their institutions of government), Propertian elegy's poet-lover appears to adopt, provocatively, the position of an Antony so enslaved by desire for a dominating woman that he is no longer capable of rendering proper service to his Roman *patria*.[52] Its elegiac mistress, however, is not figured comparably as a militant Fulvia or a sovereign Cleopatra. If the Propertian mistress is described as a *dux* it is only to position her narrator metaphorically in love's encampment. Instead of exploring recent challenges by women to male military authority, this elegiac world makes love a battlefield on which the lover-poet hopes to exercise an erotic heroism (*militia amoris*)—virilely removing his rivals, violently subjugating his beloved.[53]

On the level of poetics, the elegiac mistress Cynthia is allocated skills in poetry, music, and dance, that is, the conventional Greek triad of charms belonging to the courtesan who has been educated for the pleasure of men.[54] She is also equipped with *doctrina* but, in the elegiac world, her erudition acts as a prompt only to the male poet's literary activity, not to her own. Despite the intervention of Sulpicia, the elegiac genre constitutes itself as an enterprise that precludes its production by women. The *docta puella* operates not as a

[52] See Ch. 6 below and Miller (2001), sec. 1 on 2.16.35–40. Miller argues that the lover-poet's comparison with Antony is double-edged because the enslaving love that binds them together is described as *turpis*.

[53] See Fredrick (1997); Greene (1998), 67–92, and (2000); Sharrock (2000), 275–82; Miller (2001), sec. 3.

[54] As noted by Hemelrijk (1998), 117–21.

potential judge or rival in the field of poetic composition but as the embodiment of her author's learned subject-matter.[55]

Finally, on the level of erotics, the gender play of elegy is radically asymmetrical. Outside the fourth book of Propertius and Ovid's *Heroides*, the sexual (as well as the political and the poetic) self that is at stake is always male.[56] Within the discursive system of elegiac love, the inversion of the submission / dominance paradigm for sexual relations is not everywhere sustained (the Propertian lover-poet, for example, can equally depict his beloved as in a state of helplessness from which he needs to rescue her heroically).[57] And, when in operation, it focuses on the servitude and femininity of the narrating *ego* not on the masculinity and sexual mastery of his narrated *puella*. Any ideological charge which this unorthodox erotic system may carry rests, therefore, on the delineation of male sexual submission rather than female sexual dominance, as has been understood in discussions of the *seruitium* metaphor as a mechanism for the exploration of the elegiac poet's relations to his patron.

Critics have for some time observed that the language of the lover-poet's erotic servitude to his mistress intersects with that employed by a Roman client to his patron. There are the same declarations of loyalty, of duty performed at a door, a dinner, or on a journey; there are the same offers of praise and poetic fame in a system that expects reciprocal exchange.[58] It is not just that the language of *amicitia* can be deployed to express as strongly as possible the obligations of an ideal poetic *amor*, but also that the general failure of exchange in relations of *amor* can suggest the possibility of failure of exchange in relations of *amicitia*. Feminine servility is thus exploited by the Roman love poets to dramatize their own vulnerable position in relation

[55] See Habinek (1998), 122–36, for the differential application of the term *doctus* to men and women in Latin love poetry. On the elegiac *puella* as the incarnation of her author's poetics, see esp. Greene (1998) and Chs. 1–4 above.

[56] As Myers (1996), 1 and 11. See also Ch. 1 above.

[57] Greene (1998), 33–66, and (2000), 241–2; Sharrock (2000), 275–82.

[58] As White (1993), 87–91.

both to their patrons and to their peers (as auditors and readers of their work).[59] For the purpose of exploring the male narrator's political, poetic, and erotic stances, the only thing that matters is that he should intermittently acquire some feminine attributes.

Propertian elegy, it transpires, has three, not two, interlocking themes—love, writing, and gender. Feminine attributes are ascribed both to the narrator's erotics and to his poetics. But for all its gender play, Propertian elegy still retains (as Denise McCoskey has argued) an underlying rhetoric of biological essentialism that categorically distinguishes between the lover-poet and his mistress as male and female. He is *grauis*: stable, constant, consistent, at times even violent, heroic, and virile. She is *leuis*: unstable, fickle, faithless, dangerously passionate and deceptive, in need of supervision and control. She is vilified for the mutability her poet declares is characteristic of all women.[60] If elegy's speaking voice is generally designated as male (with the exception of some of the first-person narratives of the Propertian corpus and of Ovid's *Heroides*), then the elegiac *ego* and his genre of poetic production, whenever they are allocated feminine attributes, are both effectively constituted not as feminist, nor even as feminine, but as effeminate.

In republican and imperial Rome, *uirtus* or masculinity was a state to be achieved through oratorical performance, political competition, military victory. It was always open to assault or slippage so that its attainment and maintenance required constant care. Masculinity was centrally defined by the exercise and display of control over self and others (such as wife, children, slaves) and secured by its strong opposition to effeminacy. Effeminacy signified all that masculinity was not and included, in the crucial realm of pleasure, an excessive

[59] On the intersection of the language of *amor* and *amicitia* in Catullus and the elegists, see Skinner (1993*a*), 118–19; Gold (1993*b*); Fitzgerald (1995), 114–39, and (2000), 72–7; Oliensis (1997); McCarthy (1998); Lee-Stecum (1998); Greene (2000), 248–51.

[60] McCoskey (1999). Cf. Gold (1993*a*), 88–9, and (1993*b*), 292–3 and 287–9; Greene (1998), 59–66; Sharrock (2000), 275–82.

desire to give rather than to take. The charge of effeminacy associated its recipient with the worst of 'feminine' characteristics: with leisure (*otium*) as opposed to business (*negotium*), retirement as opposed to public life, indulgence as opposed to toil, sexual compliance as opposed to mastery, fleshy softness as opposed to muscular rigidity. In these discursive terms, therefore, for the elegiac *ego* to take on such feminine characteristics is to open him up to the damning charge of effeminacy and consequently to imply his failure to achieve the status of a Roman *man*.[61]

The whole constellation of negative values which are attached in moral writings to the effeminate man are not lost on elegy's male *ego*. Propertius' literary patron Maecenas was said, when freed from the pressures of public life, 'to dissolve into an idleness and acts of softness almost beyond what one would expect of a woman' (*otio ac mollitiis paene ultra feminam fluens*, Vell. Pat. 2.88.2).[62] The noun *mollitia* and its adjective *mollis* were the most commonly used terms to mark male behaviour considered to be effeminate and were, therefore, frequently deployed to discredit the behaviour of a male member of the Roman elite. Thus, in poem 2.22a, the Propertian narrator finds himself accused of being *mollis in omnis* (soft for them all, 2.22a.13). Sexual excess is here (as elsewhere in Roman moral discourses) a signifier of effeminacy,[63] as is indicated by the lover-poet's immediate suggestion that his condition is as inexplicable as ritual castration. He then attempts to reassert a semblance of virility by informing his accuser of his sexual prowess, a prowess that is radically undermined by the amatory laments of the surrounding poems.[64] Elsewhere the

[61] On the fragility of ancient masculinity and the charge of effeminacy, see Edwards (1993), 63–97; Gleason (1995); Corbeill (1996), 128–73; Hallett and Skinner (1997); Williams (1999), esp. 125–59.

[62] Kennedy (1993), 31. Cf. Richlin $(1992)^2$, 3–5, and (1997), 94; Miller (2001), sec. 3.

[63] See e.g. Richlin $(1992)^2$, 91–3; Williams (1999), 141–8.

[64] On the elegiac lover as *mollis*, see Keith (1999), 56–7 and 61. My attention was drawn to the defamatory use of *mollis* in Prop. 2.22 by McCoskey (1996), 36 n. 22. She, however, interprets the response of the elegiac *amator* differently. Cf. Cat. 16 for the

Propertian lover-poet describes his condition as one of *nequitia* or moral depravity. The lover of 1.7.26 longs to expire in the throes of abject *nequitia*, rather than in the (more virile) duty of military service on which his addressee Tullus is poised to embark. Similarly the lover-poet of Propertius 2.24.1–8 declares that his frustrated love and his elegiac poetry have caused him to be accused of *nequitia* and to be labelled *infamis* or 'disreputable' throughout the city of Rome. Because the male lover of Propertian elegy is aligned with supposedly perverse 'feminine' characteristics and pursuits, he too opens himself to the charge of effeminacy and its consequent loss of reputation.

The very texture of elegiac verse, its 'softness' or *mollitia*, marks the genre as effeminate. If a literary genre is a means of signification incorporated into the text, a set of rules that give form and meaning to the genre's discourse and instructions to its readers,[65] the quality of effeminacy or *mollitia* as traditionally perceived is one of the generic rules that constructs and organizes Augustan erotic elegy and works to determine its reception.[66] Epic supplies the generic and gendered norm: its subject-matter is men and warfare; it scrutinizes the conventions of *uirtus*; it trains its readers in manliness; it is, itself, hard (*durus*) and virile.[67] Satire constitutes its narrating *ego* as hypermasculine and attributes to him the threatening and extreme virility of Priapus.[68] Thus the Lucilian narrator (as John Henderson describes him)

> incarnates in his phallic brag that invariant and aggressive masculinity of bodily penetration which has been erected by modern scholars into the very condition of a normality in Roman culture. We are to know L[ucilius] as the epitome, that is, of the Male—who rapes women, buggers

lover-poet responding aggressively to a charge of effeminacy, on which see Richlin (1992)², 12–13 and 145–6; Skinner (1993*b*), 64–7; Fitzgerald (1995), 34–58; Hallett (1996), 328–9; Miller (1994), 182–4; Williams (1999), 164–5.

[65] Conte (1989), 441–2. Cf. Kennedy (1992), 47.

[66] Cf. Fitzgerald (1995), 40–1, on the engendering of Catullan poetry, in its programmatic opening poem, as provocatively effeminate.

[67] As Keith (2000).

[68] Richlin (1992)², esp. 57–63 and 164–209.

boys, repels crones and pathic adult males, and reviles all (else) in his cock-swagger.[69]

In love elegy, however, the narrating *ego* is constituted as effeminate. Paradoxically, it is sexual impotence rather than potency that marks the figure of the male lover of elegy, for he is represented as languishing almost perpetually outside his beloved's door. He submits, not imposes, is weaponless rather than armed, soft not hard, amorously lamenting not aggressively abusing, and feminine not masculine. Even the composition of elegiac poetry can be figured as a failed sexual act, for the lover's failure constitutes the poet's success. Thus in *Amores* 3.7 the Ovidian lover's literal impotence works figuratively to identify the attenuation of the elegiac writing-style and its anti-epic weaponlessness, while in *Amores* 1.1 the production of a first book of love elegies is presented in such a way as to associate that verse form with the erection and detumescence of the penis.[70]

What conclusions then can be drawn as to the politics of elegiac eroticism, if it engenders itself as effeminate? When attention is focused on the enunciative system of Augustan elegy, on the process by which the male narrator and his verse are marked out as effeminate, the male *ego* of the elegiac text could be read as exploring, in his own person, not just the specific tensions and ambiguities inherent in the relations of poetic patronage, but also a broader crisis of masculinity evident in the period of transition from republic to principate. In his study of slavery as a Roman literary topos, William Fitzgerald draws attention to the seemingly perverse Tibullan declaration *hic mihi seruitium uideo dominamque paratam: | iam mihi, libertas illa paterna, uale* (Now, for me, I see slavery and a mistress at the ready: | now good-bye to that freedom of my fathers, 2.4.1–2). He comments:

[69] Henderson (1989), 56. Cf. Hallett (1996), 322–6, on Martial.

[70] Kennedy (1993), 58–63; Oliensis (1991), 125, Keith (1994), 60–1; Sharrock (1995); Myers (1996), 10–12.

> What might be an anxious truth for the poet-courtier is a resigned, amused, or defiant acceptance of the rules of a game for the poet/lover who serves as a lightning rod for all the floating dis-ease with the increasing servility of social relationships, collected into a bolt of lightning that strikes *this* extravagant figure.[71]

By the beginning of the principate, the performance of masculinity in public competition was already felt to have become a mere pantomime. With the progressive realignment of authority around the *princeps*, elegy's metaphor of erotic *seruitium* could trope Rome's male elite as seduced from virile republican *libertas* into an abject state of feminine enslavement.[72]

Duncan Kennedy reminds us that conclusions are not self-evident, for Augustan elegy can be processed by its readers (both then as now) in such a way as to generate and emphasize contradictions which might imply opposition to the regime or, conversely, to minimize or iron them out.[73] The self-presentation of elegy's male *ego* as a depraved effeminate could be read, for example, as legitimating the moral programme of Augustus by marking out precisely the kind of behaviour which was thought to require reform if the state was to be restored to its proper virility. The reader could feel envious of or superior to the character of the lover-poet, for elegiac love (however desirable) is generally unobtainable. And even the seemingly most sincere Propertius appears to mock the provocative claims of his own elegiac persona as well as conventional moral and political behaviours.[74] But, at the very least, the first-person confes-

[71] Fitzgerald (2000), 72–3.

[72] See esp. Skinner (1993*a*) on an earlier Catullan dis-ease with the condition of masculine *libertas* and, following her on the Augustan elegists, Myers (1996), 10–11; Fredrick (1997), 172 and 179; Lindheim (1998*b*), 28; Lee-Stecum (1998), 302–3, and (2000), 179–80; Fear (2000), 234–8; Janan (2001), 7–9, on the work of Paul Allen Miller, and 45–52; Miller (2001).

[73] Kennedy (1993), 34–9.

[74] As Kennedy (1993), 42–7, on Ovid's *Ars Amatoria*. Cf. Sharrock (1995), 174–5; Fitzgerald (1995), 8–9; Platter (1995); Gale (1997); Lee-Stecum (1998); Miller (2001), esp. secs. 3 and 4.

sion of the effeminacy of both elegy's erotics and poetics keeps the conventional gender categories of Augustan Rome constantly in play in this genre. In Augustan elegy, love, writing, *and* gender are all marked out as areas of contestation—as the genre's problematic.[75]

## PLAYING THE OTHER[76]

Augustan elegy is not an obstinately male genre, because problems of gender identity (the tensions and mobilities of gender differentiation as masculine or feminine) are integral to its discursive structure. Gender play in the Propertian corpus, however, is not limited to the ascription of feminine attributes to the male narrator and his poetic practice. The gender dynamics of the fourth book are significantly different from those of the first three. Here the poems step away from elegy's earlier restricted subjectivity: the dominating perspective of a male lover-poet. The fourth book constitutes a point of departure in the corpus, for women are elaborately represented and frequently even speak. Through the characters and voices of Arethusa, Tarpeia, Acanthis, Cynthia, and Cornelia, the last book introduces into male-authored elegy a form of female subjectivity. It is for this reason that Propertius' book 4 was so crucial to Judith Hallett's case for the feminism of Latin love elegy:

> There, the poet devotes considerable space to women who are *not* his love objects—something heretofore rather unusual in Latin love elegy. There, through contrasting the behavioral roles and personal values of these various women, both legendary and contemporary figures, with those of his

[75] *Contra* Kennedy, Miller (1994), 180–4 and 193–202, argues for the gender play of Catullan love elegy that we should distinguish between the discursive strategy of 'transgression' that affirms limits by crossing them, and the strategy of 'negation' that sets out a lasting difference from what constitutes the order's limits: by means of negation oppositional discourse *is* possible. On elegy, and Propertius in particular, Miller (2001) argues that the poets simultaneously question *and* accept Roman conventions of masculinity, but through such 'double voicing' they disclose a profound dissension at the heart of Augustan discursive norms.

[76] I take my heading here from the title of an article by Froma Zeitlin (1990).

mistress Cynthia, Propertius voices his general discontent with Augustan beliefs and reaffirms the validity of his own.[77]

But the fourth book of Propertius does not form a neat continuum with the enunciative system of the earlier books. The fundamental norm of earlier Propertian elegy was that the only voice which speaks in the text belongs to the male poet-lover. The world of love was there constructed 'in an entirely exclusive perspective, in which the point of view and the "values" of other subjects (the *amica*, the rival, the *lena*) were denied expression'.[78] Female subjectivity now enters the Propertian corpus as part of a new poetic project that permits no unifying lover's perspective to bind together its disparate voices, and when women speak in the fourth book they do not reaffirm the validity of the values expressed in the first three books so much as *attack* them. When women speak in book 4 they frequently challenge the old elegiac poses of the constant lover, a fickle mistress, and his servile devotion.

As part of the programmatic opening to the fourth book, poem 4.2 offers a key to the novel techniques by which Propertian elegy is about to play with gender. A new first-person narrator, the statue Vertumnus, declares his capacity to take on diverse shapes while still retaining artistic decorum, and thus proclaims the simultaneous diversity and unity of the new book's multifarious voices that will be held together by the bipolar poetics of *Roma* and *amor*.[79] But the very first transformations for which Vertumnus playfully professes a capacity are those of gender: dressed in fine Coan silks, the statue will become a soft girl (*indue me Cois, fiam non dura puella*, v. 23); wearing a toga, no one will deny him to be a man (*meque uirum sumpta quis neget esse toga?*, v. 24). Soft girl and male citizen—these are the successful disguises Vertumnus can adopt by dressing in the appropriate

[77] Hallett (1984), 254, in the reprint of her original article.

[78] See Conte (1994), 46, who is commenting on the distinction between the techniques of Ovid's *Remedia amoris* and the *Amores*.

[79] See Ch. 3 above.

costume of silks or a toga, yet they are also recognizable as the characters who inhabit the familiar world of earlier amatory elegy—the beloved *puella* and the loving *ego*. In the first three books of the corpus, the subjectivity of the elegiac mistress was subsumed into the point of view of her amorous narrator. It was the acuteness of focus on his servile devotion to her that pointed to elegy's play with the troubles of Roman masculinity. Here, however, in poem 4.2 Vertumnus focuses equally on male and female. He thus programmatically undercuts the overriding authority ascribed to the perspective of the male lover-poet in the preceding books.[80]

Furthermore, as Vertumnus describes his technique of gender play, the presentation of the old elegiac poses now becomes a matter of putting on costumes, of play-acting. The verb *uertere* (which defines the very nature of Vertumnus and his process of gender transformation) is also employed in Roman drama to refer to the adoption of a disguise.[81] 'Taking the woman's part' in the fourth book of Propertian elegies, therefore, is represented at the outset as a process of dramatic mimesis. Like an actor on the stage, the elegiac poet is going to play the *puella* as well as the male first-person narrator. If the ithyphallic statuette of Priapus is an appropriate totem for the hypermasculine narrative of satire, cross-dressing Vertumnus is an appropriate totem for the gender ambiguities and transformations that the genre of elegy is now about to enact.[82]

Vertumnus programmatically represents the construction of character in the elegiac discourse of Propertius' fourth book as a form of dramatic disguise: if the *amator* or the *puella* speak here, it is because an author is impersonating them. The performative qualities of the elegiac genre to which Vertumnus draws attention have long been recognized, but only recently has there been sustained interest

[80] See esp. O'Neill (2000).

[81] For example, Jupiter is said to disguise himself (*uortit*) as Amphitryo, in the prologue to Plautus *Am.* 121.

[82] On Vertumnus' play with gender, see below and DeBrohun (1994); Lindheim (1998*b*); Janan (1998), 68.

in their implications for the genre's play with gender (as indicated by a special issue of the journal *Helios* published in 1998 and dedicated to the analysis of gender and genre in Roman comedy and elegy).[83]

It was not only the genres of oratory and drama that might be addressed to a live audience at Rome. While, during the republic, dinner parties or *conuiuia* had provided informal occasions and locations for the performance of poetry, performance had become more formalized by the beginning of the principate in the social institution of *recitationes*, which Asinius Pollio was said to have initiated in 39 BC. The recitation by authors of their as yet unpublished works to friends, patrons, and other members of the Roman elite had thus already taken hold as a fashionable and significant means of literary dissemination by the time Propertius, Tibullus, and Ovid were producing their elegiac poetry.[84] While the *recitatio* was culturally privileged, it should not be understood as incompatible with the production of poetry-books, which also became fashionable in this period. Different kinds of access were now available to a poet's works. Poems could be read linearly, intratextually, and recursively when collected in books, or they could be heard in performance prior to publication.[85]

The elegiac genre clearly had a stake in the institution of *recitatio*, for the poems themselves show an awareness of both a readership and an audience. The production of elegy is a matter of chanting (*canere*)

[83] For earlier advocacies of understanding Roman poetry as a performance of gender, see Richlin (1992*a*), 174–6; Skinner (1993*b*), 61–3; Hallett (1993*a*), 65. In the original article on which this chapter is based I drew extensively on Froma Zeitlin's interpretation of how women's parts were played on the Attic stage. See Wyke (1994), 121–4, and the discussion there of Zeitlin (1990).

[84] See Wiseman (1985), 124–9; Woodman and Powell (1992), 204–6; Fantham (1996), 70–1; Dupont (1997); Gamel (1998), 81–3.

[85] On the importance of poetic performance, see Sharrock (1994), 103–4; Fantham (1996), 55–101; Dupont (1997), 45; Habinek (1998), 103–21; Gamel (1998), 80–1. For renewed emphasis on the reading of poetry-books, see Miller (1994), esp. 173–7; Boyd (1997); Lee-Stecum (1998) and (2000). Fitzgerald (1995), esp. 5–7, explores the consequences of the availability of both types of access to Roman poetry.

as well as writing (*scribere*), and the reception of elegy a matter of listening (*audire*) as well as reading (*legere*). Moreover, the characters who operate in the amatory world of elegy (the crafty mistress, her young lover, the rich rival or foolish husband, the greedy madam) have been recognized as literary descendants of parts played in Roman comedy and mime. Although the recitation of Roman elegy presumably did not involve the absorption of the author into his characters' parts through the use of costume, mask, and gesture, and was therefore not of the same order of dramatic mimesis as the acting on stage of comedy or mime, there is thus justification for regarding elegy as in some sense performed.[86] Given that the fourth book of the Propertian corpus sets out its male and female voices explicitly as a form of dramatic disguise, and by giving expression to points of view other than that of the male *amator* (including that of the mistress and the madam) returns to the fuller vision of love sustained by its literary precursors in comedy and mime, it seems doubly appropriate to interpret its particular play with gender as performative.[87]

In the period of the early principate, moreover, a *recitatio* that involved 'taking a woman's part' would have been especially loaded with issues of gender. During the republic, *oratio* was a central means by which the Roman citizen elite produced, defined, or defended their *uirtus* (masculinity) and their *dignitas* (social and political standing) and contested that of their opponents.[88] As the institution of *recitatio* emerged so that of *oratio* disappeared, for with the establishment of the principate exercise of power moved to the imperial palace. *Recitationes*, however, were not public events in the civic sense and, although they appealed to their audience's judgement, were closer to the conditions of theatre, than those of the senate or the courtroom.[89] The institution was therefore already compromised as

[86] For elegy's relation to *recitatio* and dramatic performance, see McKeown (1979); Yardley (1987) and (1991); Griffin (1985), 198–210; James (1998); Gamel (1998).

[87] See Ch. 3 above for an analysis of the gender play of Propertius book 4 in terms of the operations of a poetry-book.

[88] Dupont (1997); Richlin (1997); Gamel (1998), 90–4.

[89] Dupont (1997), esp. 46–7.

an opportunity for the performance of Roman masculinity, while the male performance of femininity had always and everywhere been stigmatized. Orators were advised on the strict limits they should set to the adoption of female personae for fear of resembling actors, whose performance of female parts rendered them vulnerable to accusations of effeminacy (while their profession already precluded them from citizenship).[90] The poetic performance of a woman's part might thus call into question both the *uirtus* and the *dignitas* of its author.[91]

Commenting on the value for feminist criticism of reading Augustan love elegy as scripts for performance, Mary-Kay Gamel observes:

> As a man performed the roles of both *amator* and *puella*, putting his own voice into the pronouns and his own body into the gestures, the reader/performer of this poetry performed his own involvement in the system of gender construction more consciously and more actively than did silent readers or audience members watching comedies. And the ventriloquism involved in male authors writing 'female' roles is much more clearly on display in performance than it is in a text.[92]

On such a reading, the elegiac genre even invites both its authors and its audiences 'to question accepted ideas about gender'.[93] In an earlier analysis of the feminine presence in Attic drama, Froma Zeitlin argued that woman is assigned the role of the radically other and that the performance of this other opens up to question the masculine view of the universe.[94] When the Propertian corpus begins to 'play the other' in sustained fashion in the fourth book, when (in a break with the earlier gendered conventions for elegiac enunication) a female *ego* enters on the elegiac stage, an especially subtle and complex interrogation of gender is initiated. For here, in the last book of

[90] See e.g. Richlin (1992)$^2$, 10, (1992*a*), 174–6, and (1997); Lindheim (1998*b*), 28; Gamel (1998), 86–8 and 90–4; Williams (1999), 139–40.

[91] As Fitzgerald (1995), 34–58, and Gamel (1998), 88.

[92] Gamel (1998), 92.

[93] Gamel (1998), 94.

[94] Zeitlin (1990).

Propertian elegies, the genders which are put into play as problematic include the male poet-lover of the first three books and his construction of a courted mistress. On either side of the central poem concerning the battle of Actium, the madam Acanthis and the mistress Cynthia are both allocated direct speech only to denounce the earlier Propertian *ego*. In both cases, their departure from the erotic and poetic values espoused by the earlier male narrator is clearly marked.

In poem 4.5 the withered madam Acanthis delivers a disquisition on the erotic arts, matching one set of *carmina* against another (her magical incantations against the poetic courtship of the *amator*). The male narrator of the first elegiac book had played the role of an expert on amatory matters, telling his mistress to place the pleasures of a single mutual love for a poet and his immortal gifts of verse over multiple lovers, worldly riches, and the wearing of Coan silks. Here the audience to poem 4.5 is invited to recognize the self-interestedness of that poet-lover's expert advice, when set against the madam's economic concern not for her own but for her pupil's old age. The mistress whom Acanthis advises is told to welcome not the poet but the moneyed soldier, sailor, or slave. She quotes an early Propertian couplet (1.2.1–2) only to demand that the man who offers gifts of such verses, rather than Coan silks, should be judged artless and left unheard (*qui uersus, Coae dederit nec munera uestis,* | *istius tibi sit surda sine arte lyra*, 4.5.57–8). When Propertius now impersonates a madam, it is precisely his earlier self-presentation as lover-poet that she vigorously rejects and threatens with both erotic and poetic failure.[95]

Similarly, in poem 4.7 the dead Cynthia returns to her lover in a dream to berate him for his negligence. The male lover-poet of the first three poetry-books had declared his utter loyalty to his beloved

[95] Myers (1996); O'Neill (1998), and (2000), 273–4; Janan (2001), 28–9 and 89; Ch. 3 above. Sharrock (2000) argues that the technique of exposing the self-interestedness of the *amator* operates even in the *Monobiblos*.

despite her faithlessness. As a counter to that point of view, this mistress accuses her old lover of disloyalty and boasts instead of her own faithfulness. She discloses the falsity of her lover-poet's self-representation as an erotic *seruus* and his depiction of her as an erotic *domina*, when she reveals that the Roman amatory world is constituted instead by male dominance, female economic dependence, and the literal torture of domestic slaves. When Propertius impersonates his elegiac mistress, she constructs a rival elegiac world of female constancy and male betrayal, male negligence and female poverty. As a result, she demands that all the earlier Propertian verses that had been composed with her as their pretext—and in which she had been so misrepresented—be immediately burned (*et quoscumque meo fecisti nomine uersus,* | *ure mihi*, 4.7.77–8).[96]

## READING AND SPEAKING IN THE FEMININE[97]

When Propertian elegy plays the other, when it is momentarily engendered as feminine, the author's prior self-representation as the enslaved *amator* is both challenged and supplanted by a rival narrative. In 4.7, not only does Cynthia's ghost order the destruction of the old verse in which her lover-poet had constructed her as fickle mistress, but she also dictates a public epitaph for herself that makes no reference at all to a male lover. Concluding an article on the female voice in the Propertian corpus, Barbara Flaschenriem proposes:

> In fact, we could read the spectral Cynthia of 4.7 as a metaphor for a feminine perspective, or a subjectivity, which the poet's earlier erotic fictions acknowledge intermittently, but generally appropriate as a part of the male

[96] Flaschenriem (1998); Janan (2001), 100–13; Ch. 3 above.

[97] I borrow my terminology here from recent studies of elegy that have been indebted to the French feminist theories of Julia Kristeva, Luce Irigaray, and Hélène Cixous, such as a special issue of *Classical World* (1999), ed. Miller and Platter; Janan (2001); Miller (2001); Spentzou (forthcoming).

> narrator's literary repertoire: she signifies the existence of an autonomous, though largely unrepresented, female point of view. Through Cynthia's posthumous mandates, 4.7 alludes to a concern articulated more explicitly in the work of the elegiac poet Sulpicia: the female speaker's attempt to take command of *fama*, and to represent herself by creating authoritative texts of her own . . .
>
> . . . Cynthia's epitaph points to the difference between the poet's representations of the female and the stories that she herself might wish to tell.[98]

The Propertian poem appears fleetingly to acknowledge that missing almost completely from Augustan Rome is a different, female perspective on love, writing, and gender. If we find few Augustan speakers determined enough to launch an explicit challenge to the authorial control exercised by men over women's voices in poetic texts and their performance, feminist scholarship supplies plenty of readers who are so determined. Then, following the example set by Propertius' spectral Cynthia, such readers can reconsider and retell the dynamics of gender and female representation in the elegiac genre.[99]

In her study of Ovid's *Heroides*, for example, Efrossini Spentzou locates transgressions and interrogations of gender not so much in the author's playing of the other, as in the intersection between the other so played and her reception by feminist readers. She argues that, as with the critiques offered by Acanthis and Cynthia in the Propertian corpus, the Ovidian collection of feminine letters from mythic heroines like Penelope or Dido inscribe within themselves an invitation to read elegy against the grain—an invitation that a modern woman reader (such as Spentzou) may be especially willing to accept. Placing emphasis on the argument that meaning is constructed at the point of reception, Spentzou offers an interceptive reading (a reading in the feminine) of these mythic female voices. She cele-

98 Flaschenriem (1998), 63.

99 On the capacity of the determined reader to challenge the Roman male's poetic authority over women's voices, see Fowler (2000), 293–4.

brates the heroines' defiance of authorial control, their effort to establish their own discourse (a writing in the feminine), their will to break out of the confinement of the elegiac world.[100]

While a reading in the feminine may be regarded as especially appropriate to—because called for by—the *Heroides*, the Propertian corpus contains only two poems that completely elide the male who plays the female other (namely those in book four voiced by Arethusa and Cornelia). New, psychoanalytic interpretations of gender play in Propertian love poetry by Micaela Janan and Paul Allen Miller argue instead that the elegiac poet, even where he does not play a separable female character, speaks in the feminine. No reading against the grain is necessary if a feminine voice is already ingrained in the corpus. Here, however, following post-Lacanian French feminism, the 'feminine' or Woman is understood to exceed any reference to historical women, anatomy, or biology, and instead refers to points of breakdown in symbolic discourse or (in this particular historical context) gaps in the logical foundations on which Augustan Rome was attempting to build its ideological edifice. Propertius as woman speaks in the interstices of the masculinist dominant order, eluding or disrupting not just the binary opposition of man and woman, love and hate, but also Roman and non-Roman, pro- and anti-Augustan, epic and elegy. Thus Propertius can speak as woman even without playing one, and in his feminine voice can address questions beyond those of female representation or gender.[101]

In the broadly conceived terms of post-Lacanian psychoanalytic theory, Propertius can be found to speak in the feminine about social displacement through the highly disjunctive quality of the Gallan poems of his first book, or about gender, genre, and Augustanism through the rhetoric of ambivalence, oxymoron, and paradox evident in his second.[102] Nonetheless, Janan carefully argues

[100] Spentzou (forthcoming).

[101] See esp. Janan (2001), 71–2, 165, and n. 58 on 175–7; Miller (2001), sec. 2.

[102] As, respectively, Janan (2001), 33–52, and Miller (2001).

that Propertius speaks in the feminine most dramatically and most subversively where he also *plays* the female—that is in his fourth book. It is also in the fourth book, she observes, that the feminine voice of Propertian elegy is most concerned with issues of gender and sexuality. In *The Politics of Desire: Propertius Book IV* (2001), Janan demonstrates how poem 4.1 programmatically juxtaposes a masculine and a feminine poetics (not in the exclusively generic sense of epic and elegy, but in the epistemological sense of certainty and scepticism), and then embodies the latter in the elegiac *puella*.[103] Whether in the shape of wife, virgin, madam, or mistress, the elegiac woman of the fourth book then trains her feminine suspicion on Augustan Rome's nationalist and masculinist pretensions. Abandoned Arethusa casts a sceptical look over both military and marital relations; Tarpeia's desire for Rome's enemy collapses conventional oppositions between active man and passive woman, and between Roman and non-Roman; old, poor Acanthis challenges the erotic creed of the first three Propertian books and insists that woman is just a series of masks donned to meet man's self-regarding demands; dead Cynthia indicts the whole elegiac tradition of representing male devotion and servitude to female fickleness; living Cynthia exposes the illogicality that characterizes conventional sexual relations at Rome; Cornelia in the underworld opens up the protocols of Roman matronal life to be judged as either sublime self-sacrifice or pointless waste.[104] Given this continuing emphasis in feminist scholarship on *playing* the female as a crucial mechanism in the Propertian interrogation of Roman gender and sexuality, I wish now to conclude with a return to questions of the performance and reception of Propertius' gender play.

[103] See esp. Janan (2001), 102–3.

[104] Janan (2001), 128–45, argues that in book four the interrogation of gender is not confined to poems where women are central characters. Hercules' transvestism and Tiresias' transsexuality in poem 4.9 both disturb conceptions of gender as biologically constituted.

## TECHNOLOGIES OF GENDER[105]

Propertian elegy is not an obstinately male genre. It is engendered as masculine in its discursive mastery over the female object of its erotics and poetics, but engenders itself as effeminate in its association with softness, submissiveness, and impotence, and as feminine especially in its self-critique and its interrogation of Roman gender and sexuality. This gender play is firmly inscribed within the corpus and spotlighted as scholarly attention continues to be drawn to the performative aspect of love poetry, for acknowledgement of its performativity assists in the analysis of the elegiac genre as *itself* a technology of gender.

Duncan Kennedy has asked what rhetorical function is served by an appeal to drama or performance in the study of the elegiac genre. He argues that the hard historicism which underlies much of the critical debate concerning elegy has softened under pressure of an awareness of the textuality of love poetry. Yet that underlying historicism may create fresh devices (such as an appeal to performance) in order to escape from the elegiac texts into the terrain of context, and in this way return to the comforts of describing history or extratextual realities.[106] I would argue that, in feminist study of gender play in the elegiac genre, recent appeals to performance do not constitute a rhetorical device that might facilitate a return to some comforting sense of the 'real' world of Augustan Rome and the 'realities' of women's lives in ancient societies. Rather, as a form of poetry recited before an audience of the Roman elite, Propertian elegy was part of an institutionalized system of representation—a social technology—through which gender was performed and, therefore, constructed at Rome.[107]

[105] I take my heading here from the title of a book by Teresa de Lauretis (1987).

[106] Kennedy (1993), 21–2.

[107] See the discussion above of Roman masculinity as a state achieved through various types of social performance. Cf. now Keith (2000), 6–7, on Roman epic as a technology of gender.

Recent studies of the Propertian poems 4.2 and 4.9 have disclosed how the elegiac genre even draws attention to this conception of Roman gender as socially constructed through its performance. The rhetoric of biological essentialism is threaded through the corpus, with the lover-poet and his mistress categorically differentiated as constant male and unstable female, but first Vertumnus (in poem 4.2) and then Hercules (in poem 4.9) suggest that they can change gender merely by changing costume. The possibilities of cross-dressing or transvestism momentarily offer a dramatic argument against the apparent grounding of gender identity in anatomy. Instead they suggest that gender can only be represented sartorially or performed as masquerade. The Vertumnus poem in particular programmatically demonstrates the performativity of both elegy and gender and, therefore, Augustan love poetry's role in gender's representation and construction.[108]

Gender difference, in the view of Teresa de Lauretis, is produced and reproduced through institutionalized systems of representation such as the cinematic apparatus. The study of gender is, therefore, the study of how it is constructed in a given system of representation or social technology, of how identification is solicited and structured in that technology, and of how it becomes absorbed by each individual whom the technology addresses.[109] In this chapter, I have effectively focused on only the first of de Lauretis's approaches to the study of the technologies of gender. To explore Augustan love poetry and its elegiac mistress more fully as such a technology, it would be necessary to ask how the poems themselves structure identification with their gender play by, for example, engendering the addressees who are incorporated into their narratives. Critics have noted that the ele-

[108] Lindheim (1998*a* and *b*), following DeBrohun's analysis of 4.2 and 4.9 in terms of a 'rhetoric of fashion' (1994). Cf. Janan (1998), and (2001), 142–5, who adds that the example provided in 4.9 of Tiresias' easy transsexuality points to the instability of a system that defines gender in terms of an essential difference between Man and Woman.

[109] De Lauretis (1987), 1–30.

giac poetry of Propertius, Tibullus, and Ovid deploys a variety of strategies to engender and sexualize not just their texts but also their auditors and readers, such as directly identifying its addressees as women who require seducement or inviting its addressees as men to experience and learn from the amatory sufferings of the feminized *ego*.[110] How then were members of the Roman elite (both male and female) being asked to respond to such addresses that invited them to play out other genders for themselves? Were they being cast as distanced onlookers to someone else's love-affair or being brought more intimately, and more disturbingly, into either or both of the positions of male lover and female beloved?

The third of De Lauretis's approaches to the technology of gender is perhaps the most difficult to explore, as little evidence is available for the engendering of responses to the recitation of elegiac poetry among the Roman elite. But the first satire of Persius sets the ground for such an examination.[111] There the satiric narrator describes how, at a poetic recitation, you might see huge Roman citizens thrill as the poems penetrate their bodies (*ingentis trepidare Titos, cum carmina lumbum | intrant*, 1.20–1). If one type of poetry is humorously described as turning a strapping male audience into effeminates, what would the complex gender play of elegy (with its submissive males and dominating mistresses) have done to them?

[110] See e.g. Gamel (1989), 185–6; DeForest (1993), pp. vi–vii; Gold (1993*a*), 94–5 n. 17; Hemelrijk (1998), 62–3 and 67–79; Lee-Stecum (2000), 211–12. Cf. Sharrock (1994), esp. 8–9 and 21–86, on *Ars Amat.* 2, and Gibson (1998) on *Ars Amat.* 3.

[111] On Persius 1, see Richlin (1992)², 185–90, and (1997), 98; Dupont (1997), 51–2; Gamel (1998), 89–90. Cat. 16 is regularly compared as it also casts the relationship between poetry and its reader in highly sexual terms, both pathic and phallic. See Richlin (1992)², 12–13 and 145–6; Skinner (1993*b*), 64–7; Fitzgerald (1995), 34–58; Hallett (1996), 327–9; Miller (1994), 182–4; Williams (1999), 164–5.

# PART 2

# *Reception*

# 6

# *Meretrix regina*: Augustan Cleopatras

Propertius asks the reader of his love elegies *quid mirare, meam si versat femina vitam | et trahit addictum sub sua iura virum?* (why are you astonished if a woman drives my life | and drags, bound beneath her own laws, a man? 3.11.1–2).[1] A catalogue of dominating women of myth and history follows, culminating in a lengthy assault on Cleopatra's ambition to rule Rome and praise for Augustus who alone has released the citizenry from such a fearful prospect. But at the poem's close its narrator still remains in bondage to his elegiac mistress and, therefore, locked into the position not of a resistant Augustus but of a Mark Antony enslaved by the *meretrix regina* ('whore queen', 3.11.39). The narrator's life should be no cause of astonishment because it replays the life that Antony had recently led. Throughout the Propertian poetry-books, Jasper Griffin has

This chapter is a substantially revised and extended version of an article first published in *Roman Poetry and Propaganda in the Age of Augustus* (1992) edited by Anton Powell, and is reproduced with kind permission of Bristol Classical Press.

[1] See above, Ch. 1.

argued, a parallel is sustained between the life of the lover and the life of Antony: reckless, romantic, and tragically obsessed with a woman who degrades him.[2] Propertius 3.11 lays before its readers a seemingly vitriolic account of Cleopatra's fearsome desires and ambitions in order that they may better comprehend elegy's amatory enslavement. In so doing, the poem deploys motifs for the depiction of the last Ptolemaic ruler that have been traced back to the propaganda spearheaded by Octavian as he agitated for support in the lead up to the battle of Actium, and whose repetition has also been observed in the iambic Cleopatra of Horace *Epode* 9, the lyric Cleopatra of Horace *Ode* 1.37, the epic Cleopatra of Virgil *Aeneid* 8, and the elegiac Cleopatra of Propertius 4.6.

By the time of the battle of Actium in 31 BC, Cleopatra VII had shaped her own image as a protective queen of Egypt and been shaped by her opponents as the eastern enemy of Rome. Her own propaganda, of which there are now few remains, depicted the queen in ways that competed for authority with the propaganda of the ultimate victor, Octavian.[3] Cleopatra's power was variously represented in the verbal and visual discourses of Egypt and Rome, yet the texts that survive from the period close to her death are predominantly male, Roman, and poetic. At this distance, we seem to be witness only to the extreme partiality of the winning side for, within the discursive patterns of Augustan iambics, lyric, epic, and elegy, Cleopatra VII is the defeated enemy of the *res publica* and potent only in her sympotic and erotic perversity. She is the Egyptian whore, a drunkard, mistress of eunuchs, and (almost) of Rome itself. Both this poetic and the later historiographic tradition have been said to create around an opponent of Octavian 'a miasma of romance, glamour, sentiment, and prurience', and to invoke a form of political propa-

[2] Griffin (1985). On the double-edged comparison between Propertius and Antony in 2.16.35–40, see Miller (2001), sec. 1.

[3] Hughes-Hallett (1991), 14–15; Rice (1999), 2–3; Foreman (1999), 27.

ganda against the queen that constitutes 'one of the most terrible outbursts of hatred in history'.[4]

Although twentieth-century historians have often acknowledged the danger of their own complicity with Graeco-Roman judgements of the queen (in the absence of any surviving Graeco-Egyptian accounts), the last Ptolemy has regularly been represented in their works as only an appendage to her two Roman lovers. In the opening paragraph of her biography *Cleopatra* (1999), the Hellenistic historian E. E. Rice warns that:

> Cleopatra VII of Egypt is one of the most famous, if not *the* most famous woman of classical antiquity. Her fortune, or perhaps, misfortune, was that the chaotic historical circumstances of the first century BC—namely a series of Roman civil wars combined with a fateful clash of an increasingly powerful Rome with the Hellenistic Empires of the Greek East—brought about her meeting with two of the most famous figures of Roman history, Julius Caesar and Marc Antony. While these encounters dramatically affected the history of the Mediterranean world, it is our own irresistible fascination with love affairs between larger-than-life historical figures that has ensured Cleopatra's undying fame, for better or for worse.[5]

The marked tendency of twentieth-century historians to break into Shakespearian tragic dialogue when describing the queen's death demonstrates the pervasiveness of one particular ancient fiction, from Plutarch in a direct line of descent through his translators Amyot and North, to Shakespeare and the first 1930s edition of *The Cambridge Ancient History*.[6] Similarly, when Michael Grant, at the outset of his own biography of the queen, invites his readers into the 'story of a woman who became utterly involved, in her public and

[4] Respectively, Grant (1972), p. xvii, and Tarn and Charlesworth (1934), 98. Cf. Weigall (1923), esp. 22; Pelling (1996), 4 and 41–6; Rice (1999), 3–6.

[5] Rice (1999), 1.

[6] Tarn and Charlesworth (1934), 111. Cf. Macurdy (1932), 216–8; Lindsay (1971), 475–6; Foss (1997), 187. No Shakespearian quotation appears in the second edition of the *CAH*, although Pelling (1996), 64, does note the magnificence with which Plutarch, and following him Shakespeare, tell the story of Antony's death.

private life alike, with two men', he borrows his narrative strategy (which allows Cleopatra only the power of sexual allure and absorbs her entirely into a history of Rome) from the ancient historian Cassius Dio who centres Cleopatra's reign around her captivation of two Roman men, Julius Caesar and Mark Antony, and her destruction by a third, Octavian (Dio 51.15.4).[7]

Even where scholars have lingered over Cleopatra in their narratives of Roman history, their narrative alignments are disclosed by such comments as 'she had a wonderful voice and the seductiveness which attracts men', or 'among the women who intervene in the masculine strife for political power, she will always occupy a special position, and ever and anon excite the imagination of mankind'.[8] The Decadent critic Arthur Symons provided the interpretative key to such descriptions when he claimed that 'before the thought of Cleopatra every man is an Antony'.[9] Twentieth-century historians of ancient Rome have structured the queen as erotic object both for the male author of the narrative and for the male reader which that narrative has presupposed.

Nor is the scholar who writes a separate biography of Cleopatra VII's reign in Egypt immune from such erotic fascination. In *The Life and Times of Cleopatra Queen of Egypt* (1914), Arthur Weigall—having just completed a nine-year term as Inspector General of Antiquities for the Egyptian government—constructed for the queen an ambition to restore the lost kingdoms of the Ptolemaic empire (and even to establish world power) through her exploitation of Rome's capacity to aggrandize its clients and allies. Nonetheless he declared that as an historian shapes his picture of Cleopatra 'he cannot fail to fall himself under the spell of that enchantment by which the face of the world was changed'.[10] At the other end of the twentieth century, fol-

[7] Grant (1972), p. xv, and reproduced in the Phoenix Press paperback edition published in 2000.

[8] Tarn and Charlesworth (1934), 35, and Volkmann (1958), 219.

[9] Quoted in Hughes-Hallett (1991), 16.

[10] Weigall (1923 edn.), p. 26. On Weigall's biographies of Egypt's rulers, see Montserrat (2000), 4 and 103–5.

lowing the strategies (and the admission) of Weigall, Michael Foss in *The Search for Cleopatra* (1997) constructs a woman who deploys her sexuality as an instrument of politically perceptive statescraft; yet he invites his readers to 'Imagine her in all the variety and grace and appeal of mature womanhood taken to its utmost possibility, with the mind and a body to captivate a caesar, a world-conqueror, an emperor.'[11] Similarly a recent biography by Laura Foreman, *Cleopatra's Palace: In Search of a Legend* (1999), openly warns against the Cleopatra of the ancient sources as a seductively dramatic but hollow fiction, and observes that already by the Renaissance 'generations of educated individuals across the continent had, like Caesar and Antony before them, fallen under Cleopatra's spell'.[12] Yet a foreword by Franck Goddio, the archaeologist investigating the now submerged royal quarters of ancient Alexandria, belies the biographer's caution. He attaches considerable romantic value to his underwater investigations:

> Above all it was the home of Cleopatra, history's most fascinating woman. It was in Alexandria that she met and mesmerized Julius Caesar, in its now-drowned streets that she, a conquerer of conquerors, caroused with Mark Antony. And it was here that she chose for herself death before dishonor.
>
> More than anything else, it was the drama of Cleopatra's life and loves that drew me to Alexandria and that finally spurred me on in 1992 to undertake the daunting task of locating, mapping, and exploring the remains of the sunken city. (p. 22)

Cleopatra VII appears to have seduced scholars as well as Romans.

The purpose of this chapter is, therefore, to sketch the discursive process whereby an Egyptian queen, the 'glory of her fathers', entered the poetry of the early Augustan period in the shape of a royal mistress charged with such extraordinary political and erotic potency that it has continued to invite its readers to take up the

[11] Foss (1997), 9. He immediately poses the question 'Did such a person exist, or was she only a figment of the imagination?', but answers that 'history suggests there was such a woman'.

[12] Foreman (1999), 161 and 27.

position of either a resistant Octavian or a seduced Antony. Such an examination of the process whereby Cleopatra VII entered Augustan culture to become the most famous of Roman mistresses (whose seductions even jeopardized Rome's dominance of the Mediterranean) addresses questions of poetry's apparent complicity in the social construction of gender, ethnicity, political legitimacy and empire, its part in the formation of a founding myth of Western culture that predicated Augustan rule on a contest between freedom and tyranny, west and east, male and female.

## EMPOWERING WOMEN

The traditional strategies for representing female power which had existed in Ptolemaic Egypt and the validating fictions created by Cleopatra herself both contrast markedly with the images we have inherited from the winning, western side. These validating strategies empower 'woman' not as a despotic enemy who imperils political systems from without, but as a beneficent ruler who protects them from within.

Viewed in the context of the social structures of post-Actian Rome, the queen Cleopatra VII may seem to be a striking anomaly.[13] In ancient Egypt, however, papyri, inscriptions, poetry and prose, temple sculpture, coins, and cult implements all attest to the public powers of the Ptolemaic queens.[14] For example, linked in her coinage with the Pharaonic past, associated with the Egyptian and Olympian deities Isis and Aphrodite, Arsinoe II Philadelphos (*c.* 316–270 BC) was the first Ptolemaic queen to be worshipped in her own lifetime as a goddess. Towns were named after her, temples erected, and festivals established in her honour.[15] In Hellenistic po-

[13] Pomeroy (1984), 24 and 26; Hamer (1993), 11–12.

[14] Pomeroy (1984), 28. See, in general, Pomeroy (1984), 13–40; Macurdy (1932), 102–235; Flamarion (1997), 14; Rowlandson (1998), 6 and 24.

[15] Theoc. *Idyll* 15.106–11. Fraser (1972), 236–40; Thompson (1973), 4; Pomeroy (1984), 28–39; Quaegebeur (1988), 41–5; Rowlandson (1998), 24–33.

etry, the queens often appear as patterns of wifeliness, virtuous in their capacities to maintain the dynastic line.[16] Theocritus *Idyll* 17, an encomium to the poet's patron Ptolemy II Philadelphus, includes praise of Ptolemy's mother Berenice I as outstanding among wise women, while further defining her as a profit to her parents, devout in her conjugal love, and loyal in her production of legitimate children. Gratitude is expressed by the poem's narrator to Aphrodite, who has deified the queen after her death and endowed her with a share of divine prerogatives: placed in Aphrodite's temple, Berenice I now undertakes the goddess's offices in her kindness towards all mortal lovers. Thus queen Berenice I is represented as possessed of positive and public erotic powers.[17] Similarly, Berenice II, addressed as *numpha* ('wife' or 'bride'), provides the narrative frame for the third and fourth books of Callimachus' *Aetia*, a text of fundamental importance to the Augustan poets. The paired books begin with a tribute to a display of Ptolemaic authority on Greek territories (the victory of Berenice's horses at the Nemean games), and close with a description of the queen's conjugal devotion (the tale of the lock of her hair which she vowed for her husband's safety).[18]

The eastern representations of Cleopatra VII clearly belong to this tradition for empowering royal women.[19] The queen is nowhere named in the Augustan narratives, yet her name belongs to a pattern of 'Ptolemies', 'Berenices' and 'Cleopatras' that by its repetitions signified the continuity of the Lagid dynasty.[20] A stele dedicated in 51 BC, the year in which Cleopatra inherited the throne with her brother Ptolemy XIII, represents the queen as a bare-chested and kilted Pharaoh who wears the Double Crown and makes offerings to

16 Richlin (1992*c*).

17 Theocritus *Idyll* 17.34–52, for which see Gow (1950), 332–5. Cf. Pomeroy (1984), 31; Rowlandson (1998), 6.

18 Parsons (1977). On the *Coma*, in particular, see Fraser (1972), i. 729–30, and, on the translation by Catullus, West (1985).

19 See, in general, Hamer (1993), 5–18.

20 Pomeroy (1984), 22; Grant (1972), 31; Bowman (1996), 23.

an enthroned Isis. The accompanying Greek text lists the queen's name and her titles. The combination of Egyptian iconography and Greek inscription signals that the queen who is entitled 'a glory to her father' (*Kleopatra*) and 'father-loving' (*philopator*) is legitimate heir to the authority and political power of both her own father, the Greek-descended Ptolemy XII Auletes, and all her ancestral 'fathers', the native Pharaonic kings.[21] Furthermore, the validating power of such names was clearly recognized by Cleopatra herself for, in 36 BC, she assumed a new title not used by her predecessors. As the queen who was respecting Pharaonic ritual, building temples in upper Egypt, and regaining parts of the lost Ptolemaic empire, she became Queen Cleopatra, the Goddess, the Younger, Father-Loving and Fatherland-loving (*philopatris*).[22] In her Ptolemaic context, Cleopatra was certainly a lover of Egypt, but no seducing *meretrix*.

In her titles and iconography Cleopatra VII, like the other queens before her, played the role of daughter to all the previous kings of Egypt. She also represented herself as mother on monuments and coins, for part of her validating strategies involved the presentation of her son Ptolemy XV Caesar (better known as Caesarion) as her legitimate heir and co-regent, fit to rule Egypt in the Pharaonic tradition.[23] The birth of Caesarion was celebrated in the words and images of a temple built for the purpose at Hermonthis in Upper Egypt, where Cleopatra's role as mother to her son was assimilated iconographically to the role of Isis as mother to Horus. On the south wall of a surviving temple at Dendera (also in Upper Egypt), a monumental Cleopatra still appears in relief behind Caesarion, both in the dress and posture of the Pharaohs, as they make offerings to the

[21] For an illustration and description of the stele see the Brooklyn Exhibition Catalogue, no. 78, pp. 188–9. Cf. Rowlandson (1998), 37–8.

[22] Maehler (1983), 8; Thompson (1994), 321, Rowlandson (1998), 39. For Cleopatra's participation in Pharaonic ritual see also Tarn (1936) on the stele from Bucheum; Volkmann (1958), 60; Thompson (1994), 321.

[23] Volkmann (1958), 74–7; Flamarion (1997), 50–1; Rice (1999), 46; Southern (1999), 48.

FIG. 6.1 Cleopatra's bronze coinage from Cyprus, dated *c.*47–30 BC.

divine mother/son pairs Hathor/Harsomtus and Isis/Horus.[24] Furthermore, as the only Ptolemaic queen to coin in her own right and not as the representative of a king,[25] there appears on Cleopatra's bronze coinage from Cyprus (dated *c.*47–30 BC) a type of the queen suckling her son and crowned with a stephane, in the manner of Aphrodite/Isis nursing the infant Eros/Horus (Fig. 6.1). The image of fertility as an instrument for the authorization of Cleopatra's power is reinforced by the appearance of a sceptre behind the nursing mother's shoulder on the obverse, and, on the reverse, the type of two cornucopiae—an ancient device of the Ptolemies, employed earlier on the coinage of Arsinoe II—accompanied by the legend KLEOPATRAS BASILISSES ('of Cleopatra the Queen').[26]

Preserving the Pharaonic tradition that closely associated temporal with spiritual authority, Cleopatra represented herself as both a regal and a divine mother. She was regularly identified with the Egyptian mother goddess Isis, in her permanent monumental display on temple walls, in the typology of her coinage, and, most explicitly,

[24] Grant (1972), 99–100; Quaegebeur (1988), 52; Hamer (1993), 14–16; Rowlandson (1998), 38.

[25] Tarn and Charlesworth (1934), 67; Macurdy (1932), 8; Lindsay (1971), 245; Grant (1972), 47–8; Rice (1999), 97; Southern (1999), 21 and 69.

[26] BMC Ptolemies, Cleopatra VII, p. 122, no. 2, and pl. 30.6; Burnett (1990), n. 3901; Davis and Kraay (1973), nos. 41, 42, and 46; Volkmann (1958), 76; Grant (1972), 85; Hamer (1993), 8.

in her title *nea Isis* ('new Isis'). The queen dressed her political and social powers in the eroticism of a divine mother nurturing her child. In Egypt, therefore, Cleopatra VII assumed positive, sacred powers as the loving mother of her dynasty and her country, whereas in Rome she would become a model of meretricious perversity who thereby challenged the good ordering of the western world.[27]

Exalted by her divinity, the last Ptolemaic queen may also have been reified as symbol of the conquering East. Among the miscellaneous materials to be found in the third book of the *Oracula Sibyllina* (a collection of which is thought to have been circulating in Rome by the mid-first century BC), are a number of oracles which seem to endorse the conquests of the Ptolemaic dynasty.[28] Two of those oracles personify the powers of the Ptolemaic east in the figure of a woman. At 3.350–80 it is a woman (a *despoina*) who will exact Asia's vengeance for Roman aggression (expressed intriguingly in the invective of sexual promiscuity as if to counterpoint Rome's self-representation in terms of moral probity). Shearing Rome's hair, she will enforce a marriage of enslavement and, with that punishment complete, usher in a Golden Age of peace for both Asia and Europe:

> O Rome, luxurious Rome of gold, you Latin child,
> Virgin drunken with lust in many beds you've run wild,
> but you'll be married without due rites, a slave-slut of despair,
> while still the Queen crops off your delicate head of hair
> and uttering judgements will hurl you to earth from the sky,
> then take up from the earth and set you again on high.[29]

At 3.75–92 it is a widow (a *cherê*) who will take over the rule of the world and then bring on its destruction. A case has been argued for identifying these two female embodiments of the conquering East

[27] See Thompson (1973), 58–9 and 122; Burnett (1990), n. 1245; Hamer (1993), 10–13, and 18; Rowlandson (1998), 39; Gurval (forthcoming).

[28] Parke (1988), 144. For the eastern provenance of these oracles see Parke (1988), 2 and 6; Collins (1987), 31–2; Lindsay (1971), 355–80.

[29] The translation is taken from Lindsay (1971), 356.

with Cleopatra herself, and placing their composition respectively in an optimistic period before Actium and in a period of her supporters' disillusionment after the defeat.[30] The prophecy of a glorious world kingdom and a golden age of peace for East and West certainly parallels the discourses of conquest centred around Alexander the Great on which Cleopatra herself had drawn when, for example, she named her son by Antony 'Alexander Helios'.[31] If the identification holds, these oracles assimilate monarch with country or continent in a manner permitted by a pre-existing language for representing the power of the Ptolemaic queens, and, as part of a discourse of resistance to the power of Rome, Cleopatra is transformed into a personification of a righteous and vengeful Asia.[32]

In the years after Actium, however, the Cleopatra who appears at Rome in the poetry of Horace, Virgil, and Propertius exhibits scarcely any of the above features. No name or title is used to identify her. She is once called 'the Egyptian wife' (*Aegyptia coniunx*), but more frequently is entitled only 'queen' (*regina*) or 'woman' (*femina*, *mulier*, *illa*). She is described neither as the daughter of kings nor as a mother of kings and, in the Roman narratives, her kingdom seems to consist only of the vanquished.

In Augustan poetry, Cleopatra does not live up to the name the poems deny her: she sheds no glory on her 'fathers'. The queen of Egypt is nameless in the Roman narratives precisely because she is notorious. She has become instead the one exceptional disgrace of a dynasty that claimed descent from the illustrious kings of Macedon when, in Propertius 3.11.40, she is described as *una Philippeo*

[30] See Collins (1983), 358–61, and (1987), 433–5, who follows Tarn (1932), 137–9. Pelling (1996), 50–1, however, notes sadly that the dating of these oracles is insecure.

[31] See Tarn (1932), 144–8; Volkmann (1958), 122; Grant (1972), 142–4; Collins (1983), 358; Pelling (1988), 256; Hamer (1993), 17–18; Bowman (1996), 34–5; Foss (1997), 185–6.

[32] On the assimilation of female ruler to nation, in a country that has a history of queens, see Warner (1987), 38–60, on Elizabeth I, Queen Victoria, and Margaret Thatcher.

*sanguine adusta nota* (the single reproach scorched on the blood of Philip).[33] In Horatian lyric, it is only when confronted by her prostrated kingdom that the queen desires to act more nobly (*generosius*, 1.37.21) and to die without being stripped of her royal status (*privata*, 1.37.31).[34] Moreover, it is not Cleopatra but Octavian who, in *Aeneid* 8.681, is borne into battle resplendent with the glory of the fatherland, the *patrium sidus*.[35] Deprived of name and titles, banished from the dynastic history of Macedonian and Ptolemaic rule, Cleopatra is effectively denied both her paternal ancestral powers and her claims to patriotism.

Just as the Cleopatra of Augustan poetry is denied a role as the fatherland's loving daughter, so she does not appear as good wife, nor as fertile mother. If she is called wife (*coniunx*, *Aen.* 8.688) or described as demanding a wife's reward (*coniugis pretium*, Prop. 3.11.31), the adjectives employed to qualify these terms (*Aegyptia* and *obsceni* respectively) signal clearly that for Antony this was no legitimate marriage. Since it was not possible for him to be married to both Octavia and Cleopatra simultaneously or for his foreign 'marriage' to have any legal standing at Rome, from the Roman perspective an *Aegyptia coniunx* is no real *coniunx* at all.[36] Nor can the Augustan Cleopatra be the wedded mother of legitimate offspring, for her claim to the political authority of Julius Caesar, through the alleged parentage of her son Caesarion, conflicts directly with Octavian's claim to be Caesar's rightful heir.[37]

Julius Caesar displayed Cleopatra in Rome neither as his unlawful wife nor as his *meretrix*, but as a divine mother-figure. During the same period as Cleopatra minted her divinely maternal Cyprian coin

[33] Fedeli (1985), 377–9; Gurval (1995), 196.

[34] Nisbet and Hubbard (1970), 417; West (1995), 189–91.

[35] I am indebted to Duncan Kennedy for this observation.

[36] See Reinhold (1988), 221 on Plutarch's comments; Lindsay (1971), 240; Rice (1999), 55; Southern (1999), 50 and 122.

[37] Dio 49.41.1; 50.1.3; 51.3.5. Zanker (1988), 34; Grant (1972), 87–8; Aly (1992), 50.

type, Julius Caesar had placed her gilded statue in the temple of Venus Genetrix at Rome—thus juxtapositioning the Egyptian queen with the mother and founder of the Julian clan. While the deified Berenice I may have supplied a specific Ptolemaic precedent for such shrine sharing, in republican Rome the ascription of such divine authority to a living woman was unprecedented. In Graeco-Egyptian ritual, sacred architecture, coinage, and literature, the Ptolemaic queens exercised the fertile erotic powers of an Aphrodite/Isis mother figure, but no Augustan poem reproduces Caesar's provocative gesture.[38] Instead the texts substitute such general devices for the delineation of Octavian's eastern enemy as drunkenness (Horace *Ode* 1.37.14, Prop. 3.11.56), and excess (particularized as the unmanly luxury of mosquito nets at Horace *Ep.* 9.15–16 and Prop. 3.11.45). Where Cleopatra's sexual behaviour is mentioned at all it is in the guise of 'the whore queen of incestuous Canopus' (*incesti meretrix regina Canopi*, Prop. 3.11.39); the kind of woman who wears herself out in intercourse with her own slaves (*famulos inter femina trita suos*, Prop. 3.11.30), and emasculates the men who are present at her court (*Ep.* 9.13–14, *Ode* 1.37.9–10).

Neither daughter, wife, nor mother, Cleopatra has scarcely any physical presence at all in the Horatian and Virgilian narratives. At best the queen is drunk with sweet success (*Ode* 1.37.11–12) or pale with fear of her coming death (*Aen.* 8.709). Only barking Anubis and the rattling sistrum which, in the *Aeneid*, accompany the queen into battle might suggest the dissonance of barbarian speech. In Propertian elegy, Cleopatra takes on a little more substance. At 4.6.22, the weapons of the losing side at Actium are clutched shamefully in the hand of a woman. In 3.11, more significantly, the dying Cleopatra possesses a tongue that once had spoken, hands that are now enchained, and a body steeped in poison (3.11.52–5). When, however, the elegiac narrator claims to have witnessed the physical

[38] App. *BC* 2.15.102, and Dio 51.22.1–3. On which, see Lindsay (1971), 67–8; Reinhold (1988), 158; Aly (1992), 52.

effects of venom on the queen's body (*spectaui*, 3.11.53), it becomes apparent that the author has put on display in poetry not Cleopatra's death at Alexandria in 30 BC, but its Roman simulacrum—the visual representation of the vanquished which will have been carried in the triple triumph at Rome in 29 BC.[39] Similarly, the Cleopatra of the *Aeneid* is not presented as a woman of flesh and blood, but as a woman of metals such as silver and gold, already a visual image on a shield now further delineated in the words of a poetic ekphrasis.[40] In both poetic contexts, Cleopatra's failing body is distanced as a work of art designed for the voyeuristic pleasure of her Roman spectators.

The Egyptian Cleopatra assumed positive powers through her identification with the goddess Isis. For the poetic Cleopatra of the Augustan narratives, however, assimilation to Isis brings with it connotations of disorder, dissonance, and barbarous animality. The Roman poems do not name Isis explicitly in association with Cleopatra but bring the goddess in indirectly through her cultic attributes.[41] Virgil's epic narrative of Actium and Propertius' elegy 3.11 both depict Cleopatra in possession of a sistrum (a musical instrument used regularly in the fertility rites of Isis and appearing frequently in visual depictions of the goddess to signal her powers), and supported by Anubis (the god who in the myth of Isis assisted her in restoring Osiris to life).[42] In the *Aeneid*, the sistrum is not an instrument of worship but a native Egyptian means for summoning up armies (*Aen.* 8.696), and Anubis, in the company of all the monstrous shapes of the Egyptian gods, barks his opposition to the pantheon of Rome (8.698). The hierarchical oppositions of which the sistrum and Anubis form a part are set out in Propertius 3.11: Cleopatra loses because she dared to oppose 'our' Jupiter with her barking Anubis

[39] See Plut. *Ant.* 86, and Dio 51.21.7–8. Cf. Fedeli (1985), 384, on Prop. 3.11.53–4.

[40] See e.g. West (1975) for the ekphrastic techniques of the Virgilian narrative, and Putnam (1998), 119–88.

[41] As Malaise (1972), 246–7; Witt (1971), 55.

[42] Toynbee (1934), 41; Witt (1971), 39 and 198.

(3.11.41) and the Roman trumpet with the *crepitanti sistro* (3.11.43).[43]

Thus the Cleopatra of the Augustan poets exhibits a certain anonymity. She holds the relationships neither of daughter, nor mother, nor legitimate wife, and possesses no individuating physical features. Remaining somewhat distanced and reified, she becomes an artful and artifical symbol of an entire nation. Within eastern discourses for the authorization of imperial power, 'woman' is reified as righteous and vengeful Asia. She becomes, however, the personification of effeminate and conquered Asia in the competing discourses of the west.

The sympotic, epic, and elegiac Cleopatras of Augustan poetry all constrain the queen within the limits of a sexualized role as vanquished opponent of the Roman state, which may suggest that these texts are operating as the authoritative voice of Augustus in matters Actian. Yet the persistence with which the Horatian, Virgilian, and Propertian Cleopatras are associated with abuse of political power, with drunkenness, immorality, bestiality, effeminacy, and a perverse sexual dominance, takes on a recognizably more long-standing and entrenched discursive shape. For the rhetorical patterns of Octavian's agitational propaganda that emerged in the 30s BC (and to which these poetic motifs have been traced) could not constitute mere inventions of the moment but, in order to prove persuasive with their intended addressees (the veteran colonies, the propertied classes of Italy's towns, the Roman senate), they had to draw on pre-existing structures of thinking they then mirrored and exploited.[44]

The poetic fictions of a queen who is surrounded by the paraphernalia of an eastern despot are clearly grounded in a discursive tradition whose history transcends the immediate control of individual Augustan poets, their individual poetic utterances, and the specific political agendas of their patrons. The features of these fictive

[43] Hardie (1986), 98; Putnam (1998), 145.

[44] Pelling (1996), 41–6, and Feeney (1992), 3.

Cleopatras are clearly articulated with the overlapping structures of ancient gender and orientalism—'the complex system of signifiers denoting the ethically, psychologically and politically "other" by which the West has sought to dominate and have authority over the East'.[45] So, before literary critics attempt to discriminate between individual poetic fictions according to such categories as period of production, patronal relations, genre, context, or narrative voice, it is essential to elucidate the broad conceptual patterns which underlie the writing of Cleopatra into Augustan Rome as a *meretrix regina*.[46]

Edith Hall placed the invention of the oriental 'barbarian' in the specific historical circumstances of the fifth century BC and demonstrated the ways in which tragic drama provided cultural authorization for the perpetuation of the stereotype.[47] In Aeschylus' *Suppliants*, the sons of Aegyptus (the prototypes of the Egyptian people) are unfavourably contrasted with their philhellenic relatives the Danaids as violent, arrogant, gluttonous, and treacherous barbarians, and Egyptians are in general ridiculed as crocodiles, beer-drinkers, and papyrus-eaters.[48] The Athenian polarization between Greece and its other then became the model for subsequent constructions of Roman identity through definition of the other, or reverse self.[49] Despite its traditional depiction as the cradle of wisdom, its association with a miraculous fertility, and its gradual entry from the second century BC into Rome's sphere of political influence, Egypt nevertheless held an important place in Rome's dis-

[45] Hall (1989), 2 and 99, following Said (1985), 3. For Cleopatra's deployment in the modern orientalist discourses of colonialism, see Hughes-Hallett (1991), Flamarion (1997), 140–8, and Ch. 7 below.

[46] For the priority of conceptual systems over individual iterary expressions see Goldhill (1986), 111–13, on anthropologically based readings of Greek tragedy, and Wyke (1989) on Paul Veyne's readings of Latin love elegy. Cf. Said (1985), 13 on modern orientalist literatures.

[47] Hall (1989), 1 and 103.

[48] Smelik and Hemelrijk (1984), 1870–2.

[49] Hannestad (1988), 54; Marshall (1998), 49.

courses of orientalism.[50] The visit of Scipio Aemilianus to Egypt about 140 BC was later pictured by the Graeco-Sicilian historian Diodorus Siculus as a confrontation between the Roman general's practicality and strength and the Ptolemaic king's effeminacy and luxurious incompetence;[51] while the first documented rhetorical assault on Egypt by a Roman occurs in a defence speech Cicero delivered in 54 BC, where he attempted to undermine the testimony of Egyptian witnesses by described Alexandria as the home of all tricks (*praestigiae*) and deceits (*fallaciae*).[52]

Egypt's place in Rome's discourses of orientalism was reinforced by the subsequent civil conflicts in Alexandria and the murder of Pompey. Recording the background to his involvement in the Alexandrian wars of 48–47 BC over Cleopatra's claims to the Ptolemaic throne, Julius Caesar presaged the tactics of Octavian's propaganda campaign against Antony when he noted disparagingly that the Egyptian general's armies included Roman soldiers 'who had by now become habituated to the licentiousness of Alexandrian life (*Alexandrinae vitae ac licentiae*) and had forgotten the good name and orderly conduct of the Roman people (*nomen disciplinamque populi Romani*) and had taken wives by whom most of them had children', *Civil Wars* 3.110.2.[53] After the battle of Actium and the conquest of Egypt in 30 BC, the unique policy of isolating Egypt which Augustus pursued further fostered the pre-existing pattern. Government of Egypt was allocated to a prefect of equestrian (rather than senatorial) rank who was directly appointed by and answerable to the *princeps* (rather than the state). While members of the Roman elite were not allowed to

[50] See, in general, Balsdon (1979), 68–9; Malaise (1972), 244–51; Smelik and Hemelrijk (1984); Reinhold (1988), 227–8; Takács (1995), 33–4; David (2000), 51–8.

[51] Diod. Sic. 33.28b.1–3. On which, see Gruen (1984), 714–15; Lampela (1998), 21–2.

[52] Cic. *Pro Rab. Post.* 35, on which see Smelik and Hemelrijk (1984), 1921–2.

[53] Monaco (1992), 262.

visit Egypt without the permission of Augustus, Egyptians were not allowed to serve in the Roman army or enter the senate. Such official prohibitions marked the country as both a unique and a distant realm, and one which was now under the authority of the *princeps* (although, officially, he had added it to the empire of the people of Rome).[54] It is that particular historical context which lends a strong political resonance to the poetic construction of Cleopatra as Egyptian: she is the Egyptian wife (*Aen.* 8.688), the whore queen of Canopus (Prop. 3.11.39), nourished by the waters of the Nile (*Aen.* 8.711–3), drunk on the wine of Mareotis (*Ode* 1.37.14).

The ideological resonance of the poetic Cleopatra's identification with Isis also must be understood in a larger historical context—that of Roman religious practice and prohibition. Although the worship of Isis constituted the most popular cult that spread to Rome from Egypt, in the early principate its Italian adherents practised beliefs that were neither centred on the Augustan state nor controlled by it.[55] Three times already between 58 and 48 BC, the altar of Isis on the Capitol had been destroyed on the orders of the senate in order to affirm that only it had the right to confer official religious status. Cleopatra's presence in Rome before the assassination of Caesar may have given the cult higher visibility and encouraged the triumvirs to vote it a temple in 43 BC. But the official gesture towards the deified Caesar and his Egyptian consort was an empty one, the temple never erected. Three years after Actium, to further an atmosphere of religious renewal, Octavian himself debarred the practice of the Isis cult from within the boundaries of the *pomerium*, and, in 21 BC, from within the first milestone of the city. Isis never gained a place in the official calendar of the Augustan state religion.[56] It is in this historical

[54] Smelik and Hemelrijk (1984), 1922–4; Reinhold (1988), 227–8; Hamer (1993), 23; Bowman (1996), 37–8; Flamarion (1997), 110–11; Rowlandson (1998), 10–11; Southern (1999), 36 and 145.

[55] Toynbee (1934), 40; Malaise (1972), 159–70.

[56] Malaise (1972), 365–89; Zanker (1988), 109; Ciceroni (1992); Takács (1995), 75–80; Beard, North, and Price (1998), esp. 230–1 and 250.

context that the sistrum and Anubis become transformed by Augustan representations of Cleopatra into markers of incongruity, of exotic 'otherness', of animality and, especially, of eastern discordance. Within the logic of Roman orientalism, the alien and the bestial Anubis of Propertius 3.11 must be defeated by the familiar anthropomorphic divinity Jupiter, the bark and the rattle must be drowned out by the clear sounds of Rome's trumpet.[57]

In the narrative patterns of fifth-century tragic drama the barbarian is shaped as an inversion of Athenian civic ideals and is associated, therefore, with tyranny and female power.[58] Societies that marginalize women in the political arena locate female rulers outside their own political stuctures in an alien social order, as a means of highlighting that order's perceived peculiarity and their own 'normality'.[59] In Athenian drama, women are ascribed political authority in proportion to the perceived barbarity of the community to which they belong and Athens is being opposed.[60] In the ethnographic tradition as well as in drama, gender roles are reversed in the world of the other: Egyptian customs and laws, according to the account of Herodotus, were 'for the most part the converse of those of all other men' and required, for example, that women go out to trade, while the men remain at home weaving.[61] Similarly, Diodorus Siculus (who lived in Egypt between 60 and 56 BC and wrote his universal history at Rome in the period of the second triumvirate) imputed to the worship of Isis Egypt's now notorious gender reversals: 'This, they say, is the reason that it was handed down that the queen should receive greater power and respect than the king and that, among

[57] Roman abhorrence for the Egyptian theriomorphic gods is detailed in Smelik and Hemelrijk (1984), 1854–5. Cf. Malaise (1972), 211 and 246–8.

[58] Hall (1989), 1 and 50. See also Hartog (1988), 212–14, for the schema of inversion in the historiographic tradition.

[59] Macdonald (1987), 8; Hall (1989), 201.

[60] Hall (1989), 95.

[61] Herod. 2.35. On which, see Hartog (1988), 213; Hall (1989), 202 and 208; Smelik and Hemelrijk (1984), 1873–80; Rowlandson (1998), 3.

private individuals, the woman should be master of the man, and in the dowry-contracts husbands should agree to obey the wife in all matters.'[62]

Tyranny and aberrant female power are likewise the two principal features which give shape to the Egyptian queen of Augustan poetry. In the political writings of the late republic, the championship of *libertas* against the threat of *seruitus* or *regnum* became the validating slogan for insurrection. After Actium, *libertas* was appropriated (and redefined as a form of *securitas*) to validate the incipient autocracy, so that Augustus commenced his *Res Gestae* with a claim to have liberated the republic.[63] Confronting long-standing constructions of oriental tyranny with the republican slogan of liberty, the poetic narratives of Actium construct an anomalous and eroticized female despotism by which the *libertas* of the Roman male is dangerously imperilled. If, in *Epode* 9, the Antonian soldier is in bondage to a woman (*emancipatus feminae*, 9.12) and in service to wrinkled eunuchs, Octavian is thereby rendered the champion of male liberty in the Actian sea-battle, seeking to free the Antonian slave from a woman's chains.[64] In Virgilian epic, Augustus sails into that battle made radiant by the star of his fathers—both the deified Julius Caesar and the fatherland (*patrium sidus*, *Aen.* 8.681). He is also escorted by the fathers (*patribus*, *Aen.* 8.679) and the people of all Italy and partnered by his trusted general Agrippa. Whereas, instead of the Roman fathers and a named general, Antony brings the assorted hordes of the orient and a nameless Egyptian 'wife' (*Aen.* 8.685–688).[65] In Propertian elegy, after the battle is won, sea nymphs clap the freed standards (*libera signa*, 4.6.62) of the fatherland (*patriae*, 4.6.24) which had been

[62] Diod. Sic. 1.27.1–2; the translation is taken from Rowlandson (1998), 11. On the passage, see Smelik and Hemelrijk (1984), 1895–8.

[63] Wirszubski (1960), esp. 87–91 and 100–6; Earl (1967), 59–60 and 64; Reinhold (1988), 108; Kennedy (1992), 31; Galinsky (1996), 54–7.

[64] Otis (1968), 59; Pelling (1996), 42; Gurval (1995), 147–50.

[65] Smelik and Hemelrijk (1984), 1853–5; Quint (1989), 6–7 and 9; Hardie (1986), 98; Putnam (1998), 142; Keith (2000), 76.

forced shamefully to confront a woman's javelins (*pilaque femineae turpiter apta manu*, 4.6.22), and Rome, thanks to its saviour Augustus, becomes a city no longer terrified by woman's warfare (*femineo Marte*, 3.11.58).[66] By demanding a sympotic celebration of the death of Cleopatra and a dance beaten out with a freed foot (*pede libero*, *Ode* 1.37.1), the Horatian ode points a parallel with the Alcaic celebration of the death in battle of the hated tyrant Myrsilus.[67] This time, however, death has come to a female tyrant, a *regina*, whose court once consisted of diseased men.

This persistent equation of the relation of West to East with that of male to female provides, within the logic of ancient orientalism and gender, the necessary authority for domination and conquest.[68] The womanish Easterners enthralled by their Egyptian queen need imposed upon them the masculine order of the West, embodied in the figure of Octavian/Augustus.[69] A sense of urgency then attends the whole process for, following the orientalist pattern that calls for the West's control of the East in order to stop the East's designs on the West,[70] the Capitol is depicted as compelled to conquer Cleopatra in order to prevent Cleopatra's plans for subjecting it (*Ode* 1.37.5–12, Prop. 3.11.39–46).

In the Augustan narratives, Cleopatra is a nameless, scarcely individuated *meretrix regina*, a dangerous anomaly who represents the 'otherness' of the East and whose characteristics thereby lend poetic authority to the supremacy of the West. Positive images of the political power of women were not, however, entirely alien to the Roman state. Precisely in this same period, a representational language was being developed for some specific women as good servants of Rome's political interests, despite a republican historiographic tradition that had deployed women in possession of political power as

[66] Mader (1989), 190–7.

[67] Otis (1968), 54–5; Nisbet and Hubbard (1970), 411; West (1995), 182–3; Lowrie (1997), 145–6; Oliensis (1998), 143; Gurval (forthcoming).

[68] Cf. Said (1985), 206 and 309 on the discourses of modern orientalism.

[69] Quint (1989), 8–9 and 21.

[70] See Hall (1989), 195–7.

signifiers of moral decline and the breakdown of social order. Whether, for example, the participation of Sallust's Sempronia in the Catilinarian conspiracy of 63 BC is an historiographic fiction or the documentation of an elite woman's genuine political interests, her characterization in *Bellum Catilinae* 25 underscores the dubious character of the conspiracy and demonstrates by counterpart its leader's lack of *virtus*. Sempronia's departure from the matronly norm expected of a consul's wife into the domain of political intrigue is categorized in terms of financial extravagance, an aggressive sexuality (her desires were so ardent that she sought men more often than she was sought by them), and transgressions of gender; Sempronia was, in sum, a woman *quae multa saepe uirilis audaciae facinora conmiserat* (who had often committed many crimes of masculine daring, 25.1).[71] In the early principate, even members of the imperial family such as Augustus' wife Livia and his daughter Julia, who were shaped by the state machinery as paragons of the wifely virtues, could attract the charge of excessive political authority (especially in the matter of control over the dynastic succession) and with it the invective pattern of promiscuity and poisoning.[72]

Nonetheless, in the 30s BC, a language was being created to endorse the role of specific women in Roman political activity. Already, shortly after the marriage of Antony and Octavian's sister in 39 BC, silver cistophori and gold aurei were minted in the East to commemorate the treaty of Brundisium that the marriage had been designed to seal. Innovatively Antony's coinage celebrates Octavia's role in forging a political alliance by displaying her head on the

[71] See Paul (1985); Boyd (1987); Bauman (1992), 67–8; Hemelrijk (1999), 84–6 and 90; Ch. 1 above. For the collocation of social and political disorder with transgressions of gender roles in the cultural discourses of Augustan Rome, see also Wallace-Hadrill (1985); Edwards (1993); Bauman (1992), esp. 10–11.

[72] See Purcell (1986); Richlin (1992c); Bauman (1992), 99–129; Bartman (1999), 35–40; Hemelrijk (1999), 80–1; Wood (1999), 38–9 and 75–141. Cf. Ch. 9 below, on historiographic accounts of the political intrigues and sexual excesses of the empress Messalina.

reverse, his on the obverse.[73] It is also clear that, in the years immediately preceding Actium, still more audacious attempts were made by Antony to incorporate Cleopatra within Roman political structures and, particularly, to exploit her authority in the East within Roman systems for designating and sustaining power.

Two sets of coin types disclose the distinct techniques employed by Cleopatra and Antony to integrate each other into their respective political and iconographic systems. One series of bronze coins from Chalcis, dated around 31 BC, has Cleopatra for its mint authority. A portrait head of the queen appears on the obverse accompanied by her name and title BASILISSES, on the reverse appears a type of Antony, who is evidently the subordinate figure of the pair since it is Cleopatra's regnal year 21 which is inscribed first around Antony's portrait head, instead of year six of a new dating system designed to declare their joint sovereignty over the East and Rome.[74] Another series, this time of silver denarii, dated around 32 BC, has Antony for its mint authority (Fig. 6.2). A head of Antony appears on the obverse with an Armenian tiara behind him and the legend ANTONI ARMENIA DEVICTA (of Antony, Armenia conquered). The coinage is linked iconographically to the republican tradition for signalling Roman victories over Eastern despotism. On the reverse, however, there appears a portrait of Cleopatra redesigned to look like her Roman patron's, yet crowned with a diadem and accompanied by the legend CLEOPATRAE REGINAE REGUM FILIORUM REGUM (of Cleopatra, Queen of Kings and of her Sons who are Kings). A ship's prow lies in the foreground. While Cleopatra's coinage attempts to endorse Antony's role in the East by assimilating it to the Ptolemaic dynastic system, Antony's coinage attempts, remarkably and paradoxically, to incorporate Cleopatra's royal powers and dynastic ambitions within

[73] Carson and Sutherland (1956), 151–2; Kleiner (1992*a*), 361–3; Bartman (1999), 59 and 213–14; Wood (1999), 41–51.

[74] Brett (1937), 460–61. BMC *Phoenicia*, 54 no. 15 and pl. 7.10, identifies the origin of the coinage as Berytus, but see Burnett (1990), n. 4771.

FIG. 6.2 Silver denarius of Antony, dated *c.*32 BC.

Roman republican strategies for designating a general's triumph: a client queen's Egyptian ships have brought aid to another Roman victory over oriental tyranny (for which she and her sons have been rewarded with additional territories by the triumvir).[75]

It was apparently to counter such extraordinary moves as these (and motivated most immediately by Antony's rejection of Octavia when she visited him in Greece to supply troops) that from 35 BC there began to accrue to Octavian's sister and to his wife extraordinary and innovative honours which served to elevate them both above other Roman *matronae*, and to distinguish them from Antony's Egyptian *meretrix*. They were provided with freedom from *tutela*, tribunician sacrosanctity, and public statuary—the latter connected in the past almost exclusively with male service to the state. If, as has been conjectured, the statues of Octavia and Livia were placed on public display in the temple of Venus Genetrix near that of Cleopatra, they would have provided viewers with an opportunity to make tangible and unfavourable comparison between the gilded whore of Antony's Egypt and the loyal wives of Octavian's Rome.[76] During the

[75] BMCR 2, no. 180. See Volkmann (1958), 148; Kent (1978), 275; Smith (1988*b*), 132–4 and pl. 75.21–4; Smith (1991), 209; Lindsay (1971), 59–60; Kleiner (1992*a*), 364–5; Hamer (1993), 8–10; Pelling (1996), 41; Wood (1999), 46; Southern (1999), 113–16; Rice (1999), 56–7 and 98.

[76] Volkmann (1958), 138; Purcell (1986), 85; Bauman (1992), 91–8; Flory (1993); Bartman (1999), 62–7; Wood (1999), 27–35.

course of the principate, Livia was to become assimilated to personifications of *iustitia* and *pax* on Augustan coinage and the *Ara Pacis* reliefs of 9 BC, and marked out as an emblem of chastity and marital harmony, fertility, and prosperity. By the final years of the regime, Livia would even be appealed to in poetry as the *Romana princeps*, a guide to the appropriate public virtues for women. The most important woman in the Augustan state thus became identified gradually as a model of chaste womanhood, the first wife and mother, and a benefactor of family life, in a manner that (somewhat ironically) closely resembles Ptolemaic strategies for validating female rule.[77]

Any attempt to accommodate Cleopatra within Roman systems for political validation and to justify her public powers in these new Roman terms would, however, have been fraught with difficulty, because her state functions extended far beyond the limits that were being laid down carefully even for Livia (as benefactor, mediator, and mother of the people). While Livia was only ever associated with victory and carefully distanced from acts of war or their triumphal aftermath,[78] the Ptolemaic queen exercised authority in the military sphere.

Within Roman discursive systems, a militant woman was traditionally and persistently a transgressive figure, a non-woman or a pseudo-man, who overturned all established codes of social behaviour. The patterns of invective which could be brought to bear on a specific woman operating in the military domain can be seen at play in the abuse heaped on Antony's previous wife, Fulvia, when in 40 BC she summoned reinforcements for his brother besieged in Perusia. Sling-bullets employed during the siege of Perusia, the *glandes Perusinae*, are inscribed with insults against both sides, but include threats of sexual assault against Fulvia such as *Fuluiae landicam peto* (I aim at Fulvia's cunt). An epigram of Martial (11.20), which claims to quote

[77] Purcell (1986); Bauman (1992), 124–9; Bartman (1999), esp. 72–101; Wood (1999), 75–141.

[78] Bartman (1999), 84–6.

a poem composed by Octavian himself at the time of the battle, follows a similar pattern, denigrating Fulvia's military activities through her supposedly parallel sexual initiatives. Fulvia, portrayed as jealous of her husband's philandering with Cleopatra, demands of Octavian *aut futue, aut pugnemus* (fuck me or let's fight). The battle of Perusia then takes place only to ensure the continued health of Octavian's *mentula*.[79] In subsequent historiographic texts, Fulvia's participation in warfare is bound up closely with fictions of the 'non-woman'. According to Velleius Paterculus, the only part of the militant Fulvia that was female was her anatomy: *nihil muliebre praeter corpus* (2.74.2). Plutarch's Fulvia not only lacks due feminine interest in spinning and housekeeping, but plays the man in wishing to rule the ruler and command the commander: *archontos archein, strategountos strategein* (10.3). The potential for this form of invective to be transferred wholesale to the figure of Cleopatra is fully realized in Plutarch's biography of Antony, where his wife passes on to his whore a man already thoroughly trained in the habits of *gynaikokratia* (feminine rule).[80]

The Horatian, Virgilian, and Propertian Cleopatras can seem to operate within precisely such invective patterns as these. Their Egyptian queen transgresses all the social and political constraints which Roman society imposed (ideally) upon its women. Operating outside cultural structures construed as 'natural', she is a fatal monstrosity (*fatale monstrum*, *Ode* 1.37.21), both deadly and doomed.[81] Nameless, in possession of no individuating physical features, represented largely in terms of political, religious, ethnic, and gender difference, the Cleopatras of Augustan poetry can be read as part of a narrative of Actium and Alexandria which turns Roman civil war

[79] Hallett (1977), 154–5 and 160–3; Lindsay (1971), 171–6; Welch (1995), 193–4; Galinsky (1996), 372; Pelling (1996), 16.

[80] Volkmann (1958), 96; Bauman (1992), 83–9; Hemelrijk (1999), 90–1; Bartman (1999), 58–9.

[81] Pomeroy (1984), 26–7.

into an heroic Caesar's fight against tyranny, female dominance, and the perils of the orient. The poetic reification of Cleopatra renders her a suitable second term in the binary oppositions between West and East, male and female, which these texts appear to articulate.[82]

## AUGUSTAN VICTORY

There are aspects of the Augustan poems, however, which do not seem to be straightforwardly critical of Cleopatra nor unambiguously supportive of Octavian. Many critics have hesitated over the double poetic similes which lead into the second half of the Horatian ode on Cleopatra's defeat (1.37.17–20), where the hawk and the soft doves, the hunter and the hare, illustrate Octavian's pursuit of Cleopatra across the sea from Actium back to Egypt. Some have read the next stanza's *fatale monstrum / quae* (1.37.21) as a pivotal phrase that now turns the reader's point of view and sympathies away from the cruel Roman hunter and toward his defenceless quarry, restoring to the 'fateful marvel' humanity, gender, nobility, and courageous agency.[83] As noted at the opening of this chapter, Jasper Griffin has argued that the first-person, authorial voice of the Propertian elegy 3.11 effectively pushes the love poet into the role of an Antony who willingly accepts submission to his dominating beloved. For the poem employs Cleopatra as an example of the kind of woman who can hold men like the narrator voluntarily enchained.[84]

[82] See Quint (1989), 3–4, on the Roman texts. The Greek conceptual system of hierarchical oppositions based on male/female is discussed by DuBois (1982). Maclean (1980) surveys its impact on the Renaissance structuring of femininity. See also Said (1985), 7, on orientalism; Greene and Kahn (1985), 3–4, on gender; Yeğenoğlu (1998) on the importance of their intersection.

[83] As e.g. Commager (1958); Johnson (1967); Otis (1968), 51; Mader (1989), 184–8; DeForest (1989); Monaco (1992), 263; Hendry (1993), 143–7; West (1995), 187–91; Oliensis (1998), 139–45; Gurval (forthcoming). Cf., more cautiously, Lowrie (1997), 150–64.

[84] Griffin (1985), 32–47. Cf. discussions of the political ambivalence of Prop. 3.11 in Mader (1989), 188–200, and Gurval (1995), 189–207.

More tentatively, Page duBois has explored the implications of the ekphrastic narration of Roman history in the *Aeneid*—a verbal description of visual images on a shield—and observes that the poetic convention allows the epic hero (who gazes on the shield) to mediate the audience's relationship to narrated history, and places in the foreground the hero's act of incomprehension; while Robert Gurval has argued that, despite its exaltation of Actium as a cosmic struggle for order over chaos, *Aeneid* 8 locates the frightful gods Mars, Dirae, Discordia, and Bellona (War, Furies, Discord, and Battle) neither on one side nor the other, but at the centre of the struggle.[85] Propertius 4.6 has been read as a witty parody of the triumphal celebration of Actium, or at least as a depiction of a winnerless victory since it entails merely the defeat of a woman.[86] Even Horace's *Epode* 9, which has generally been read as an unequivocal and immediate celebration of Antony's flight from Actium, has been closely scrutinized by Gurval for potential political ambivalence: introduced as a *mixtum carmen* (a poem of shifting tones, 9.5), it opens optimistically but ends with the enemy not yet captured, the narrator fearful for the renewal of civil war.[87]

In seeking to put these apparent poetic ambiguities or ambivalences into an historical context, it is important to note that surviving depictions of Cleopatra occur at Rome only in the *poetry* composed around and after Actium. Yet, in the aftermath of Actium, the Augustan poetry which began to create its own fictions of Cleopatra was only one of many sites that displayed and explored the new powers and political authority vested in the *princeps*. After Octavian's victories at Actium and Alexandria, his ascendancy was also articulated through civic ceremonies and religious rituals, through the changing topography of the city of Rome, through new monuments, coin types, inscriptions, and testimonials that proclaimed

[85] DuBois (1982); Gurval (1995), 209–47; Putnam (1998), 119–88.
[86] Johnson (1973); Gurval (1995), 249–78.
[87] Gurval (1995), 137–59.

Augustus himself as their author.[88] Yet, where we might expect to find attempts to produce wholly unambiguous images of Octavian's victory, in these state rituals, monuments, coins, or inscriptions, Cleopatra scarcely figures at all.

Augustan poetry and, therefore, its fictive Cleopatras should not be read in isolation from the whole system of discourses within which validation of Augustan autocracy was played out. Firstly, the Augustan state itself continually recognized the word and, specifically, the poem as a tool for sustaining political power. According to the evidence of the later historians and biographers such as Suetonius, from the death of Julius Caesar in 44 BC to the suicide of Antony in 30 BC, graffiti, lampoons, letters, speeches, pamphlets, and edicts were all employed as instruments in the pursuit of political power.[89] After the initial deployment of invective to undermine the credibility of Antony, and after the declaration of war against Cleopatra in October 32 BC for which legitimacy was sought through the re-enactment of an ancient (perhaps even fabricated) fetial ritual,[90] the post-Actian period witnessed numerous instances of the spoken word and the displayed text employed to buttress the new regime. Most pervasively, the personal name 'Augustus', once voted by the senate and people in 27 BC, lent to the *princeps* a sacred aura of venerability on every repetition as one divinely bestowed with the power to foster growth.[91] Official narratives, stamped with the authority of an Augustus who speaks for himself in the first person, were prepared and publicized throughout the relevant period: an autobiography was composed to deny any usurpation of power, and this was

[88] Brunt and Moore (1967); Yavetz (1984); Millar and Segal (1984); Zanker (1988), 79–339; Reinhold (1988); Gurval (1995); Galinsky (1996); Habinek and Schiesaro (1997).

[89] See esp. Scott (1929) and (1933); Charlesworth (1933); Zanker (1988), 33–77; Pelling (1996).

[90] See Reinhold (1981–2); Reinhold (1988), 94; Volkmann (1958), 170; Pelling (1996), 54.

[91] Millar (1984), 37; Galinsky (1996), 315–18.

followed by the monumental *Res Gestae*. Itself both word and image, the *Res Gestae* were engraved on two bronze columns and displayed in front of Augustus' Mausoleum as a permanent epigraphic key for understanding the other visual displays of Augustan achievement by which it was surrounded.[92]

Testimony to a belief in the persuasive powers of oracular poetry is to be found both in the new location provided for the Sibylline books and in the constraints attached to their consultation. Recopied in 18 BC, and transferred by Augustus six years later to two gilded bookcases deposited in the base of Apollo's cult statue in the new Palatine temple, the *libri Sibyllini* were brought physically adjacent to the residence of Augustus and effectively under his jurisdiction. Consulted only by decree of the senate, the political importance of these texts was both manifest and unparalleled.[93] Yet the establishment of a library adjoining the Palatine temple, to house works in both Greek and Latin (and in later years to hold meetings of the senate), demonstrates that a much broader range of literature was also subjected to Augustus' public ratification and formed part of a strategy for his own cultural accreditation.[94] Furthermore, any sharp distinctions in Augustan culture between the propagandist possibilities of monument, religious ritual, and poetic production would have been blurred at least temporarily when, in 17 BC, a Horatian choral ode (the *Carmen Saeculare*) was performed first before Apollo's temple on the Palatine and then before Jupiter's on the Capitoline as the culminating point of the three-day celebration of the Secular Games, of which Augustus, along with Agrippa, was the chief officiant. An oracle calculating the length of a *saeculum*, cataloguing the order of the ceremonies, and specifying the performance of a choral hymn had conveniently been found in the recopied Sibylline books.[95]

92 Elsner (1996). Cf. Yavetz (1984).

93 Parke (1988), 141; Collins (1983), 319–20; White (1993), 124; Galinsky (1996), 102 and 216.

94 Galinsky (1996), 218; Yavetz (1984), 32 n. 131.

95 See Fraenkel (1957), 364–82; Zanker (1988), 167–72; White (1993), 123–7; Galinsky (1996), 100–6; Feeney (1998), 28–38.

Secondly, while the Augustan state can recognize the political strength of poetry alongside that of rituals and monuments, Augustan poetry often ascribes to itself a parity with those same rituals and monuments, or even offers itself as a challenge to their presumed superiority.[96] A passage of Virgil's *Georgics*, most likely written around the time of the triple triumph of 29 BC and the dedication of the Palatine temple to Apollo in 28 BC, deploys metaphors of a triumph and a temple to characterize an envisaged epic narrative as a Caesarian temple of poetry and its poet as a triumphator, parading a hundred chariots before it in victory games (3.10–36). In the metaphoric idioms of the Horatian and Propertian texts, lyrics are a loftier monument than pyramids (*Odes* 3.30.1–5), and elegiacs are more lasting (Prop. 3.2.17–26).[97] The Augustan poems categorize themselves as social acts rather than personal artforms when they address directly Maecenas, Augustus, or the Roman populace at large. They also characterize their poets as priests or prophets of public ceremonial, rather than as private artists, when they use the title *uates*.[98]

The poetic narratives of Cleopatra's defeat themselves dissolve distinctions between ritual, monument, and poem. The Horatian Cleopatras of *Epode* 9 and *Ode* 1.37 appear in the context of a call for the ritual, sympotic celebration of victory. The Propertian elegy 3.11 offers its own verbal simulacrum of Cleopatra at the same time as it makes its poet witness to the ritual display of her visual simulacrum in the triumphal procession of 29 BC. As part of an ekphrasis on the shield of Aeneas, the Cleopatra of Virgilian epic takes on material shape and monumental proportions. Similarly, the subsequent and dependent elegiac Cleopatra of Propertius 4.6 appears within a poetic aetiology of an Augustan monument (the ubiquitous temple of Apollo on the Palatine) and within a narrative which describes itself simultaneously as poetic performance and act of ritual worship.

[96] See Fowler (2000), 193–217.

[97] Vance (1973), 112; White (1993), 175–7; Galinsky (1996), 240, 275, and 350–1; Kraggerud (1998), 1–20; Habinek (1998), 110–14.

[98] Santirocco (1986), 22.

Thus, at the precise points where the Ptolemaic queen enters Augustan poetry as the *meretrix regina*, those narratives relate the poetic to both ritual and monumental celebrations of Roman victory.

Augustan poetry thus *demands* comparison with other contemporary discursive mechanisms for the propagation of an image of the principate. Ever since Ronald Syme claimed, in *The Roman Revolution* (1939), that the Augustan poets were merely fulfilling a requirement to design formulas by which the Roman elite could accept the new regime, the relationship between poetry and the *princeps* in the post-Actium period has been much debated.[99] Many critics have observed that, on Syme's model, literature and art concede second place to politics: Augustan culture can only be responsive, for (or, more infrequently, against) Augustus. In *The Roman Cultural Revolution* (1997), Thomas Habinek and Alessandro Schiesaro have called for a more holistic approach to Augustan cultural production—as Augustan poetry itself demands—in which culture ceases to be construed as a purely aesthetic activity independent from, and subordinate to, politics. Augustan culture is instead a process, and a set of intersecting practices and discourses: verbal and visual, closer to or more distant from the orbit of the *princeps*. On this definition, Augustan poetry does not merely reproduce the propaganda of Augustus, but refracts, interrogates, or even enables the social, political, and economic changes that were taking place under the new regime. In order better to analyse whether the Cleopatras of Augustan poetry are refractions, interrogations, subversions, or creations of the new cultural order, it is therefore necessary to compare them to other mechanisms for representing the victor and the vanquished in the post-Actium period, mechanisms to which they allude and respond.

Outside the narratives of the Augustan poets, most of our evidence for ancient constructions of Cleopatra as vanquished enemy of

[99] A representative sample would include Powell (1992), White (1993), Gurval (1995), Galinsky (1996), Barchiesi (1997), Habinek (1998), Fowler (2000), 173–92.

the *res publica* comes from historians and biographers such as Velleius Paterculus, Plutarch, or Dio.[100] These historiographic works reproduce, in one form or another, the same chauvinisms of sex and race as appear in the Augustan poetry-books. The speech which Dio assigns Octavian before the commencement of battle at Actium, for example, encourages the Roman soldiers to fight on two counts; because the opposing commander is an Egyptian woman (and it would be unworthy of the Roman ancestors who overthrew the likes of Pyrrhus, Philip, Perseus, and Antiochus for their descendants to be trodden underfoot by a female), and because the opposing armies are Egyptian (and it would be disgraceful to bear the insults of the sort of people who are a woman's slaves). Cleopatra once again is mannish and her orientalized Antony unmanned.[101]

Yet it is difficult to extract from these later accounts Cleopatra's precise function in the consolidation of Augustus' position at Rome during the years immediately after his victory.[102] In the absence of substantial extracts of both Augustus' autobiography and contemporary prose histories, few later statements regarding his direct propagandist strategies can now be corroborated except, perhaps, by their widespread repetition: in one case, we are told by Dio's history that Augustus claimed Antony's Roman legions were made to guard Cleopatra's palace in Alexandria (50.5.1) and by Servius' commentary on the *Aeneid* that this claim appeared in Augustus' own account of the period (*ad Aen.* 8.696). The later prose narratives, moreover, are often composed for a different audience of Greeks in the East and shaped by the political perspectives, analogical interests, and literary traditions (such as the Greek romance) of different cultures and centuries.[103] Finally, in both ancient and modern studies, lurid

[100] For which see, respectively, Woodman (1983); Pelling (1988); Reinhold (1988). The full range of texts are reviewed by Becher (1966).

[101] Dio 50.24.3–7. Cf. Vell. Pat. 87.1 and Plutarch *Life of Ant.* 53–5. See Reinhold (1988), 109–10; Brenk (1992), 160; Flamarion (1997), 82–3.

[102] As Tarn (1931), 173.

[103] Reinhold (1988), 6–7; Pelling (1988), 8; Brenk (1992); Pelling (1996), 4.

depictions of Antony's captivation and Cleopatra's suicide have a tendency to overshadow the few details which the texts also supply for Cleopatra's propagandist functions in the immediate post-Actian phase of celebration and consolidation.

As part of a propagandist scheme closely associated with Augustus himself, most attention seems to have been focused on Cleopatra in a limited period immediately before and after the battle of Actium, when she appears within a larger discursive pattern of political agitation that articulates Octavian's pursuit and achievement of power as a war of liberation by Italy against an external, eastern enemy.[104] In the many public rituals and ceremonies of this period, Cleopatra has an integral function only in the declaration of war and the triumphal celebration. Several of the ancient historians agree that in October 32 BC war was declared formally against Cleopatra alone, using the full panoply of fetial rites, and thus was proclaimed a national crusade in defence of *Romanitas*, the West, and the Male Principle.[105] Similarly, during the triple triumph of August 29 BC, celebrated for victories over Illyria, at Actium, and (climatically) in Egypt, an effigy of Cleopatra is said to have been present in the parade of the vanquished, in addition to two of her surviving children Alexander Helios and Cleopatra Selene.[106]

All the other surviving evidence suggests that, in the public celebrations of Actium, victory and the struggle to obtain it were signified by more abstract tokens—it was Egypt or the East, not a specific Ptolemaic queen, that had been defeated. It was the day of Alexandria's capture (and Antony's death), not the day of Cleopatra's suicide, which was declared a holiday by resolution of the senate, and the day of Octavian's entry into that city was recorded publicly in the *Fasti* as one on which he had saved the state not from the clutches of a

[104] On which, see Galinsky (1996), 39–41.

[105] Plut. *Ant.* 60.1; Suet. *Aug.* 31; Dio 50.4.4, 6.1, 26.3–4. See Reinhold (1981–2), 102; Flamarion (1997), 80–1.

[106] Dio 51.21.7–8; Prop. 3.11.53–4. See Gurval (1995), 4–5 and 19–36; Hamer (1993), 20–1.

female despot but simply from 'terrible danger' (*rem public. tristiss. periculo liberauit*).[107] The monumental taxonomy of domination which constitutes the *Res Gestae* follows a similar pattern of abstraction. Not one of Augustus' opponents appears in it by name. Sextus Pompeius becomes an anonymous pirate supported by runaway slaves, and Antony a faction. Cleopatra, however, is rendered completely impersonal—a territory rather than a political party—when her defeat becomes the addition of Egypt to the empire of the Roman people (*Aegyptum imperio populi Romani adieci*, *RG* 27.1).[108]

There is also little evidence to suggest that Cleopatra had a role to play in the monumental iconography which featured so significantly in Augustus' refurbished Rome. The Palatine temple to Apollo which was dedicated on 9 October 28 BC (and which has often been interpreted as the most visible and prominent monument to the Actian victory in Rome) commemorated victory exclusively in the abstract or mythological idioms of Apollo's achievement as saviour and divine avenger of mortal hybris. A votive statue of the god before the temple signalled victory at sea metonymically, in the shape of ships' prows, while the depiction in ivory on the temple doors of Apollo's rout of the Gauls at Delphi in 278 BC and his mythic slaughter of the Niobids constitutes at best a veiled metaphor for or allegory of Octavian's divinely sanctioned defeat of Antony, as does the depiction on terracotta plaques of Apollo confronting Hercules.[109] Similarly, the statues of the Danaids (set between the columns of the temple portico according to Propertius 2.13) could only at best allude indirectly to the conquest of Egypt, and even the detail of their allegorical function has been much disputed. While, for some, the gender of the

[107] For references to the appropriate Augustan documents see Volkmann (1958), 213; Tarn and Charlesworth (1934), 108 and n. 3; Gurval (1995), 19–85.

[108] Brunt and Moore (1967), 2; Gurval (1995), 15–16 and 146; Elsner (1996), 39–40.

[109] See, Zanker (1988), 85–9; Kellum (1997), 159–61; Fantham (1997), 127–8. Gurval (1995), 213–24 argues that such imagery would have been resonant beyond any immediate reference to Actium.

Danaids, their Graeco-Egyptian ethnicity, and their traditional condemnation in art and literature for the impious slaughter of their husbands might evoke Cleopatra, for others their earlier function as prototypes of the Greeks battling against the barbarous other (enacted in Aeschylus' *Suppliants*) renders the slaughter of their Egyptian relatives an evocation and legitimation of civil war between the western Octavian and the eastern Antony.[110] The statues and reliefs belonging to the temple of Apollo focus on the quality of divine victory over anonymous hubristic hordes or purge, through myth, the conflicts of Roman civil war, but they do not focus, as does Augustan poetry, on the mortal specifics of a particular Ptolemaic queen's defeat. Here Cleopatra is concealed rather than revealed as Rome's enemy.

The precise design and location in Rome of an arch to commemorate the Actian victory are still much disputed. This renders its identification with arches illustrated on some denarii equally contentious. If, as is generally the case, the Actian arch is thought to have been single-vaulted, it may be identifiable with a coin type that displays an arch crowned by a triumphant statuary group of Octavian standing in a quadriga, and exhibiting additionally only disembodied standards on its socles. A high degree of abstraction would then be attached to the monumental iconography for victory. Moreover, it is now disputed whether such an arch was ever erected, and archaeological study of the *forum Romanum* suggests that, if erected, it was soon supplanted by a much grander, triple-vaulted arch celebrating Rome's triumph over Parthia.[111]

Aligned with other public discourses of the principate explicitly through their illustration of monuments or ritual acts or literary

[110] Contrast Kellum (1997), 159–61 with Galinsky (1996), 220–2. Gurval (1995), 124–6, argues instead that the sanctuary simply honoured Apollo and the myths associated with him.

[111] See Nash (1961), 92–101; Coarelli (1985), 258–308; Nedergaard (1988); Hannestad (1988), 58–62; Reinhold (1988), 146; Gurval (1995), 5, 8, and 36–47.

topoi (such as the departure of Aeneas from Troy), and minted to pay the army and generally to support the economic life of both Italy and the provinces, coins nevertheless were not the foremost instruments of Augustus' validation at Rome. Coin types and their slogans which proclaimed military success often relied for comprehension on the detail provided previously by the celebration of a triumph. Nevertheless, Augustan coins were invested with substantial discursive power and were designed to draw on images of maximum political potency.[112] Yet no coin throughout this period depicts a vanquished Cleopatra.

Of the coins minted during the triumviral period and the early principate many depict the victor of a sea-battle or the fruits of victory, but nowhere is Cleopatra a part of the victory symbolism. There appear, instead, impersonal tokens such as ships' prows and marine creatures, divine patrons such as Venus and Apollo, or personifications such as Victory standing on a globe. So impersonal is the typology and so detached from the specific features of the sea-battle at Actium that it is difficult to distinguish it (if at all) from that designed to celebrate Octavian's earlier sea-battle at Naulochus in 36 BC.[113] One coin type shows, standing on a ship's prow, a copy of the 'Victory of Samothrace'—a statue which the Macedonian Antigonus had set up to commemorate his victory over Ptolemy II at Cos (Fig. 6.3). If it can be reliably dated to the post-Actium period, the design implies that Actium belongs to a celebrated tradition of victories over the Ptolemaic dynasty, but suppresses any detail of that dynasty's most recent representative and subsumes the queen Cleopatra into a more comfortable history of victory over kings.[114] On coins which celebrate the capture of Egypt (and can, therefore, be more reliably

112 See Wallace-Hadrill (1986), 68–70, for this description of the status of coins. Cf. Consigliere (1978), 7–11 and 120–1.

113 Sutherland and Carson (1984), 30–1; Zanker (1988), 82; Gurval (1995), 8–9 and 47–65.

114 BMC 1, nos. 616 and 617. Tarn (1931), 179–83; Tarn and Charlesworth (1934), 113; Hannestad (1988), 57; Simon (1986), 84; Kent (1978), 18–19 and plate 35.123.

FIG. 6.3 Coin issued to celebrate the Actian victory.

FIG. 6.4 Coin issued in celebration of the capture of Egypt, dated *c.* 28–27 BC.

dated), it is a crocodile that takes Cleopatra's place. Some rare gold and silver coins dated to 28–27 BC, but of uncertain mint, display a head of the then Octavian Caesar on their obverse and, on the reverse, carry the legend AEGYPT. CAPTA accompanied by a crocodile (Fig. 6.4).[115] Similarly, abundant coppers from the mint at Nîmes which were distributed widely through the West in the period 10 BC to AD 14 display on the reverse a captive crocodile and a palm tree and, on the obverse, heads of Augustus and Agrippa.[116]

Victories at Actium and in Egypt, and the forces ranged at that time against Octavian, are all depicted, in this iconographic pattern, in terms of material or animal tokens, divine personifications, or—more distantly still—in terms of illustrations of monumental depictions of tokens and personifications. They are never depicted in terms of vanquished opponents or suppliant peoples. Yet opponents and peoples do appear in Augustan coin types signifying conquests and submissions when those conquests and submissions have ceased to be associated with either Cleopatra or Antony. The supplicating barbarian, for example, becomes an especially popular image after the

[115] BMC 1, no. 655, and cf. nos. 650–4. See also Kent (1978) no. 124; Wallace-Hadrill (1986), 68; Sutherland and Carson (1984), 38; Gurval (1995), 64.

[116] Sutherland and Carson (1984), 26–7 and plate 3.154–5.

restoration of the Roman standards from Parthia in 20 BC, an event which is far more personalized in the *Res Gestae* than was the conquest of Egypt: 'I forced the Parthians to restore to me the spoils and standards of three Roman armies and to ask as suppliants for the friendship of the Roman people' (29.2). The triple-vaulted Parthian arch (thought to have soon replaced the simpler 'Actian' arch in the Roman forum) was elaborately carved with suppliant bowmen and slingers.[117] Large numbers of denarii issued at Rome show on the obverse the head of a divinity such as *Liber* or *Honos* and on the reverse the legend CAESAR AUGUSTUS SIGN. RECE. (Caesar Augustus, the standards restored) accompanied by the type of a bareheaded Parthian—perhaps king Phraates himself—who kneels in breeches and cloak offering a standard and holding out his left hand in supplication.[118] The installation of a client king in Armenia was also commemorated in a coin series minted at Rome in 18 BC, showing the head of *Liber* on the obverse and, on the reverse, the legend CAESAR DIVI F. ARME. CAPT. (Caesar, son of the Divine, Armenia captured) accompanied by the type of an Armenian king who, wearing the tiara and long robe that signified an eastern monarch, kneels and extends both hands in a gesture of submission.[119]

Although this intersecting network of rituals, monuments, coins, and writings testify to the importance of military victories and conquests in Augustus' claims to power,[120] there seems to be a certain hesitancy in authorizing the political ascendancy of the *princeps* through the representation of a specific woman as vanquished opponent. The discourses of power most closely supervised by Octavian and the subsequent Augustan state are not static but change through time. The agitational rhetoric of the triumviral period of the 30s BC changes, in the post-Actium period, into a more restrained rhetoric

[117] Galinsky (1996), 155–6; Gurval (1995), 282.

[118] BMC 1, nos. 10–17 and 56–8; Zanker (1988), 183–92. Cf. Kent (1978), 277–8 and no. 131.

[119] BMC 1, nos. 18 and 19, and Hannestad (1988), 55. Cf. BMC 1, nos. 43 and 44.

[120] Smith (1987), 98; Zanker (1988), 185.

of integration that would allow for both the legitimation of new government and the reconciliation of former foes. In this shifting scheme, Cleopatra herself carries only a brief ideological potency centred around the time of the military campaigns, and by the time of the triumphs in 29 BC is already being subsumed into a less problematic celebration of the conquest of Egypt. Even that conquest gradually ceases to possess its original political resonance, being replaced soon after 20 BC by 'the suppliant Parthian' as a more pervasive representation of surrender to Augustan military might.[121] In the post-Actium period, no lasting image of Cleopatra has survived in the discourses of power closest to the *princeps*. Within the framework of the representation of Actium and Alexandria as moments of victory in a war of liberation from the tyranny of the East, the Roman Antony could not be represented, but neither, it would seem, could Cleopatra. In games, festivals, libations, dedications, public statuary and monuments, there are only Apollos and Victories, and a general triumphant, while ships' prows and crocodiles stand in for the actual opponents. Why, then, does Cleopatra VII appear so briefly in the most 'official' victory symbolism?

## THE PROBLEMATIC FEMALE

One explanation for the abstraction of the coin types which celebrate Actium and Egypt lies in the evident gendering of the iconography of victory and the vanquished which traditionally occurred in Roman coin issues. Coins which mark conquest or submission disclose a spectrum of types ranging from named enemies through to material tokens and personifications of Victory. In that spectrum, representations of women are more closely aligned with the general than the particular.

One of the earliest examples of a coin type which marks the specific military achievements of a living magistrate is a series of silver

[121] Gurval (1995), esp. 135–6. Cf. Yavetz (1984), 1–5; Feeney (1992), 1–2.

denarii minted at Rome in 58 BC jointly by M. Scaurus and P. Hypsaeus. The side devoted to Scaurus records the surrender of the Arabian king Aretas of Nabataea, who appears on his knees holding an olive branch beside a camel and is identified clearly by name.[122] Many similar designs followed, such as the silver denarii of 56 BC which were minted by Sulla's son and display on the reverse an enchained Jugurtha being surrendered by king Bocchus of Mauretania to an enthroned Sulla.[123] None such design displays a woman as the specific conquered opponent.

In the spectrum of coin types depicting conquest and submission, and in order of increasing abstraction, women first appear not in the category of 'specific opponents' but in that of 'typical prisoners' and, even here, their iconographic function is still differentiated from that of their more substantial male counterparts. An issue of denarii minted in Spain around 46–45 BC, for example, celebrates Julius Caesar's conquests in Gaul by displaying a portrait head of Venus on the obverse and, on the reverse, Gallic trophies surrounded by two figures—a kneeling or seated male whose hands are tied behind his back, and a seated female who, in a gesture of grief, rests her head in her right hand. Since only the male is enchained, the female figure has been read as signifying both a captive Gaul and a grieving *Gallia*. It is then as both representative prisoner and personification of the province that the woman mourns.[124] Gallic female is similarly differentiated from Gallic male on a pair of silver denarii minted around 48 BC. On one coin, the portrait head of a bearded (and therefore barbarian) male displayed on the obverse is matched, on the reverse, with the type of a charioteer leading a naked warrior who brandishes spear and shield (Fig. 6.5). On the other coin, the portrait head of a long-haired (and therefore barbarian) female on the obverse is

[122] BMCR 2, 591, no. 16, or RRC 2, 422, no. 1b. See Kent (1978), 15 and pl. 17.60; Hannestad (1988), 26.

[123] BMCR 1, 471, no. 3824, or RRC 2, 426, no. 1. See Hannestad (1988), 22; Kent (1978), 16 and pl. 18.69.

[124] See Hannestad (1988), 22–3 on RRC 2, 468, no. 1.

FIG. 6.5 Coin issued in celebration of Julius Caesar's Gallic victories, dated *c*.48 BC.

matched, on the reverse, with the type of Artemis, the goddess of Massalia, who holds a spear and rests her right hand on the head of a stag (Fig. 6.6).[125] While the male is associated with the ferocious military agents in Caesar's Gallic wars, the female is linked more impersonally to the symbol of an acquiescent Gallic city.

Further along the spectrum, where victory is designated by the category of 'personified countries' rather than 'typical prisoners', the female replaces the male altogether on the standard coin type. Instead of representative inhabitants of surrendered or restored territories, the coinage displays ideal female personifications of whole peoples.[126] A denarius minted at Rome in 71 BC, for example, carries on the obverse the helmeted bust of *Virtus* and, on the reverse, the legend SICIL. accompanied by an armed warrior raising up a fallen female figure. The gesture towards the woman alludes symbolically to the benefits conferred on Sicily by Marius, the grandfather of the minter, when he ended Sicily's second slave war.[127]

In conventional patterns for the Roman iconography of the vanquished, therefore, the female form functions largely as a personifi-

[125] BMC 1, 513, nos. 3994 and 3996; RRC 2, 448, nos. 2e and 3. See Kent (1978), 271.

[126] See Toynbee (1934), 7–23; Smith (1988*a*), 71.

[127] RRC 2, 401, no. 1. See Hannestad (1988), 23.

FIG. 6.6 Coin marking Julius Caesar's victories in Gaul, dated *c.*48 BC.

cation or at best as a representative prisoner in coin types, never as a specific opponent, and her attributes characterize a nation not an individual.[128] The figure of Cleopatra VII clearly cannot fit into such a system and is absent from the coinage which pays tribute to the powers of Augustus.

This pattern for gendering the iconography of victory and the vanquished extends into every visual sphere. Thus on the breastplate of the famous statue of Augustus from Prima Porta, the centrepiece is devoted to the representation of a Parthian surrendering the standards to a Roman commander (or the god Mars) (Fig. 6.7). Persian dress, bow and quiver, and royal diadem identify the suppliant male figure as the Parthian king Phraates IV. On the edges of the breastplate, on either side of the Parthian king, appear figures of grieving females (Fig. 6.8). Their attributes, instead of marking the women as specific vanquished opponents, assist in the process of reification. The eagle-sword and the dragon-trumpet are additional signifiers of client states restored or territories captured in both East and West.[129] Thus the specific male opponent and the specific military achievement lie, literally, at the heart of a monument which sets out the anatomy of Augustan victory symbolism. The female personification and her generalized gestures remain marginalized on either side.

[128] Toynbee (1934), esp. 9–10.

[129] Zanker (1988), 188–92; Hannestad (1988), 55; Galinsky (1996), 107 and 155–64.

FIG. 6.7 Statue of Augustus from Prima Porta.

FIG. 6.8 Detail of breastplate of statue of Augustus from Prima Porta.

The relative abstraction of such 'official' discourses celebrating victory at Actium and the conquest of Egypt is, thus, explained by the requirements of victory symbolism at Rome. Depictions of Roman Antony would have resonated with civil war associations, while the Egyptian foe Cleopatra VII was highly problematic as a *female* opponent. In Rome's traditional displays of military conquest, the female functions as an abstraction, and the entire possibility of differentiating between a symbolic order of female personifications such as Victory, Justice, or the Nation Vanquished, and the actual order of soldiers, generals, and defeated foes depends largely on the absence of women from the military sphere.[130] Where war is defined

[130] See Warner (1987), for a more general discussion of the role of women in victory symbolism.

as a masculine activity and highly-esteemed masculine qualities are attached to military pursuits, a specific female opponent is suggestive of a paired and perverse gender reversal, and she can therefore operate as a derogation of her male military opponent: Dio portrays the militant Boudicca as transgressing the bounds of normal female behaviour, and sets up her opposition to Rome as an illustration of Nero's effeminacy and Rome's social disorder.[131] Thus the delineation of a specific female opponent would fit uneasily into the intricate symbolic network of gender and imperialism which constitutes Rome's validating system for warfare, and would disturb the system's operations. If any dignity accrues to Cleopatra in the poetic description of her death at the end of Horace's *Ode* 1.37 it is, from the Roman perspective, because in her final moments she *transcends* the condition of woman—*nec muliebriter / expavit* (1.37.22–3).

It is not only as a result of the Roman grammar of conquest that Cleopatra VII is rendered problematic as a symbol of Augustan claims to power. The queen's suicide also generates substantial difficulties as an image of Augustan victory, for in the ideology of conquest a Roman general would kill a king in battle, or accept his submission and lead him and his children in a triumphal procession of the vanquished. Cleopatra's suicide thus denied to the triumph of 29 BC her physical presence as an assured token of that submission.[132] Some historians have argued that Cleopatra's death may have been ordered or connived at by Octavian, since (according to Dio 43.19.3–4 and Appian *BC* 2.15.101–2) the appearance of her sister Arsinoe in the triumphal procession of Julius Caesar in 46 BC had stirred Roman spectators to sympathy rather than patriotic pride.[133] Cleopatra, however, had been constructed as the cause of war, and the story of her death by snake-bite left space for a defiant and regal figure to

[131] See Macdonald (1987*a*), 6, and (1987*b*), 44–5 on Dio 62.

[132] Smith (1987), 115–17, and see *Res Gestae* 4.3 for Augustus' own boast that he led nine kings or children of kings in triumph.

[133] On which, see Aly (1992), 51; Gurval (1995), 22–5.

emerge: in prose narratives, epitomes, and commentaries, the tale is repeated that Cleopatra herself cried out against appearing in a Roman triumph (*ou thriambeusomai*); while the circumstances of her death could be read as entirely in keeping with the emblematic apparatus of the Pharoahs, a conclusive reassertion both of royalty and godhead which boldly denied that the final victory belonged to Octavian.[134]

Finally, the potential ambiguity in exposing for Roman consumption representations of the Ptolemaic queen is not lost even on ancient commentators. Dio notes that in 29 BC, by senatorial decree, Octavian removed many public dedications but not the gilded statue of Cleopatra that Julius Caesar had placed in the Temple of Venus Genetrix. Dio relishes the paradox that in continuing to display the sculpted image of the defeated queen, the Romans might yet be adding to her glorification (51.22.1–3).[135] It is as if, for Dio, the visual discourses of Augustan victory lacked the register of invective, but could only be viewed as positive assertion.[136] There inhere within the Augustan Cleopatras elements which can contradict and throw into question her once dominant ideological function at Rome as a validator of civil war. The queen can frustrate attempts at representational conquest.

Earlier in this chapter, a certain anonymity was observed in the poetic representations of Cleopatra during the years that followed Actium. She possesses no name, no individuating physical features, and none of the physical presence customarily accorded the poetic barbarian such as the golden locks and golden dress, the striped

[134] See Pelling (1988), 318–19, and (1996), 64–5, where he argues that modern scepticism about the ancient accounts of Cleopatra's death may be misplaced. Cf. Volkmann (1958), 205–7; Lindsay (1971), 431–6; Reinhold (1981–2), 136; Pomeroy (1984), 28; Hamer (1993), 21–2; Whitehorne (1994), 186–96; Marasco (1995), 320–1; Rowlandson (1998), 40–1; Southern (1999), 143–5; Gurval (forthcoming).

[135] See Reinhold (1988), 157–8; Flory (1993), 295–6.

[136] I am grateful to Andrew Wallace-Hadrill for this point. Cf. Powell (1992), 148 on the relative incapacity of Augustus' iconographic propaganda to register apology.

cloaks and the milky-white necks, the spear-carrying hands and the protected bodies of the Gauls who, elsewhere on the shield of Aeneas, are caught ascending the Capitol (*Aen.* 8.657–62). The extent of Cleopatra's reification, moreover, grows with time. In the later poetic narratives of the *Aeneid* and Propertius 4.6 there are no mosquito nets and no eunuchs, no drunkenness or sexual depravity, only the conflict of divine forces embodied in the sanctified Augustus and the Isiac Cleopatra. Nonetheless, after the triumphs of 29 BC, the very presence of Cleopatra in these poetic narratives marks a significant departure from other modes of cultural production of the period, whether rituals, monuments, coin issues, or inscriptions. For Augustan poetry plays with its fictions of Cleopatra long after she has ceased to carry any burden of validation in more 'official' spheres. Long after her image had once been carried in the triumphal procession of 29 BC, poetic fictions of Cleopatra continue to be composed and distributed.

In the absence of the historiographic Cleopatras of the contemporary prose tradition, the poetic Cleopatras of the Augustan age are an important and intriguing anomaly. Furthermore, the Augustan poets focus precisely on those issues that elsewhere render Cleopatra problematic as a signifier of victory. They engender and individuate the battle of Actium as the defeat of a specific militant woman: Propertius, in particular, reminds his readers that for Romans a triumph over one woman (*una mulier*) is no real triumph at all (4.6.65–6). They frequently colour the queen's regal suicide in tragedy or pathos: Horace, most famously, concludes his call for sympotic celebration in *Odes* 1.37 not with Augustus Caesar the hunter, but with the Egyptian quarry who, with calm resolution (*voltu sereno*, 1.37.26), manages to elude him in death. And by explicitly linking their poetic Cleopatras to other Augustan mechanisms for the depiction of victory—triumphs, temples, decorative armour, religious ritual—they everywhere draw attention to the question of *how* to represent Cleopatra publicly and to the *difference* of poetry.

The difference of Augustan poetry could be read in two distinct ways. On the one hand, it works towards creating a new more abstracted representation of Cleopatra and Actium better to suit the early principate's political climate of integration rather than agitation. From Horace *Epode* 9 through to Propertius 4.6, ambivalence and ambiguity are gradually weeded out to culminate in a confident myth of cosmic struggle, where the point of view rests with a divinely favoured Augustus ever resisting the forces of femininity and barbarism. On the other hand, Augustan poetry interrogates (and, in places, subverts) the validating strategies of the regime through its continued display of the troublesome *meretrix regina*, persistently putting a tragic Cleopatra before its readers in order, like a remonstrating Antony, better to disclose the uncomfortable truths of a civil war. Yet, either way, the depiction of Cleopatra in the poetic narratives of Augustan Rome, the position from which her features are assembled, is always that of the Roman and the Male and the texts themselves work to construct a reader according to that model. Nowhere do they deploy Cleopatra's own Ptolemaic strategies for validating female rule, as Julius Caesar and Antony in turn had cause to do, nor do they write from her point of view (however imagined). It is only in the much later tradition of the *meretrix regina* that mechanisms are employed (poetic or otherwise) to solicit from her consumers an identification, as woman, with the female seducer of the masters of Rome.

# 7

# Oriental Vamp: Cleopatra 1910s

On 4 November 1913, the newspaper *Giornale d'Italia* carried an account of the recent production of a silent Italian film about Cleopatra. According to its director Enrico Guazzoni, he chose to make *Marcantonio e Cleopatra* because

> no theme could better attract and move an artist than that which, through the figures of Mark Antony and Cleopatra, had so much weight over the destinies of the ancient world. It provided above all the opportunity to parade before the eyes of the spectator the most distinctive places of ancient Rome and ancient Egypt, which everyone has imprinted in their minds at their school-desks, but has never seen, nor would have any way of really seeing, not even if they spent the treasures of Croesus. Next it offered the possibility of reconstructing landings and battles which have remained among the most memorable of those times, and which will be seen reproduced on the cinema screen not without trembling emotion. And, finally, the loves of Mark Antony and Cleopatra, besides being of themselves one of the most passionate subjects of history, lent themselves magnificently to the reconstruction of the life led at the sumptuous

This chapter is a substantially revised and extended version of part of a chapter in my book *Projecting the Past: Ancient Rome, Cinema and History* (Routledge, 1997).

court of the Ptolemies, with scenes of intimacy full of fascination for their magnificence . . .[1]

Love and passion play a surprisingly subordinate role in the director's catalogue of what attracted and moved him in the story of Antony and Cleopatra (and, by implication, what should attract and move the audience he is trying to solicit for his film). Spectators are invited to attend a weighty narrative of the Mediterranean's historical destiny, to visit through the magic of moving pictures the ancient places where that destiny was determined, and to experience for themselves the landings and battles that preceded Rome's historic triumph over Egypt. The playing out of Cleopatra's seduction of Antony on screen is here explicitly stated to be instrumental to a parade of Ptolemaic sumptuousness, as if newspaper readers who saw *Marcantonio e Cleopatra* would be able to experience vicariously first the treacherous thrill of an Antony and then the patriotic disdain of an Octavian for the pleasures imagined to reside on North African shores. For Guazzoni (and the Italian spectators on whom he presumed), what mattered most was not so much the erotic seductions instigated by a politically-motivated and passionate queen, but the spectacle of Egypt—its fascinating magnificence and its conquest by Rome.[2] In that respect, Guazzoni chose to promote an image for his film which showed a substantial debt to the rhetorical figuring of the *meretrix regina* in ancient, Graeco-Roman sources.

In different periods, cultures, and media, representations of the Ptolemaic queen Cleopatra VII and her relations to Rome have ceaselessly shifted in structure and meaning. Depictions of Cleopatra's encounters with Julius Caesar and Mark Antony, her departure from the battle of Actium, her suicide, and the subsequent triumph of Octavian, have taken on many diverse forms by virtue of, for

[1] Quoted in Prolo (1951), 55.

[2] Cf. Bertellini (1999), 41, on nationalistic allusions in a similar interview given by Guazzoni to the New York-based Italian newspaper *Il Progresso Italo-Americano* for 27 November 1913.

example, specific technologies for the representation of the queen, and distinct cultural conditions for viewing gender, race, empire, and female power. In 31 BC, at the time of the battle of Actium, Cleopatra had already become two competing sets of images designed to validate either her rule or her overthrow. To her Graeco-Egyptian subjects, in honorific titles, inscriptions, coins, temple reliefs, religious ceremonial, public spectacle, and oracular writings, Cleopatra VII was a loving daughter of her country and its previous kings, a protective and fertile mother-figure, a goddess, a liberator and a messiah. The Ptolemaic queen came to symbolize resistance to the aggression of the West: she embodied a vengeful Asia who would conquer Rome and, with that victory, bring unity. She was to establish a glorious world kingdom and initiate a golden age of peace. To Cleopatra's Roman enemies, however, in the propaganda disseminated by Octavian before the battle of Actium, in the ritual of the subsequent triumph, in contemporary Roman poetry, and in later historiography, the Egyptian queen was a barbaric debauchee, a whore and a drunkard, the mistress of eunuchs. She was the eastern enemy of Rome and the embodiment of an effeminate Asia. She was represented as having seduced one Roman into her eastern ways, only to be deservedly overcome by another. In Roman narratives, Octavian became the defender of Rome against the assaults of Egypt. He was the conqueror of Asia, and the founder of a new kingdom of peace and of Roman imperial rule.[3]

In the vicious propaganda campaign waged by Octavian before the battle of Actium, Cleopatra was constructed as an enticing but monstrous character who had lured Antony away from his proper Roman duties and thus endangered the welfare of the whole Roman state. That representation of the Egyptian queen and the Roman lover over whom she made herself mistress was sustained and elaborated in the later histories of Plutarch and Cassius Dio. Plutarch's *Life of Antony* is a case study in the moral disintegration of its hero, whose love for

[3] See above, Ch. 6, for detailed discussion.

Cleopatra is described as his life's 'final and crowning evil'.[4] The narrative of Octavian's victory over the erotic and political tyranny of Cleopatra, of masculine Rome's ultimate triumph over feminine Egypt, then became a founding myth of western culture. It is that myth of western victory over the East which lies at the core of Enrico Guazzoni's *Marcantonio e Cleopatra* (1913). This and the next chapter explore the function of Cleopatra in twentieth-century film production. As in Dominic Montserrat's analysis of the reception of the Egyptian Pharaoh Akhenaten and his city Amarna, these two chapters constitute a 'metabiography', that is an examination of the process whereby Cleopatra's life has been represented in modern culture.[5] Such an analysis of canonic moments in the western cinematic tradition for ancient Rome's quintessential mistress throws into relief her popular deployment as a site for the formulation and exploration of modern imperialism, ethnicity, gender, and sexuality, and demonstrates her adaptability to changes in their articulation.

## ITALY'S COLONIAL CLEOPATRA (1913)

From antiquity, manifold representations of Cleopatra and her seductions have pervaded western cultural production, in, for example, paintings and sculpture, poetry, plays and operas, biographies and historical novels, ballets and burlesques, from tapestries to snuff-boxes, from theatrical tragedies to music-hall sketches, from fancy-dress balls to cabaret acts, from circus spectacles to cigarette labels.[6] But the title of Enrico Guazzoni's film, and its association with the Roman production house Cines, suggests at first that the primary source material for *Marcantonio e Cleopatra* consists in Shakespeare's

[4] Plutarch, *Life of Antony* 25.1, and see Brenk (1992).

[5] Montserrat (2000), esp. 2.

[6] See esp. Hughes-Hallett (1991); Hamer (1993) and (2001); Ziegler (1994), 552–61; Lant (1995), 77–8; Hoberman (1997), 137–49; Pucci (forthcoming). My thanks are due to both Mary Hamer and Pino Pucci for kindly giving me access to their articles prior to publication.

authoritative Roman play *Antony and Cleopatra*. In the early years of the film industry preceding the first world war, in the face of considerable hostility to the new medium, both European and American film-makers transformed Shakespeare's plays into moving pictures as a means of demonstrating the significant contribution film could make to culture. The plays of Shakespeare were perceived as free source material of wide cultural circulation, familiar from numerous editions, school versions, theatrical productions, and even ephemera such as advertising. Both thrilling and culturally respectable, Shakespeare was powerfully attractive as source material for film production. Adaptations of his plays could be marketed not only as entertaining, but also as uplifting and educational. Such film adaptations selected the most familiar phrases, scenes, and images from individual plays, constructed their *mise en scène* to accord with the Shakespearean iconography established by contemporary play productions, and trumpeted their capacity to substitute for Shakespearean dialogue the representation on screen of off-stage action—the transformation of verse into spectacle.[7]

In November 1908, the American Vitagraph Company had already released its own version of *Antony and Cleopatra*. The film was structured, packaged, and consumed as an adaptation of Shakespeare's play. The director, Charles Kent, had for some thirty years previously played Shakespearean roles on the American stage. The action, according to the research of the film historian Robert Hamilton Ball, consisted of about a quarter of the play compressed on screen into thirteen tableaux. A favourable review (which Ball quotes from *Moving Picture World* of 7 November 1908) reads the Vitagraph film unequivocally as an attempt to transform Shakespeare into moving images:

If Shakespeare could only realize the fate of the works he left behind, the modern use of them would cause his prophetic soul to weep. Just think of

[7] Pearson and Uricchio (1990). For a survey of the silent era's film adaptations of Shakespeare, see Ball (1968), and Rothwell (1999), 1–27.

it! Antony and Cleopatra given in its entirety, with the vocal parts and other details of the regular production cut out, in less than twenty minutes! What a vast difference between the older presentation and that represented by the modernized form of amusement. But with all the condensation, the magnificence was retained, and I heard several in the audience say the film had created in them an appetite for more of the same kind. The Vitagraph company can take pride in the production.[8]

Like the Vitagraph Company, which continued its cycle of Shakespearean one-reelers with, for example, *King Lear* (1909) and *Twelfth Night* (1910), Cines had regularly released Shakespearean adaptations before the launch of the feature-length film *Marcantonio e Cleopatra* (1913). As the most prestigious film company of the time in Italy, Cines rivalled Pathé and Gaumont for distribution of its films in the European film market and for their exportation to the United States. It therefore exploited the high international cultural value of a whole string of Shakespearean productions such as *Romeo and Juliet* (1908), *Hamlet* (1908), *Othello* (1909), *Macbeth* (1909), *A Winter's Tale* (1910), *All's Well That Ends Well* (1912), and *A Comedy of Errors* (1912), and specialized in spectacular stagings that borrowed from the nineteenth-century's extravagant theatrical conventions while utilizing the additional cinematic resources of location shooting, chiaroscuro lighting, huge casts and their movement in deep space.[9] Consequently, by 1913, Cines had established a whole programme of spectacular Shakespearean films to which *Marcantonio e Cleopatra* might have been a predicted addition.

Some of the publicity for the American and the British launch of *Marcantonio e Cleopatra* packaged the film as Shakespearean,[10] yet when, for the Italian launch, Enrico Guazzoni described the merits of his production in the *Giornale d'Italia*, the director demonstrated a greater interest in battles than passion, and in ancient places rather

[8] Ball (1968), 47–8. Cf. Rothwell (1999), 6–13.

[9] Ball (1968), 96, English titles and release dates are listed in Ball's index. Cf. Uricchio and Pearson (1995); Rothwell (1999), 14–17; Bertellini (1999).

[10] Ball (1968), 167.

than tragic plot. According to Guazzoni (in the Italian press at any rate), the fidelity that needed to be secured was to ancient architecture and art rather than English literature:

> Every part of this reconstruction has been studied with the greatest scruple, on sites, in museums, in libraries. This research completed, a legion of artists and labourers from Cines patiently set to work reconstructing whole sections of cities, palaces, monuments, court-yards, halls, fountains, ponds, furniture, weapons and clothing, so that everything would be in keeping with the most absolute historical truth.

Furthermore, the film text itself proves to be less grounded in the Shakespearean Cleopatra than in her refiguring within nineteenth-century, orientalist discourses of nationalism and empire.

Published around the beginning of the seventeenth century (*c.*1606), Shakespeare's *Antony and Cleopatra* operates in a direct line of descent from Plutarch's *Life of Antony* (via Sir Thomas North's English rendition of the earlier French translation by Jacques Amyot that had given Plutarch's dramatic narrative of mad passion a wide diffusion across Europe). The play opens with a description of Antony as 'The triple pillar of the world transformed | Into a strumpet's fool' (1.1.12–13). Octavian's Rome, which Antony deserts, is depicted as a soldierly, asexual, masculine world of civic duty, politics, imperialism, and history. Cleopatra's Egypt, whose embrace Antony accepts, is depicted as a disorderly, passionate, and feminine world of private pleasures, love, and theatrical excess. But critics have observed how Shakespeare's representation of the contrasting domains between which Antony vacillates is less censorious than that of Plutarch. The consistent and pervasive political moralism supplied by the authorial voice of the ancient historian is replaced by the contesting perspectives of the dramatic characters themselves. However ventriloquized, Cleopatra gains a voice that mocks Rome's pretensions to authority and empire. Although the overall drive of the play may be towards a demonstration for Jacobean England of the folly of political rebellion, imperious passion, and female rule, nevertheless, in the course of that demonstration, Octavia is colourless, Octavian ruthless, Antony great-hearted, and Cleopatra both captivating and majestic. Love has been gifted with moments of sublimity, as Cleopatra herself recalls:

> Eternity was in our lips and eyes,
> Bliss in our brows' bent; none our parts so poor
> But was a race of heaven. (1.3.36–8)[11]

Not only does the narrative of the film *Marcantonio e Cleopatra* bear little correspondence to the tragic plot of Shakespeare's play, but it also attempts to close down the kind of ambivalences which the Renaissance drama manifests. Guazzoni's Cleopatra is visualized at the beginning of the film as a sinister enchantress (lit from below by the flames of a cauldron, she seeks out a love potion from an old witch around whom a snake slithers). At the close of the film, like the nineteenth-century, sexually voracious killer-Cleopatras of Alexander Pushkin, Pietro Cossa, Victorien Sardou, Théophile Gautier, or Rider Haggard, she has become a murderous sorceress (returning to the witch to obtain poisons which she proceeds to test out on her slaves).[12] The Roman Octavia, the touchstone of wifely virtue, is indignantly rebuffed by the mistress Cleopatra in a direct confrontation on Egyptian soil.[13] The romantic plot is shifted away from the figure of Cleopatra onto one of her innocent slave-girls, who rescues Antony from a conspiracy of Egyptian courtiers only to be whipped and thrown to the crocodiles by a savagely jealous queen. Finally, the

[11] On Shakespeare's *Antony and Cleopatra* see e.g. Thomas (1989); Martindale and Martindale (1990); Bloom (1990); Hughes-Hallett (1991), 169–202; Charnes (1993), 103–47; Wilders (1995); Wood (1996); Miles (1996), 169–88; Kahn (1997), 110–43; Bielmeier (2000), 109–61; Hamer (2001).

[12] For the 'killer-Cleopatra' of the 19th cent. inherited from the account supplied by Sextus Aurelius Victor in the 4th cent. AD, see Hughes-Hallett (1991), 252–311; Ziegler (1994), 559; Pucci (forthcoming).

[13] The motif is inherited from Dryden's *All for Love*, for which see Hughes-Hallett (1991), 212–14; Martindale and Martindale (1990), 140–1; Madelaine (1998), 26–30.

narrative closure of *Marcantonio e Cleopatra* exceeds the limits of Shakespeare's play. While *Antony and Cleopatra* concludes with Caesar (Octavian) pitying the dead lovers and giving orders for his army to attend their funeral in Alexandria, the film continues on to Rome where the Italian audiences of 1913 could witness the Roman leader parading on horseback in triumph, accompanied by fasces- and standard-bearers, trophies of shields and spears, and a procession of the vanquished. The final shot is of Octavian high up beneath a statue of winged victory, standing and saluting the cheering crowds. On this concluding image is imposed the Latin words AVE ROMA IMMORTALIS (Hail Rome the Eternal City).[14]

Guazzoni's *Marcantonio e Cleopatra* evidently shifts away from the cinematic strategy of Shakespearean adaptation and attempts to contain Cleopatra within a narrative of Roman conquest. The film's historiographic mode is connected to a wider set of discourses which had taken on a great intensity in Italy in the period leading up to the first world war—namely that of nationhood and empire. From the time of unification, Italy had been constructed as legitimate heir to ancient Rome—the new nation imagined itself antique. *Romanità* was called upon to supply the new state with a national identity, to affirm the importance of that state in Europe, and to legitimate territorial expansion in the Mediterranean.[15] During the course of 1911 in particular (the year that marked the fiftieth anniversary of Italian unity), nationalists urged, in a widespread and vociferous press campaign, that the country had an historic right and obligation to assert sovereignty over territories once ruled by ancient Rome. With the

[14] The sequence of the triumph at Rome survives in the print at the Library of Congress (Washington) but is missing from the print at the Cineteca archive (Rome)—a clearly mutilated version with scarcely any intertitles. But, as if to elide the film's difference from Shakespeare's play, publicity for the American launch of *Marcantonio e Cleopatra* fails to conclude its plot summary with mention of the triumphal procession.

[15] On the political deployment of *romanità* in Italy in the period before the first world war, see Cagnetta (1979), 15–33; Bondanella (1987), 165–6; Bosworth (1996), 95 and 97; Wyke (1997).

most 'Roman' parts of North Africa already under the control of other European powers, in September 1911 Italy declared war on Turkey and invaded the Ottoman provinces of Tripolitania and Cyrenaica. A year later, when Turkey surrendered those territories, Italy at last could boast possession of a colony in north Africa that, following due Roman precedent, it renamed Libya.[16]

Before, during, and after the annexation of Libya, Rome and its ancient empire were appropriated by Italian imperialists as a validation of Italy's territorial expansion into Africa. Thus the poet Giovanni Pascoli, when accompanying Italian troops on their advance toward Ain Zara in Libya on 26 November 1911, was said to have proclaimed: 'O Tripoli, O Beronike, O Leptis Magna . . . you see again, after so many centuries, Doric columns and Roman legions! Look above you: even the eagles are there!'[17] Similarly, in one of his poems Giuseppe Lipparini gave voice to a Roman soldier buried at Leptis Magna:

> After a silence of centuries I am awakened, and I hear whinnying
> above my head the dash of Lazio's horses.
> Rome returns. I feel the most ancient gods roaming
> above the desert: the glory that once was returns today.[18]

The discourse of historical continuity between the Roman conquests in Africa and the victory of the modern Italian state circulated widely, and the Italian film industry, with its already thriving reconstructions of Roman history, played a significant role in further disseminating for years to come this conception of a modern Italian empire arising out of the rediscovered traces of ancient Rome.[19]

Released only one year after the conquest of Libya, the cinematic narration of Cleopatra's defeat in *Marcantonio e Cleopatra* (1913) was

[16] Bosworth (1979), 135; Del Boca (1986), esp. 54; Childs (1990), 36–42; Bosworth (1996), 103–4.

[17] Quoted in Cagnetta (1979), 17.

[18] Quoted in Del Boca (1986), 149.

[19] See Brunetta and Gili (1990), 9–13, and (1993), 160–77; Wyke (1997) and (1999); Bertenelli (1999).

a uniquely appropriate vehicle for both the legitimation and the celebration of Italy as once again mistress of the Mediterranean. Already in antiquity, the narration of Antony's supposed subjection to Cleopatra had been teleologically structured to lead to the just triumph of Rome over Egypt. But the cinematic representation of that triumph could also draw on the much more recent refiguring of Cleopatra and her kingdom within a nineteenth-century 'colonialist imaginary'.[20] As the western nations looked to occupy the fragmenting Ottoman empire, there was a significant series of adjustments to the Cleopatra narrative and an adscription to it of fresh currency. In her survey of western traditions for representing the Ptolemaic queen, Lucy Hughes-Hallett delineates the numerous ways in which Cleopatra was refigured in the nineteenth-century European imagination as an Orient inviting penetration.[21] A bronze medallion struck in 1826 to commemorate the completed publication of Baron Denon's influential *Description de l'Égypte*, displays on the obverse the Napoleonic invasion of Egypt which had taken place in 1789. The Napoleonic campaign constituted a defining moment in the development of the modern discourse of orientalism and its specific figuring as 'Egyptomania'.[22] On the medallion, France is seen to take possession of an Ottoman province in the guise of a Roman general unveiling a bare-breasted Egyptian queen. She lies reclining passively on a crocodile, before a cluttered scene of pyramids, palm trees, and temple reliefs, gazing up at the conquering Roman—a Cleopatra on display before Julius Caesar, Mark Antony, or, most suitably, Octavian (Fig. 7.1).[23] Similarly, if less explicitly, *L'Illustrazione Italiana* for

[20] For discussion of the 19th-cent. 'colonialist imaginary' and its structuring of film narratives, see esp. Shohat (1991*a*), and Bernstein and Studlar (1997).

[21] Hughes-Hallett (1991), 252–80. Cf. Ziegler (1994), 558–9, and Pucci (forthcoming).

[22] On orientalism, and the importance of the Napoleonic campaign in its specific figuring as Egyptomania, see Said (1985), 42–3 and 76–88; Humbert (1994*a*); MacKenzie (1995), 1–50; Turner (2000), 1–31.

[23] Curl (1994), 132.

FIG. 7.1 France unveils Egypt. Bronze medallion of 1826.

19 March 1876 gave notice of its blessings on an Italian expedition that had just left Naples for the African equatorial, side-by-side with an advertisement for and illustration of an opera about Cleopatra that was currently running. Appropriated for nineteenth-century orientalism, Cleopatra authorizes the articulation of the Orient as Woman, as separate from and subservient to the Occident. Feminized, the Orient can take on, under a gendered western gaze, a feminine allure and penetrability. The colonialist project is provided with an ancient and successful precedent, and geographical conquest of a land is naturalized as sexual possession of a woman's body.[24]

Late nineteenth-century orientalism generated 'a systematic accumulation of human beings and territories' not just through their domination by western adventurers, armies, and administrations, but also through their visual reproduction within western culture.[25] From paintings and drawings to magic-lantern shows, dioramas, and panoramas, from photography on into the new medium of cinema itself, there was an explosion of images of the Orient. The spectacle of Egypt, particularly in France and Great Britain, became an extension of the colonialist project of mapping and photographing and classifying the country in order to claim ownership of it. Thus, in the 1840s, Britain opened up an overland trade route to India which crossed Egyptian soil. Shortly after, British audiences were treated to the spectacle of a panoramic trip up the river Nile provided for them in the comfort of the Egyptian Hall in London. Alexandria, Cairo, and Suez all appeared as moving images.[26] Along with the landscape of Egypt, the mechanisms of nineteenth-century orientalism transformed its queen Cleopatra into a visual spectacle to be desired and

[24] For the feminization of the Orient, more generally, see Said (1985), 188 and 206–8; Shohat (1991*a*), 46–62; Bernstein and Studlar (1997); Yeğenoğlu (1998), esp. 10–11 and 56.

[25] Higashi (1994), 90, who extends Said's definition of orientalism to include its more theatrical forms. Cf. Stevens (1984); Lant (1992), 96; Humbert (1994*b*); Bernstein and Studlar (1997).

[26] Lant (1992), 93–8; Hodgdon (1998), 87–91. For the spectacle of Egypt generally, cf. Curl (1994), 187–206; MacKenzie (1995), 189–92.

FIG. 7.2 *Antony and Cleopatra* (1883), by Sir Lawrence Alma-Tadema.

possessed by watching Europe: in Jean-Léon Gérôme's painting *Cleopatra before Caesar* (1866), a crouching Nubian slave unwraps a bare-breasted Cleopatra from her sumptuous Persian carpet for display before the discerning eyes of both Caesar and the painting's viewer; in Lawrence Alma-Tadema's *Antony and Cleopatra* (1883), the queen appears in the foreground languidly awaiting possession by an approaching Antony (Fig. 7.2). In both paintings, as on the earlier medallion, the visual accumulation of exotic clutter around the body of Cleopatra—the dark-complexioned slaves, the leopard skins and silks, the animal-headed idols, the Pharaonic architecture and hieroglyphs—also operates as a western claim to ownership (through Egyptological knowledge and its visual reproduction) of a mysterious and ancient Egypt.[27]

[27] Hughes-Hallett (1991), 266–70; Ziegler (1994), 574–5 and 558–9; Humbert *et al.* (1994), 488–90. Cf. Pucci (forthcoming) on Italian orientalist depictions of Cleopatra.

The orientalist patterns of such visual reconstructions of ancient Egypt's seductions were reproduced in the pictorial set designs for stage productions of Shakespeare's play at the turn of the century, and carried over into Egypt's iconography in the later screen adaptation by the Italian director Guazzoni. Shakespeare's *Antony and Cleopatra* only gained a secure hold on the British stage from the mid-nineteenth century, when his Cleopatra—that 'Egyptian dish' (2.6.123)—could now feed imperial appetites. Spectacular, pictorial performances of the play were favoured, culminating in the London production by Herbert Beerbohm Tree in 1906 that included, according to astonished reviewers, magic-lantern projections of a sphinx at opening and close, silken canopies and cushioned divans, costumes of shimmering silver with headdresses of gold, exotic dancing girls, and a barge whose scented sails drifted across the stage before a backdrop of the Nile. Throughout its imperial history Britain had compared itself to ancient Rome as a world power, and in recent years had vigorously pursued its own colonial enterprise in Egypt that led to military intervention in 1882 and, by the time of the first world war, the formation of a protectorate. The staging of *Antony and Cleopatra* thus provided a pretext for an oriental pantomime of great political topicality for British audiences and, as a synecdoche for the Orient, Cleopatra was played as languorous and luscious, and as satisfyingly overcome at curtain fall by the belligerent mastery of her western opponent.[28]

The new medium of film emerged during the height of Europe's imperial project between the late nineteenth-century and the beginning of the first world war.[29] The colonizing power of cinema, and the Cleopatra narrative in particular, does not appear to have escaped the Cines production house or the director Enrico Guazzoni. Cines was controlled by the Banco di Roma which had acted as a covert

[28] On the cultural imperialism of turn-of-the-century British stage productions of *Antony and Cleopatra*, see Lamb (1980), 72–98; Madelaine (1998), 44–74; Hodgdon (1998), 74–109.

[29] Shohat (1991*a*), 45.

government agency in developing substantial shipping, banking, and agricultural investments throughout North Africa during the early years of the twentieth century, and whose financial interests were therefore served by the Italian occupation of Libya.[30] During the Libyan campaign of 1911–12, the Italian production house released documentaries on Egypt along with footage of the Libyan war zone. The following year, its historical film *Marcantonio e Cleopatra* opened with actuality shots of Pharaonic monuments borrowed from Cines documentaries such as *Paesaggi egiziani* and *Regno dei Faraoni*. The camera pans around the avenue of ram-headed lions (or *criosphinxes*) at Karnak, and roams over a series of temple ruins, statues, and a pyramid, before initiating the historical narrative proper with the disembarkation of Antony's Roman troops on Egyptian shores.[31] The film literally cannot escape a colonialist intertext. The documentary footage helps to authenticate the ensuing historical reconstruction but, positioned within a narrative of Roman conquest, the footage is itself authenticated as a display of legitimate Italian territorial possession. The historical film, and the narrative image of it promulgated in the Italian press by Guazzoni, also discloses what has been called colonialist cinema's 'visual infatuation with Egypt's material abundance'.[32] The director parades, and draws attention to the parade of, 'the most distinctive places of ancient Rome and ancient Egypt'. The painstaking labour involved in reconstructing 'the sumptuous court of the Ptolemies' is emphasized both in the press and in the film's *mise en scène*, which is cluttered with reproductions of Egyptian architecture and artefacts. This reproduction of the Egyptian past suppresses the colonial conditions of the Libyan present, and the narration of Octavian's victory in Egypt invites the Italian spectator of 1913 on a visit to an Orient that has long since been won.

[30] Bosworth (1979), 139–40; Clark (1984), 153–4; Del Boca (1986), 38–45; Simon (1987), 49–50; Childs (1990), 32–4.

[31] de Vincenti (1988), 25. The opening documentary sequence survives in the Cineteca print, but not in that of the Library of Congress.

[32] Shohat (1991*a*), 49.

In *Marcantonio e Cleopatra*, the narrative of Cleopatra's seduction of Antony is embedded within a spectacle of politically resonant landscapes, monuments, *and* troop movements. Parades of Roman troops appear on numerous occasions and for long sequences of the film. The skill and care with which Enrico Guazzoni attended to the scenography of warfare—the location shooting, artificial lighting, camera movement, and crowd control—were highly praised in reviews of the film, both in Italy and abroad. In *The Moving Picture World* of 10 January 1914, for example, James McQuade wrote:

> Superb scenes are the fall of Alexandria before Octavius; his triumphal entry afterwards at Rome; the landing of the Roman troops in Egypt by moonlight; the long and silent march to Alexandria . . . What terrific scenes are shown on the lofty flight of steps leading up to the royal palace entrance, and on the Nile within the city! The carnage has all the show of blood and death. The Cines supernumeraries—and there are 3500 of them in the scene showing the fall of Alexandria—are really a marvellous force. Seldom, if ever, do they fail to do the right thing, in the right way, at the right time; and this, it must be remembered, is largely due to able direction . . . Those beautiful moonlight effects, taken in the eye of the sun, in the afternoon of a cloudy day, with a veiled lens, are so convincing and artistic that one must cry 'bravo!'. I refer to the scenes showing the landing of the Roman troops in Egypt and to the showing of the beginning of their march to Alexandria. One of these scenes is finely tinted, and gives the effect of an exquisite and gigantic land and sea view in water colors . . .[33]

The central segments of *Marcantonio e Cleopatra*, however, offer its audiences a lesson in how to read such beautifully crafted troop movements morally.

The moral disintegration of Antony, and his oriental entrapment, is marked externally by Amleto Novelli's costume changes in the course of the film, from commanding Roman soldier in military uniform, to romantic Roman civilian in a toga, to subservient 'Egyptian' in Pharaonic headdress and robe. Cross-cutting neatly juxtaposes

[33] Quoted in Martinelli (1993), 42–5, along with a number of other reviews.

Antony's life of leisure and subservience at the savage, feminine Ptolemaic court with Octavian's life of authority at the just, masculine senate house at Rome and Octavian's life of activity commanding the Roman troops on their way to war and victory. The message that Roman civilization is about to triumph over Egyptian barbarity is clearly signalled by the anachronistic presence on screen of a quotation from Virgil's *Aeneid*, seen engraved around the senate-wall high above the heads of the senators as they vote for war in Africa. In Virgil's famous definition of Rome's imperial mission, Aeneas is told

> tu regere imperio populos, Romane, memento
> (hae tibi erunt artes), pacique imponere morem,
> parcere subiectis et debellare superbos. (*Aeneid* 6.851–3)
>
> [but yours will be the rulership of nations,
> remember, Roman, these will be your arts:
> to teach the ways of peace to those you conquer,
> to spare defeated peoples, tame the proud.][34]

The Roman conception of its civilizing mission was used as a constant cover in all the history of Italian expansionism, even at the official level of Italy's ultimatum to Turkey in September 1911 when Italy was presented as providing Tripolitania and Cyrenaica with the *civiltà* which Turkey had denied them.[35] Significantly, in the senate-house sequence of *Marcantonio e Cleopatra*, only part of the last line of the Virgilian mission appears visible in the film frame (E SUBIECTIS ET DEBELLA). The injunction 'to spare' is missing.

The closure of *Marcantonio e Cleopatra*, in order to keep the moral high ground for ancient Rome (and thus, by extension, for modern Italy), works to diminish any pathos or majesty which might accrue to the suicide of Cleopatra and the defeat of Egypt. Towards the end of Shakespeare's play, the queen appears to achieve a form of triumphant apotheosis, asserting that through death she will be united

[34] The translation is that of Mandelbaum (1981).
[35] Cagnetta (1979), 22–5.

in marriage with Antony (5.2.282–6).[36] In its closural aftermath, Charmian famously comments that her mistress' suicide was 'Well done, and fitting for a princess', and Caesar, when he catches sight of her body, says of Cleopatra

> Bravest at the last,
> She levelled at our purposes and, being royal,
> Took her own way. (5.2.334–6)

As if in defiance of the Shakespearean tradition, the intertitle in *Marcantonio e Cleopatra* that follows on Octavian's discovery of Cleopatra's body declares 'truly an inglorious ending for the last of the Ptolemies, the setting of Egypt's star salutes the dawn of Roman rule'.[37] The final shot of *Marcantonio e Cleopatra*, in which Octavian's triumphant parade through Rome dissolves into a salutation to the 'immortal' city, provides a further key to the political resonance of this film for the Italy of the 1910s. It also suggests why Italian audiences in 1913 might have viewed the troop movements of the film with a 'trembling emotion' that was not generated purely by the aesthetic perfection of the military reconstructions. If Rome is eternal, then (in the historical film's terms) what endures for ever is glorious military victory over the Orient: according to Guazzoni, in an interview conducted for a New York-based Italian newspaper that year, his production is capable of persuading its spectators to applaud 'the glories of the Roman eagles everywhere triumphant'.[38] The cinematic language of justification for Octavian's conquest of Egypt, the necessity of saving Rome from oriental emasculation and depravity, can easily translate into a justification for and celebration of the more recent conquest of Libya. Italy's current imperial project here, as elsewhere, is sustained by an appeal to Roman origins and historical continuity: modern Italy is doing nothing less than carrying on Rome's legitimate mission.

[36] Wilders (1995), 3 and 61; Kahn (1997), 137–9; Hamer (2001).

[37] This intertitle, as well as the subsequent triumph in Rome, is missing from the Cineteca print of the film.

[38] Bertellini (1997), 37.

*Marcantonio e Cleopatra* was a huge commercial success, both in Italy and abroad. From the end of 1913 and during the course of 1914, it was distributed throughout Europe, the United States, Latin America, Russia, Asia, Africa, and Australia, often accompanied by grand premières, huge quantities of publicity, and enthusiastic accolades.[39] While reviewers at the time of the film's release dwelt largely on the fine cinematography and careful historical reconstructions of *Marcantonio e Cleopatra*, two years later the film critic Vachel Lindsay drew attention to the imperialist ambition that underlies Guazzoni's display of ancient sites, oriental magnificence, and battles on African soil. According to Lindsay, Guazzoni's historical film 'is equivalent to waving the Italian above the Egyptian flag, quite slowly for two hours'.[40] It would be a mistake, however, to read *Marcantonio e Cleopatra* as unequivocally and unifocally imperialist in design. Even Italian reviewers and Enrico Guazzoni himself (when commenting on the film in the Italian press) focused explicitly on the film's artistic merits rather more than its political ambitions. The film was largely discussed as an attempt to improve upon the cinematographic virtuosity of Guazzoni's earlier success in historical reconstruction, *Quo Vadis?* (1913).

Before the emergence of cinema, its ancestral forms (panoramas, dioramas, magic-lantern shows, and photography) were frequently utilized for the visual reproduction of Egypt within western culture. The material culture of Egypt, meanwhile, gained the status of a silent and mysterious spectacle as ancient tombs were excavated, interpreted, and exhibited throughout the nineteenth century and into the twentieth. From the advent of cinema, its form and content were linked with the discursive constructs of Egyptology. The blackened enclosure of the silent cinema auditorium was assimilated to the dark depth of the Egyptian necropolis, and that assimilation was reinforced through the use of a pseudo-Egyptian architectural style in the construction of some of the new moving-picture palaces. Like

[39] Ball (1968), 166.

[40] *The Art of the Motion Picture* (1915; rev. edn. 1922), 54–5.

a western traveller to the monuments of ancient Egypt, the cinema spectator entered a silent world which spoke through pictorial images akin to hieroglyphs, and saw a kind of immortality preserved on screen akin to the secrets of mummification. The constructs of Egyptology explained, legitimated, and conceptualized the new medium, lending cinema mystery, grandeur, history, and an artistic aura.[41] Reconstructions of ancient Egypt on screen, therefore, could acquire a self-reflexive status as celebrations of cinema's quasi-archaeological powers. With regard to *Marcantonio e Cleopatra*, the skilful reconstructions of ancient Egypt, and discussion of them in the press, drew attention to and celebrated the operations of Italian cinema, and arguably positioned the film's spectators not just as conquering Romans, but also as Romans surrendering to the oriental splendours of film spectacle itself.

The film's representation of Cleopatra, moreover, does not consistently promote a narrative drive towards the just triumph of Octavian. At one point, for example, Cleopatra visualizes the coming Roman victory and draws back in horror as she watches togaed crowds jeering a procession which includes herself and her bound Egyptian subjects. It is this vision of public humiliation that compels her to suicide. Thus, juxtaposed with the final scene of Octavian's victory parade at Rome, film spectators are offered, for at least a brief moment, Cleopatra's tragic point of view. Beyond the film text, the Italian actress who played the Egyptian queen (Gianna Terribili Gonzales) sometimes promoted *Marcantonio e Cleopatra* through personal appearances at screenings or in magazine interviews, since erotic display of the female body was not an insignificant attraction Cleopatra's narrative gave to the film (although scarcely alluded to by the director in his nationalistic press interviews) (Fig. 7.3).[42] The use

[41] Lant (1992) and (1995), 78–80; Shohat (1991*a*), 49–51; Pantazzi (1994), 513–4; Bernstein and Studlar (1997).

[42] Prolo (1951), 56; Martinelli (1993), 46. On the eroticism of the Italian films of this period, see generally, Renzi (1991); Brunetta (1993), 71–91 and 169; Sorlin (1996), 32–4; Ch. 9, below.

FIG. 7.3 Poster advertising Gianna Terribili Gonzales in *Marcantonio e Cleopatra* (1913).

of the actress as a promotional vehicle to sell the film further restructured the cinematic Cleopatra into a pleasurably seductive but sadly tragic figure with whom the *diva* could then claim much sympathy and whose exotic aura she could then inherit for her developing star persona. Both the Egypt reconstructed by Guazzoni, and the Cleopatra performed and disseminated by Terribili

Gonzales, exceed the requirements of colonialism's representational conquests.

## HOLLYWOOD'S VAMPIRE QUEEN (1917)

In the particular case of Cleopatra, Roman history provided the film industry with a narrative of great cultural prestige, with a seemingly momentous justification for cinematic imperialism, eroticism, and the spectacle of the female body, and, as a star system developed in the course of the 1910s, even with a biography that could be appropriated to shape and enhance the public personae of some of cinema's first female stars. In 1914, in the same year as Gianna Terribili Gonzales expressed a passing sympathy with the figure of Cleopatra, the American Fox film studio initiated a far more elaborate and sustained association with the queen and her kingdom for the actress Theodosia Goodman.

According to film historians, no discursive apparatus existed before 1907 for the production of film stars. By 1914, however, a star system was already in place as knowledges concerning the picture-players were expanded and transformed to include not only their acting skills and their personality as constituted across their films, but also questions of their extra-cinematic existence.[43] Goodman was the first American film actress to have a star image manufactured for her by studio press agents, and it was one which was heavily invested in nineteenth-century orientalist structures of meaning.

Nineteenth-century orientalism was a discourse of desire as well as empire. It troped the relationship between colonizing West and colonized East as one of sexual dominance, and represented the western explorer, scholar, or soldier as a masculine subject penetrating either inviting virginal landscape or resisting, libidinal Nature.[44]

[43] See esp. de Cordova (1990).

[44] Said (1985), 188 and 309; Shohat (1991*a*), 46–62 and 69–70; Hughes-Hallett (1991), 93; Yeğenoğlu (1998), esp. 2–3.

But if the Orient could be figured as Woman, so too could Woman be figured as the Orient. The 'other' sex could take on the characteristics of the 'other' culture—mysterious and threatening, sensual and alluring.[45] Offering a ready-made gendered narrative of oriental temptation, seduction, and conquest, the Cleopatras of the nineteenth-century were often figured as capable of affording transcendent, terrifying sexual pleasures to their lovers. In an act of identification rather than possession, an act that assaulted the western displacement of assertive female sexuality onto the elsewhere and the elsewhen, many would-be femmes fatales chose to enhance their own attractions by adopting some of those which had accrued to Cleopatra. Thus Sarah Bernhardt, who performed the role of Cleopatra in productions of Victorien Sardou's play at the turn of the century, claimed that the snakes she used on stage in the death scene were live and kept in her house adorned with jewels. She walked, it was said, a crocodile on a leash. In the 1910s, as the star system emerged and was exploited to market films, the film industry appropriated and then elaborated the personae of nineteenth-century theatrical stars such as Bernhardt for a new kind of 'diva'.[46]

As an industrial marketing device to create and organize audiences for its films, the Fox studio invented an alluring past and an exotic, occult lifestyle for its actress Theodosia Goodman. Her public image was designed to introduce American audiences to a cinematic character which had been successfully launched a few years earlier by the Danish film industry, namely the dangerous yet alluring modern 'vamp' or homebreaker who takes pleasure in ruthlessly seducing men, and then abandons them once drained of their fortunes, their will to live, and their blood.[47] Goodman was to star in almost forty such Fox films from 1915 to 1919, but she was placed under contract to both play and seemingly be the part.

[45] Yeğenoğlu (1998), 56.

[46] Hughes-Hallett (1991), 263 and 346–8; Renzi (1991), 121.

[47] Renzi (1991), 121, and Lant (1992), 109.

While, from 1914, Goodman began to play film roles as a voracious, serial mistress, using a (usually) married man sexually and then abandoning him for her next victim, Fox press releases that were fed to newspapers and fan magazines proceeded to wrap her up in orientalist publicity. Although the actress was the daughter of a Jewish tailor from Cincinnati, the studio claimed fantastically that the star had been born at an Egyptian oasis, in the shadow of the Sphinx, and had sucked the venom of serpents as an infant. They noted that her name—now converted to Theda Bara—was an anagram of Arab Death. While the actress lived with her parents, the Fox publicists generated a star image for Bara as a heartbreaker, a 'torpedo of domesticity', whose dark and voluptuous beauty would bring 'suffering and ruin to thousands of sturdy labourers and their families'. Her home in Los Angeles (to which she moved in mid-1917) was reportedly furnished in 'Early Vampire' ottomans, rugs, and beaded curtains, and reeked with musk. In the presence of the press she would stroke a snake and speak of her attachment to a statue of Amen-Ra. She was not to be seen outdoors in daylight.[48] Drawing on nineteenth-century fantasies of Egypt, the Fox studio dressed its star in the aesthetics of occult ritual, despotic power, a dripping and languid sexuality, and perverse death.[49]

The culmination and apparent legitimation of this procedure, whereby a Hollywood studio articulated the vamp's aggressive eroticism in orientalist terms, came with the release of *Cleopatra* in 1917. Directed by J. Gordon Edwards, the historical film constituted a vehicle for the visual display of Theda Bara's sensual exoticism (and its narrative punishment) (Fig. 7.4). The Fox Film Corporation's publicity bureau now identified Cleopatra as 'the most famous vamp in history' and Theda Bara as her 'reincarnation'. Thus, to advertise

[48] For accounts of Theda Bara's star image, see Parish (1971), 17–47; Bodeen (1976), 13–28; Golden (1996); Genini (1996).

[49] For a convenient summary of 19th-cent. fantasies of Egypt, see Meskell (1998), 64–7. For more detailed discussion, see Curl (1994); Humbert *et al.* (1994); Montserrat (2000).

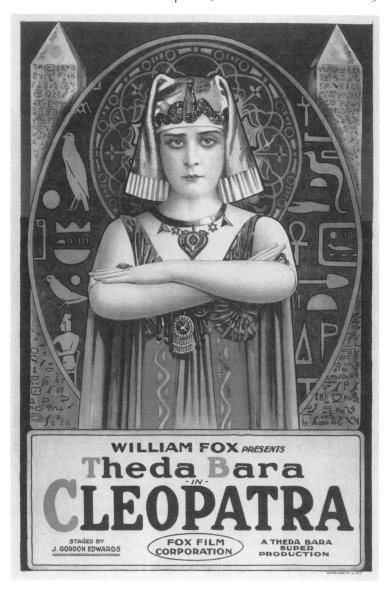

FIG. 7.4 Poster advertising Theda Bara in *Cleopatra* (1917).

the opening of its spectacular epic in October 1917 and to shape spectators' readings of the film, the studio's press department asked moviegoers portentously: 'What will be your verdict after you see Theda Bara's portrayal of the passions and pageants of Egypt's vampire queen?'[50] Simultaneously, in numerous press releases, Fox claimed that Bara had received a tribute in hieroglyphs from a reincarnated servant of Cleopatra, posed her in a museum gazing reflectively at 'her own' mummified remains, and quoted their star as proclaiming: 'I know that I am a reincarnation of Cleopatra. It is not a mere theory in my mind. I have positive knowledge that such is the case. I live Cleopatra, I breathe Cleopatra, I *am* Cleopatra.'[51] Both film (now sadly lost) and marketing framed the cinematic representation of the Ptolemaic ruler as promised authentication of the star image long since established for the American actress.[52]

In the economy of the film industry star images are marketing devices, but they are also cultural commodities or discursive sites for the exploration of threatened social values.[53] The particular star image of the vamp (so popular in the 1910s and early 1920s) has been interpreted as an index of the struggle at the beginning of the twentieth century to define appropriate genders and sexualities for an America that, faced with the growth of immigration, female emancipation, and a multicultural urban life, could no longer sustain a picture of itself as an agrarian, small-town, Anglo-Saxon republic of domesticated wives and puritan husbands.[54] In the early decades of

[50] Quoted in Magill (1982), 322. Cf. the very favourable verdict on *Cleopatra* in *Moving Picture World* for 3 November 1917, which reproduces the studio description of Theda Bara as acting 'the Egyptian vampire'.

[51] Quoted in Golden (1996), 130.

[52] No print of *Cleopatra* (1917) survives, but its content can be deduced from surviving stills, contemporary publicity, and reviews.

[53] For theories of film stardom, see esp. Dyer (1987) and (1998); Gledhill (1991). For the intersection of star images with contemporary discourses of femininity, and the importance of that intersection for reading filmic representations of Cleopatra and Messalina, see also Chs. 8 and 10 below.

[54] On Hollywood cinema's vamps, see Higashi (1978), 55–78; Staiger (1995), 147–62; Studlar (1997), 115–17.

the twentieth century, the hegemony of native-born Americans was seemingly threatened by the arrival of millions of immigrants from eastern and southern Europe and by the emergence of the phenomenon of the 'new woman'. The 'new woman' was a term that began to circulate in the United States from the 1890s, its coinage signalling a recognition of (and debate about) an evident shift away from the nineteenth-century conception of woman's sphere of operation as properly limited to the home, marriage, and the family. Concern about women's emancipation from domesticity into the public world of work, about women's demands for the right to vote, to limit their fertility, and actively to express their sexual desires, was assimilated to concern about immigration, and expressed by eugenicists in terms of the dangers of miscegenation. Cinematically, the modern woman and the new immigrant were conjoined as an urban other or Orient within: located in an exotic *mise en scène*, they were characterized as consumed by an obsessive taste for sybaritic luxury and depraved sex.[55]

The discourse of 'internal orientalism'—the orientalizing of races and genders that are subordinated or marginalized *within* western nations—gave the Hollywood film industry an array of defensive mechanisms with which to assuage concerns about sexualized femininity and mongrelism.[56] Such orientalism suffused the contemporary sexual comedies directed by Cecil B. DeMille in the silent era. Two years after the release of *Cleopatra*, for example, *Don't Change Your Husband* (1919) dealt with a bored wife who abandons the dissatisfactions of her marriage for the exotic and luxurious world of a gigolo only to be satisfactorily restored to husband and marriage at film's close. The artwork employed to promote DeMille's film included the image of a sphinx and a pyramid, and the title 'The

[55] On the 'new woman', see Smith (1989), 317–63; Heller and Rudnick (1991). On her assimilation to the new immigrant in American cinema, see Higashi (1994), esp. 3; Studlar (1997), esp. 100.

[56] For the mechanisms of 'internal orientalism', see Turner (2000), 12–14.

Eternal Feminine', in order to advertise its concern with the question of what the new woman wanted.[57] Similarly, to advertise her screen image as a contemporary vamp or husband-stealer, Theda Bara was photographed surrounded by skulls and snakes (for the 1914 release of *A Fool There Was*) and (in a *Photoplay* article of September 1915) labelled a 'daughter of the Sphinx'. In such films, the modern Orient within is structured as a locus of decadent passion to which wives are lured by gigolos or husbands by vamps and where, frequently, they are destroyed. More specifically, given early cinema's close alignment with the rhetoric of Egyptology, the perceived problem of female gratification beyond or outside marriage is clothed in Egypt's antiquity and occult mystery. The modern woman projected on screen is reassuringly figured as a social hieroglyph: her desires an eternal riddle as indecipherable as the silent Sphinx.[58]

In 1917, on posters advertising *Cleopatra*, Theda Bara's face was superimposed over that of a sphinx and, according to surviving descriptions of the film's opening sequence, after a long shot of the 'desert wastes' of Ventura County, the camera raced towards the studio-built pyramids and a monumental sphinx, the latter of which then dissolved into the features of Bara/Cleopatra suddenly opening her eyes.[59] The cinematic troping of the sexualized new woman as decadent Orient and mysterious sphinx, and its embodiment in the star Theda Bara, is here provided with an explanatory origin in 'real' Egypt and 'legitimate' history. The Orient of Fox's *Cleopatra* provides an imaginative field of free play for a shamelessly paranoid, hyperbolic elaboration of American traumas about gender, sexuality, ethnicity, and race,[60] set safely in a distant elsewhere and elsewhen that offers the historical guarantee of the Occident's ultimate supremacy.

[57] Higashi (1994), 151–2.

[58] Lant (1992), 109–10, and (1995), 78–80. Cf. Higashi (1994), 3 and 108.

[59] As catalogued in Ball (1968), 239; Hughes-Hallett (1991), 330–1 and 340; Lant (1992), 109–10.

[60] I here adapt Peter Wollen's description of the functions of the Orient in early twentieth-century visual arts including the scenography of dance, (1987), 17.

In the absence of the urgent colonial investments of the Italian *Cleopatra* released four years earlier, the Hollywood representation of the Ptolemaic queen becomes an account of a woman more than a war, and its visual pleasures those of erotic seductions more than military manoeuvres.[61] Drawing on and adding to the nineteenth-century 'mankiller' fantasies of Rider Haggard and Victorien Sardou (as well as the more customary Plutarch and Shakespeare), the film's narrative drive displays no less than three major examples of transgressive female sexuality. For sandwiched between the expected unveiling of the queen's physical charms before Julius Caesar in the palace at Alexandria, and her sumptuous strategies for enticing Antony on board her barge at Cydnus, is the wholly fictitious captivation of the Egyptian Pharon who steals from the tombs of his ancestors, the Pharaohs, in order to please his demanding mistress.[62] In an earlier draft of the scenario, still preserved in the archives of the University of Southern California, explicit instructions are given that Cleopatra's love scenes 'should be as strong and "Oriental" as will be allowed. Cleopatra when she did love must have been a "bear".'[63]

In a film that generally cast Mexicans as Egyptians, 'fair-haired Americans' as Romans, and 'real negroes' as slaves, Cleopatra is shaped as an alarmingly literal and authenticating version of the twentieth-century's metaphoric vamp.[64] This vamp and her foolish victims play out in the classical past contemporary, conservative fears that capitulation to the social and sexual demands of women would

[61] Obeidat (1998), 127, and MacKenzie (1995), 9–10, note that until the United States became a prime political actor in the Middle East from the late twentieth century, its Orient was largely experienced indirectly and patterned on French and British discourses of colonialism.

[62] The character is inherited from an earlier *Cleopatra* released in 1913 by the Helen Gardner Picture Players.

[63] USC Film and Television Archive, 20th-Century Fox Collection, Box 41, Item 1464.

[64] To operate as the origin of America's 'urban other', however, Hollywood's Cleopatra cannot be represented as the black African queen that, for example, MacDonald (1996) finds suggested by the description of her as of tawny front and pinched black by love in the first act of Shakespeare's *Antony and Cleopatra*.

threaten the vitality of men and the American nation—for this mistress 'wrecked empires'. But spectators could consume the film's visual pleasures safe in the knowledge that Cleopatra eventually succumbed to a 'pure love', and ultimately wrecked not a western, masculine empire but merely her own.[65] A review in *Motion Picture News* of 3 November 1917 imagines the thought-processes of one such spectator on leaving the cinema where he has just seen Theda Bara's Cleopatra in action:

> His mind will drift back to the first half of the picture when Miss Bara wore a different costume in every episode. Different pieces of costume rather; or better still different varieties of beads. His temperature will ascend with a jump when he recalls the easy way in which the siren captivated Caesar and Pharon and Antony. If he knows the picture business he may wonder about Pennsylvania and Chicago and other places with censor boards that have no appreciation for the female form in a state that so nearly approaches nudeness that only a few strings of beads stand in the way. He might suddenly realize that his mother back in Hohokus would shut her eyes once or twice for fear the beads might break or slip, but then—mother never did understand Egyptian history after all.

Such extratextual discourses of costume disclose that in J. Gordon Edwards' *Cleopatra* (1917), in contrast to Enrico Guazzoni's *Marcantonio e Cleopatra* (1913), Cleopatra/Bara has become the focus of the look, her body the centre of spectacle rather than 'landings and battles' and 'the most distinctive places of ancient Rome and Egypt'.

Similarly, alongside claims that the production cost over half a million dollars, the Fox pressbooks illustrated and dwelt lovingly on the numerous exotic costumes in which Theda Bara could be viewed seducing her on- (and off-) screen admirers:

> It was an age of barbaric splendour in everything, and with all the ruby and sapphire mines of the East to call upon, a Queen went robed in brilliance.

[65] The quotations all come from the Fox pressbook produced for the British release of the film that can be found in the Special Collections of the British Film Institute, London.

> There is one filmy robe of gold tissue, and with it are worn a perfect outfit of pearls and rubies which are so remarkable a specimen of jeweller's art that they must be seen to be believed. The headpiece of massed pearls with its great cabochon rubies inset in it, matched by the great ruby star worn at the breast, must be seen to be realised; and another wonderful effect is when Cleopatra leads her forces to battle against the Romans, when she goes habited in a bodice and apron piece of gold scales, and a headdress in the form of the Sacred Bird surmounted by the sign of Osiris.[66]

The accompanying photograph displays Theda Bara so costumed, seated majestically so as to look back and down at the humbled viewer of her jewelled splendours (Fig. 7.5). The star image, film, and marketing which encourage the identification of Theda Bara with Cleopatra can all be read as conforming to the structures of an orientalist cinema that solicit a 'gendered Western gaze'.[67] The spectator is constituted as a western traveller undertaking an initiation into the barbaric splendours of an unknown culture, their gendered male gaze drawn to an East embodied as a mysterious but alluring woman who feeds an imperialist appetite for her possession.[68]

What, then, of the female spectator of *Cleopatra* (1917)? The Fox pressbooks do not offer details of jewellery and fabric in terms that most women could or would attempt to reproduce in their lives outside the cinema—despite the precedent of a nineteenth-century tradition that regularly saw aristocratic women attending fancy dress balls richly attired in Cleopatra costumes.[69] Nor did the studio attempt to solicit from female audiences their own practical identification with the star-as-Cleopatra. Instead the press agents fed to fan magazines representative 'examples' of audience responses to Bara's

[66] Ibid. [67] See esp. Shohat (1991*a*).

[68] Cf. Hodgdon (1998), 91–101, on the extratextual discourses of costume that surrounded Tree's staging of Shakespeare's *Antony and Cleopatra* in 1906.

[69] Described in Hughes-Hallett (1991), 346–8. Hodgdon (1998), 95, notes that by 1907 Cleopatra had already become dispersed into mass culture in, for example, fashion exhibitions held in American department stores. Yet the advertisement she quotes for such an exhibition concedes that 'American women cannot be gowned in the flowing draperies of Cleopatra', but can be dressed in Egyptian motifs.

FIG. 7.5 Theda Bara displays a costume from *Cleopatra* (1917).

image as oriental vamp. In *Picture-Play Magazine* for 15 February 1916, for example, an article supposedly written by the star herself talks of letters of abuse received from angry wives and letters of love from desirous husbands. One of the latter, writing all the way from Australia, is said to have declared: 'I have gone insane over dreams of you, my Egyptian queen, soul of my soul! Without you, life is but a void, and earth a desert drear. Come to my arms, oh, Cleopatra; my heart is burning for you! I want you. I want you!'

Yet such fan magazines constitute an index of how women were frequently positioned as more distanced, sophisticated, and sceptical consumers of star images than the above 'responses' would suggest.[70] The same *Picture-Play* article also clearly concedes that any identification of Bara with a vamping Cleopatra is merely an entertaining charade. Bara professes herself amused by the letters which suggest some spectators have been duped by her star image. The photographs which illustrate Bara's account of her birth in the desert sands of Egypt and her subsequently strange life carry undercutting captions such as 'Theda Bara's greatest ambition away from the screen is to live down her film reputation—and look as unlike a vampire as possible'. The largely female readership that magazines like *Picture-Play* acknowledge explicitly through their mode of address is drawn into a community of women utterly aware of the film industry's illusionistic strategies for star-making, and placed in pleasing complicity with the star herself. They understand with Bara that her brand of femininity is playfully performative and therefore, if anything, it is more appealing. Divested of any real danger or sin, her masquerade as Cleopatra offers a momentary escape from the everyday domestic constraints of traditional femininity into an Orient figured (both on- and off-screen) as home to a woman of formidable power and sexual passion. Too extraordinary to be imitable, Theda Bara's performance of *Cleopatra* was the biggest American box-office success of 1917. The

[70] For this and the argument below, see more generally Studlar (1996) and (1997) on silent era fan magazines and their address to female spectators.

most advertised, written-about, and talked-about film of the year constituted an early form of twentieth-century Cleomania that concerned spectatorial desire but only the star's identification.

The Hollywood Cleopatras of subsequent eras did not continue to be shaped along the contours of an exotic and destructive vamp. With, for example, the further development of the Hollywood star system and the classical Hollywood style of film production, with the advent of the new technology of sound, with the rise of consumerism, and the increasing intervention of women in the public domain, the Hollywood Cleopatra came to be structured along the lines of a less outlandish, more glamorous figure. She was now to be looked at, consumed, and even identified with—a role-model for female spectators in the art of seducing their own modern-day 'Romans'.

# 8

# Glamour Girl: Cleopatra 1930s–1960s

While Elizabeth Taylor was in Rome shooting the spectacular Hollywood epic *Cleopatra*, women's magazines began to advise their readers on how to construct for themselves a new Egyptian look. An article in *Look* magazine for 27 February 1962 predicted:

> Superimpose two such famous glamour girls as Elizabeth Taylor and Cleopatra, and you are in for a beauty boom. In her role as Egypt's seductive queen, actress Taylor's exotic eye makeup, diverse hair styles (devised with 30 wigs), magnificent jewels and gowns are bound to inspire a new Egyptian look every bit as sweeping as the recent tousled B.B. and pale-lipped Italian looks.

Alongside a glamour photograph of two models, the text indicates what the magazine's staff have done to provide them with 'the new Egyptian look reminiscent of the regal, exotic beauties seen on ancient bas-reliefs': eyes lined with kohl to cultivate a sensuous, cat-like look; mouths boldly painted to create the illusion of a full lower

This chapter is a substantially revised and extended version of part of a chapter in my book *Projecting the Past: Ancient Rome, Cinema and History* (Routledge, 1997).

FIG. 8.1 Photographic illustration to article on 'the new Egyptian look', for *Look*, 27 February 1962.

lip; eyebrows heavily outlined in black; Nile-green eye shadow, henna-coloured powder, and a Cleopatra coif applied to the blonde; white shadow, very pale powder, and a high-rising Nefertiti hair style applied to the brunette; the necks of both decorated with elaborate beaded collars made out of costume-jewellery (Fig. 8.1). The following page offers detailed instructions addressed directly to the magazine's readers on 'How to change American girls into Egyptian beauties—with new hairdos', while the last displays 'a Liz Taylor look-alike' successfully kitted out for the evening in the Cleopatra look.[1] The purpose of this chapter, following on from the last, is to explore this most personalized and intimate cinematic technology of

[1] Cf. an earlier article in *Vogue*, for 15 January 1962, which focuses rather more on the supposed Cleopatran life-style of Elizabeth Taylor but also predicts 'a new Cleopatra complex' in fashions, hairstyles, and cosmetics.

Cleomania that was widely disseminated and even inscribed on the bodies of modern women, kitting them out to seduce their twentieth-century 'Roman' lovers.

The preceding chapter disclosed a shift in the cinematic representation of the Ptolemaic queen: first located in Guazzoni's *Marcantonio e Cleopatra* (1913) within the geography of colonialism as Italy's African other, she is then brought into a western cultural landscape as America's troubling urban other in Gordon Edward's *Cleopatra* (1917). In the first case, Cleopatra is appropriated to feminize an Orient now awaiting possession by her new Roman conquerors, in the second she facilitates the exoticizing of western Woman who, Cleopatra's history suggests, is to be feared but can be mastered. While both films of the 1910s largely solicit a gendered male gaze, later Hollywood productions of the 1930s and 1960s appear to solicit a new mode of looking at their Egyptian queen. This chapter explores the mechanisms by which Hollywood domesticated, glamourized, and commodified Cleopatra, inviting female spectators to consume that image, identify with it, and adopt it in their lives outside the cinema. The boundaries between past and present are breached: Cleopatra becomes an American girl, and American girls become Cleopatras.

## HOLLYWOOD'S GLAMOUR GIRL (1934)

When Cecil B. DeMille's *Cleopatra* was released in 1934, journalists frequently commented on the modernity and humour of its dialogue, as if the director had produced a sexual comedy about a modern woman, even though set entirely in antiquity. A review in *The New York Times* of 17 August 1934 observed that 'When a gathering of Roman women are talking about Caesar, it is done in the modern fashion, with one of the fair ones remarking that "the wife always is the last to hear" of her husband's love affairs.' While, in the censorious judgement of *Variety* for 21 August 1934, the same Roman social gathering was played ill-advisedly 'like a modern bridge night', and Claudette Colbert, in the role of Cleopatra, conducted herself like 'a cross between a lady of the evening and a rough soubrette in a country melodrama'.

It was not only the colloquial dialogue of *Cleopatra* that appeared to elide any significant distinction between the social habits of the past and those of the American present. The film was a product of the pairing of a distinctive director with a distinctive studio, Paramount. By the 1930s Paramount had become celebrated for its regular production of an array of elegant comedies characterized by a witty script and an opulent *mise en scène*—a house style that derived from the studio's success throughout the 1920s in producing and distributing contemporary sexual comedies directed by DeMille.[2]

From the 1890s on into the 1930s, there occurred in the United States a significant increase in the proportion of women in paid labour or with access to higher education and the professions, a dramatic rise in maternal and infant health, in wealth, and in the purchase of consumer goods such as cars, leisure activities, cosmetics, and home furnishings. DeMille's romantic comedies of the silent era had projected on screen the radical changes in family and sexual life that accompanied these developments, such as an increase in pre- and extra-marital sex, and in rates of divorce. By the 1920s, when American women had already achieved general suffrage, and were now campaigning for legalized birth-control and for an Equal Rights amendment to the constitution, DeMille was pioneering a fresh marital ethics for Hollywood cinema. DeMille's modern woman, on gaining access to the new middle-class lifestyle of conspicuous consumption and secular hedonism, is, by the close of each film, safely restored to marriage as a fashion plate and passionate sexual playmate.[3] In several of these films, historical flashbacks, such as a

[2] Elley (1984), 93; Izod (1988), 87–8. On Paramount in the 1930s more generally, see Baxter (1993).

[3] On the modern woman of the early twentieth-century, see Smith (1989), 317–453; Heller and Rudnick (1991). On DeMille's representation of her in his silent films, see esp. Higashi (1994), and cf. May (1980), 200–36; Black (1994), 26–8; Christie (1991), 20.

Babylonian fantasy in *Male and Female* (1919) or a Roman orgy in *Manslaughter* (1922), suggest a key to DeMille's deployment of antiquity to project modern sexualities on screen: as both wish-fulfilment and warning. Scenes set in the ancient world give an opportunity for more ostentatious display than the contemporary ones into which they are inserted. Historical flashbacks also provide a suitably salutary lesson for the present, since the films imply that it is the sexual and material excess exhibited in these sequences which once led to the downfall of civilizations.[4]

Dialogue and director, studio and casting all helped to mark *Cleopatra* (1934) as a comedy of modern manners in fancy dress. The casting policy for the film, especially regarding the opening half where Warren William is seen playing Julius Caesar, connects the scenes in ancient Rome with contemporary life in New York. For the star image of both William and Colbert, by which audiences would have been attracted into the cinema to see *Cleopatra*, included their previous appearances on screen as members of urban America's smart set. William was already famous for taking on roles as a refined New Yorker, and Colbert had just played a sophisticated modern American wife in the Academy Award winning *It Happened One Night* (1934).[5]

Some of the promotional material which followed the release of *Cleopatra* (despite claiming for the film the accuracy of a Plutarchan biography, and the cultural prestige of a Shakespearian or Shavian drama) even drew explicit attention to DeMille's cinematic modernization of the ancient Romans and Egyptians, and attempted to solicit from its young addressees a suitably prestigious justification for that process. Paramount set up a contest for college students and high-school seniors offering prizes, or 'Cleopatra scholarships', of five hundred dollars each for the three essays which best respond-

[4] May (1980), 212–13; Higashi (1994), 100; Black (1994), 28, Christie (1991), 20.

[5] Hamer (1993), 119–21. On Colbert's star image, see also Parish (1972), 92–141; Everson (1976); Balio (1993), 149–50; Viviani (1997).

ed to a range of questions the studio posed concerning the film director's treatment of history. Question 44 of the *Study Guide and Manual* (which Paramount distributed to schools in order to launch the contest) asked:

> R. H. Case calls Shakespeare's 'Antony and Cleopatra' 'an extraordinarily vivid presentment in Elizabethan terms of events and characters of the ancient world'. Would it be fair to describe DeMille's 'Cleopatra' as 'an extraordinarily vivid presentment in *American* terms of events and characters of the ancient world?' Justify your answer.[6]

DeMille's *Cleopatra* was thus closely bound in its production, packaging, and reception to the representation of contemporary American social mores—whatever the studio's attempted justifications, reviewers persisted in remarking unhappily upon the film's privileging of the present: 'all the early Romans and Egyptians seem so definitely like modern Americans, all ready for the costume ball' (*New York Herald Tribune*, 17 August 1934). Yet the Egyptian setting and the Cleopatra narrative were not just arbitrary pieces of fancy dress, as such reviews might imply.

DeMille's *Cleopatra* was made in a climate of ever increasing national concern about the moral content and effects of Hollywood films. According to the Republican reformer Will Hays, at the time of his appointment by the major studios in 1922 as an internal regulator of the film industry, films had to be made 'giving the public all the sex it wants with compensating values for all those church and women groups'.[7] DeMille is regarded as having found a shrewd film formula to meet Hays's requirements during the 1920s, namely romantic triangles, spiced with liberal displays of sex and consumption, and diluted by the triumph of marriage at the film's close.[8] The early years of the Depression, however, witnessed a proliferation of films visualizing (and *talking* about) divorce, adultery, prostitution,

[6] See Paramount's *Study Guide and Manual* (1934), 16, and compare question 47.

[7] Quoted in May (1980), 204–5.

[8] Izod (1988), 69–70; Black (1994), 27–34.

crime, and violence, despite the installation in 1930 of a formal Production Code which clearly stipulated that the Hollywood studios should promote the institutions of marriage, home, and family.[9] When DeMille released *Sign of the Cross* in 1932—starring Colbert as the cruel and licentious empress Poppaea who incites Nero to the persecution of the Christians—he might have anticipated that he could display sex, nudity, arson, homosexuality, lesbianism, mass murder, and orgies relatively uncontentiously. For they were all clothed in religious history and all marked as pagan depravities, nobly scorned or endured by the heroine and (ultimately) the hero, who are seen in the closing moments of the film virtuously conjoined in spiritual union as they ascend into the blazing light of Christian salvation. But, however pious the film's conclusion, and despite its enormous box-office success, the spectacular sex and sadism of *Sign of the Cross* only exacerbated the already intensifying national debate over the morality of motion pictures.[10]

*Cleopatra* was released in July 1934, just three months after the Catholic Church had launched its pressure group the Legion of Decency, which pledged millions of Catholics to boycott films judged immoral, and in the same month as the industry felt compelled to appoint a lay catholic as head of a new Production Code Administration with considerably greater powers to police the content of Hollywood films and to enforce adherence to the Code.[11] Facing the pressure of a more restrictive Production Code, the seeming historicity and literariness of *Cleopatra* provided DeMille with a less objectionable formula than that of *Sign of the Cross* with which to attract spectators. The seductions of Colbert/Cleopatra were now displayed in a milder and more indirect form than those of Colbert/Poppaea, and they received their proper punishment at the film's close. Encased in a secular narrative, they were also less likely

[9] Izod (1988), 105–6; Baxter (1993), 3–5; Black (1994), 1 and 39–83.

[10] Black (1994), 65–70; Wyke (1997), 131–7.

[11] Izod (1988), 106; Maltby (1993), 37–72; Black (1994), 149–97.

to aggravate the powerful lobbying forces of organized American religion. Cleopatra was thus a highly appropriate vehicle for the display and exploration of contemporary concerns about female sexuality in 1930s America, without fear of significant censure.

Cast in Graeco-Roman historiography as a woman who lived outside the bounds of marriage, in her later western reception Cleopatra VII always provided a challenge to concepts of the good wife and mother.[12] But the union in her person of a transgressive sexuality with political power gave the Ptolemaic queen an additional, special currency for the America of the 1930s. Between the two world wars, with the increasing entry of women into the public domain and an associated intensification of debates about women's political role, there was a significant increase in the number of western reassessments of the queen's reign.[13] An academic redefinition of Cleopatra had already begun in 1864, with the publication of a biography defending the queen by the German historian Adolf Stahr. His work was followed by a series of histories and novels which ridiculed the Roman portrait of a wicked seductress, such as that by the Inspector General of Egyptian Antiquities, Arthur Weigall. Weigall's *The Life and Times of Cleopatra Queen of Egypt* (1914, revised edition 1923) undercut the exoticism and decadent sensuality of the West's Cleopatra by emphasizing her identity as Greek (rather than Egyptian or African) and drew sympathetic attention to her political vision of a pan-Hellenic empire subsuming East and West: 'statecraft made a strong appeal to her, and as Queen of Egypt she served the cause of her dynasty's independence and aggrandisement with passionate energy' (p. 21); she was 'consumed at times with desire for world power' (p. 22).[14] More radically still, in *Scenes from the Life of Cleopatra* (1935), the British novelist Mary Butts depicted the queen, in the words of one recent critic, as a woman who could 'wield power

[12] Hamer (2001). [13] Hamer (1993), 109–10.

[14] On Weigall, see Hughes-Hallett (1991), 315–16; Hoberman (1997), 148 n. 2; Montserrat (2000), 4 and 103–5; above, Ch. 6.

while remaining autonomous, maternal, and sexual', and sought through her feminist fiction 'to make room in Western culture for the very concept of a female maker of history'.[15]

During the course of the 1930s, among an array of plays, novels, and biographies about the queen,[16] a corresponding reaction to these revisions surfaced with, for example, Oscar von Wertheimer's *Cleopatra—a Royal Voluptuary* (published in an English translation in 1931, three years before the release of DeMille's film). The biography's preface begins:

> Cleopatra, Queen of Egypt, has from time immemorial made the strongest appeal to the imagination of men. She is the most outstanding example of the sphinx in woman—the creature designed by nature to shed lustre and enchantment on life, but also to prove its undoing. Even hundreds of years after her death men of the highest intellectual attainments continued to fall beneath her magic spell. And could any woman fail to envy her powers of fascination? We judge men by their achievements and women by the love they have inspired.[17]

Paramount's *Study Guide* for the college-aged audiences of DeMille's *Cleopatra* clearly engages with this historical debate and comes down expressly in favour of Wertheimer's restoration of orientalism's cruel but fascinating voluptuary. In the studio's promotional literature, despite references to Shakespeare, Dryden, and Shaw as source material, Wertheimer's becomes the master-text against which to test the veracity of DeMille's film adaptation. Contestants for the 'Cleopatra scholarship' are encouraged to read the German historian's biography before responding to the set questions, passages from *The Royal Voluptuary* are quoted (including criticism of Weigall), and several scenes or characterizations in the film are justified as

[15] Hoberman (1997), 137 and 148 respectively.

[16] Hamer (1993), 148 n. 19, provides a useful list.

[17] Oscar Von Wertheimer, *Cleopatra. A Royal Voluptuary* (1931, trans. H. Paterson), London: George G. Harrap, 5. On which see Hughes-Hallett (1991), 276, 287–8, 296, and 319–20.

carrying out Wertheimer's conception of events. Following the historical model offered by Wertheimer, Paramount's *Study Guide* describes Cleopatra's political policies disdainfully as an example of the 'unbridled ambition of women'.[18] For Wertheimer, Paramount, and DeMille narratives of Cleopatra can play out the problem of Woman, now articulated in contemporary terms of claims on sexual independence and political authority: 'she was a magic mistress and a regal ruler, able to satisfy the demands of the night, but also every claim of the day'; a woman 'seizing pleasures while pursuing ambition'.[19]

Like Wertheimer's biography, DeMille's film initiates an exploration of the eternally fascinating 'sphinx in woman'. The orientalist structures of meaning which refigured the representation of Cleopatra from the time of the Napoleonic campaigns in Egypt, persisted into her cinematic depictions in the silent era of the early twentieth-century, and re-emerged in biographies of the 1930s, continue to bolster the expression of contemporary social concerns in DeMille's *Cleopatra*. The film's first image is of two stones drawn back like curtains to reveal the action behind them, its last image that of the stones drawn together to conceal the preceding spectacle. Cleopatra's story is thus framed both as spectacle and as penetration of the exotic mysteries of Woman, for the queen is first revealed in a desert landscape amid Pharaonic monuments covered in hieroglyphs and last seen silent, remote, and majestic in death, enthroned in the royal palace at Alexandria beneath a giant winged scarab.[20]

Before *Cleopatra*, however, orientalism had already suffused DeMille's cinematic practice, as a means to mark out not just a new and troubling feminine identity, but also a new and troubling ethnic identity. In sectors of the American urban communities of the early

[18] See Paramount's *Study Guide and Manual* (1934), 15, question 34.

[19] Wertheimer (1931), 107–8.

[20] Cf. Hamer (1993), 124–6; above, Ch. 7. Lant (1992), 91–3 and n. 19, argues additionally that the film's frame constructs the spectator's experience, as in early lantern shows, in terms of entering an Egyptian necropolis.

twentieth century, concern about the huge new influx of immigrants from in and outside Europe was assimilated to concern about the increased independence of women, since both were construed equally as threats to the existing social formation. Both 'modern' women and new immigrants were often figured cinematically in orientalist terms. As the collective urban other—the Orient within—they were often set in luxurious boudoirs indulging their taste for the exotic and the erotic.[21] In the first half of DeMille's *Cleopatra*, the Egyptian queen seduces Julius Caesar in Alexandria and then comes to Rome, where Caesar is planning to divorce his wife Calpurnia, set himself up as king, and make Cleopatra his queen. Articulated with wider discourses of gender and ethnicity, DeMille's representation of the oriental queen's arrival in Rome and her impact on the Romans would have had a special hold on urban American audiences. For the United States is a society where ethnic composition and immigration exist at the core of its historical and cultural formation.[22]

In the Roman sequences of DeMille's *Cleopatra*, at the dinner-party (which *Variety* scathingly compared to 'a modern bridge night'), the gossip concerns Julius Caesar's rumoured divorce and his designs to convert the republic into a monarchy. During Cleopatra's ensuing triumphal procession through the streets of Rome, when the more familiar images of Julius Caesar's Roman soldiers and chariots, trumpets, and magisterial *fasces* are swiftly supplanted by the bizarre music, black attendants, animal iconography, and canopied sedan of the enthroned queen, cinema audiences are offered the opportunity to identify with the Roman crowds on screen who have cheered their Roman leader but observe the arrival of his Egyptian mistress in bemused silence. In subsequent scenes, at the Roman baths and in the house of Julius Caesar, first the conspirators and then Mark Antony express volubly their anxieties about the

[21] See above, Ch. 7.

[22] For the importance of ethnicity and immigration in both American society and Hollywood cinema, see Shohat (1991*b*), esp. 217–18; Higashi (1994); Bernstein and Studlar (1997); Bertellini (1999).

malign influence now exerting itself on Caesar and the city at large. 'Rome', they protest, 'cannot be turned into another Orient with golden thrones for a king and queen.' 'That woman', they complain to Julius Caesar, 'is making an Egyptian out of you' and 'a fool'. In these film sequences, Rome is characterized as a republican, masculine world, where women are domesticated wives and only men have political authority: of women, Mark Antony vehemently declares 'They've no place among men. They can't think and they can't fight. They're just playthings for us.' That virile world is perceived to be under threat from the intrusion of the tyrannical, feminine world of Egypt, where women are rulers of both the state and their menfolk: 'Look at the Roman eagle, with half the world in his claws, tamed by a woman!'[23]

In its 'hegemonic national imaginary' the United States has been projected as essentially an Anglo-American nation whose purity is endangered by other, subordinated ethnicities seeping in or already lurking inside.[24] If at times those subordinated ethnicities were figured as a feminine Orient, from its inception the hegemonic Nation was figured as a virile Rome.[25] The long-standing and widely disseminated practice of utilizing the virtues of the Roman republic to underscore the heroism of America's Founding Fathers enhances the cultural competence of spectators to read the appalled Romans of DeMille's film as historical analogies for themselves—here positioned with the old Anglo-aristocracy of America's cities whose hegemony appears to be threatened by the arrival of an urban other. Set in antiquity, the urban other is structured as foreign, decadent, and dangerous, and any attempt to master the republic as doomed to

[23] Cf. Elley (1984), 93.

[24] See esp. Shohat (1991*b*), 215–16.

[25] On the United States' invented tradition of *romanitas*, see Hobsbawm and Ranger (1983), 279–80; Reinhold (1984); Bondanella (1987); Vance (1989); Richard (1994); Edwards (1999). On the use of Rome in Hollywood cinema as an historical analogy for the United States, see Wyke (1997) and Joshel *et al*. (2001).

failure, since spectators already know that Cleopatra's stratagems will not succeed—Julius Caesar will be assassinated and the queen will be forced ignominously to leave the city. The first half of DeMille's *Cleopatra* thus acts out an extreme version of a current fear that the social fabric of modern America is endangered. Historical analogy fosters an hyperbolic articulation of gender and ethnic conflicts in terms of the rescue of western masculine civilization from eastern feminine corruption.

The second half of DeMille's *Cleopatra* increases and then appears to remove the fears articulated in the first half concerning the challenge posed to traditional gender roles by the advent of the modern woman. The Mark Antony who, in the earlier Roman sequences, had bitterly protested that both Caesar and the Roman eagle had been tamed by a woman, and who had concluded the first half of the film with a declaration that he would take vengeance for Rome on the Egyptian, is himself vanquished by her. Through the use of DeMille's visual system of objective correlatives,[26] Antony is represented as engulfed and unmanned by a woman's body in the sequence where the Roman visits Cleopatra's barge at Tarsus. When Antony enters the feminine ship, he passes between a double line of women waving soft fans to reach within a Cleopatra who reclines before a vulvaic mass of plumes. On the way to being sexually possessed by the queen—a 'gorgeous piece of cinematic euphemism' involving the rhythmic thrusting and retracting of her ship's banks of oars[27]—Antony loses all the emblems of his Roman virility, namely his soldier's helmet, his huge wolfhounds, and his upright stance.

The conservative narrative drive of DeMille's *Cleopatra* later restores Antony reassuringly to full manhood and Cleopatra to a very traditionally conceived femininity. When news reaches Antony in

[26] For DeMille's use of 'objective correlatives' as a mode of filmic characterization, see Christie (1991), 20.

[27] Hughes-Hallett (1991), 363. See further Hughes-Hallett (1991), 362–4, and Hamer (1993), 128–30, for a more detailed analysis of the barge sequence.

Alexandria that the Romans have declared war, he springs to attention again as an aggressive Roman general. At that precise moment, Cleopatra falls to her knees, caresses, and kisses her lover's hand, and (with the camera looking down on her) gushes 'At last! I've seen a god come to life. I'm no longer a queen. I'm a woman.' Through dialogue, camera-angle, and gesture, cinema spectators witness the empowerment of Antony and Cleopatra's submission to love. In the concluding sequences of the film, Cleopatra now works not in the interests of her country but of her man. The second half of DeMille's *Cleopatra* thus displays a minatory vision of the modern American woman only to contain her eventually within the safe bounds of conventional romance.[28] Once again the message that social order could be disrupted by modern women's claims to political and sexual freedom is made more rhetorically pointed by the use of Roman historical analogy. The lesson that Woman is dangerous but defeatable is lent an air of authority and venerability by its apparent antiquity and historical truth.[29]

Filmic representations of Cleopatra cannot, nor would they want to, limit her significance to the espousal of imperialism, ethnic purity, or patriarchy. The cinematic tradition for depicting Cleopatra has often closed with the defeat of the oriental queen, but, at the same time, it has lingered lovingly over her attractions. Thus DeMille's *Cleopatra* (in contrast to Guazzoni's *Marcantonio e Cleopatra*) is framed as the story of the queen, not her Roman opponents. The characterization of Cleopatra through casting, dialogue and gesture, camera-work and lighting, often invites audience identification with her point of view.[30] In the barge sequence, for example, DeMille's 'Rembrandt style' of film aesthetics provides highlighted

[28] Cf. Babington and Evans (1993), 113, on the representation of Mary Magdalene and her submission to Christ in DeMille's *King of Kings* (1927).

[29] Compare the use of the Greek myth that Amazon women were once defeated by Athenian men in the comedy *The Warrior's Husband*, which was produced by an associate of DeMille, Jesse L. Lasky, and released the year before *Cleopatra*.

[30] As noted by Hamer (1993), 117–18.

close-ups of Cleopatra's face, as we are made privy to a clever double bluff by which she entertainingly seduces a gruff and naive Antony.[31] At the end of the film, moreover, its diegetic world is left in suspended animation as DeMille's camera slowly recedes back from the visually opulent image of a motionless Egyptian queen clothed in full Pharaonic costume, enthroned on high in the royal palace beneath the giant winged scarab. The closure of *Cleopatra* (1934) reveals an evident conflict between the film's narrative and stylistic codes. In this cinematic biography of the queen, rich visual detail of glamorous costumes and luxurious decor are furnished, and Cleopatra is figured as herself a seductive spectacle, often through moments of narrative stasis that permit voyeuristic access to her dressing, banqueting, embracing, parading, or sitting enthroned, all in exotic surroundings. The historical film invites a consumer gaze that visually appropriates the commodities showcased in the film and apprehends the image of the woman on screen as an ideal of female beauty and a consumer lifestyle.[32]

Studies of American consumer culture have drawn attention to a progressive tightening of the bond between the institutions of Hollywood cinema and the department store through the second and third decades of the twentieth century. Film historians generally place the director DeMille at the point of origin of this process whereby a department-store aesthetic entered American cinema. During the course of the 1920s, DeMille perfected a technique for turning the film frame into a living display window occupied by marvellous mannequins. His stylish sex comedies regularly showcased modern fashions, furnishings, accessories, and cosmetics in fetishized form as commodities. In numerous bathroom and bedroom scenes, DeMille's glamorous heroines ostentatiously put products to use in an appeal to middle-class, female spectators with incomes to dispose of. His chic sets and costumes against and in which love affairs were

[31] For DeMille's lighting techniques see May (1980), 221; Higashi (1994), 15.

[32] For Hollywood cinema's solicitation of a consumer gaze, see esp. Doane (1989).

played out received such strong and attractive visual emphasis that they set American consumer trends.[33]

Cleopatra and her Egypt could very easily submit to such DeMille treatment. As part of the nineteenth-century's colonialist project to claim territories and subjects by their visual reproduction and display, ancient Egypt had already been reified and turned into a spectacle of material abundance in museum and world's fair exhibitions, in magic-lantern shows, panoramas, dioramas, photography, and documentary footage.[34] And in the first two decades of the twentieth century, the Orient (with its connotations of luxury, sensuality, impulse, and desire) became the most attractive of merchandising tropes for America's developing consumer industries.[35] Even Cleopatra herself made a tentative entry into American consumer culture. An advertisement in the *New York Daily Tribune* for 22 March 1907, for example, drew attention to a fashion exhibition being held at a New York department store to display 'The Egyptian Tendency': 'Of course, American women cannot be gowned in the flowing draperies of Cleopatra: but the graceful dress allurements of those days that ring of Caesar, Ptolemy, and Antony, have given the *motif* for witching and daring originality.'[36] In the same period, another New York store held a six week 'Carnival of Nations' that concluded with a spectacular oriental show comprising a Turkish harem, dancing girls, a genie, and Cleopatra of the Nile.[37]

More recently still, the discovery of Tutankhamun's tomb and the widespread and persistent dissemination of details of its contents in

[33] The first history of the relationship between the Hollywood film industry and department-store fashions is that of Eckert (1978). His famous article has been followed by numerous other studies, such as Allen (1980); Doane (1989); Gaines (1989); Gaines and Herzog (1990); Herzog and Gaines (1991); Stacey (1994), 176–223. On DeMille in particular, see also Higashi (1994), 2–4 and 142–78, and May (1980), 200–36.

[34] Lant (1992), 91–8 and (1995). See also Ch. 7 above.

[35] Leach (1993), 104–11.

[36] The advertisement is reproduced in Hodgdon (1998), 97, and discussed on 95.

[37] See Leach (1993), 138.

the mass media from the famous first report in *The Times* on 30 November 1922 into the early 1930s, as well as the excavation during this entire period of el-Amarna (city of Akhenaten and Nefertiti), gave impetus to the mass production and consumption of Nilotic designs, from ashtrays to ocean liners, from evening gowns to pseudo-Egyptian cinemas. Already in April 1923, American *Vogue* carried the headline 'The Mode Has a Rendezvous by the Nile' and predicted that New York fashions would soon be gripped by a taste for the Egyptian. While Tutmania gave modern mass-produced objects and fashions a sheen of luxury, exoticism and exclusivity, Amarnamania rendered them accessible as everyday yet beautiful bourgeois comforts.[38] Given this range of ancient Egypts made available by popularized archaeology in the 1920s and 1930s, it is unsurprising that by the mid-1920s American women were shopping in emporia laden with examples of an Egypt simultaneously commodified, glamourized, and domesticated. Consequently the spectacular art deco sets of DeMille's *Cleopatra*, awash with feathers, fans, pearls, and leopard-skins, would have evoked for their spectators the orientalist aesthetic of the department store, while Travis Banton's designs for Cleopatra's costumes (elegantly understated, cut on the bias, in soft, smooth fabrics that clung to the contours of Colbert's slim body) could appear to be simultaneously of an other and of this world.

The narrative of Cleopatra's relations with Rome could also be adapted very easily to suit the commercial concerns of the Hollywood film industry. For, in her western tradition, this Ptolemaic ruler was already the supreme historical embodiment of Woman engineered as seductive spectacle. Essential topoi inherited from classical sources include a queen unravelled from a rug for the pleasure of Caesar, a Venus riding on her barge to seduce Antony.[39] Such

[38] On Amarnamania, see Montserrat (2000), esp. 83–91 and Wyke and Montserrat (forthcoming). On Tutmania, see also Frayling (1992), esp. 10–28; Curl (1994), 211–20; Higashi (1994), 90–2; Pantazzi (1994), 506–51; Montserrat (2000), 8 and 74–6.

[39] For a more extensive list, see Hughes-Hallett (1991), 88–92 and 102–43.

FIG. 8.2 Poster advertising Claudette Colbert in *Cleopatra* (1934).

accounts of the queen provide historical justification for sequences in DeMille's *Cleopatra* (1934) where a woman poses self-consciously for the admiration of a male, on-screen audience (Fig. 8.2). Framed within a consumer gaze, Cleopatra and the Orient undergo a slippage in signification. By a metonymic process, they supply showcased products with the sheen of a mysterious and venerable eroticism and luxury.[40] For the consuming spectator, mastery of the Orient involves not occupation but consumption.

By the 1930s, the Hollywood film industry envisaged the spectators who consumed its films to be predominantly female. For both

[40] On the 'metonymic' process of consumerist cinema, see Doane (1989), 24–7.

the film and retail industries were aware that women were the primary motivators of cinema attendance and that they made between eighty and ninety per cent of all purchases for family use. The industry assumption that women constituted its core audience affected all aspects of film production: from an increase in films set around female protagonists, and the elaboration of a machinery for selling women goods, to the development of the star system.[41] Hollywood gave female stars a central role both on- and off-screen in differentiating its mass production of films, and in glamourizing commodities and activating their consumption.[42] With the advent of the technology of sound, and in the era of the Depression, such stars had also become less divine and extraordinary in status and appearance, their screen characters more commonly motivated by a credible psychology than by occult possession. Stars continued to be special but now combined the exceptional with the ordinary and the everyday.[43] The Paramount star whose function it was to display and endorse a Cleopatra vogue was among the top five female box-office draws of the early 1930s (and by 1938 Hollywood's highest earner). Claudette Colbert's star image was that of an modern American woman who was sleek, sophisticated, witty, resourceful, and chic.[44] Thus it was not difficult for Claudette Colbert, in keeping with her star image and aided by the modernity of the dialogue in *Cleopatra*, to play the Ptolemaic queen as a sassy, easy-going, glamour girl who finds herself on a journey between public responsibility and romantic love, nor for female spectators of the thirties to consume Colbert/Cleopatra as deserving of imitation off screen.

Beyond the cinema screen there now lay a massive apparatus to tie up commodities with particular films.[45] In cinema shops and other

[41] See Stokes (1999), 43–4.

[42] On the importance of the star system in 1920s and 1930s Hollywood, see Balio (1993), 143–77; Studlar (1996) and (1997); Stokes (1999).

[43] Dyer (1998), 21–3.

[44] Parish (1972), 92–141; Everson (1976); Balio (1993), 149–50; Hamer (1993), 120–1; Viviani (1997).

[45] See Eckert (1978), 11–17; Gaines (1989); Doane (1989), 25–7; Stokes (1999), 44.

retail outlets, Colbert/Cleopatra was deployed to sell a range of products such as hats, cigarettes, shoes, and soap. Campaign books supplied by Paramount to theatre managers suggested ways of exploiting such tie-ups with department stores to advertise their film. For example, a press sheet released by Paramount around November 1934 (and designed to aid exhibitors in selling the Hollywood studio's new release *Cleopatra* to British audiences) carried the dramatic headline 'Season's Styles Go "Cleopatra"! From Head to Toe Fashionable Ladies Emulate Egypt's Queen.' Below examples of 'Egyptian' styles inspired by Paramount's film, exhibitors were also conveniently supplied with a sample article for placement in national newspapers and women's magazines:

> 'Cleopatra' has gone to the ladies' heads! And to their feet—and into almost every article of apparel, judging by the growing vogue of 'Cleopatra' styles, following the release of the Paramount picture of that name, which comes ...... to the ...... Theatre. Directed by Cecil B. DeMille, it features Claudette Colbert, Warren William and Henry Wilcoxon.
>
> A few of the highlights of the 'Cleopatra' vogue are illustrated here in the two dresses designed by Travis Banton for Miss Colbert, and the 'Cleopatra' hat and coiffure, the marked influence of Egyptian style and designs is evident in the sandals, jewelry and buckles selected to illustrate the new season's offerings.[46]

Elsewhere in the studio's publicity, British exhibitors were notified that Selfridge's department store had brought out a special 'Cleopatra' hat that had been posed on a wax model of Colbert-as-Cleopatra and displayed in a dedicated window of its Oxford Street store in London, while Dolcis had brought out a special sandal for evening dress wear and, for the duration of the film's run, was displaying it and other 'Cleopatra models' in all its shoe shops throughout Great Britain. Similarly, the manufacturers of Lux soap and Marcovitch

[46] Several such campaign books and press sheets for *Cleopatra* (1934) can be viewed in the Special Collections of the British Film Institute, London.

FIG. 8.3 Illustrations of merchandising campaign tied to *Cleopatra* (1934).

Egyptian cigarettes were running special advertising campaigns which, by utilizing stills of the star of *Cleopatra*, tied up their products with the glamour of Hollywood's Egypt. It would be a different and more difficult project to establish whether these tactics did indeed generate a genuine Cleopatran vogue or sell more soap and cigarettes, but proof that they were actually deployed is much easier to find. Another Paramount campaign book, for example, illustrates its suggestions for selling the film with photographs of those shop-windows of R. H. Macy & Co. (the smart New York department store) that had been given over to 'Cleopatra' gowns and shoes, or 'Egyptian' backgammon sets, and to copies of newspaper advertisments for 'Jewel-Studded Cleopatra Sandals' or the evening dresses worn by Colbert as the 'Queen of Glamour' (Fig. 8.3). By 1934, Cleopatra and her Egypt had been commodified as a glamorous fashion-style which was now widely available for purchase in all good department stores across the United States and Great Britain.

Hollywood campaign books of the 1930s included articles on the costumes and cosmetics of female stars suitable for reprinting in women's magazines that were designed to encourage a *practical*, not just a fantastical, identification between female spectators and the characters who appeared on screen.[47] From 1930 the Modern Merchandising Bureau, acting as a middleman between studios and retailers, regularly adapted screen fashions for promotion in an international mass market. Reproduced in a Paramount campaign book, the Bureau's suggested copy (in connection with the costumes designed by Travis Banton for *Cleopatra*) declares:

> They are lavish, glamorous gowns with authentic details in jewels and trimming. From these we have made exciting adaptations in evening gowns and accessories. Our copies have all the allure of the original with exotic edges rubbed down and subdued into fashions that are definitely 1934 and wearable.

The campaign books for DeMille's *Cleopatra* provide vivid evidence of how Hollywood's Egypt was brought out of the film frame and the cinema and, after slight adjustments, transferred to retail outlets throughout the United States and abroad in order to encourage a very personal (and purchasable) Cleomania.

Women in the audiences to DeMille's historical film were encouraged to identify with the Cleopatra on screen in order to carry over that identification into their lives outside the cinema through the

[47] See esp. Herzog and Gaines (1991).

purchase of Cleopatra gowns and other 'style accessories'.[48] Such marketing strategies have been condemned by some feminist film historians as examples of how Hollywood cinema's commodity logic was designed to deflect women's dissatisfaction with their social conditions onto an intensified concern with their bodies and an overriding interest in romance.[49] Identification also constituted a useful mechanism for socializing ethnically diverse spectators into 'a more homogeneous nation of consumers'.[50] To that end, the features of the actress chosen to play Cleopatra, Claudette Colbert, adhere more closely to dominant American conventions for female beauty than to those required of an orientalized urban other. Both the film's diegesis and consumer retailing, moreover, market a traditionally conceived femininity for the queen and her spectators. The narrative resolution of DeMille's *Cleopatra* and the extra-cinematic consumer discourses that surrounded the film deny the queen any political authority. Any societal concerns the female spectator may have is deflected onto an intensified concern with her own body, and the need to dress it and shape it in line with the demanding requirements of the oriental glamour of Hollywood. The Roman conquests that consumers might make, thanks to the Cleopatra style accessories they can buy, belong purely to the domain of romance.

Other feminist theorizations of the relationship between Hollywood cinema's spectacle and female spectatorship have considered how women moviegoers actually (and actively) responded to the invitation to purchase an apparently traditional feminine identity.[51] On this basis, contradictions have been explored between the narrative drives, visual styles, promotional literature, and marketing strategies of films directed at women. Although the narratives of Hollywood cinema often closed with a last-gasp reassertion of male

[48] Hamer (1993), 121–4 and 132–4.

[49] Eg. Doane (1989), 25–7, and Gaines (1989), 49–50.

[50] Allen (1980), 487. Cf. Baxter (1993), 23–5.

[51] See e.g. Stacey (1994); Studlar (1996) and (1997); Bruzzi (1997); Stokes (1999). Cf. also Chs. 7 above and 10 below.

dominance (in DeMille's film Cleopatra eventually gives up politics and patriotism and submits to personal love for a newly virile Antony), their discourses of clothing and cosmetics often transcended such conventional narrative structures and frequently paraded before spectators a vision of femininity as masquerade, that is, as a mask or dress that must be worn to hide female strength from anxious males. Thus, although DeMille's *Cleopatra* closes with the apparent submission of the queen to tragic romance, Colbert-as-Cleopatra acknowledges in the film that the paraphernalia of her glamorous femininity are designed to seduce Roman statesmen to her political ambitions. In an amusing double bluff, she even talks to a foolish Antony explicitly of the plans she had had to dazzle him at the very moment that she proves their usefulness. If we had access to the recollections of those female moviegoers who might once have bought and worn Cleopatra sandals, gowns, hair curlers, and hats, who washed with Lux soap or smoked Egyptian cigarettes, it is just possible that they too may have thought of these rituals of femininity as cunning acts of public empowerment. The reviewer of *The New York Herald Tribune* may have caught a glimpse of just such a response to *Cleopatra* when he wrote with clear irritation of its double romance: 'In each case the conquering Roman is determined to break the will and the spirit of the Egyptian woman only to find that her wiles are just a bit too much for him.'

## LIZPATRA (1963)

Similarly, the infamous *Cleopatra* released in 1963 by 20th Century-Fox offers a heterogeneous set of appropriations of Roman history, a conflicting array of lessons in gender and sexual politics, and a range of different identifications, as a result of the competing discourses of, for example, the film's diegesis and visual style, associated newspaper publicity, and studio press-releases and promotions. In the case of Fox's *Cleopatra*, even the diegesis itself is not a very stable entity. The film finally distributed by the studio in 1963 was a substantially cut version of that originally made by the director Joseph L. Mankiewicz.

Mankiewicz's *Cleopatra* appears to have been conceived as a response to DeMille's, one more suited to the social and political climate of the early 1960s. A souvenir programme from the film's charity première in Los Angeles (held on 20 June 1963) opens with a quotation from the biography of the queen by Arthur Weigall.[52] As the film's historical master-text, Wertheimer's depiction of an oriental royal voluptuary is jettisoned in favour of Weigall's political visionary who had just recently resurfaced in a novelistic biography by Carlo Maria Franzero, *The Life and Times of Cleopatra* (1957). Both souvenir programme and film credits state that, beyond the accounts supplied by ancient historians, Mankiewicz's representation of Cleopatra on screen is most deeply indebted to the novel. In its preface, Franzero asks:

> Of all the great women in History the most famous is Cleopatra. Her name is a legend; and yet, we know almost nothing of her. Down through the ages the legend of Cleopatra has been retold by historians and poets, the tale of a woman who was called the incarnation of the Sphinx; and we are left wondering at the enigma of a fascination which is still alive after two thousand years. What irresistible charm and enchantment did Cleopatra possess that made her name immortal?[53]

Franzero immediately answers his own question and authorizes it as a response to Roman material culture. One day the novelist had stood gazing at the ruins of the Temple of Venus Genetrix in Rome:

> In that temple Caesar had placed the statue of Cleopatra, deified as Venus—Cleopatra who had borne Caesar his only son; Cleopatra who in those fateful months before the Ides of March held Court for Caesar in the Villa

[52] The programme can be found in the production files for *Cleopatra* (1963) at the USC Film and Television Library (Los Angeles).

[53] Carlo Maria Franzero, *Cleopatra* (1962), London: Panther Books, 9. The novel was first published in 1957 as *The Life and Times of Cleopatra*, on which see Hughes-Hallett (1991), 345.

Transtiberina; Cleopatra who was urging Caesar to crown himself a King and rule the World with her as his Queen.

The sight of those three beautiful columns seemed to give to me the key to the mystery of Cleopatra. For, when I read and reread all the ancient historians and chroniclers of the events in which her brief life was involved, I felt impatient with the stilted and disparaging picture that dramatists and poets, not excluding Shakespeare and Bernard Shaw, have made of Cleopatra to suit popular tradition. I felt convinced that Cleopatra was certainly a woman of great beauty and charm, but also a woman of immense political ambition; a Queen who thought politically and at the same time loved passionately; vital, vivid, scheming and imperious, an enchantress prompted both by passion and greatness.[54]

In the climate of the early 1960s, Cleopatra could be depicted more comfortably as a woman of considerable political authority, whose great ambition it was to achieve the unity of East and West.

In surviving footage of a scene at Alexander's tomb, in the first half of Mankiewicz's *Cleopatra*, the queen attempts to persuade Julius Caesar of the merits of Alexander's grand design—that there should arise 'out of the patchwork of conquests, one world, and out of one world, one nation, one people on earth living in peace'. In an early draft of the screenplay, the director labelled this Cleopatra 'an early-day Kennedy',[55] a newspaper review at the time of the film's release derided the apparent banality of her political pleas for unity and peace as making of the queen 'a World Federalist at heart',[56] while ten years later a film historian observed her to be 'a kind of Eleanor Roosevelt captivated by the ideal of one-world unity'.[57] The election of President Kennedy in 1960 had seemed, to some Americans, to hold out the hope of an end to the cold war antagonism between the Unit-

[54] Carlo Maria Franzero, 9–10. On Julius Caesar's dedication of a statue to Cleopatra in Rome, see above, Ch. 6.

[55] In the USC Film and Television Archive (Los Angeles), 20th Century-Fox collection 5042.17. The item is dated 1961.

[56] *New York Herald Tribune*, 13 June 1963.

[57] Hirsch (1978), 101.

ed States and the Soviet Union (although confrontation continued unabated).[58] While, perhaps more pertinently, Mrs Roosevelt had worked for the United Nations from its inception in 1945 until her death in late 1962 (during the final stages of shooting *Cleopatra*), during which time she had campaigned vigorously in the international arena for the cause of human rights, nuclear containment, and world peace.[59] For that work, and for the attention she drew to the effectiveness of women in world politics (particularly though her syndicated newpaper columns and television shows), she had been lauded as the 'First Lady of the World'.[60]

Western representations of ancient Egypt are not monolithic. They have their own history and their own distinct national configurations.[61] Until the 1950s, unlike France or Great Britain, the United States had no concrete colonial or political connection with Egypt, and American cinematic visions of its ancient past had often appropriated the structures of nineteenth-century orientalist discourse to serve their own ends. Once the United States took on its new post-war imperial role and became heavily invested in the Middle East, present American political concerns came to the surface of Hollywood's histories of the eastern Mediterranean.[62] Thus desires for an Arab–Israeli settlement enter the epic film *Ben-Hur* (1959) in the shape of an amenable sheik who offers support to the film's fictional Jewish hero.[63] But, given American concerns about the presidency of Gamal Abdel Nasser in Egypt and his vision for the country of an Arab nationalism, it is no surprise that the *Cleopatra* released by 20th Century-Fox in 1963 constructs the political vision of Egypt's earlier leader in less problematic, utterly western

[58] Luard (1989), esp. 1–17 and 514–48.

[59] On the role of Eleanor Roosevelt in international politics, see Berger (1981); Cook (1993); Spangenburg and Moser (1997).

[60] Spangenburg and Moser (1997), 89–90.

[61] See Said (1985) on the western representation of the Orient more generally. Cf. MacKenzie (1995), 24; Yeğenoğlu (1998), 29–38; Turner (2000), 8–9.

[62] Said (1992), 276–85.

[63] On *Ben-Hur* (1959), see most recently Cieutat (2000) and Winkler (2001).

terms—the world peace of a Kennedy or a Roosevelt, rather than the Arab nationalism of a Nasser.

The characterization of Cleopatra as 'captivated by the ideal of one-world unity' was apparently woven tightly through the original film shot by Mankiewicz. Yet, although this visionary Cleopatra can still be glimpsed in some of the studio's press-releases and in première programmes, little survives of a coherent political diegesis in the film which was finally exhibited in 1963. Most commentators on the film have observed that its attempt at a contemporary political resonance is both fragmentary and fragile, because the film was radically cut before and after its release, and because whatever political narrative it once possessed was utterly swamped by the film's spectacular values, and by extra-cinematic publicity concerning the troubled production of the film and the lifestyle of its female star, Elizabeth Taylor.[64]

A mass of extra-cinematic discourses began to accumulate around Mankiewicz's *Cleopatra* long before its release, as the film was in production on and off for almost two years. Shooting began in England in October 1960, and culminated in the loss of some five million dollars, a change of director, and a serious illness for its big-name star. In September 1961, with a new director and a new one million-dollar contract negotiated for Taylor, shooting restarted in Italy. Having failed to meet a pressing studio deadline of June 1962 for completion, the film's producer was fired and the head of Fox resigned. Finally, under the authority of a new studio head, a considerably edited version of Mankiewicz's *Cleopatra* was premiered in June 1963.[65] The *Motion Picture Herald* for 26 June 1963 thus claimed 'never before in motion picture history, perhaps, has a film come to the public with a greater degree of expectancy than "Cleopatra".'

[64] As Geagley (1984); Bertoni (1987); Beuselink (1988); Hughes-Hallett (1991), 345.

[65] On the production history of Mankiewicz's *Cleopatra*, see Baxter (1972), 160–4; Solomon (1978), 45–6; Elley (1984), 92–5; Smith (1991), 44–6; Hughes-Hallett (1991), 355–9; Bernstein (1994); Finler (2000), 82. See *Newsweek*, 25 March 1963, for a contemporary account of the film's misfortunes.

In the long and costly absence of a film on which to peg an advertising campaign, 20th Century-Fox solicited consumer interest during production through the star image of Elizabeth Taylor. Star images, such as Taylor's, continued to have an important function in the economy of Hollywood in the 1950s and 1960s, as they had in the 1930s. The film star's persona now entered into extra-cinematic circulation, in studio publicity and promotion, newspapers and magazines, in advertisements, on radio and television chat-shows, then continued into the films themselves and subsequent commentary on them. Images of female stars, especially, continued to be exploited by the studios and the associated retailing industries as a means of selling fashion and beauty products. Representations of the star's supposed personality and lifestyle were organized around themes of consumption, success, and sex. The star was also defined, paradoxically, as being both an extraordinary and an ordinary individual, so that she might become a model of beauty and consumption to be imitated, on a humbler scale, by readers of her image. Simultaneously, Hollywood studios structured the images of their stars in extra-cinematic texts as a vehicle for describing forthcoming films—as an invitation to readers to enter the cinema where they might expect to see those images vividly enacted.[66]

At the start of 1962, the Fox studio began an attempt to pre-sell interest in its troubled film by feeding publicity into women's magazines like *Vogue* and *Look* (cited at the opening of this chapter) that twinned Taylor and Cleopatra as two legendary glamour girls, who both enjoyed a fabulously luxurious lifestyle and who together would now initiate a new 'Egyptian look' or 'Cleopatra complex'. The *Vogue* article, accompanied by photographs of Elizabeth Taylor dressed in both historical character and in some 'non-cinema coifs', described the star's daily life off-set while shooting of the epic film was taking place in Italy:

[66] Dyer (1998) and Ellis (1982), 91–108. Cf. the discussion of female star images in Chs. 7 above and 10 below.

Cleopatra, at the height of her fascination and power, sailed with Caesar to Rome where, the record shows, her potent, volatile charms turned the *vox pop* decidedly pettish. Her experience, in fact, was quite the reverse of Cleopatra Taylor's. . . . To *this* Cleopatra the Romans seem anything but hostile; their designers are plotting some not-too-broody Cleo clothes; the papers are full of Liz; and the Queen of the Nile coiffure can be felt at least as far north as Paris. . . . To all challenges, Miss Taylor presents an on-location manner that's disciplined and direct. Off-set she's as languid as a cheetah, relaxing, cat-like, at her Via Appia villa with her husband, three children, four dogs, two Siamese cats, sipping champagne by the pool, letting the world come to her—and it does.[67]

By means of an elision between the Egyptian queen and the Hollywood film star, Taylor inherits Cleopatra's commanding power, her immense celebrity, and her legendary lifestyle. The champagne and the pool take on the fabulous quality of Cleopatra's banquets by virtue of being sited at a Roman villa. The langour of a cheetah and the pose of a cat recall the animal iconography of Pharaonic Egypt and hint at a feral sexuality to match that attributed to the oriental queen. Dissolving the boundaries between historical character and film star considerably enriches Taylor's star image and, by extension, the fashions she promotes, as well as soliciting interest in the elusive film where the 'new Cleopatra', it may be assumed, will act out all the extravagance and excess of the old.

At the very same time, however, the rhetoric of an identity between star and Egyptian queen began to be explored in other extra-cinematic texts without any attempt to promote Mankiewicz's *Cleopatra* or its proposed merchandising. The Taylor/Cleopatra link was taken out of the hands of the studio and redirected to signify not glamour and luxury but wastefulness and adultery. On these occasions, a correspondence was observed not just between the extravagance of the queen and the film star who was now playing her part, but also between their respective sexual relationships with their

[67] *Vogue*, 15 January 1962.

lovers. An article in *Show Business Illustrated* of 2 January 1962 noted these different and disturbing parallels at length:

MOVIE OF "CLEOPATRA" curious case of destiny at work. Film now underway again after series of appalling mishaps—e.g., near-death of Elizabeth Taylor, loss of $5,000,000. Why was unlucky project not abandoned altogether? Reason: Elizabeth Taylor fated to play Cleopatra. Parallels in life of two girls spooky . . . LIZ ALSO FOUND NEW REGENT. Also man whose wife was paragon of sunny domesticity. Eddie Fischer. Party boy like Antony. Left wife, married Liz . . . Both queens accused of stealing husband from nice wife. Liz replied: "What am I supposed to do, ask him to go back to her?" Cleopatra would have said the same. She and Liz are classic Other Woman. Can't help it. Metabolism.

Taylor, at the time when she was cast to make *Cleopatra*, was already notorious for being seen to break up the marriage between Eddie Fisher and Debbie Reynolds, whose star image was that of America's perfect young wife. The studio's assimilation of the film star to her film character here provides an opportunity to equate Cleopatra's enticement of Antony away from his wife Octavia bathetically with Taylor's past affair. Parallels with Roman history enstate her as America's scandalous mistress.[68]

But more and better parallels with the seductions of Roman history were to come as rumours began to break of a new sexual scandal now occuring on the set of *Cleopatra*. Already in January 1962, the article in *Show Business Illustrated* concluded by hinting tantalizingly at fresh possibilities:

But does small voice of Cleopatra whisper to Liz across the centuries: "You really *can* rule the world. Get a barge! Roll yourself in an Oriental rug and have it sent to . . ." But who? MANY FASCINATING possibilities. But no concern of scholarly work. Stick to facts. Future will reveal them in own time. Notes put aside to then.

[68] See Hughes-Hallett (1991), 341–2. For the development of Taylor's star status as a serial adulteress, see more generally Walker (1966), 131–45, and (1990); Hirsch (1973); Bernstein (1994), 351.

Elizabeth Taylor's star status as an infamous serial adulteress was swiftly reinforced as rumours broke that she was conducting an on-set affair with Richard Burton, who was now apparently playing Mark Antony to her Cleopatra both literally and metaphorically. By February 1962, for example, *The Perry Como Show* ran a comic sketch in which a slave going by the name of Taylor's husband kept getting in Mark Antony's way. The opportunities provided by the rhetoric of studio promotions to trope a modern affair in terms of Cleopatran high farce were too splendid to miss, and in the excitable gossip of newspapers, magazines, and television shows the Ptolemaic queen was reconfigured exactly to match Elizabeth Taylor as a classic Other Woman or homebreaker.[69] This Cleomania, unlike that concerning Theda Bara or Claudette Colbert, operated outside the control of the Hollywood studio. Its apparent escape from the star image 20th Century-Fox had attempted to promote made it seem more authentic and, therefore, more like a privileged glimpse of a real 'Lizpatra' and her modern 'Roman' seductions.[70]

Within a matter of months the Taylor / Burton affair had grown into an international sex scandal condemned by both members of Congress and the Vatican. According to a recent résumé of the events in *Vanity Fair*, 'When Liz Met Dick', the celebrity scandal was taken up so intensely in the popular press that on front pages world-wide it soon superseded news of John Glenn's orbiting of the earth or details of the US–Soviet tensions that by year's end would lead to the Cuban missile crisis.[71] Star images often embody social values perceived to be in crisis.[72] Discourses of stardom are littered with the exploration,

[69] For further discussion of the salacious press links made between Cleopatra/ Taylor and Antony/Burton, see Hughes-Hallett (1991), 348–50 and 357–60.

[70] See Dyer (1987), 61, on the apparent credibility of uninvited publicity concerning star scandals. 'Lizpatra' was coined by Dwight MacDonald in *Esquire*, February 1965, to describe Taylor's performance of the Ptolemaic queen.

[71] *Vanity Fair* 452, April 1998. Cf. Bernstein (1994), 368–9.

[72] On the social significance of star images, see Dyer (1987) and (1998). For the intersection of star images with discourses of femininity and sexuality, and for the importance of that intersection for the filmic representation of Cleopatra and Messalina, see also Chs. 7 above and 10 below.

in particular, of sexual behaviours. Elizabeth Taylor's star image as a modern-day Cleopatra and her performance of it in Mankiewicz's film became a useful reference point in the early 1960s for discussion of the frailty of heterosexual monogamy and the perceived problem of widespread adultery. The Kinsey reports of 1948 and 1953 on the sexual behaviour of males and females respectively had aroused enormous interest and debate in an era that idealized the family as a refuge against social change. Moral panics about the fragility of conventional sexuality, about the success of *Playboy*, and the introduction of the oral contraceptive, about increases in adultery and divorce, had already begun to be troped in the language of Roman history: the president of the Union Theological Seminary, for example, had observed that interest in Kinsey's work (including his revelation of persistent adultery among middle-class American women) was symptomatic of 'a prevailing degradation in American morality approximating the worst decadence of the Roman era'.[73] Now extra-cinematic discourses on Taylor's playing of Cleopatra could draw on, and perhaps even support, the argument that modern America was confronting the same crisis of moral decline as ancient Rome.

If, during the early months of 1962, modern adultery was being troped as a replay of Roman history, the process of *filming* that history began to be read in turn as the performance of modern adultery in ancient costume. More explicit and detailed reports of the affair between Taylor and Burton poured forth in the European and American press from early 1962. Both the couple and the *Cleopatra* film-set were besieged by the world's press. By the spring, 20th Century-Fox became concerned whether such massive and persistent press interest in the film would provide good box-office returns or encourage the American public instead to boycott the film on its eventual release.[74] In a letter dated 7 June 1962 (published in 1963 in

[73] Quoted in Whitfield (1991), 184–7. See also Dyer (1987), 19–66, and (1998); Biskind (1983), 250–333; Nadel (1993), 422.

[74] See Brodsky and Weiss (1963), 64, for a letter apparently sent to Rome by the Fox publicist Weiss, dated 17 April 1962, expressing anxiety about press scorn for the conduct of Taylor and Burton.

a collected edition entitled *The Cleopatra Papers: A Private Correspondence*), the Fox publicist Nathan Weiss wrote slightly less anxiously from Rome to a colleague in New York on just such a press visit to the film's Alexandria set:

> After lunch there was a short but eloquent scene in which Antony divorces his wife after the fashion of the time—by proclaiming it three times to the multitudes. Partly because the writing is so overnight-contemporary, to coin a new period, there were regrettable connotations from the point of view of stirring up the press—regret that is from the puritan Fox viewpoint, but not damaging I suspect to the box office. It is, in just about every sense, a most peculiarly ambivalent production.[75]

Provided on set with such gloriously neat connections between Roman history and a modern sex scandal, the press continued to figure their accounts of the Taylor/Burton affair in the extravagant terms of a Cleopatran romance. But, in the same year as (and preceding) the release of the film *Cleopatra*, another insider account of its production was published and widely sold. *My Life with Cleopatra*, written by its producer Walter Wanger (with the aid of the reporter Joe Hyams), worked to suggest that such extra-cinematic discourses of film-star adultery had infected the film-making process itself, in particular the overnight revisions of the script by Mankiewicz and the performance of its two stars.

In a vivid diary-format Wanger recalls what happened on 5 March 1962:

> Today we filmed the bath scene . . .
>
> Cleopatra comes in to see Antony, who is in the bath . . . They commence a beautiful love scene.
>
> JLM's dialogue is right out of real life, with Cleopatra telling how she will feel if Antony leaves her. "Love can stab the heart", she says.
>
> It was hard to tell whether Liz and Burton were reading lines or living the parts.[76]

[75] Brodsky and Weiss (1963), 117.

[76] Wanger and Hyams (1963), 134.

Similarly, in an entry for 13 April 1962, Wanger duplicates his notes on that day's shooting, which had been immediately preceded by an attack on Elizabeth Taylor in the Vatican weekly *Osservatore della domenica*, where she had been castigated for making a mockery of the sanctity of marriage and threatened with a future of 'erotic vagrancy':

> Filmed one of the most dramatic scenes in the movie and one of the most dramatic real-life scenes I have ever witnessed. Again the parallel between the life of Cleopatra and the life of Elizabeth Taylor is incredible. The scene filmed in the Forum calls for Cleopatra to make her entrance into Rome sitting with Caesarion on top of a huge (more than thirty feet high) black Sphinx drawn by 300 gold-covered slaves. The entrance into Rome was Cleopatra's big gamble. If the Romans accepted her with an ovation, she had won Caesar. If they refused to accept her, she had lost him, and very possibly her life. There were almost 7,000 Roman extras milling about in front of the Forum. All of them presumably had read the Vatican criticism of Liz. Not only would these Roman extras be accepting Cleopatra, but they would also be expressing their personal acceptance of the woman who plays Cleopatra . . . I saw the sense of relief flood through Liz's body as the slave girls, handmaidens, senators, guards, and thousands of others applauded her—personally.[77]

Wanger's biographer notes that his account of events (published before the film opened) is full of petty deceptions designed to help publicize the much-criticized film and its much-maligned star. Given the immense public fascination with the sex scandal, the producer took up the trope of a Cleopatran romance in order to suggest that cinemagoers could now see that notorious adultery played out before their eyes in Technicolor and on widescreen.[78]

Finally, to coincide with the month in which *Cleopatra* was at last released, 20th Century-Fox cooperated in the reprint of the source novel by Carlo Maria Franzero and illustrated it with stills from the

[77] Wanger and Hyams (1963), 146–9.

[78] Bernstein (1994), 375–80.

FIG. 8.4 'Elizabeth Taylor as Cleopatra relaxes between shots'. From C. M. Franzero, *Cleopatra, Queen of Egypt* (1963 edn.).

film and production photographs showing Taylor-as-Cleopatra *between* takes, as if Taylor had lived Cleopatra both on set and off (Fig. 8.4).[79] Stars are cast in Hollywood's histories not as characters but in character, and thus people the represented past with the present, while extra-cinematic discourses about them and about the moment of film production further extend the temporality of the time represented into the here-and-now.[80] Reviewers certainly read Elizabeth Taylor's performance of the title role in Mankiewicz's *Cleopatra* as utterly of the present. In a blistering critique, *The New York Herald Tribune* of 13 June 1963 said of Taylor that 'out of royal regalia, en negligée or au naturel she gives the impression that she is really car-

[79] See the British Panther Books reprint whose publication is dated to June 1963.
[80] Sobchack (1990), 35–6.

rying on in one of Miami Beach's more exotic resorts rather than inhabiting a palace in ancient Alexandria or even a villa in Rome'. For this critic, even the elaborate detail of the sets did not help to place the performances in the past of ancient Egypt: 'Even in their most dramatic moment, when Cleopatra and Antony are slapping each other around in her tomb, one's immediate image is of Miss Taylor and Mr. Burton having it out in the Egyptian Wing of the Metropolitan Museum.' Such criticism of Taylor's performance in reviews of the film—her perceived 'commonness' and inability to know 'the difference between playing oneself in an Egyptian costume and playing Queen of Egypt'[81]—exposes the contradiction between the role of Cleopatra as it may have been originally conceived (political visionary) and the star performance of it (cruelly hounded Other Woman). Thus, the extra-cinematic development of Taylor's star image from legendary bon viveur to legendary adulteress and her performance of that image in Mankiewicz's *Cleopatra* overwhelmed any attempt by the film's diegesis to characterize the queen as a state leader dreaming of world empire.

## CLEOPATRA'S SPECTATORS

Hollywood rarely acknowledges the discursive operations of the star system: that the star personality is a construct built up and expressed only through films and associated extra-cinematic texts, and that the person and the image are two separable entities.[82] Mankiewicz's *Cleopatra*, however, appears to offer a glimpse of that duality, and in doing so sets up an identification between the Roman within the film who looks at Cleopatra and the spectators in the cinema who look at the screen. Near the beginning of the Cleopatra/Antony half of the film, during the sequence where Cleopatra sumptuously entertains Antony on board her barge at Tarsus, she tantalizes the drunk Roman

[81] *New York Times*, 23 June 1963.

[82] Dyer (1998), 20. Cf. the analysis below, Ch. 10, of Susan Hayward as Messalina.

with a mock-Cleopatra, a scantily dressed and lascivious imitation, whom Antony grabs and passionately kisses only to turn and find that the real Cleopatra has left the shipboard banquet-hall. Angrily, he abandons the fake queen and tracks down the real one to her boudoir. There he confronts Cleopatra directly, after having first slashed the diaphanous hangings which screen her from him. *Cleopatra* here hints self-consciously at the strategies of the Fox publicists and the press who, for many months before the release of the film, had been constructing the star image of 'Cleopatra Taylor' for an avid readership. The dynamic between the characters on screen reproduces that between the film and its spectators. The play-acting on the barge suggests that there are two Taylors just as there are two Cleopatras, and that Antony's search for the real queen behind the gauzy curtain mirrors the spectator's search for the real Taylor behind the star image. *Cleopatra* shows us what Antony sees, first his blurred vision of the Cleopatra double, then, after the veil which fills the whole film frame is cut away, his direct uncluttered gaze on the sleeping queen. Thus Mankiewicz's *Cleopatra* encourages its spectators to believe that their desirous look, like that of Antony/Burton, will cut through to and finally take possession of the elusive star.

A similar scene also occurs in the Cleopatra/Julius Caesar half of the film. During an early sequence set in Alexandria, Cleopatra is shown fully clothed, seated on a plain bench, drinking from an unassuming cup, as she listens to a recitation of Catullan poetry. Realizing that Julius Caesar is on his way to her palace-chamber, she declares 'We must not disappoint the mighty Caesar. The Romans tell fabulous tales of my bath, and my handmaidens, and my morals.' The queen then stages a titillating spectacle of herself for the benefit of Caesar's gaze, posing supine and sensuous on a couch, now naked but for a sparsely decorated, transparent covering, surrounded by handmaidens who dance, or fan their seductive mistress, or paint her finger- and toe-nails. The scene not only hints self-consciously at the discourses of stardom that have shaped the Taylor image, but also foregrounds the way female stars have been made to function in Hollywood cinema, including past cinematic Cleopatras. The 'fabulous tales' the Romans tell signify the sensational accounts of Taylor's star lifestyle off set (her pool-side champagne, her eight-hundred-dollar-a-week hairdresser, her perpetual debauch with Burton)[83] as well as the Roman histories of an oriental whore. Attention is also drawn to Hollywood cinema's mechanisms for fetishizing and objectifying its female stars for the desirous spectator.[84] We are offered the double pleasure of a sophisticated laugh with Cleopatra at the hackneyed, DeMillean tactic of 'the bedroom scene', as well as the scopophilic act itself, when the body of Cleopatra/Taylor is viewed admiringly by the approaching Roman/camera.[85]

Interestingly, the film critic for *The New York Herald Tribune* (cited above) scoffs at the 'orgy' which takes place on Cleopatra's barge:

> skimpy—and not helped one bit by having one of the dancing girls decked out as a double for Cleopatra. We should not be reminded that other girls can look just like Elizabeth Taylor, particularly when she is trying to portray the Queen of Queens.

In her effort to deride the film, the critic clearly missed the full significance of the sequence. Here, I would argue, is made visible the outcome of the film's opportunistic promotional strategies. By placing so much emphasis on Taylor's new superstar image as Lizpatra, the studio solicited from spectators a hermeneutic reading of Cleopatra's representation on screen, that is an interpretation directed at the discovery of a 'real' Lizpatra lying behind the screen performance.[86] The attempt to solicit a Cleopatra look for 'other girls' is abandoned, recognised as fake, as a matter of superficial appearance, while the film itself invites us instead to track down the only woman who can now truly embody the Egyptian queen and her Roman seductions.[87]

[83] For which see Hughes-Hallett (1991), 357–60.

[84] Those mechanisms were first analysed in terms of the fetishistic and voyeuristic look by Mulvey (1975).

[85] Cf. Hughes-Hallett (1991), 343–4.

[86] For the concept of the hermeneutic reading of the performance of stars on screen, see de Cordova (1990), 112–13.

[87] According to Bernstein (1994), 372–3, after the promotion of hairstyles and costumes in *Look*, *Vogue*, and *Life* early in 1962, Wanger continued to suggest merchandis-

In the 1960s, at a time when a visit to the cinema had become only one of a number of possible leisure activities, a large number of Hollywood films exhibited narrative self-consciousness about the artifices involved in filmmaking.[88] The historical epic had always been a genre in which cinema could display itself and its powers through showpiece moments of spectacle, such as (in the case of films reconstructing ancient history) chariot races, gladiatorial combat, triumphal processions, or land and sea battles, the persecutions of Nero, or the seductions of Cleopatra.[89] The ancient world of such Hollywood films was, as Michael Wood has argued, 'a huge, many-faceted metaphor for Hollywood itself' and, throughout the 1950s, the spectacularly reconstructed ancient world (with its lavish production values, and the visually enticing technology of Technicolor and widescreen) also signalled the hope of salvation for a film industry suffering from the depredations caused by the large-scale retirement of the American public into do-it-yourself pursuits and domestic television viewing.[90] Mankiewicz's *Cleopatra*, in particular, was widely discussed in its long pre-release period as a last ditch (and ultimately unsuccessful) attempt by a Hollywood studio to bring back audiences to the cinema following the by now outdated production techniques of the old studio system, and the generic codes of hugely expensive historical construction which had last won the industry significant commercial success in 1959 when MGM released *Ben-Hur*.[91]

ing ideas to sell in connection with *Cleopatra*, but they were all dismissed by the studio.

[88] Thumin (1992), 40.

[89] Neale (1983), 35. Cf. Wood (1975), 168–72; dall'Asta (1992), 31; Wyke (1997); Joshel *et al*. (2001); above, Ch. 7.

[90] Wood (1975), 173. See also Houston and Gillett (1963); Wood (1975), 166–77; Belton (1992), 183–210; Babington and Evans (1993), 6–8; Wyke (1997), 24–32; Joshel *et al*. (2001).

[91] See e.g. the account of the film's production in *Newsweek*, 25 March 1963, and cf. Biskind (1983), 336–7.

FIG. 8.5 Poster advertising Elizabeth Taylor in *Cleopatra* (1963).

Aided by the intense expectation generated by pre-release discussion of the film, Mankiewicz's *Cleopatra* positioned its spectators as Romans waiting to see the oriental splendour that is Hollywood cinema itself. Details of the magnificence of the Forum scene were fed to the press long before spectators had an opportunity to judge its visual pleasures for themselves. At the moment when Cleopatra is finally seen arriving through a triumphal arch, the crowd on screen express their amazement at the oriental spectacle of the black, half-naked dancing girls, the emissions of brightly coloured smoke, the scattered rose petals, the birds released from false pyramids, the massive sphinx float, and, finally, the queen and her son enthroned on high, dressed in cloth of gold. The reaction of the Roman crowd on screen to Cleopatra's spectacle attempts to solicit a similar reaction in contemporary spectators to Fox's long-awaited historical epic.

Two alluring features of Cleopatra for Hollywood cinema were her legendary reputation as a creator of fabulous and seductive spectacle and the long-standing association of her kingdom with the mysteries of moving-image projection. Through the representation of Cleopatra and the Orient both on screen and off (in film promotion, and in cinema architecture and foyer-design), the Hollywood studios could proclaim cinema's own visual seductiveness to its awed 'Roman' spectators (Fig. 8.5). But, given that the production of Mankiewicz's *Cleopatra* led to the financial ruin of the 20th Century-Fox studio and was ever after marked as having ushered in the end of the historical epic genre, it is perhaps unsurprising that one scene edited out of the exhibited version of the film shows the queen seducing Julius Caesar with a display of Egypt's extraordinary inventions, including the marvellous, moving images of a zoetrope.[92]

[92] See Beuselink (1988), 6–7, for details of the cut scene.

# 9

## *Meretrix Augusta*: Messalina 1870s–1920s

A lustful empress reclines in a steaming bath. Sliding her hands up over her body—naked but for the ropes of pearls that dangle from her hair—she stares directly out of the cinema screen. A Roman soldier announces to her his love for a Christian girl, as she warns of the seductive pleasure revenge can bring. Next the beloved girl is seized and dragged away, while the empress smirks sadistically in extreme close-up. On her imperial command a gladiator vigorously twists his trident into another's body, before Christian girl and Roman soldier walk serenely to their death through the corpse-strewn arena. This ironic black-and-white epitome of Roman historical films unfolds during the initial sequence of Federico Fellini's *Roma* (1972), in which the film director recalls his childhood in the small Italian coastal town of Rimini during the 1930s and the various ways in which he learned his Roman history: from the landscape and its monuments, from theatre, school, and radio, but most of all from the discursive power of cinema. Fellini focuses on the emotional impact of film spectacle and the process of spectatorship. A mother violently drags her protesting son out of Rimini's cinema as soon as the empress begins to smirk. Fellini's pseudo-autobiographical family eagerly scuttle to the emptied seats from their awkward position straining to see the screen from a side aisle. The father gapes, the mother cries, and the young boy sits completely transfixed until he turns from the screen to gaze with fascination at the chemist's wife behind him in the auditorium. As the glamorous woman, dressed in a scarlet coat with fur-trimmed collar, signals voracious desire to her male companion, a voice-over informs us that 'everyone used to say she was worse than Messalina'. For Fellini, the insatiable Roman empress constitutes part of the modern cultural production of the sexual.

The imperial depravity projected by early Italian historical film is made to intersect with and shape the erotic fantasies of a young boy in 1930s Rimini. For this sequence of *Roma* next cuts away from the cinema to a parked convertible, inside which the chemist's wife is now smothering her boyfriend in kisses, pausing only to wave with intense eagerness at a neat queue formed behind the car. Like the spectators in the cinema who had twisted their necks to get a good look at the empress on screen, the men all lean forward awkwardly to catch a glimpse of the woman whose services they await. Finally, the scene transforms into an explicit blend of Roman past and Rimini present: the insatiable chemist's wife/Messalina dances on the seat of the convertible dressed in a gauzy, scarlet stola over which she slides her hands, staring voraciously off screen oblivious to her togaed clients seated below (Fig. 9.1). Thus the exotic images of Roman historical film are appropriated for and acted out by the citizens of Fellini's Rimini.[1] The recollections of the Italian film director demonstrate that cinema is an important form of popular historiography for ancient Rome, an historiography that draws spectators into its vividly depicted imperial world and flows out into their lives beyond the cinema. They also serve to remind us that (as well as

[1] On this sequence of *Roma*, see Bondanella (1987), 246–51, and Wyke (1997), 3–4. Cf. Hay (1987), pp. xi–xiii, on Fellini's *Amacord*.

FIG. 9.1 'Messalina' and her lovers, from Fellini's *Roma* (1972).

Queen Cleopatra) Empress Messalina has held a significant place in Italian popular cultural production and that her representation has shaped, and been shaped by, modern constructions of femininity and female sexuality. This chapter traces back from Fellini's vision of fascist Italy the origins and development of the popular representation of Valeria Messalina, third wife of the emperor Claudius, as a site for the display, exploration, and consumption of modern femininity and sexuality (as well as tyranny and empire).

## MERETRIX AUGUSTA

The account of Messalina provided by the ancient historians is strictly relational. She lasts for no more than ten years, emerging in the record at her marriage to Claudius (dated variously by modern scholars between 37 and 41 AD) and disappearing after her execution in 48 for adultery and treason. Married at a tender age (according to modern guesswork, at either 14 or 18 years old) to a man at least thirty years her senior, she nonetheless produces a daughter Octavia and a son and potential heir Britannicus—born, most usefully, in 41 the very year of Claudius' accession to power. For the period 41 to 48, classical narratives of Claudius' reign are littered with Messalina's purges of her enemies (the collated list is long but includes most notably Caligula's sister Livilla; the Governor of Eastern Spain, C. Appius Silanus; the praetorian prefect Catonius Justus; Tiberius' granddaughter Julia; the ex-consul and ex-husband of Livilla, M. Vinicius; Claudius' son-in-law Pompeius Magnus; the senator and ex-consul Valerius Asiaticus; and the imperial freedman Polybius).[2] But this fragmentary narrative for Claudius' third wife is also driven by the sexual: 'the Messalina of the sources is one of the great nymphomaniacs of history.'[3]

Fellini's depiction of female sexual voraciousness (ancient Roman and modern Italian) finds its origins in prurient tales of Messalina in the works of Juvenal, the elder Pliny, and Dio.[4] In his satire on the faults of women, the poet Juvenal places Messalina at the climax of a catalogue of unchaste wives (*Sat.* 6.114–32), for Messalina is no ordinary adulteress but an insatiable whore and an emperor's wife. While the emperor slept, the poet notoriously asserts, the empress (disguised beneath hood and blonde wig) used to seek out a mat in a brothel in preference to her Palatine bed. There she would trade to

2 On Messalina in the ancient sources, see the classical materials conveniently collated by Herzog-Hauser and Wotke (1955) and, for their analysis, see Levick (1990), 53–67; Bauman (1992), 166–79; Joshel (1995); Barrett (1996), 71–94; Wood (1999), 252–5 and 274–85.

3 Bauman (1992), 168. Messalina does indeed appear as one of the great courtesans of history in the catalogue produced by Alexandre Dumas *père*, *Filles, lorettes et courtisanes* (Paris: Dolin, 1843; p. 125 in the 1881 edn.).

4 For a collation of the ancient sources on Messalina's supposedly perverse sexual character, see Herzog-Hauser and Wotke (1955), cols. 247–8, and Barrett (1996), 78–9.

the last under the name 'Lycisca' (evoking the Greek for wolf and, thereby, the Roman slang for prostitute), until tired by men but still unsatisfied (*lassata viris necdum satiata*, 6.130), dirty and reeking, she withdrew to her imperial couch.[5] Similarly bestial is the brief reference to Messalina's desires in the elder Pliny's *Natural History*. In a discussion on the mating periods of animals, Pliny notes the relative baseness of humans who neither have fixed seasons nor feel satiety. Claudius' wife provides the single outrageous example: over a day and a night she competed with a celebrated professional prostitute and triumphed with her twenty-fifth coupling (*quinto atque vicensimo concubitu*, 10.171–2). The historian Dio piles on the meretriciousness: Messalina was the most whorish and licentious of women (*pornikotata te kai aselgestata*, 60.14.3), who was not just herself unchaste but required it of others. She compelled many wives to commit adultery, in the palace itself, with their husbands both present and watching (60.18.1–2). Thus while Cleopatra becomes the regal whore of Egypt (*meretrix regina*, Prop. 3.11.39), Messalina more disturbingly becomes the imperial whore lying at the heart of Rome (*meretrix Augusta*, Juv. 6.118).[6]

In the works of the ancient historians, furthermore, in the narratives of Dio (60.31) and especially Tacitus (*Annals* 11.12 and 11.26–38), Messalina's insatiable sexual desire is given an extraordinarily dramatic momentum—so much so that Tacitus even admits his account of it may seem 'fictional' or, perhaps, 'theatrical' (*fabulosus*, 11.27).[7] In the final year of her life, the emperor's wife advances

[5] On the characterization of Messalina in Juv. *Sat.* 6.114–32, see esp. Joshel (1995), 77–8.

[6] In his commentary on Juvenal 6.114–35, John Ferguson (1979), 190, notes that the phrase *meretrix Augusta* used of Messalina is indebted to Propertius' use of *meretrix regina* for Cleopatra. The epithet *Augusta* has particular satiric value because, in the political domain, it was an honorific title awarded to women of the imperial family. Dio 60.12.5 states that the title was considered but rejected for Messalina at the time of her son's birth, see further Saunders (1994).

[7] A detailed analysis of the Tacitean narrative appears in Joshel (1995). Cf., most recently, O'Gorman (2000), 115–21, on Messalina's *damnatio memoriae*.

beyond mere acts of adultery (*emoicheueto*) and prostitution (*eporneueto*), to conceive the perverse, and ultimately treasonable, desire to have many husbands (*epethumese kai andras . . . pollous echein*, Dio 60.31.2). Messalina begins to burn with a new love that verges on madness (*novo et furori proximo amore*, Tac. 11.12) for the consul-designate Gaius Silius. First she drives his wife away, showers him with gifts, and makes no attempt to conceal her adultery. Then, bored by simple adultery, she suggests to Silius (or, alternatively, accepts his suggestion) that they marry, for—in the neatest of paradoxes—the name of wife would bring with it the greatest disrepute (*infamia*, Tac. 11.26). Later, as the emperor's wife openly celebrates a bacchic revel with her new husband, Claudius rushes back to Rome from Ostia, terrified by the warnings of his freedmen. Messalina crosses the city on foot and by refuse cart to reach Claudius on the Ostian road, but is blocked from throwing herself on his mercy. Claudius orders that Silius and other associates of Messalina be put to death but, after too much wine, concedes that his wife may plead her case the next day. That night, therefore, the freedman Narcissus arranges for her immediate execution. Too lust-corrupted in character to take her own life (*per libidines corrupto*, Tac. 11.37), the dishonourable empress is run through. An emotionless (or merely forgetful) Claudius soon marries Agrippina the Younger, while the senate decrees that Messalina's name and image be removed from all public and private places.

## DONNA DELINQUENTE (1870S–1900S)

Messalina's name and image have not, of course, disappeared from the historical record, and, during the course of the nineteenth century, her name even came to signify, and her image to embody, the sexual delinquency of modern women. The use of Messalina to mark the sexual behaviour of Italian women can be traced back beyond the early cinema which Fellini recalls at least to the early years of the new nation. Under the heading 'Messalina' in the *Grande dizionario della lingua italiana* (vol. x, 1978, p. 214) can be found the definition 'donna malvagia, corrotta, dissoluta' (a woman who is wicked, depraved, dissolute). The first example of such a linguistic usage offered by the dictionary is from a polemical article written by the professor of Italian literature Giosuè Carducci and printed in the Bologna newspaper *La voce del populo* for 6 November 1872, in which he attacks another critic and considers in passing the appropriateness of labelling Lucrezia Borgia a strumpet, a Messalina, or a Locusta, during her years as wife of the Duke of Ferrara.[8] The collocation of Messalina and Locusta indicates that, in this debate about the notoriety of an extraordinary Renaissance figure, the critics drew on the Roman exemplars of extreme female wickedness to be found in Juvenal's *Satires* (Messalina from *Sat.* 6 as the great whore, Locusta from *Sat.* 1 as the great poisoner). By the turn of the century, however, 'Messalina' and the adjective 'messalinesco' were being used to mark the licentiousness of ordinary, present-day women, although in the following case one who was comfortably on the margins of the Italian empire: on 7 March 1902 the Governor of the colony of Eritrea, Ferdinando Martini, noted in his diary that he had been informed of the 'scandalous news of Asmara and the truely Messalinian gestures of Signora X'.[9] By 1905 'Messalina' had even become established in a dictionary of modern Italian as said, on the basis of Juvenal *Sat.* 6.130, 'autonomasticamente di donna rotta ai piaceri o sessualmente degenerata' (autonymically of a woman inured to pleasures or sexually degenerate).[10] From the late nineteenth century

[8] *Opere di Giosuè Carducci*, xxvii. *Ceneri e faville* (Bologna: Nicola Zanichelli editore, Serie Seconda, 1938), 358. The *Dizionario etimologico italiano*, iv (Florence: Università di Firenze, 1954) also places the start of this linguistic usage in the nineteenth century, while the *Dizionario della lingua italiana* (Turin: Loescher editore, 1995), more specifically, also gives 1872 as a start date.

[9] *Il diario eritreo*, ii (Florence: Vallecchi editore, 1946), 533.

[10] Alfredo Panzini's *Dizionario moderno*, iv (Milan: Ulrico Hoepli, 1905). By 1989, however, the *Vocabolario della lingua italiana*, iii (Rome: Istituto della Enciclopedia italiana) has added that the usage is neither common nor often serious.

into the early twentieth, a signifying process developed in Italy whereby Messalina *named* delinquent female desire.[11]

During that same period, Messalina also came to *embody* such delinquency. In 1893 the Italian doctor Cesare Lombroso, with the assistance of the young historian Guglielmo Ferrero, published a book that was to become a central text in the new science of criminal anthropology and grant physiology a place in popular culture, *La donna delinquente, la prostituta e la donna normale*.[12] Its title-page was illustrated with a line-drawing of a Roman portrait bust labelled Messalina (Fig. 9.2*a*) which, after sections on the normal woman and female criminology, reappeared on page 346 within a discussion of 'the anatomy, pathology, and anthropometry of the female criminal and the prostitute', and among a series of photographs of female murderers, poisoners, arsonists, brigands, drunks, prostitutes and transvestites whose prison records Lombroso had examined. According to Lombroso and Ferrero, Messalina belonged in their topology of the criminal face as an example of the type whose youth often disguises the masculine and savage features that will inevitably develop in maturity. Juxtaposed with photographs of apparently attractive criminals as young as twelve and nine, Messalina's face worked to support a theory of nineteenth-century woman as trickster or falsification personified, under whose attractive surface lies an atavistic savagery.[13] To the expert eye, however, Messalina's youthful

[11] The *Oxford English Dictionary*, 2nd edn., ix (Oxford: Clarendon Press, 1989), gives as its first example of Messalina 'used allusively for a licentious and scheming woman' a passage from *The Athenaeum* for 8 October 1887: 'his heroine is a New York Messalina who fastens herself upon a villain of the worst type'. However, opening her article on the Tacitean Messalina, Joshel (1995) quotes an earlier description of Edward Rochester's wife in Charlotte Brontë's *Jane Eyre* (1847) as 'my Indian Messalina'.

[12] Turin: Editori L. Roux, 1893; partially trans. into English in 1895 as *The Female Offender*. On Lombroso, see esp. Harrowitz (1994); Dijkstra (1986), 212, 277, and 289; Magli (1989), 95; Bruno (1993), 69–72. Joshel (1995), n. 3, pp. 51–2, notes in passing Lombroso's interest in Messalina.

[13] Harrowitz (1994), 17 and 34. On Roman articulations of woman as falsification personified, see Wyke (1994).

FIG. 9.2*a* Title page of C. Lombroso and E. G. Ferrero, *La donna delinquente* (1893).

portrait disclosed the features of the criminal and born prostitute—a low forehead, very thick, wavy hair, and a heavy jaw (pp. 344–6). Deceit and sexual delinquency are mapped onto the body of Messalina, whose infamous career in historical (rather than prison) records speaks to the accuracy of her physical identification as criminal, and operates as an unspoken but authoritative warning against the deceitfulness and delinquency of modern women for those men who open Lombroso and Ferrero's book. The Roman portrait bust on the title-page of *La donna delinquente* is thus coded as a kind of visual ideogram of female criminality and is to be understood as a term in the discursive categorization and regulation of nineteenth-century femininity.

## MONSTROUS MESSALINA RECONSIDERED

Retrospectively, the historical authenticity of Lombroso's exemplary Roman criminal may have seemed to be secured by the involvement in this scientific project of his son-in-law Ferrero, who was soon to achieve world-wide fame for a five-volume study of the manners and morals of the late republic and early principate, *Grandezza e decadenza di Roma* (1902–7) and, among many other works, a history of the imperial women, *The Women of the Caesars* (1911).[14] Ferrero was concerned to find equivalences between the past and the present, such as the growth and collapse of societies in *Grandezza e decadenza* and, in *The Women of the Caesars*, the dangers attendant on women's liberty. However, both twentieth-century historical scholarship (including Ferrero's own) and iconographic autopsy have discredited any claim to truth of the nineteenth-century's paradigmatically delinquent Messalina.

Modern scholars generally concede that the identification of Messalina's iconography is especially problematic, because of later attempts to vandalize or obliterate her imagery, and because of the absence of an official prototype of the empress on coins of the Roman mint against which to judge the questionable representations of

[14] *Grandezza e decadenza di Roma* (1902–7); trans. into English by Alfred E. Zimmern as *The Greatness and Decline of Rome* (London: William Heinemann, 1907–9). *The Women of the Caesars* (New York: The Century Co., trans. Christian Gauss, 1911); reissued in 1925 in both English and Italian editions. On Ferrero's historiography and political thought, see Sorgi (1983) and Giannetti (1989).

provincial issue.[15] In fact, the marble bust which is the source of the drawing that fronts Lombroso and Ferrero's *La donna delinquente*, and which is to be found in Florence's Uffizi gallery, was once identified as a portrait of Messalina but is now commonly regarded as that of Claudius' next wife, Agrippina the Younger.[16] The nineteenth-century misidentification somewhat undercuts the scientific value of the criminal anthropology the portrait was supposed to illustrate as, in the historical record, Agrippina is motivated by excessive political ambition rather than excessive lust.[17] Furthermore, Susan Wood's recent autopsy of female imperial portraiture distinguishes significantly between the relatively well-attested features of Agrippina and those she more speculatively ascribes to Messalina: while Agrippina's likenesses (such as the bust in Florence, and other sculptural replicas and cameos) exhibit a square jaw, a sharp, jutting chin, thin, rather pinched lips, and low-level eyebrows, the two marble portraits tentatively identified as being of the young Messalina (a statue in Paris and a damaged bust in Dresden) display the same low forehead but a small, slightly retreating chin, a soft, delicate mouth with cupid bow's curve, large, round eyes, and gracefully arched eyebrows (Fig. 9.2*b*). The face, according to Wood, reveals a pleasantly open expression within its smooth, child-like features.[18] Such a Messalina would be, for nineteenth-century criminology, an even more alarming example of feminine trickery than previously thought possible.

[15] Wood (1992), 230, and (1999), 274–6. Cf. Barrett (1996), 215–16, on the problem of identifying Agrippina's portraits.

[16] I am greatly indebted to my colleague Peter Stewart of the Courtauld Institute for identifying the marble bust portrayed in Lombroso's volume, and for supplying me with further details about the original. On the Uffizi website it is mentioned as 'Bust with head of Agrippina the Younger (15–59 AD), formerly believed to be Messalina, inv. 1914 n. 115', http://musa.uffizi.firenze.it/Ambienti/corridoio3.htm, downloaded 14 April 2000. See also Kleiner (1992*b*), 140, fig. 116, where the bust is labelled Agrippina the Younger but in the photograph the old label 'Messalina' is still attached visibly to the sculpture. The bust is still identified as Messalina at www.idn.it/orgoglio/foto/misteri3.htm, downloaded 14 April 2000.

[17] Barrett (1996), 78–9, 90–1, and 206.

[18] Wood (1992), and (1999), 276–82.

FIG. 9.2*b* Roman portrait bust of Messalina.

If Messalina's criminal physiognomy has been undermined, so has her career as a sexual libertine. Writing *The Women of the Caesars* in 1911, the historian Ferrero declared his interest in the problem of woman and her freedom, and explained his purpose consisted in placing 'before the eyes of this pleasure-loving contemporary age' the salutary tragedies of ancient Rome's imperial women (pp. 44–5). He warned that when the moral advance of equality for women is not accompanied also by social discipline, and political and economic responsibility, woman's liberty can be a terrible force for dissolution (pp. 40–2). Yet, after stating that 'everyone knows that the name of Valeria Messalina has become in history synonymous with all the faults and all the vices of which a woman can be guilty', Ferrero did not piece together from her biography a salutary tragedy of monstrous dissolution. He suggested, rather, that Messalina's notoriety was the result of the malevolence and fabulous infamies of the ancient sources (p. 251). He sought for a political, rather than a sexual, motivation for Messalina's marriage with Silius (pp. 265–73), and downgraded her from monster to mere woman, though one 'capricious, gay, powerful, reckless, avid of luxury and money', and prepared to exploit the weakness of Claudius to obtain them both (p. 252).

Scholarship at the end of the twentieth century has gone much further in its reconsideration of the Messalina of the sources and construed her representation in terms of the rhetorical structures of ancient historiography. In particular, the Tacitean narrative—the most extensive and influential source for all subsequent Messalinas—discloses its senatorial bias against the imperial system by structuring the latter's tyranny and corruption in moral terms: proper senatorial authority and masculine power is gradually usurped by the uncontrolled women and scheming freedmen of the imperial household. Such unconstitutional and unnatural transgression of Roman boundaries emasculates emperors and leads inexorably to the fall of the house of the Caesars. Female abuses of power are recycled across a history of dominating wives. The bedroom trials of their enemies, for example, are more than once motivated by a desire to possess the gardens of their victim. For Messalina, the Tacitean plot is truely *fabulosus* (theatrical), for it bears the stamp of comedy in the old man deluded by his adulterous wife and clever slaves, and the stamp of tragic irony in the death of the leading lady in the very gardens she had once so coveted.[19]

[19] On Messalina in the sources, see above, n. 2. On imperial women in Roman historiography, more broadly, see Santoro L'Hoir (1994); Fischler (1994); Laurence (1997); O'Gorman (2000), 122–43.

Modern scholars have read through the strategies of such narratives and substituted for the Messalina of sexual recklessness one of shrewd political intelligence. They note that after an accession to imperial power achieved by military force, Claudius found himself in a precarious position: not a member of the Julian dynasty, estranged from the senate, without prior military, political, or administrative accomplishment, physically handicapped, ageing, and in poor health. Messalina was an advantageous match (the great-granddaughter of Octavia, Augustus' sister, on both her maternal and paternal sides) and could therefore embody both the past of the Julio-Claudian dynasty and its potential future. Her relationship with her husband can be reread as one not of domination but collusion; her actions as propelled not by lust but by fear for her husband, herself, and her son; the deaths of 41–8 (most notably that of Valerius Asiaticus) as motivated not by petty sexual jealousy or greed but by the imperial couple's sensitivity to sedition; the marriage to Silius in 48 as driven not by the need for a new sexual thrill but by the need for a new political alliance after the empress had lost the support of the imperial freedmen. Messalina had to be executed not because she fell victim to her own debauched passions, but because finally she entered into a political conspiracy against Claudius pressed by fear of Agrippina's ambitions and her son Nero's growing popularity.[20] Sandra Joshel, however, has argued persuasively that the sexual and the political cannot be so easily disentangled, either in the informal mechanisms to power available to Roman women under the principate or in the narrative stategies of Roman historiography. Any attempt to reconstruct a real Messalina out of Tacitean fictions is extremely difficult, because the only Messalina to which we now have access is a sign in interlocking discourses of gender and empire.[21]

[20] Griffin (1984), 28–9; Levick (1990), 53–67; Joshel (1995); Barrett (1996), 71–94 and 196–229; Wood (1999), 252–5. Contrast Bauman (1992), 166–79, who considers Messalina's actions to be politically motivated, except where he concurs with Tacitus that her marriage to Silius was purely a love affair.

[21] Joshel (1995), 52 and 77–8.

## ITALIAN THEATRE'S MESSALINA (1876)

Thus the ancient narrative of Messalina constructs a sensational Roman drama of both sexual excess and political injustice that was to gain particular significance when restaged for the new Italian nation. On 3 January 1876, just fifteen years after unification, Pietro Cossa's *Messalina* was first performed in the Teatro Valle at Rome, and became so popular that it provoked much contemporary comment, was staged once again in 1907, inspired a ballet by Luigi Danesi, and clearly influenced the cinematic tradition to which Fellini alludes in *Roma*.[22] After a prologue in which the lovers of republican liberty Valerio Asiatico and his (fictional) freedman Bito participate in the assassination of the emperor Caligula, Cossa's plot draws heavily on the extant sections of Tacitus' *Annals*. Thanks to the vagaries of textual transmission, the *Annals* are missing for the first six years of Claudius' reign and resume at the year AD 47, when Asiaticus is put on trial for treason (11.1) and Messalina has become more disturbed by Agrippina and the popularity at the secular games of her son Nero (11.11–12).[23] Cossa's Messalina begins Act 1 similarly disturbed. She is also in love with Silio, but is herself loved by Bito (now turned gladiator). To take vengeance on the gladiator for his confrontation with her when in disguise in the Suburra, she forces his patron to take his own life on a charge of treason. After her marriage with Silio and its discovery, Bito—torn between his desire for liberty or the empress—dies protecting her from Claudius' freedmen. At the palace, Messalina pleads with her husband persuasively for pardon

[22] All subsequent references are to Pietro Cossa, *Messalina: commedia in 5 atti in versi con prologo* (Turin: F. Casanova editore, 1876). For discussion of Cossa and his play, see *Commemorazione di Pietro Cossa* (1881); Trevisani (1885), 82–94; Arcari (1899), 15–29; Costetti (1978 edn.), 341–8; de Blasi (1911), esp. 74–88; Croce (1914), 145–66; Barbiera (1931), 321–40; *Enciclopedia dello spettacolo*, iii (1956), cols. 1547–9; Momigliano (1960), 538–9; Calendoli (1967), 70–4; La Penna (1990), 576–8.

[23] On the significance of *Annals* 11.11 and 12 for constructing Messalina's political motivations, see Barrett (1996), 89–90. Cf. Griffin (1984), 28–9, and Levick (1990), 65–6.

and is therefore swiftly executed at the imperial freedmen's orders to prevent her reinstatement. The tragedy ends in Act 5.9 when Claudius invites Agrippina to take his wife's empty seat at dinner.

Pietro Cossa was recognized by his contemporaries as an ardent Italian nationalist and patriot. On his death in 1881, he was commemorated as a 'caldissimo idoleggiatore di libertà' (a most heated worshipper of liberty) and as Italy's pre-eminent revolutionary poet.[24] The *romanità* he staged in Rome's theatres constituted part of the discursive terrain on which the Risorgimento revolutionaries had struggled for Italy's independence as a nation-state of civic rather than religious virtue, of triumvirs and consuls, not tyrants. After unification in 1861, the new secular body politic continued to seek its historical justification and continuing legitimacy in the institutions of the Roman republic. Designed to give Italians a common national heritage, Roman history novels and plays proliferated in the latter part of the nineteenth century, to which Cossa contributed the staging of ancient Italy's struggles against tyranny and corruption.[25] The work of the Italian dramatist was also recognized as part of a movement to supply a *popular* national culture: in Cossa's Roman plays, exalted historical figures get off their traditionally pompous 'pedestals of togaed rhetoric' to speak spare verses with an everyday and domesticated realism.[26] Following his proclamation of adherence to the laws of *verismo* in the prologue to the earlier tragedy *Nerone* (1872), Cossa's Romans are neither extravagantly heroic nor extravagantly villainous, and the lives of the great are made to intersect with those of the most lowly.[27] Thus the whole of *Messalina* Act 2

[24] Raffaello Giovagnoli in *Commemorazione di Pietro Cossa* (1881), 30 and 32–3.

[25] On *romanità* and the Risorgimento, see Springer (1987), esp. 65–74 and 136–57; Bondanella (1987), 158–65; Vance (1997), 49–53; Wyke (1997), 17–18, 37–41, and 125–6; Wyke (1999), 189–90.

[26] As Lopez-Celly (1939), 212–16, on nineteenth-century Italian historical novels.

[27] On Cossa's *verismo*, see esp. Croce (1914), 152–4; *Enciclopedia dello spettacolo* (1956), cols. 1547–8; Momigliano (1960), 538–9; Calendoli (1967), 70–4. Cf. Brunetta (1993), 165 and 169, on the topos of social permeability in Italian historical film.

takes place in the Suburra, where the fictive Bito meets again the empress who had once invited him to her secret room in the imperial palace (the role is probably moulded from references in Dio 60.28 to Sabinus, a lover of the empress who had been saved by her from death in gladiatorial combat, and in Tacitus *Annals* 11.35 to Sulpicius Rufus, procurator of gladiators, who was among the conspirators executed in 48). The importance to Cossa's drama of this lowly character's choice between the restoration of republican liberty and the protection of his imperial love is highlighted by an illustration advertising the spectacular production in a contemporary Italian magazine, *L'illustrazione italiana* 26 November 1876, p. 412. Its two central panels display Bito's role in the assassination of Caligula above his defence of Messalina from her would-be executioners (Fig. 9.3).[28]

Many imaginative representations of imperial decadence and decline that were produced during the course of the nineteenth century (and became regular sources for the emplotment of cinema's histories of pagan Rome) positioned Christianity as the driving force behind their accounts.[29] The highly inventive historiography contained in the tragedy *Caligula*, which was staged in Paris by Alexandre Dumas *père* in 1837, and to which the subsequent Italian tragedy could be compared, gave a central role to the martyrdom of Caligula's sister Stella, before the play culminated in the death of the emperor—an assassination orchestrated by his wife (there identified as Messalina) but finally accomplished by Stella's vengeful fiancé and Christian convert, Aquila the Gaul. As befits the anti-clerical stance of Italian nationalism, however, Cossa's *Messalina* acknowledges in passing the purity of early Christianity (if not that of the Catholic Church) while giving it no role to play in the empress's last days.[30] In Act 2, Bito meets in the Suburra not only the empress Messalina (there at her pleasure) but also a young convert Silva (there under

[28] On the importance of Bito, see Arcari (1899), 19.

[29] See, e.g. Turner (1999).

[30] Costetti (1901), 342, suggested that Cossa's *Nerone* was inspired by Dumas, for whose *Caligula* see Schopp (1985), 298–300, and Hamel and Méthé (1990), 124–5.

MESSALINA
A. BONAMORE dis.
La *Messalina* di Pietro Cossa. (Vedi la *Conversazione*).

FIG. 9.3 Advertisement for Pietro Cossa's play *Messalina* (1876).

duress). The latter expresses movingly her wish to escape to the secret Christian community where she can be a sister instead of a slave but, unlike the Christian beloved of Dumas' tragedy or Fellini's epitome of film, she never interacts romantically with the protagonists.[31]

In a further contrast to the drama of Dumas, Cossa's is intra- rather than inter-national: it is not Gallic virtue that Rome needs to bring tyranny to an end. The play opens with the conspirators' cries of 'viva la libertà!' and 'viva l'antica | Repubblica!' (long live liberty!; long live the republic!, Prologue Scene 1). At the play's core, before his enforced suicide, the patriot Asiatico warns the emperor that, though the senate is a useless assembly of the corrupt, the spark of republicanism yet remains in the armies (Act 3.7). Tacitean longing for senatorial *libertas* is here translated into the popular slogans of Italian nationalism. Cossa's Messalina, like that of Tacitus, is capable of embodying the regime since possession of her should bring 'imperio' and the title 'Cesare' (Act 4.3), yet, as the uncontrolled wife of an imbecilic husband, she dares declare to her rival and her lover respectively 'son io | Cesare, io sola' (it is I who am Caesar, I alone, Act 1.3) and 'impero io sola' (I alone rule, Act 3.10). Like Tacitus, Cossa lingers over the eradication of his sign of autocratic government—the excessively desirous woman—and leaves the audience of 1876 satisfied in the knowledge that, while the Romans of the imperial age could not restore the republic, liberty (if not republicanism) has at last been achieved by the virile men and virtuous women of new Italy.[32]

Cossa's *Messalina* is articulated with modern discourses of femininity, as well as that of Italian nationalism. Womanhood is a fundamental topos of the play that domesticates the Roman past and

[31] For a discussion of the scene, see de Blasi (1911), 86; Croce (1914), 155–6; La Penna (1990), 576–8.

[32] On Messalina's role in Tacitus as a sign of bad government, see Joshel (1995). For the influence of Tacitus on Cossa's play, and its consequently patriotic tone, see de Blasi (1911), 76–81 and 85–6.

translates the Tacitean annals of political and military maladministration into an intimate record of adultery and death.[33] It is to the justification of being a woman that Messalina appeals when begging her husband pardon in the final scenes of the tragedy:

> Sono una donna. Voi le forti imprese,
> Voi le battaglie allettano, i trionfi,
> Gli ardui perigli, noi meno superbe,
> E fatte gioco dell'Iddio fanciullo,
> Amiamo! (Act 5.3)
> I am a woman. You, brave deeds,
> You, battles tempt, triumphs,
> Great dangers. We, less proud,
> And made the plaything of the child god,
> We love!

The empress is played not as Juvenal's monstrously voracious whore, but as an amorous adulteress driven by ruinous passions to open betrayals of her husband. It is the vulgarity of Messalina's escapades outside the palace on which Bito comments and for which he condemns her in their Suburra encounter: 'come femmina del volgo | Inseque smaniosa il drudo infame, | E contamina Roma' (like a common woman, she eagerly chases the vile lover, and pollutes Rome, Act 2.8). Such appeals to woman's essence as wholly amorous, along with frequent comparisons of Messalina to the vulgar herd of women, encouraged contemporary commentators to interpret Cossa's empress as a personification of the horror of her sex's instincts, and his play as a meditation in ancient dress on the shamelessness of modern women.[34]

This Messalina understands her predicament in terms of the nineteenth-century rhetoric of the separation of the spheres: man's

[33] Cf. Chard (1999), 127–9, on the use of the topos of the feminine in eighteenth- and nineteenth-century travel writing to create a bridge between the antique and the personal.

[34] As Trevisani (1885), 85 and 89, and de Blasi (1911), 74.

place, it was argued, is to participate in public life and representative politics, woman's to care for the home (and not, therefore, for the world of work or the vote).[35] Voiced fifteen years after the unification of Italy, such rhetoric might seem to some theatre-goers to have a reactionary flavour. Shortly after the formation of the new nation, the feminist Anna Maria Mozzoni had published *La donna e i suoi rapporti sociali* (1864) in which she conjoined rights for Italian women with the very right of Italy to exist.[36] Women had been substantially involved in the campaign for the formation of the secular state (even fighting in the revolutionary armies). Politicized by the struggle, and disappointed by the new constitution of the 1860s, Italian women in the 1870s were now fighting for emanicipation, education, and the reformation of legislation on marriage and divorce.[37] Yet nowhere in the nationalistic drama of Cossa does a woman struggle for political or social liberty.

*Messalina* (1876), however, is not unambiguously reactionary in the way it addresses nineteenth-century femininity through its tragic delineation of the empress. The performance of her death on stage might constitute a fitting punishment for a woman who has misunderstood the separation of spheres, since she has ceased to domesticate her sexuality within the virtuous bounds of home and husband. Yet, following Ferrero, we could read Messalina's tragedy as a warning of the social dissolution that results from *not* giving women political and social responsibility, as a lesson in what goes wrong when women can only exercise sexual agency. It may be significant that, while appropriating antiquity's gendered structures for the exploration of bad government, Cossa's play constructs a more vulnerable and empathetic *meretrix Augusta*. In the Tacitean account, as Messalina races across the city to seek her husband's pardon, the ancient historian states categorically that the horror of her crimes

[35] Smith (1989), 181–3.
[36] Smith (1989), 257; de Giorgio (1992), 495–6.
[37] Smith (1989), 222–4, 236–8, and 256–8; de Giorgio (1992), esp. 7–8.

outweighed anyone's capacity to show her *misericordia* (pity, *Ann.* 11.32), whereas the Italian playwright consistently presents the empress as a woman cruelly duped by her lover and desperately concerned for the safety of her son.

Firstly, Claudius pointedly discloses to his wife at the close of the play what the theatre spectators of 1876 and 1907 would have already observed: that all along Silio had been using her as a stool to climb up to the emperor's throne (Act 5.3). Secondly, considerable emphasis is placed throughout the play on Messalina's point of view as mother (a status rarely exploited elsewhere in Messalina's modern reception, but familiar enough from the Roman tragedy *Octavia* in which, as mother of the heroine, Messalina had been represented sympathetically as the misguided victim of Venus).[38] The machinations of Agrippina and the imperial freedman Pallante frame the play proper. In the first scene (following the prologue), Agrippina is assured that she will become the emperor's wife by the day of his triumph, and in the last she is summoned to dine with the temporary widower. In between Messalina is represented as justifiably afraid for her son. Such an emphasis on motherhood was arguably influenced by its contemporary importance as a source of identity and anxiety for Italian women, whose letters began to appear, from the 1870s, in the pages of women's magazines cataloguing betrayals by husbands and sacrifices for children that had to be endured in the absence of an entitlement to divorce.[39] In such a context, we can begin to understand the full emotive force for some spectators of the empress's plea in Act 1.3 of Cossa's play: that she not be blamed for the unique, jealous mother's love that can sublimate the vilest woman.

The nineteenth-century tragedy also appears to equate Messalina with the actress who played her (Virginia Marini) by embedding within itself an invitation to star-worship. The lowly gladiator Bito acts as the Italian spectator's stage surrogate. He sees through

38 On the point of view of *Octavia*, see Levick (1990), 192.

39 Smith (1989), 168 and 181; de Giorgio (1992), 344.

Messalina's Suburra disguise to the 'real' woman behind it, and speaks of watching, following, and distantly adoring the dazzling and proud woman (Act 2.6)—like a theatre (or later, cinema) spectator trailing a *diva* off set.[40] The star-system to which this scene self-reflexively draws attention became, from the early decades of the next century, a central mechanism of cinema, and one that enabled the *meretrix Augusta* to participate yet further in the popular cultural production of Italian femininity.

## ITALIAN CINEMA'S MESSALINA (1923)

When Countess Rina de Liguoro starred as the heroine of Enrico Guazzoni's historical film *Messalina* (premiered in Rome 31 March 1924, but with a release date of 1923), the Roman empress had already been the subject of a number of Italian films on which Fellini could have drawn for his recollections of cinema-going in Rimini, but this was by far the most successful both in Italy and abroad.[41] From the early years of the twentieth century, the Italian film industry had picked up on and developed the previous century's nationalistic discourse of *romanità*, first to celebrate unity, and then, as in Guazzoni's *Marcantonio e Cleopatra* (1913), to make claims to empire in Africa. Utilizing popular sources such as Pietro Cossa's acclaimed Roman plays (as well as native and foreign novels, operas, paintings, and circus shows set in ancient Rome), cinema became a privileged mechanism for the transmission of Roman symbols of national identity to a vast domestic audience, and the creation of Roman spectacle a means to advance the Italian film industry on the international market. By the time Guazzoni's *Messalina* was released in 1923, however, that industry was deep in economic crisis, and attempting to rebuild

[40] For the significance of this speech for the mechanisms of cinema spectatorship, see Calendoli (1967), 72–4.

[41] See e.g. Bernardini and Martinelli (1996), 259–60, on *Messalina* (dr. Mario Caserini, 1910), and Brunetta (1991), 107–9, on the star of *La moglie di Claudio* (dr. Giovanni Pastrone, 1918). I have not been able to view either of these films.

itself by releasing a series of remakes of the Roman films that had gained for it such national and international prestige in the preceding decade.[42] Despite its desired success, *Messalina* (1923) seems stylistically and thematically arrested, and its explorations of femininity in ancient dress out of keeping with the emancipationism to which the first World War had given such tremendous momentum.

In *Messalina* (1923), history operates as a framing device on which to hang a plot whose convolutions have been rendered even more complex for modern viewers of the film by the accident of its survival as a heavily edited sound print.[43] The film opens with an apprehensive Claudius saluted as emperor thanks to a plot against his predecessor headed by Messalina's love-sick admirer (Marco, Captain of the Praetorians), and draws to a close with Messalina's suicide after she has plotted through another rival admirer (Caio Silio, Praetorian Officer) to overthrow Claudius. In between and motivating the narrative is the wholesome (and wholly fictional) love formed between two slaves—the Persian charioteer Ennio and the Greek handmaid Egle—which is placed in jeopardy by the competing desire for Ennio of the Roman empress and her Egyptian rival Mirit, priestess of Isis. The film features multiple rescues of the innocent slave-girl from her lecherous master or the jealously sadistic priestess, and confrontations between Messalina and Mirit over possession of Ennio. Both women are portrayed elaborately as worshippers of pagan gods (Venus and Isis respectively), both are aggressive, jealous, and vengeful lovers, both are cruel killers punished finally by death (Mirit by fire and lion, Messalina by the sword).

Directed by Enrico Guazzoni, by now a renowned specialist in cinematic reconstructions of ancient Rome, the historical film is

[42] For these developments in silent Italian cinema, see esp. Rognoni (1952), 63–75; Bernardini and Martinelli (1979); Bernardini (1986); Brunetta (1986) and (1993); Sorlin (1996), 16–54.

[43] My analysis of Guazzoni's *Messalina* is based on examination of the surviving sound print produced by Vittorio Malpassuti and to be found in Cineteca Nazionale, in Rome.

formulated as an intertext not with Tacitus, or even Cossa, so much as with earlier historical films about Rome. Like Fellini in his later epitome, Guazzoni recalls and incorporates into *Messalina* (1923) the tradition's favoured topoi: chariot-racing from an American *Ben-Hur* (1907); conflagration and the worship of Isis from *Gli ultimi giorni di Pompei* (1908, twice in 1913, and again in 1926); arena-fighting and the rescue of an innocent girl by her giant protector from *Quo Vadis?* (1913, and again in 1924); an oriental seductress from *Marcantonio e Cleopatra* (1913). Faint surviving traces of the theme of early Christianity can also be discerned in the prayers to the Virgin of the distressed Egle, and in the plot summary provided in a campaign book for the British release of the film where closure comes with the fictional lovers departing 'for the land of promise'.[44]

*Messalina* (1923) appears to place Egyptian, Roman, and Christian cultures in sequence as successively higher stages of history, and their respective femininities in ascending order of moral value. In its narrative excess and plot doubling, Mirit always exceeds the 'Augusta' in cruelty, while vulnerable and innocent Christian girlhood finally triumphs over both mature oriental decadence and imperial meretriciousness. In the 1920s this cinematic formulation of the discourse of *romanità* was much less politically resonant than in preceding decades. It held little appeal for liberals, as a struggle for political liberty was nowhere at issue, nor for imperialists, as oriental corruption is matched by Roman, nor for the newly installed fascist regime which, even before the March on Rome in 1922, had been deploying completely different Roman precedents for political action (such as the supposedly benevolent dictatorship of Julius Caesar). Nor could this *romanità* have even had much appeal for the Catholic Church, since its display of innocence triumphant is achieved only after many preparatory reels of sensuality and sadism. But Guazzoni's *Messalina* was repeatedly lauded for its spectacular visual pleasures: fine

[44] Special Collections (small and large pressbooks), British Film Institute, London. The sound print in Cineteca Nazionale ends earlier with the suicide of the empress.

photography, magnificent sets, gorgeous costumes, thrilling action, vast crowds of extras, and the abundant eroticism of its principal *diva*, Rina de Liguoro.[45]

The Roman empress is here played as a tragic *femme fatale* who, by the film's close, has lost the love of the populace because of her political ambitions, open adulteries, and night-time promiscuities, as she patrols the streets of the Suburra 'da baccante lusinghiera' (like an alluring bacchant). Whereas the opening acclamation of Claudius as the new Caesar is immediately followed by his *wife's* glorious triumph, parading through the heart of Rome in spectacular long shot to the acclaim of huge cheering crowds (although that triumph is already coded as an improper usurpation of power because, according to the accompanying intertitle, it constitutes the triumph of Messalina's beauty), her plot to overthrow Claudius is intercut with her public denunciation from the rostrum to a similarly vast, turbulent throng. While Cossa's Messalina had been duped by her lover, Guazzoni's dupes hers. A dispenser of death, deceitful and devious, she is not attributed with any of the selfless, compensatory anxieties of a mother but only with one final, true love for the humble charioteer. She is captured and frozen in advertising stills posed before her mirror, a symbol of female beauty and elegance, but also arrogant self-admiration and self-containment (Fig. 9.4).[46] This Messalina—who first appears on screen fetishized as a charming foot on to which a slave is strapping a sandal—was partly designed as a successful marketing device to resell the beauty and elegance of Italian cinema to a worldwide audience, and to solicit interest in Countess Rina de Liguoro as the next (and last) great *diva* of the silent era.

[45] On *Messalina* (1923) and other Roman films of the 1920s, see Bernardini and Martinelli (1979), 51–3; Martinelli (1981), 75–8; Gili (1985), 23–5; de Vincenti (1988), 25–6; Gori (1988), 16–19; Brunetta (1993), 314–17; Wyke (1997), 128–30 and 166–71. Martinelli (1981) includes representative quotations from contemporary Italian reviews of *Messalina*.

[46] On the mirror as prop of Italian cinema's *femme fatale*, see Renzi (1991), 126, and for its role in Roman discourses of femininity, see Wyke (1994).

FIG. 9.4 Countess Rina de Liguoro in Messalina (1923) or *The Fall of an Empress.*

In the 1910s, Italian *dive* had been idolized in their distant silence and luxurious surroundings, exalted as an aristocracy above the masses, and frequently sold to spectators as languid of pose, slow of gesture, mysterious, and sensual. Relatively early in the film career of the Countess, *Messalina* (1923) helped imprint on her still rudimentary star persona the features of a vamp through a carefully controlled contamination of the off-screen persona by the person she played on screen. Thus while Italian reviewers of the film described the Roman empress as 'corrotta, depravata, bella' (corrupt, depraved, beautiful), chroniclers of *divismo* recalled the star as 'vasta, bruna, ardente, estenuante' (opulent, dark, passionate, and enervating).[47] The more exotic excesses of vamping are performed in

[47] The film review is quoted in Martinelli (1981), 76, the chronicle of *divismo* in Bianchi (1969), 224.

Guazzoni's film by a *diva* of the previous generation, Gianna Terribili Gonzales (who here plays Mirit as she had Cleopatra in Guazzoni's earlier film of 1913, *Marcantonio e Cleopatra*). Nonetheless, the success in Italy of de Liguoro's performance of Messalina could be read as a form of cinematic nostalgia on the part of filmmakers and audiences confronted in the 1920s with a flood of Hollywood imports that encouraged female spectators not to adoration, but to imitation of stars who now embodied urban modernity and a consumer aesthetic.[48] The campaign book for the British release of *Messalina* (1923) declared that the empress had 'lived such a life that even today her name is a byword for a particular type of femininity' but, however much it may have excited the fantasies of Fellini's schoolboy spectator, that femininity was now both literally and metaphorically antiquated, scarcely relevant to the new economies of the star system or to the conditions of women in the inter-war years.

In the early years of the twentieth century, liberal Italy had paid no special regard to the status of women despite challenges by emancipatory movements to its denial of suffrage and its strict sexual mores, and to the paternalistic attitudes of the Catholic Church. As in other western societies, mobilization in the wartime economy secured a place for women in the public domain but led, in the aftermath of war, to anxious new discourses on woman's condition. The narrative drive of *Messalina* (1923) toward the capital punishment of an extravagantly transgressive woman might have better suited fascism's later development of a cult of motherhood (in keeping with the moral codes of the Church), than its earlier self-presentation as a modern, liberatory force for women. The rights of the 'nuova italiana' (new Italian woman) were being recognized as well as her duties, her entitlement to physical freedom and more emancipated behaviour, as

[48] For developments in cinematic *divismo* between the 1910s and 1920s, see de Miro (1978), 12–13; Bernardini (1985); Gili (1985), 22–3; Brunetta (1991), 97–118, and (1993), 71–91; Renzi (1991). On the development in Cleopatra films from audience admiration of the 1910s vamp to imitation of the glamour girl, see discussion above, Chs. 7 and 8.

well as her responsibility to care for the family. But the film's representation of a weak and acquiescent emperor-husband dominated and duped by his empress-wife would always be wholly incompatible with the Duce's nationalization of gender—the identification of a strong fascist state with militant male virility and female domestic reproduction.[49]

## MODERN MESSALINAS (1910S–1920S)

Already in 1918, an American film had made explicit the redundancy for modern audiences of depicting Messalina as a vamp and as an historical warning of the punishment meted out to female sexual dissolution. In the prologue to Maurice Tourneur's *Woman* (1918), a good-natured, modern husband searches through an encyclopaedia after a tiff with his angry wife. It brings to life for him five episodes visualizing man's eternal temptation by vamps of myth or history, of which Messalina (played by Flore Revalles) is one. According to a review in *Variety* for 1 November 1918, just as 'you grow indignant at the deliberate insult being offered to the fair sex' an epilogue comes to her defence, explaining 'that woman was a slave before slavery existed—that it needed the present war for us to realize what women are and to appreciate them'. The film closes with inserts from official weekly newsreels detailing women's work and sacrifice in industry, in the Red Cross, behind the battlelines. Like Ferrero in his earlier history, *The Women of the Caesars* (1911), the American film suggests that female sexual excess has been the result of economic and political repression, and it goes on to propose, even if only for propagandistic purposes, that the war has been woman's glorious emancipator from a genealogy of dangerous seductions.[50]

[49] De Grazia (1992), 1–44; Smith (1989), 365–453; de Giorgio (1992) esp. 4–5 and 334.

[50] Cf. the review in the *New York Times*, 28 October 1918, and, for the film's director, see Amengual (1989).

In addition, some of the American reviews of Guazzoni's *Messalina* drew attention to new possibilities for the Roman empress in the changing discourses of twentieth-century femininity. According to *Variety* for 27 August 1924: 'The title itself brings to mind hazy suggestions of a vamp ne plus ultra; the most profligate of the naughty Roman empresses and a character sufficiently wicked to cause the yellow newspapers to refer to our present humdingers as "modern Messalinas".' A book-length example of one such sensational representation of a 'modern Messalina' is available for that same year from Britain—*Messalina of the Suburbs* (London: Hutchinson & Co., 1924), published under the pseudonym E. M. Delafield. At no point in the work is an explanation given for the title it carries, but its relevance becomes clearer on reading through the chapters. Young, precocious Elsie Palmer lived in a London suburb. Possessed of considerable sexual power over men, she led on a married doctor, enjoyed the caresses of a stranger in the park, and eventually married an elderly widower. Soon she became bored, and found true love elsewhere, only to end up in a sensational trial at the Old Bailey in 1918, standing in the shadow of the scaffold, charged with inspiring her lover to her husband's murder. Delafield, speaking from Elsie's point of view, concluded 'she would never know how it was that these things had become inevitable—had happened' (p. 182). The reader, by implication, does know, since the explanation lies in the historical record of the executed Roman empress. Here Messalina is deployed not to signify the historic wickedness of woman but, as in Lombroso's *La donna delinquente* (1893), the sexual delinquency of one exceptional woman.

By the late 1920s, however, even in Italy 'Messalina' could be used to name not scandalous sexual delinquency but a relatively harmless, even attractive sexual sauciness. *Messalina!* a comedy in three acts by Piero Angelo Mazzolotti was first performed at the Teatro Carignano in Turin on the evening of 10 February 1928 (as detailed in the text published that year by Libreria Cosmopolita). Set in contemporary Italy, the comedy effectively charts the formation of a new female sexual subjectivity that is neither sacrificing mother nor chaste maiden. A demure girl exhibiting the modesty of yesteryear, Renata Altieri, arrives at a casino to find that her boyfriend is in financial difficulties. She comes across a book entitled *Storia delle sirene celebri: da Cleopatra a Messalina* (History of the Famous Sirens: From Cleopatra to Messalina) on which she draws to help him by playing the *cocotte*. She returns in elegant evening-wear and a grand feather-fan, and gives her name as Messalina. According to the stage-directions 'è scollata e dipinta come vuole la moda, è un altra donna, irriconoscibile' (she wears a low-necked gown and make-up as fashion dictates, she is another woman, unrecognizable, p. 49). By the end of Act 3, Renata has learned how to combine her bold sensation-seeker and her passive maiden in the same person with splendidly romantic results. The play steers a middle course between old and new sexual ideologies for women, between traditional sexual restraint and new possibilities of sexual desire.[51] While in Fellini's *Roma* Messalina is a kind of exotic costume imposed on a modern woman to render her a sexual grotesque, in Mazzolotti's comedy she has become a thoroughly modern woman's modish masquerade.

[51] Cf. Studlar (1996), 278, on a story in an American magazine of 1925, in which the answer to the question 'Which do our American men really prefer—the bold modern flapper, or the demure girl of yesteryear?' is *both*. I am here much indebted to her analysis.

# 10

# Suburban Feminist: Messalina 1930s–1970s

A search on the internet for information about Valeria Messalina leads to a webpage in which her biography is briefly summarized: full name, parentage, connection to Augustus, marriage to Claudius, motherhood, supplementary marriage to Silius, suicide (*sic*). The bulleted list on the left receives visual authentication from its juxtaposition with a Roman cameo on the right which bears the profile of a Claudian woman flanked by two tiny, child-like figures.[1] Underneath, however, in a chiastic arrangement is a colour photograph of a woman's face on the left juxtaposed with a caption on the right: 'REALITY CHECK: She looks innocent enough. Girl next door? She's nothing but a tramp' (Fig. 10.1). The webpage belongs to a site set up in January 1999 through the department of Classics at St Anselm College in New Hampshire, USA, as part of a student project to analyse and evaluate the British television serial *I, Claudius* (first broadcast in 1976, and adapted from the two historical novels on

[1] The gem is from the Bibliothèque Nationale in Paris, and the attribution of its portrait type to Messalina has been disputed, for which see Wood (1992), 230–1.

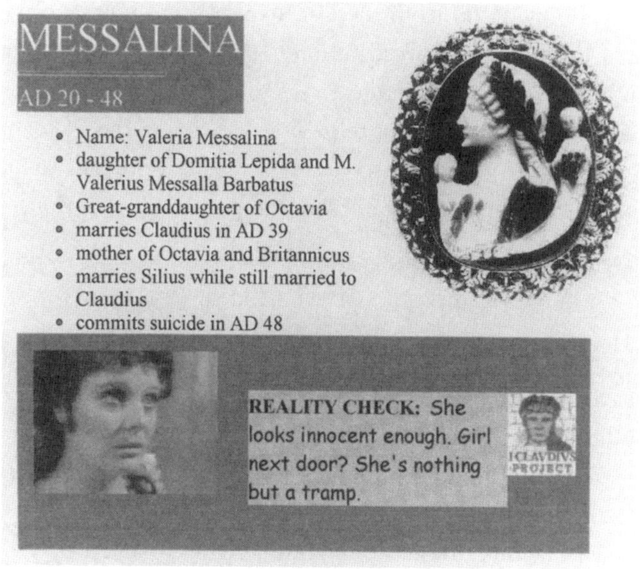


FIG. 10.1 Webpage on Messalina from *I, Claudius* project. Set up in 1999 at St Anselm College.

Claudius by Robert Graves which were published in 1934): 'Fact or Fiction? From the Ancient Historians to the BBC. An Electronic Reference to Sources for *I, Claudius*'.[2] The photograph is a still of Messalina as played by the actress Sheila White in the television production, the webpage part of a catalogue of the television serial's various 'personae'. Although the caption created by the American college students recalls Cesare Lombroso's late nineteenth-century reading of the face of the Roman empress as a map of female sexual delinquency disguised by youth, the webpage usefully reminds visitors in search of Messalina of the dominating position Graves's novels have held (and continue to hold) in the Anglo-American popular cultural production and consumption of the *meretrix Augusta*. This

[2] http://www.anselm.edu/internet/classics/I,CLAUDIUS/Personae/messalina.html (downloaded 24 May 2000).

chapter, following on from the last, explores the further development of the popular representation of Messalina (from the publication of Graves's novels in the 1930s to her appearance within the intimate domestic routine of television-viewing in the 1970s) as an engagement with modern discourses of femininity, female sexuality, and feminism, as well as dictatorship and political corruption.

## A NOVELISTIC MESSALINA (1930S)

The webpage caption neatly summarizes the characterization of the televisual Messalina inherited from Robert Graves's twin narratives of the life of Claudius (from his experience of living precariously under the rule of the first three emperors in *I, Claudius* to his own exercise of imperial power in *Claudius the God*). Graves's Messalina surfaces in Claudius' life as the embodiment of a sly and progressively more insatiable female desire for both sex and power, as a clever *performance* of wifely support and affection by which her husband is completely taken in for the nine years of their marriage. Towards the end of *I, Claudius*, after a brief description of their initial encounter and immediate marriage at the demand of a demented Caligula (Ch. 32, 324–5), Graves opens the next chapter with his first detailed description of the future empress:

> Messalina was an extremely beautiful girl, slim and quick-moving with eyes as black as jet and masses of curly black hair. She hardly spoke a word and had a mysterious smile which drove me nearly crazy with love for her. She was so glad to have escaped from Caligula and so quick to realize the advantages that marriage with me gave her, that she behaved in a way which made me quite sure that she loved me as much as I loved her. This was practically the first time I had been in love with anyone since my boyhood; and when a not very clever, not very attractive man of fifty falls in love with a very attractive and very clever girl of fifteen it is usually a poor look-out for him. (Ch. 33, 326).[3]

[3] Page numbers refer to *The Claudius Novels* (London: Penguin Books, 1999). For convenient reference, I also include chapter numbers.

Composed in the first person, the two novels adopt the generic conventions of a statesman's private memoirs. The narrator Claudius explains conspiratorially in the first chapter of the first volume that 'this is a confidential history', while adding that it is written under the oracular authority of the Sibyl, not for Roman readers but for 'you, my eventual readers of a hundred generations ahead, or more' (Ch. 1, 6)—that is for the consumers of the novels in the 1930s and beyond. Invited to consider themselves directly addressed by the emperor himself, modern readers consequently encounter a Messalina who can seem both vividly present and authentic.[4]

Graves explicitly presented the Claudius novels as both a direct *and* a factual narrative. Against the criticisms of early reviewers of *I, Claudius*, the author included in his preface to *Claudius the God* a lengthy catalogue of all the classical writers he had consulted. Aided by a relatively spare writing-style, Graves granted the insinuations and conjectures of the ancient sources the authority of historical truth (as well as his own imaginative elaborations, such as Messalina's jet-black eyes and enigmatic smile, her motivating intelligence and opportunism), as they were now re-presented in the form of personal testimony or direct reportage.[5] Yet the novels also constitute a highly idiosyncratic, revisionist history of Claudius' early life and reign. For the shambling imbecile to be found in the sources is here transformed into an engagingly self-deprecating yet principled narrator of the tragic process whereby he traded on his infirmities in order to survive the otherwise fatal machinations of the imperial family, and established a benevolent and reforming rule, but came to realize that only by playing the fool once again could he hope to bring

[4] On *I, Claudius* and *Claudius the God* see, in general, Snipes (1979), 173–88; Cohen (1987), 31–9; Bondanella (1987), 218–24; Graves (1990), 187–191; Seymour (1995), 212–25; Seymour-Smith (1995), 227–33; Burton (1995); Spivey (1999); Joshel (2001).

[5] On the author's claims to historical accuracy, and later reviewers' acceptance of those claims, see esp. Snipes (1979), 180–1; Cohen (1987), 34; O'Prey (1982), 236–7; Spivey (1999), pp. viii–ix.

autocracy and empire into disrepute and speed the restoration of the republic, even at the cost of his own life.[6]

While Graves's Claudius is rewritten to become better than the buffoonish emperor of the sources, his imperial women stay the same, if not become worse. As in the works of the ancient historians, accounts of Messalina's dishonest activities are progressively threaded into the (auto)biography of Claudius—starting with a few brief paragraphs in the first novel and culminating in whole chapters towards the close of the second—but throughout Graves's readers are positioned against the deceiving wife and in favour of the deceived husband. The first-person narrator of *Claudius the God* engages the sympathies of his modern readers with regular apologies for his persistent credulity: 'I was deeply in love with Messalina, you must know' (Ch. 6, 412); 'you must remember how clever she was and how slow-witted I was' (Ch. 15, 515). And constant distinction is made between the credulity he had exhibited in the past and the disillusionment now reached at the point of his retrospective narration: 'I realize now . . . but at the time' (Ch. 7, 423); 'I could not have been expected to guess the truth' (Ch. 15, 492); 'it was years before I learned the true facts' (Ch. 22, 585); 'I know now that this sort of trick was constantly played on me' (Ch. 25, 631).[7]

While in *Annals* 11 Tacitus had bestowed on Messalina's last year a dramatic momentum leading from mad love to execution, Graves utilizes the sources to construct a tragic momentum for Claudius leading from loving belief to disillusion. The way an empassioned Messalina baits and traps her wary, last lover in *Claudius the God* replicates in minature her cunning methods for playing her husband ('frankly I cannot blame Silius for being deceived by her: she deceived me daily for nine years', Ch. 28, 662). Her husband now

[6] Snipes (1979), 186–7; Seymour-Smith (1995), 227–9; Spivey (1999), pp. ix–x; Joshel (2001).

[7] Cf. Snipes (1979), 178–9, on the credulity exhibited towards Messalina by Graves's Claudius.

has the capacity both to chronicle for his readers and to interpret correctly his wife's seductive performance with other men. Graves's narrative of Messalina culminates in the emperor's full acknowledgement that he had repeatedly failed to read her accurately, even when all around him knew her to be 'a born whore'. Claudius wearily reports to us the revelatory words of his freedman Narcissus:

> he had resolved to spare me the pain of disillusionment so long as Messalina did nothing which endangered my life or the safety of the country. He had hoped that she might mend her ways or else that I would find out about her for myself. But as time went on and her behaviour grew more and more shameless, it became more and more difficult to tell me. In fact, he could not believe that I did not know by now what all Rome, and all the provinces for that matter, and our enemies over the frontier knew. In the course of nine years it seemed impossible that I should not have heard of her debaucheries, which were astounding in their impudence. (Ch. 28, 665)

Instead of becoming distanced spectators at Tacitus' tragicomedy of an old husband deluded by his young adulterous wife and clever slaves, Graves's readers are turned into the confidants of a distraught husband divulging his final, painful discoveries.

This revelation of the emperor's epistemological progress as husband from belief to discovery and disillusion has been interpreted by later critics and biographers as only part of the narratives' wider re-education in Roman history, supplied by Robert Graves to his readers as an instructive lesson for the 1930s. Messalina is here located within a feminine genealogy of sexual and political perversity in the Julio-Claudian family, headed by the literally poisonous Livia (wife of Augustus), followed most notably by the licentious Julia (daughter of Augustus) and Livilla (sister of Claudius), and completed by 'Agrippinilla' (last wife and murderer of Claudius). As in the gendered rhetorical structures of ancient historiography, woman's depravity and dominance within the imperial household can stand metonymically for the ubiquitous corruption of empire (although far more of the two novels is concerned directly with political and military, rather than sexual, matters).[8] Discovery of the empress Messalina's true corruption is thus bound up in discovery of the true corruption of imperial Rome.

In the cultural discourses of the late nineteenth and early twentieth centuries, ancient Rome regularly stood (however ambivalently) as a model for British empire. In school rooms, Livian histories of republican heroism were deployed as an inspiring guide to civic responsibility, patriotism, courage, and sacrifice of self for the state. By the 1930s, ancient Rome had become an even more potent and troublesome symbol of imperial grandeur or decline, and was utilized by or held up against a number of the nations of Europe. The critique of military heroism generated by the First World War, followed by Britain's loss of Ireland and the growth of Indian nationalism, challenged the values of British imperialism that had been previously troped in the rhetoric of *romanitas*, while the rising dictatorships of Mussolini and Hitler were now appropriating Graeco-Roman antiquity to legitimate their own military strength and foreign expansionism.[9] Better to suit the cultural crisis of the inter-war years, Robert Graves deconstructed Livian historiography through his erudite and authenticating first-person narrator (who at one point in *I, Claudius* sides with Asinius Pollio against Livy in a debate he finds them holding on the writing of history, Ch. 9, 85–94). The familiar Livian story of a virtuous republic on the rise is displaced by a cynical and urgent Claudian lesson in the corruption of absolute rule and the decline of empire.[10]

According to one critic, the recognized modernity of the English in which Graves's Roman characters speak in the novels *I, Claudius* and *Claudius the God* helps cumulatively to build up 'the impression that the Romans of the empire were no more than twentieth-

[8] See esp. Joshel (1995) and (2001).

[9] On the reception of ancient Rome in Britain and the rest of Europe in this period, see esp. Bondanella (1987), 152–206; Ades (1995); Vance (1997); Edwards (1999).

[10] Bondanella (1987), 218–24; Cohen (1987), 34–5; Burton (1995); Joshel (2001).

century people in period costume',[11] while incidental habits and experiences attributed to the first-person voice of the texts have led the author's biographers to conclude that Claudius somehow constitutes Robert Graves himself in a toga. Claudius then dignifies Graves with the aura of an historian on a mission to educate and reform the values of his readers.[12] This perceived elision between narrator and author has also justified some biographers in reading the imperial women of the novels, especially Livia and Messalina, as hyperbolic versions in a stola of Graves's American partner Laura Riding. The incident in *Claudius the God* when Messalina asks her husband for separate accommodation (Ch. 13, 488–91) was written, they note, in the very year that Riding chose to end her sexual relationship with the author. The subsequent execution of the empress then becomes a form of fictionalized therapy, a bitter revenge on Riding's manipulations.[13] If, however, critics have been prepared to read incidental correspondences between Claudius and Graves as a narrative strategy that helps drive a critique of modern empire, there has been little interest in reading seeming parallels between Messalina and Riding, correspondingly, in terms of a critique of modern femininity.

The duping of Claudius by Messalina is made intelligible to the novels' readers as a specific example of the general outcome of amorous relations between a credulous older man and a clever young girl. When Messalina has matured, at a central point in the narrative of *Claudius the God*, she proceeds to claim an exceptional entitlement to transcend the traditional reproductive duties of woman. She desires to have a public role (and to sleep apart):

She stroked my face. 'And I'm not like any ordinary woman, am I, whose business is merely to have children and children and children until she wears out? I am your wife—the Emperor's wife—and I help him in his

[11] Cohen (1987), 37.

[12] Cohen (1987), 35; Seymour (1995), 215–16; Seymour-Smith (1995), 231–2. On this autobiographical identification, see Joshel (2001).

[13] As in the biographies by Seymour (1995), 213–17, and the author's nephew, Graves (1990), 190–1.

Imperial work, and that should take precedence over everything, shouldn't it? Pregnancy interferes with work terribly.'

I said rather ruefully: 'Of course, my dearest, if you really feel like that, I am not the sort of husband to insist on forcing anything on you'. (Ch. 13, 488–9)

Graves also considerably elaborates on the political capacities Messalina had been disdainfully described as exercising in the ancient sources (such as Dio 60.17) and represents them as, in every case, the result of her treacherously seductive wiles: curator of public morals and adviser on membership of the senatorial role (Ch. 6, 412–13); ratifier of public documents such as applications for Roman citizenship (Ch. 13, 488–9); reviser of the citizens' roll, adviser on the choice of magistrates, governors, and commanders, granter of monopolies to trade (Ch. 15, 513–17). The politically astute Messalina of the 1930s historical novels is to be distinguished from the fearful mother of the 1870s historical drama by Pietro Cossa, who had justified her utimately tragic position as compelled by the amorous condition of woman, and the rhetoric of the separation of the spheres.

Graves's Messalina draws on contemporary discourses of femininity and its relation to reproduction and the world of work, advocating for herself the role of career woman instead of (imperial) housewife and mother. As Graves himself recalled in *The Long Weekend: A Social History of Great Britain 1918–1939* (written with Alan Hodge, 1940, 36–49 in the 1985 edn.), the ever increasing emancipation of women from the old ideal of domestic, wifely virtue and restraint was an important social phenomenon of the inter-war years. The modern notion of womanhood was constituted by efficiency at work (not just in the home), companionship with (rather than subservience to) a partner in marriage, and energy in marital sexual life (now no longer limited to reproductive purpose).[14] Although the novels' Messalina

[14] See e.g. Lewis (1984), and Smith (1989), esp. 411.

appeals to such concepts, she also perverts them all: she damages the public functions the trusting emperor generously bestows on her by accepting money or sex as bribes, dupes her husband by play-acting at wifely support, and dedicates her considerable sexual energies to everyone but him. The discourse of modern womanhood is here mouthed as a piece of meretricious treachery: 'This was how Messalina played, very cleverly and very cruelly, on my blind love for her . . . It was seven years before I heard so much as a whisper of what went on in her suite.' (Ch. 13, 491)[15] Woman's recent claims to equality in the workplace, political power, and control over her fertility operate in Graves's novels as symptom or index of the disintegration of empire, ancient and modern.[16]

Despite the author's own disparagement of his Claudian novels, *I, Claudius* and *Claudius the God* were hailed as masterpieces on their publication in 1934. The novels won literary prizes, were subsequently translated into at least seventeen languages, and have been in print ever since. Shortly after their original publication, Graves also sold the film rights to Alexander Korda, head of London Films.[17] Shot by Josef von Sternberg at Denham Studios in the early months of 1937, the British epic *Claudius* was never completed. Only twenty-five minutes of rushes now survive, incorporated into a BBC television documentary broadcast in the 1960s that catalogues the various disasters which accompanied the attempt to make the film, *The Epic that Never Was* (written and produced by Bill Duncalf, and narrated by Dirke Bogarde). That footage, however, and the various drafts of the film script still extant are revealing indicators of how London Films proposed to adapt Graves's Messalina to screen and attract spectators to see her.[18]

[15] Compare the articulation of Cleopatra in Hollywood cinema of the 1930s with discourses of modern womanhood, for which see Ch. 8 above.

[16] As Joshel (2001).

[17] Cohen (1987), 34; Seymour (1995), 222–3; Seymour-Smith (1995), 232.

[18] The documentary is available for viewing in the British National Film Archive, while various drafts of the *Claudius* script survive in the British Film Institute Special Collection on London Film productions, catalogued as e.g. S8753 and S8754. On the

The scripts and, to a lesser extent, the rushes disclose a plot line that jettisons most of Graves's narrative to concentrate on the years a noble and kind-hearted Claudius spent with his lascivious Messalina, from her seduction of him at the time of their enforced marriage, through her gradual achievement of new power as 'the mistress of Rome', to her involvement in conspiracies against Claudius, and his torment following her execution for marriage to Silius. The planned opening voiceover appeals to spectators explicitly in terms of similarities between then and now: over shots of present-day Rome, it would have declared that '1,937 years ago Rome was the centre of the world and its emperor ruled territory from Persia to the British Isles—from the cold north to sunny Egypt. These ruins were once magnificent palaces and peopled with men and women like you and I.' Furthermore, the director, evoking the strategies and agenda of the novels' author, later recalled in his memoirs that he had planned 'to bring to life the old empire and to depict the arrogance and decay of its civilization, and to hold it up as a mirror to our own tottering values and to investigate the diseased roots of excessive ambition'.[19]

Traces of the potential for a more specific and dramatic parallel between crises of sovereign power in ancient Rome and present-day Britain come to the surface in an anecdote, reproduced in the 1960s documentary and elsewhere, that the actor Charles Laughton found the key to his characterization of the Roman emperor in the abdication speech of Edward VIII (broadcast on radio 10 December 1936), a record of which he played daily in his dressing room during filming. Both Korda and the actress chosen to play Messalina, Merle Oberon, knew Edward and Mrs. Simpson, and the constitutional crisis which followed on from their affair overlapped precisely with preparations for shooting *Claudius*. But Korda, it is claimed, forbade any attempt to imitate or satirize the anguished hesitancy and romantically

scripts, see Presley (1999) and, on *Claudius*, see Sarris (1966), 46, and Solomon (1978), 52–3. The documentary is reviewed in the American trade journal *Variety* for 12 January 1966.

[19] Von Sternberg (1965), 171.

bruised dignity of the king, who had been compelled to renounce the throne in order to marry his mistress, a foreign, doubly divorced commoner.[20] Additionally, the initiation of an attempt by the studio to present Oberon as cast 'perfectly' in the role of Messalina—the drive, within the discourses of the star system, profitably to match star persona to screen character—appears to have been taken up some years later and turned against the actress by her biographers. Reporting rumours of Oberon's seduction on set of Alexander Korda (though herself committed elsewhere), the biographers Charles Higham and Roy Moseley clothe her in the characteristics of Graves's Messalina: the Oberon of that period is 'an experienced courtesan looking for a man of wealth and position'; the director lays claim to the ability to see 'through Merle's mask of carefully composed, genteel politeness and good breeding to the ambitious, restless and daring creature underneath'. Von Sternberg is described as having seen through to Merle's consuming sexuality and her streak of ruthlessness at the precise time she was due to play Messalina, the Roman empress who for antiquity, and throughout most of the twentieth century, embodied those very qualities.[21]

## TWO CINEMATIC MESSALINAS (1950S)

Two Messalinas who appear in the cinema of the 1950s, however, manifest less debt to Graves and parallels for British empire than to other traditions and other empires, as well as to evolving discourses of femininity and feminism: namely *Messalina* (1951, dr. C. Gallone) and *Demetrius and the Gladiators* (1954, dr. D. Daues). The *Messalina* directed by Carmine Gallone was a co-production shot in both

[20] The immense international interest the constitutional crisis and abdication drew is described by Graves himself, in the book he co-authored with Hodge (1985 edn.), 360–6. On the filming of *Claudius* and the impact of the royal affair on cast and crew, see Von Sternberg (1965), 171–87; Higham (1976), 74–5; Higham and Moseley (1983), 57–63; Callow (1987), 111–21.

[21] Higham and Moseley (1983), 59 and 61.

French and Italian versions and premiered during December 1951 in various cities of Europe. Some years earlier, during the same period as the Claudius novels were being adapted to screen in London, Gallone had shot the historical epic *Scipione l'Africano* (1937), a work heavily financed by the fascist regime in which republican victory in Africa had been made to glorify the virility of present-day Italian imperialism. While Graves had constructed a feminized Roman empire to demonstrate ancient and modern political corruption and the dangers of autocracy, Gallone reconstructed a muscular, masculine Rome triumphing under Scipio's populist leadership over a feminized Carthage infested by adulterous affairs and political intrigues.[22] As a review of his later *Messalina* notes, for this service to the regime Gallone had been lauded as cinema's 'esaltatore del Genio Italiano' (the extoller of Italian Genius).[23]

In the aftermath of the Second World War, a number of Italian directors (including Gallone) revisited the genre of the Roman historical film in the hope of reinstating their film industry nationally and internationally by matching the huge economic and cultural success the genre had achieved in the 1910s. *Fabiola* (1948, dr. Alessandro Blasetti), *Gli ultimi giorni di Pompei* (1948/50, dr. Paolo Moffa with Marcel L'Herbier), *Messalina* (1951), and *Spartaco* (1952, dr. Riccardo Freda) all invoked titles and characters of the silent era and attempted to provide Italian cinema and its spectators with a representation of *romanità* that would no longer be bound up in the glorification of fascism. In the year *Messalina* was released, for example, the director Blasetti responded to the hostility currently being shown by reviewers towards the revival of the genre. Apart from spectacular profit, he argued, the representation of history could also supply the kind of documentation of wartime human suffering currently undertaken by neo-realist directors, and provide from the

[22] On *Scipione*, see Cardillo (1987), 158–62; Hay (1987), 155–61; Bondanella (1987), 210–13; Gori (1988), 16–25; Gili (1990); Dalle Vacche (1992), 27–52; Quartermaine (1995); Becker (1995).

[23] *Rassegna del Film* 1/1 (1952), 39.

experience of the past 'answers and advice for our problems' today. True to his brief, in *Fabiola* (a film produced with Vatican capital), the director had invited Italians to unify behind identification with the gritty courage of the Christian martyrs, who were presented as suffering heroically a Roman tyranny reminiscent of recent wartime persecution and post-war intolerance.[24]

The opening titles of *Messalina* (1951)—themselves presented in the form of an inscribed wax tablet—lay claim to the ancient authority of Tacitus, Seneca, Suetonius, Martial, and Juvenal for their narrative, and adapt *Annals* 11.27 so that Tacitus' voice appears to become the film's own: 'the extraordinary circumstances of the marriage of Messalina are not invented, the facts that I shall recount I heard from the mouths of our elders and read in the memoirs of the time'.[25] Like the preface to Graves's *Claudius the God* (1934), this preparatory tablet bestows a seeming credibility on the subsequent narrative even, in this case, on a wholly fictious subplot concerning the innocent love of two slaves, Cynzia and Timo, who survive the prospect of martyrdom in the arena thanks to the girl's sudden faith in Christ. The film proper opens with an emperor like that of Graves, whose concern for wisdom, culture, and good politics is corrupted by his adoration for a dominating, materialistic, and deceitful Messalina.[26] When, however, Messalina expresses her concern in the opening sequence with the problems of the Suburra (she is off, she declares, 'to investigate our slum problems'), film spectators are not invited to identify with her still credulous husband. Instead they are swiftly made to understand that the empress is not talking about

[24] Blasetti (1951), 55–6. On *Fabiola* and Italy's post-war historical films, see Siclier (1962); Brunetta (1982), 499–505, and (1991), 359–60 and 419–20; Spinazzola (1985), 59–61; Wyke (1997), 49–56.

[25] I quote (and translate) from the copy of *Messalina* I have seen in Cineteca Nazionale, Rome and make additional reference to the English-language version in the Library of Congress, Washington.

[26] He is so characterized in the multi-lingual programme that accompanied the European premières of *Messalina*, a copy of which can be seen in the Special Collections of the British Film Institute, London.

schemes for urban regeneration. As the film's title indicates, it then pursues an interest not in Claudius, but in Messalina and her relentless pursuit of sex and imperial power. Reaching back beyond fascism's deployment of *romanità*, the film evokes that of early Italian nationalism, emphasizing in its plot line—as did Pietro Cossa's play of 1876—a struggle to re-establish Roman republicanism against the seductions of Messalinian empire.[27]

Messalina inexorably destroys or corrupts Rome's lovers of liberty. First Valerio Asiatico is compelled to take his life, but not before he speaks wistfully about his dream of a new republic and passes on to Caio Silio the responsibility for achieving it. Despite Valerio's warning that he should not fall in love with the empress and become her plaything, Silio (like Cossa's fictional gladiator Bito) is seduced (Fig. 10.2). After their public marriage, Silio is murdered by his fellow republicans as an amorous collaborator, and Messalina, abandoned by both lover and populace, falls on a sword when hemmed in by soldiers sent to arrest her.[28] Both in the film and in accompanying programme notes, the corruption of autocratic power is made flesh in the pleasure-seeking, sensual Messalina. It is she who actually rules 'to all intents and purposes', she who can bestow empire on whichever lover she chooses, and she who must be resisted and destroyed by lovers of liberty. Silio, according to the European programme notes, 'muore vittima del conflitto tra questa passione imperiale ed il suo ideale repubblicano' (dies victim of the conflict between this imperial passion and his republican ideal)—matched against his republican ideal, his passion is thus for the body of the

[27] The film's debt to Cossa is explicitly recognized in the Italian review cited above, n. 23.

[28] Plot summaries and other details are supplied in the programmes for both the European and the American premières. A copy of the latter can be seen in the USC Cinema-Television Library, Los Angeles. *Messalina* (1951) has received little critical attention beyond that shown to the genre of Italian post-war historical films as a whole (see above, n. 24).

FIG. 10.2 María Félix in *Messalina* (1951).

empress and for her empire. In the context of post-war Italian cinema, it is easy to see how Gallone here tries to parallel the recognized strategies of Blasetti's *Fabiola* (1948/50) and address the political wrong done by his earlier Roman film *Scipione* (1937). The earlier protagonist who embodied the triumphant masculinity of Mussolinian Rome is here substituted by one who flaunts its now defeated feminine decadence, and that substitution is brought home to Italian spectators by Gallone's clear invitation to compare the scene of Messalina's triumph (parading prostrate and bejewelled in a sedan) with that of the upright and virile Scipio in the earlier fascist film. Like Mussolini's, Messalina's death is a ritual of public humiliation: at the film's close, the camera rises up to reveal an aerial view of the corpse encircled by a now disenchanted populace and then, in imitation of post-war Italy's proposed trajectory, sweeps away to the happy young lovers' escape into a future beyond the gates of Rome's bad government.[29]

*Messalina* (1951) was a potentially discomforting experience for Italian spectators of the immediate post-war period. Throughout the film, especially in its most spectacular moments, the empress is associated with pleasure—the delights of love, food, dance, entertainment, and luxurious living—her subjects with poverty and urban squalor. In an early sequence as Messalina trawls through the city streets in disguise, the camera first turns away from the 'Augusta' to focus on the faces of the Romans she passes, so that their salacious comments are now addressed out directly to Italian audiences in the cinema as if they momentarily inhabit her point of view, before Valerio Asiatico pronounces that she (and by implication they) are a disgrace to Rome. However, the film's extra-cinematic discourses undercut the otherwise disturbing identification of modern Italians with autocratic government. In the programme notes distributed for the film's European release, the actress who plays Messalina (María Félix) is described at the outset as Mexican,[30] for the star persona of María Félix had already constituted her as an incarnation of Mexican nationalism and Latin American womanhood.[31] Additionally, the notes on *Messalina* and their attendant illustrations (as well as the film's opening display of the jewels Claudius buys to adorn his wife) everywhere draw attention to the artifice required to play the empress—the complexity of the hairstyles, jewellery, and costumes the actress must don in order to bring the character alive. The foreign artificiality of this femininity can be contrasted with that being played out simultaneously in Italian neo-realist cinema as an outline of the nation's future. Feminist critics have observed that the female body pervasively on display in such cinema of the 1940s and early 1950s is

[29] In the context of an analysis of contemporary allusions in Graves's Claudian novels, Philip Burton intriguingly notes in passing the similarity of sound between 'Messalina' and 'Mussolini', (1995), 199.

[30] 'Il Messico' opens the biographical note on María Félix.

[31] On the star persona of María Félix, see Castillo (1989) and Dever (1992).

deliberately uncontaminated by the look of fascist ideology: a creature of the earth, generous in proportion, warm and naturally erotic, she is located harmoniously in the landscape of rural Italy.[32] By contrast, the glacial Messalina played by María Félix ceases in some sense to be either natural or Italian, and displays the look of fascism as if it were an alien costume (however attractive) that the post-war Italian nation could now discard just as easily as it had put it on.[33]

Such strategies, however, were insufficient to win for Gallone's *Messalina* the enormous success achieved by Blasetti's *Fabiola*. Italian reviewers could not readily forgive Gallone the propagandistic function of his earlier Roman epic, and generally described his cinematic apologia as laughable, grandiose, and redundant.[34] The film received an even more scathing response in the American press on its release there in 1953, despite its distributors (Columbia Pictures) billing it as 'The Affairs of Messalina—History's Most Wicked Woman', or 'Empress of Love in an Era of Sin!'.[35] The representation of Messalina as a noirish femme fatale and embodiment of autocratic government proved empty of significance for the American market, where Messalina reappeared within the year incorporated into a different cinematic tradition and played, according to one reviewer, like 'a suburban feminist having a fling'.[36]

When, in 1958, London Film Productions were in negotiation over the sale of their exclusive right to film Robert Graves's Claudian novels, the potential buyer's lawyer pointed out in correspondence that a substantial piece of Graves's account of Caligula,

[32] See esp. Grignaffini (1988).

[33] It is noteworthy that in the European programme for *Messalina*, costume is explicitly described as functioning to typify characters: the costume of the true republican Valerio Asiatico (the severe toga of the Roman citizen) is explicitly contrasted with that of the collaborator Caio Silio (refined elegance).

[34] See the review cited above, n. 23, and cf. the brief comment in *Intermezzo*, 6/24 (1951), 5.

[35] See e.g. *The Hollywood Reporter* 124/41 (12 June 1953), 3 and the earlier review in *Variety*, 12 March 1952, when on European release.

[36] *Films in Review*, 5 (August–September 1954), 365.

Claudius and Messalina, as well as some of the novels' dialogue, seemed already to have been included in the 20th Century-Fox film *Demetrius and the Gladiators* (1954, dr. Delmer Daves), rendering another Claudius film 'repetitious and possibly unsaleable'.[37] Yet both the title of the American film and its precredits sequence clearly mark it as a sequel to the Hollywood biblical epic *The Robe* (1953), an adaptation to screen of an immensely popular novel written during the Second World War by the minister Lloyd C. Douglas, in which a Roman soldier witnesses the crucifixion of Christ, converts, and accepts martyrdom thanks, in part, to the powers of Christ's robe to recall for those who touch it the sacrifice its owner had made for them.

The precredit sequence of *Demetrius* replays the conclusion of *The Robe*, now intercut with the new figure of Messalina watching the Roman soldier and his beloved walking to their death on the command of the emperor Caligula. While the first film pursued the religious novel's theme of a Roman soldier's acquisition of faith, its sequel scripted by Philip Dunne expanded on the character of the soldier's slave Demetrius (played, as in the earlier film, by Victor Mature) and provided him with a trial of faith at the hands of a mad Caligula and a rapacious Messalina. Like its predecessor, *Demetrius and the Gladiators* was sold primarily as a vehicle for the display of the new technologies of CinemaScope and stereophonic sound, developed by the Hollywood film industry to demonstrate the superiority of cinema over television in an increasingly urgent competition for audiences. Grand narratives of religious history were thought capable of accommodating and naturalizing this new widescreen aesthetics. Trade reviews of *Demetrius* thus drew attention to the commercial potential of its presentation of a struggle for Christian good in the face of pagan evil in terms of spectacle and the pleasures of the look:

[37] The letter is addressed to Sir David Cunynghame of LFP from Denise Sée and dated 20 January 1958. It can be found in the LFP Collection at the British Film Institute under items B/016 (ii).

the 'hunk-o'man heroics' of the ferocious arena combats; 'the sweeping panoramas of pagan court life'; and 'the code-breaking carnality' of Messalina's seductions.[38]

After the credits, *Demetrius* opens with a crazed, effeminate Caligula and a carefully obsequious, Gravesian Claudius who display contrasting interests in the mysterious properties of Christ's robe and the Christians' capacity to endure death fearlessly: Caligula expresses a desire for immortality, Claudius philosophical curiosity. Demetrius is arrested after Roman soldiers assault his sweetheart when searching for the robe, and then finds his religious and sexual fidelity tested by Messalina's political and amatory desires.[39] She orders him to fight in the arena and sends him back there when he rejects her advances, but the gladiator loses his faith after the attempted rape and apparent death of his beloved Lucia. Falling completely from grace, Demetrius becomes an efficient killer, renounces his God, takes up a tribuneship and the embrace of his imperial temptress. Sent now to find the robe, he rediscovers Lucia, remorse, and reconversion, and is sent a third time into the arena on attacking the emperor. His fellow-soldiers assassinate Caligula and enthrone Claudius. The film closes with Messalina pronouncing wifely support for her newly invigorated husband, and with Demetrius the tribune marching off to tell the Christian community that the emperor wishes to make peace with them. The characterization of Messalina is here subordinated not to a British narrative of the recognition of imperial

[38] See e.g. *Variety* for 2 June 1954 and *Boxoffice* for 5 June 1954. My thanks are due to Ned Comstock of the USC Cinema-Television Archive for collating for me the reviews of *Demetrius* in its Philip Dunne Collection. On *Demetrius* and the Hollywood biblical epics, see further Hirsch (1978), 22–4; Babington and Evans (1993), 177–226; Wyke (1997), 27–32; the articles by Bourget, Rousseau, Cieutat, and Chanudaud collected in *Positif*, 468 (2000), 80–104; Joshel *et al.* (2001).

[39] The cinematic topos of the imperial temptress who attempts to lure a man away from both his beloved and his faith goes back, via earlier Hollywood representations such as *Quo Vadis* (1951) and *The Sign of the Cross* (1932), to the characterization of the empress Poppaea in late nineteenth-century popular religious fiction. See Wyke (1997), 110–46.

corruption, nor an Italian narrative of the fight for republican liberty, but to an American one of achieving Christian virility. *The Hollywood Reporter* for 2 June 1954 calls *Demetrius* 'the story of an individual inspired by the Most Revered Man and seduced by the most evil woman in human history'. In Cold War America, religion and morality had become the new, national politics: Dwight Eisenhower had inaugurated his presidency in the preceding year with the declaration that 'the recognition of the Supreme Being is the first, the most basic expression of Americanism', and the fight against Communism was regularly troped as a struggle between freedom and totalitarianism, godliness and immorality, Christ and the anti-Christ.[40] In *Demetrius*, national superiority is also constructed in terms of masculinity: the effeminacy and weakness manifested by a dictatorial, irreligious empire is destined to cede (set in terms of ancient Rome's relations to early Christianity) to the robust muscularity of a pious, free new world constantly combating a decline into decadence. America has God, History, Morality, and Manhood on its side.

National superiority is also embodied and enacted in *Demetrius* through a hierarchical contrast between femininities and female sexualities. During the era of the Cold War, American political institutions and popular cultural discourses (including Hollywood cinema of the early 1950s) frequently expressed anxieties about containment in relation to both the spread of Communism *and* the growth of American women's independence. Women's emancipation (particularly their hugely increased participation in paid labour and its effects on traditional gender roles) was perceived, in conservative cultural texts, as a threat to the American way of life. The re-establishment of the family unit and the restoration of women to the domestic sphere were thus urged as a matter of national security.[41] In *Demetrius and the*

[40] Whitfield (1991), 77–100. On America's Cold War rhetoric in Hollywood's Roman epics of the 1950s, see also Babington and Evans (1993); Wyke (1997), 23, 28–9, 63–72, and 142–5.

[41] See e.g. French (1978) and Byars (1991).

*Gladiators* (1954), the ideal femininity and sexuality embodied by the cherished Lucia (played by Debra Paget) counterpoints their perversion by Messalina (played by Susan Hayward). 'Lucia' names the pure light of Christian morality. She is sweet, childlike, and constantly helpless: in need of her lover's protection from male sexual assault, she offers Demetrius the redemption of wholesome, spiritualized monogamy and traditional male authority. 'Messalina', in contrast, has traditionally named female sexual delinquency. Here she is politically ambitious, deceitful, sensual, and rapacious, and constantly in control of the body of the male protagonist and those of his fellow gladiators. The perversity of her aggressive desires and their consequences for gender are marked by her appropriation of the masculine scopophilic gaze, as she voyeuristically takes pleasure in the gladiators' pre-match carousing and their fatal arena combats. This Messalina literally treats male bodies as her property and her plaything.[42]

Unusually for a film belonging to a socially conformist phase in Hollywood cinema, *Demetrius* provides its spectators with a fleeting glimpse of the self-justification of a so-called 'suburban feminist'.[43] Having just witnessed Messalina's public disavowal of complicity in a conspiracy against the emperor Caligula, spectators now witness, in the privacy of Messalina's lavish boudoir, her response to Demetrius' presumption of her innocence:

MESS: Innocent? Who said I was innocent? Caligula was right, I put those two up to it, and they bungled it. Oh, if I were a man, if I were Claudius, I would have killed Caligula long ago. I'd have won the gods to my side and taken the empire for my own. But he's no better than the rest of them.

Approaching her slave across the wide CinemaScope frame, Messalina grips his shoulders tightly in her hands and declares 'For ten years I've been married to a man old enough to be my father. I've never been close to another man. I've never wanted to. I need you

[42] Babington and Evans (1993), 188–99 and 219–23. Cf. Hark (1993) on the perverse operations of the female gaze on male bodies in *Spartacus* (1960).

[43] As noted by Babington and Evans (1993), 222.

Demetrius. I need your strength.' Demetrius, however, disentangles himself from her ensuing kiss (while a sequence of shot/reverse shots renders visually the moral chasm that lies between them) and sarcastically exposes his temptress as a liar:

DEM: You don't need me Messalina. A woman with your wit, your courage, and your reputation. All Rome knows why you married Claudius. If anything should ever happen to Caligula, Claudius would become emperor. And since then all Rome knows a steady procession of men has stood guard at your door.

Both Messalina and Demetrius merge political with sexual frustration in their respective accounts of her transgressive behaviour, thereby evoking the reactionary rhetorical strategies of commentators on 1950s American society. The dissatisfaction with domesticity they observed in suburban housewives was construed as mere loneliness and sexual starvation, the pursuit of a career outside the home as motivated by moral inadequacy. A more vigorous marital sex-life should therefore be sufficient to reroute and to answer the question posed by 'suburban feminists'—'Is this all?'.[44]

The description of Messalina/Hayward in reviews of *Demetrius* as 'a suburban feminist having a fling' or, in later biographies of the star, as 'draped in beaded '50s "formals" and the cunning authority of an over-compensating woman executive' demonstrate that at least some viewers have read the film as a morality tale (however hyperbolically expressed) for 1950s femininity and feminism.[45] After the precredits replay of *The Robe*, *Demetrius and the Gladiators* is framed by representations of marital relations in the imperial household: the film proper opens with Caligula, in his search for the abject Claudius, asking Messalina why her husband does not sleep with her; it closes with Claudius now proudly erect at the top of the throne-room steps

[44] On the exploitation of women's sexuality in 1950s American popular culture to disavow their economic and political frustrations, see French (1978), esp. pp. xxii and 152–3; Dyer (1987), 23–7; Byars (1991), esp. 89.

[45] *Films in Review*, 5 (August–September 1954), 365, and McClelland (1975), 122.

FIG. 10.3 Susan Hayward as Messalina in *Demetrius and the Gladiators* (1954).

calling down gently to his wife to join him (Fig. 10.3). In Gravesian accents, the new emperor solemnly proclaims 'I am not quite the fool that I have pretended to be all these years in order to preserve my life. That has ended. You have made me Caesar and I will act the part.' Before she steps up to seat herself beside her husband, Messalina (who stands out from the crowd of soldiers behind her in the pale and dark blue drapes of a Virgin Mary) turns to inform the assembly: 'It's no secret from any of you that I have mocked my marriage vows, that I've openly disgraced my husband and myself. That too is ended. I am Caesar's wife and I will act the part.' Seemingly tamed by contact with virile Christianity (a breast-plated Demetrius/ Mature can be seen immediately behind and below her, full of admiration), the *meretrix Augusta* walks up (and out of history) back into the institutions of marriage and heterosexual monogamy. Even 'the most evil woman in human history' can ultimately be contained.

The conservative closure of *Demetrius and the Gladiators*, however, is not without its ambiguities and contradictions. The trade journal *The Hollywood Reporter* (2 June 1954) considered the implied reformation of 20th-Century Fox's Messalina 'a minor mistake' for audiences sufficiently informed of their Roman imperial history. It is not only Roman history, however, that casts doubt on the sincerity of Messalina/Hayward's final speech. On the level of film narrative, in the earlier seduction scene, both the temptress and her victim have already exposed her preparedness to lie in order to achieve power, while the speech itself (recalling Graves's characterization of the empress) proclaims her willingness only to *act* the part of a loving and supportive wife.[46] Furthermore, on the level of extra-cinematic discourses of stardom, a new, companionate role for Messalina constituted a singular mismatch with the persona of Susan Hayward then in circulation. For, by the time of the release of *Demetrius*, Hayward's star image had become a site on which to play out 1950s concerns with female independence and its attendant dangers for traditional gender roles within the American family.

In the early 1950s, Susan Hayward and Marilyn Monroe were among Hollywood's most popular box-office draws and their star images had become reference points in current debates about female sexuality.[47] But, whereas Monroe's star image had been defined in terms of a desirable sexual playmate for men, dumb, innocent, and without menace, Hayward's 'fiery redhead' (through casting, performance, film reviews, studio promotions, and mass media publicity) operated instead as an index of an abrasive and aggressive female sex-

[46] The possible irony embedded in the final scene is noted by Babington and Evans (1993), 222.

[47] On Monroe's star image and its intersection with 1950s' discourses of sexuality, see Dyer (1987), 19–66. Cf. Chs. 7 and 8 above on star images, discourses of female sexuality, and film representations of Cleopatra.

uality, at once dominating and dangerous. From 1953, moreover, that star image had been radically reinforced by headline reports in the press progressively cataloguing violent fights between the actress and her husband, adultery, and the initiation of divorce proceedings. While film reviewers were assessing Hayward's on-screen characterization of Messalina in June 1954, simultaneously other journalists were drawing on published court testimony to delineate the Hayward household as a perversion of gender, irreparably damaged by a woman whose coldhearted desire for money had made her an unconventional breadwinner and reduced her husband to the pitiful status of 'Mr. Mom'.[48] By the end of 1955, the English *Daily Express* readily acknowledged that its readers were now familiar with the star as a 'spitfire' and included in the caption to an article about her a sonorous reference to the fascination of 'wayward Hayward'.[49] Such extra-cinematic discourses of stardom inflect spectators' understanding of the film narratives in which stars appear.[50] Thus one reviewer of *Demetrius* observed that Hayward played Messalina 'looking petulant and sultry all at once and at the same time, as if she were just hearing that testimony from the maid from across her backyard'.[51] Any attempt by *Demetrius and the Gladiators* to contain the extravagantly aberrant Messalina at the film's close within a 1950s vision of wifely reponsibility is therefore undercut by history and by wayward Hayward's apparently empathetic performance of imperial meretriciousness and its necessary deceits.[52]

[48] Testimony from the Hayward divorce case was extensively quoted in e.g. the June 1954 edition of *Modern Screen*. Its consequences for Hayward's star image are discussed in McClelland (1975); Moreno (1979); Agan (1979), 181–219; Laguardia and Arceri (1985); Hannsberry (1998), 241–51.

[49] *Daily Express*, 24 November 1955.

[50] See e.g. Stacey (1991), and Thumim (1992), 48–56.

[51] *The Morning Telegraph*, 19 June 1954.

[52] The sympathy with which Hayward played Messalina is noted in *The Hollywood Reporter* (2 June 1954) and *Boxoffice* (5 June 1954), and Hayward's performance is paralleled with her star image in McClelland (1975), 60 and 121–3, and Babington and Evans (1993), 221–2.

How female spectators might now read the seemingly intimate relationship between Messalina and Susan Hayward clearly troubled those advertisers whose brief it was to sell audiences consumer products through the exploitation of Hayward's image as a glamorous star. The Hollywood film industry regularly deployed technologies of gender that extended beyond the process of film narration. Through its marketing strategies stars placed on display ideals of feminine beauty to be admired, consumed, and imitated by female spectators in their lives outside the cinema.[53] Thus *Picturergoer* for 22 January 1955 (28) carried an advertisement detailing Hayward's advocacy of Lux Toilet soap, while directly confronting the issue of female spectatorship, mechanisms of identification, and the troubling intersection of Hayward's star image and her current screen character (Fig. 10.4).[54] Under the caption 'How do you see Susan?', the advertiser claimed for Lux soap the properties of snowy whiteness, purity, mildness, gentleness, and fragrance. A distinction is everywhere made between the star's performance in local cinemas 'as one of the hardest women in history', 'as wicked Messalina', and her own personal sweetness and charm—authenticated as genuine by use of the seemingly intimate first name 'Susan'. In the accompanying photograph, Susan stands apart from her construction as Messalina and gazes on it like a spectator of her own screen image. Sculpture becomes a convenient metaphor through which female consumers are invited to understand cinema's construction of Hayward as Messalina: identity between model and imperial portrait is recognized only on the level of surface beauty ('that fabulous complexion') not on the level of inner character. To the question 'How do you see Susan?', the advertisement solicits from the readers of *Picturegoer* the answer as a charming and pure star who merely *plays at* imperial wickedness.

[53] Cf. Ch. 8 above, on marketing strategies linked to film representations of Cleopatra.

[54] My attention was drawn to this advertisement through its use by Stacey (1991) to illustrate her discussion of forms of identification in star-audience relations.

How do you see Susan ?
HERE'S SUSAN HAYWARD as the sculptor saw her—sweet and fresh as a spring morning.
But you'll be seeing her as one of the hardest women in history—playing Messalina in her latest film!
However much Susan may change character, one thing remains familiar: that fabulous *complexion*. Why? Because she's never changed her mind about what's best for beauty. That means she's never wavered in her choice of the *whitest* soap—Lux Toilet Soap—to keep the lovely sparkle in her skin.
It's the snowy, white look of Lux Toilet Soap that tells you worlds about its *purity*. You can be sure that it is mild, is gentle—and that every day of Lux Toilet Soap care proves your first impression right!
When 9 out of 10 film stars use it, you can be sure that pure, white Lux Toilet Soap lives up to its appearance!
LUX TOILET SOAP
LUX TOILET SOAP
"DIVINELY FRAGRANT!" *Film star Susan Hayward sings the praises of Lux Toilet Soap's exciting perfume, which lingers so deliciously on the skin. In the new French handy-shaped, and easy to hold tablet for long-lasting economy, as well as the familiar size.*
9 out of 10 film stars use pure, white Lux Toilet Soap
A *LEVER* PRODUCT
SUSAN HAYWARD sees her usual charming self, captured in sculpture. You'll see her in another guise, as wicked Messalina in the new 20th CENTURY FOX FILM "DEMETRIUS AND THE GLADIATORS."

FIG. 10.4 Lux soap advertisement, from *Picturegoer*, 22 January 1955.

Such an advertising strategy, however, is highly vulnerable to a reading against its grain, since a central topos of the Messalinian tradition in popular culture has lain in an invitation to consumers of the image of the *meretrix Augusta* not to be deceived by her surface beauty. From Cesare Lombroso's study of criminal anthropology in the 1890s, to Robert Graves's historical novels in the 1930s (and on into their television serialization in the 1970s), Messalina has personified sexual excess (and a 'masculine' ambition) wrapped in an attractive package. The effort expended in the *Picturegoer* advertisement to separate star from screen character effectively acknowledges the possibility that they were not being so separated by female spectators, and that in purchasing products endorsed by Hayward / Messalina consumers were seeking to buy into not just a fabulous complexion, but also sexual freedom and economic independence. Feminist film critics have recorded how fans of 1940s and 1950s Hollywood cinema frequently colluded with cinematic examples of female power and confidence, failing to remember narrative closures in which such characters were killed off, punished, or restored to marriage, monogamy, and motherhood.[55] Such a history opens up the possibility that some female spectators chose to remember *Demetrius and the Gladiators* and its associated marketing as an invitation to become like Messalina (their screen surrogate who takes pleasure in looking at and controlling male bodies), and to transform themselves into that 1950s 'suburban feminist having a fling'.

## A TELEVISUAL MESSALINA (1970S)

Writing in 1975, a biographer who had noted parallels between the persona of Susan Hayward and her screen performance of Messalina summed up her star image in terms of present-day (rather than 1950s) discourses of feminism: '[She] projects feminine come-hither with a masculine wallop. She can appear to be the prettiest, clingin-

[55] See esp. Stacey (1994).

gest of vines . . . then, when it's time for action, she can become a landmine that today's Women's Liberation Movement might profitably skip a bra-burning to observe.'[56] Contemporary discourses of feminism also appear to be at issue in the characterization of Messalina broadcast on British television the year after this biography was published.

*I, Claudius* (dr. Herbert Wise) was produced for the minority channel BBC 2 as a quality television drama adapted from both Graves's Claudius novels. Scheduled for broadcast on Monday nights at 9pm and repeated on Wednesdays, it serialized the novels into a number of discrete television 'plays' of 50 minutes each (with the first two broadcast back to back as an opening, double-length episode) and ran over a period of twelve weeks from September to December 1976.[57] Early British reviews were lukewarm, so long as the serial was judged for its invented dialogue against the reported action of the historical novels, and for its visual limitations against Hollywood's convention of screening ancient Rome as widescreen spectacle. Critics commented unfavourably on the obvious modesty of the budget, the small cast, their stagy acting and (sometimes humorous) modern idiom, the focus on studio shooting, interior palace sets, and the consequent atmosphere of claustrophobic intensity.[58] But their comments grew much more favourable as they adjusted to the conditions of television production, eventually heaping praise on the serial's aesthetics of immediacy.[59] A central determining condition of the television medium is its status as a domestic technology that inhabits neither a specialized time nor place, and whose consumption occurs as part of the everyday life of the house-

[56] McClelland (1975), 36.

[57] The BBC Written Archive contains a shooting script and a large number of reviews of *I, Claudius* (1976), but its production records were not yet available in 2000. In what follows, I am considerably indebted to Sandra Joshel's analysis of the serial in its American viewing context (2001).

[58] See e.g. *Daily Telegraph*, *Daily Mail* and *The Guardian*, all for 21 September 1976.

[59] e.g. *Daily Telegraph*, 4 November 1976.

hold. Reflecting the circumstances of its reception, domesticity and the quotidian inform the aesthetics of the television image.[60] Thus *I, Claudius* domesticated Roman imperial history, translating the geographical sweep of the novels (which included, for example, substantial military and ethnographic histories of Germany, Judaea, and Britain) into a small-scale, intimate drama of family interactions.[61]

Intersecting with discourses of BBC television as a national utility through which to provide information, education, and cultural improvement for the British public,[62] *I, Claudius* was soon celebrated in the press as a popular hit and significant social event: viewers talked about it, anticipated the events of the next episode, and made sure to catch one of each week's transmissions.[63] The serial went on to win a number of television industry prizes, was repeated on several occasions during 1977, and reshown on BBC 1 in 1978 and 1986. It was also repeatedly broadcast in the United States on the PBS network, within the prestigious Masterpiece Theatre slot for presenting classic BBC TV dramas to American audiences, and was the most widely requested rerun when Masterpiece Theatre celebrated twenty years of transmission in 1991. In the same year, it became available as a series of videotapes from Princeton Films for the Humanities and Sciences, which were then reviewed in a classical journal in terms of their utility for lively classroom discussion of imperial Roman history.[64]

However, while *I, Claudius* came to take on the status of a prestigious and highly prized quality television drama, a translation to screen of an important literary work, and a helpful stimulus to study

[60] Tulloch (1990), 191–209; Corner (1999), 15–16 and 87–90; Caughie (2000), 19–21.

[61] Joshel (2001).

[62] Corner (1999), 14–15 and 20; Caughie (2000), 25–30; Miller (2000), 85–6.

[63] As *Sunday Telegraph*, 21 November 1976. See Seymour-Smith (1995), 229–30.

[64] On PBS and Masterpiece Theatre, see Miller (2000), 75–109. On the American reception of *I, Claudius*, see Cooke (1982), 11–21; *TV Guide* 39/24 (15 June 1991), 16; *Classical World* 85.2 (1991), 142–3; Joshel (2001).

of ancient Rome, at the time of its initial broadcast it was also constituted by troubled reviewers as an intertext with the more derided television genres of the soap opera or family saga, such as *Coronation Street*, *Brothers*, and *Upstairs / Downstairs*. The classicist Oswyn Murray noted that, despite obvious fidelity to the novels, the narrative of the Julio-Claudian dynasty now explicitly 'falls into the standard shape of the serial: "It's about a family business called ruling the world", the producer said—an everyday story of imperial folk possessing all the compulsive monotony of life upstairs, downstairs and in my lady's chamber.'[65] And one journalist complained that the television serial 'has reduced the rulers of the world to the status of characters in a newly discovered soap opera "Via Corona". Or, perhaps, "Fratres".'[66] The generic conventions of soap opera thus organized viewers' readings of the historicism of *I, Claudius*.

The point-of-view strategies for identification provided by cinema are replaced by television's mechanisms for establishing the pleasures of familiarity. Viewers' engagement is held not by the drive of the (now interrupted) narrative, but by the repetitive observation of recognizable incidents in an intricate community of characters played out at the level of the family unit. The central thematic of the soap opera is the everyday life of the home (strongly gendered as a feminine sphere) in which the position of women is consistently interrogated.[67] As Sandra Joshel has observed in her analysis of *I, Claudius* in the American viewing context, the television serial reduces the two novels to the stories of the imperial wives. The women of the imperial household theaten the stability of the family by wielding transgressive powers. Livia's duplicitous schemes to control the dynasty, culminating in the poisoning of her husband

[65] *Times Literary Supplement*, 5 November 1976, 1394.

[66] *Daily Telegraph*, 21 September 1976. Cf. *Eastern Daily Press*, 21 September 1976; *Yorkshire Post*, 21 September 1976; *Variety*, 29 September 1976. See Bondanella (1987), 222; Joshel (2001).

[67] Tulloch (1990), 31–57; Brunsdon (1997), 14–17; Corner (1999), 58 and 89; Caughie (2000), 203–25; Joshel (2001).

Augustus, dominate the first seven episodes while the last closes the serial with the poisoning of Claudius by his wife Agrippinilla. In between appear a cycle of exiles, murders, adulteries, and orgies largely motivated by female members of the family, including two whole episodes (wholly in disproportion to the political interests of the novels) dedicated to the manipulations and betrayals of a sexually voracious Messalina.[68]

Sandra Joshel argues further (in relation to the American reception of *I, Claudius*) that, located within the flow of television scheduling and permeated by the news broadcasts with whose facticity it intersected,[69] the serial's emplotment of imperial disintegration became available to be read as an address to the current crises of empire which news bulletins had been bringing vividly into American homes; while the contemporary, gendered political rhetoric of the New Right provided an entry-point for reading the serial's focus on a troubled family metonymically for the troubled empire it was described as ruling. Failures of American imperial authority abroad and social order at home—economic recession, revelation of the corruption of government (leading to the resignation of President Nixon in 1974), the humiliating conclusion to the war in Vietnam (culminating in the North's recapture of Saigon in 1975)—were regularly blamed in part on black and feminist activism, and the restoration of national security troped in terms of a return to traditional family values. In such a discursive context, Livia's pseudo-feminist complaint in episode 4 of *I, Claudius* that her capacities for government had been overlooked because of her gender (delivered at the very moment viewers observed the fatal poisoning of her husband) could be read by Americans as an educative indicator of the threat contemporary feminism posed to the nation. Since, however, Masterpiece Theatre's costume dramas (through source, setting,

[68] Joshel (2001).

[69] On the concept of television's flow, see also Corner (1999), 60–9.

casting, acting style, and accent) have functioned particularly to dissseminate images of Britishness into the American imaginary,[70] American viewers of *I, Claudius* could always resort to the more comforting proposition that its lessons were not, after all, meant for them. And British newspaper reviews did, in fact, regularly suggest parallels between BBC television's small-screen rendering of ancient Rome and the political scandals of modern Britain. In a sustained analysis, a reporter for the *Birmingham Post* (7 December 1976) argued that, as the Victorians had studied Roman history for models of imperial success, so (following the author Robert Graves) more recent Britons 'may well be studying the other side of Rome to see how it failed'. With failure of empire long since acknowledged, however, the political lessons of *I, Claudius* for 1970s Britain are restricted considerably to the dangers of intrigue and the corruption of government—Harold Macmillan's 'night of long knives' or Harold Wilson's rumoured formation of a 'kitchen cabinet'.[71] The journalist even concedes a likely shift of interest by the serial's viewers away from ancient Rome's articulation with modern discourses of empire to those of gender and sexuality: 'It could be seen, I suppose, as a penetrating study of the vulnerability of the Emperor-principle, the isolation and corruption of men in lonely power, the danger of overweening imperialism. I suspect it will be remembered, apart from the splendid acting, for the blood and sex and Messalina, like Oliver Twist, asking for more.'[72]

In *I, Claudius* (1976) the characterization of the *meretrix Augusta* is embedded into an episodic narrative that displays the gradual erosion of Claudius' trust in his wife's behaviour and brings him, finally, into

[70] Caughie (2000), 6 and 206.

[71] Cf. *Broadcast* (15 November 1976) on evocations of internal manoeuvrings in the Labour, Tory, and Liberal parties; and both *Broadcast* and the *Daily Mail* (20 December 1976) on the loss of Parliament's authority against that of the party of government.

[72] Compare such a shift of interest from issues of empire to those of gender in the consumption of cinematic representations of Cleopatra, above, Chs. 7 and 8.

line with the viewers' privileged knowledge of her sexual deceits. Messalina first appears at the close of episode 9 (*Hail Who?*) as a beautiful, young, seemingly demure girl who utilizes her erotic skills to entrap her future husband. Script directions for their first encounter catalogue the visual cues to her trickery that Claudius overlooks: 'Messalina smiles, then leans forward and kisses him softly on the mouth, parting his lips with just the tip of her tongue. Quivering. He daren't look at her. Pause . . . He clutches her hand suddenly and presses it to his lips. His subjection has been instant and complete.' Similarly, one reviewer of the episode's ensuing marriage ritual remarked of Messalina's red wedding-veil that 'it flamed with a gorgeousness tantamount to professional pride'.[73] Whatever concession this headdress might have made to historical authenticity, like the sexually voracious empress of Fellini's *Roma* (1972), at the point of marriage television's Messalina is colour-coded as a scarlet woman. With Claudius now elevated to the position of emperor and advised to trust no one, episode 10 (*Fool's Luck*) displays the foolishness of his continuing trust in a Messalina identified for viewers as negligent mother, monstrous daughter, and clever play-actor of wifely devotion (Fig. 10.5). Her ambition for political power necessitates fostering out her son, and initiates a generational conflict with her mother on notions of womanhood not to be found in Graves's historical novels. While the older woman argues that matters of state are 'not a woman's place', Messalina declares that they are and that access to them can best be achieved through the prevention of pregnancy. The empress then plots to gain access to a reluctant lover by marrying him to her own mother; when she lies to Claudius to cover her tracks the victim sarcastically praises her performance of marital fidelity, while her still deluded husband concludes the programme by praising the softness of her heart. Only in episode 11 (*A God In Colchester*), after viewers have witnessed Messalina's progressively more desperate search for sexual fulfilment (the close-up nudity of violent

[73] *The Times*, 16 November 1976.

Fig. 10.5 Sheila White as Messalina in 'Fool's Luck', episode 10 of *I, Claudius* (first broadcast 22 November 1976 on BBC 2).

sex with the actor Mnester, two subtantial scenes dedicated to her debauched tournament with the prostitute Scylla, both much discussed in the British press as challenging the moral limits of television),[74] does the retrospectively knowing voice of Claudius intrude to guide viewers in voice-over through his wife's final acts

[74] See e.g. *The Sun*, 29 November 1976; *The Times*, 7 December 1976.

of meretriciousness including the clever enslavement of her last lover Silius.[75] Television viewers and protagonist are finally united intersubjectively as Messalina's transgressive femininity is punished and, in the final episode (*Old King Log*) the trickery of Agrippinilla is deliberately manipulated by her husband to bring down the Julio-Claudian dynasty and cleanse the empire of its moral corruption.

For British audiences to make sense of Claudius' televisual journey to knowledge of the dangers of transgressive femininities, they were required to deploy their own cultural knowledge of the socially acceptable codes and conventionals for gender that had been elaborated elsewhere but whose traces might be discerned in the serial's representation of Messalina.[76] The first national Women's Liberation conference held in 1970 made newspaper headlines with its demands for equal pay, equal education and opportunity, free contraception and abortion, and twenty-four-hour nursery provision. Over the following years, those demands became emblazoned on banners, printed on badges, and paraded in mass demonstrations.[77] While the feminist movement did not accept woman's primary duty as domestic, demanded that women should be free to control their own fertility and to explore their sexual freedom, and argued that maternity was compatible with greater responsibility and independence in the world of work, right-wing movements of the same period, such as the evangelical Nationwide Festival of Light, were simultaneously attacking Britain's 'permissive' society and calling for a return to a national morality grounded in Christian ethics and the traditional nuclear family.[78] As *I, Claudius* began to draw to its close, the press reported that Mrs Mary Whitehouse, one such moral

[75] On the serial's technique of employing Claudius' retrospectively knowing voice-over, see further Joshel (2001).

[76] Cf., more generally, Brunsdon (1997), 17–18, on the cultural competences required by audiences to read the femininities played out in television soap opera.

[77] Caine (1997), 225–71.

[78] Newburn (1992), 17–48.

entrepreneur and energetic campaigner against the supposedly devastating powers of television to undermine values, had criticized the serial for the Roman depravity it was currently transmitting into the nation's homes. Under the headline 'This depraved Rome is a lesson to us all', a journalist for the *Manchester Evening News* (4 December 1976) countered: 'I, Claudius is not a cheap porn show . . . This television series is really a moral lesson. Sexual obsession is one of the signs of a decaying society, and looked at this way, I Claudius, should actually have suited Mrs Whitehouse's book.'[79] Thus *I, Claudius* is read as a site for the construction of a moral consensus, and television's Messalina as a kind of Women's Libber hyperbolically constructed as hell-bent on political power and sexual revolution. The proportionately extravagant punishment of the *meretrix Augusta* provides a history lesson in how to counter challenges to conventional femininity and restore 1970s Britain to social order.

The American webpage on Valeria Messalina set up in January 1999 (with which I opened this chapter) follows the British television serial in marking the empress whom Sheila White played as the embodiment of a transgressive femininity against whose treachery all men (not just Claudius) need warning. Two months before the transmission of *I, Claudius*, one British tabloid newspaper described Sheila White as having won the part of 'the wickedest wife who ever lived' precisely because she always used to play the nice girl, 'a sort of bouncy blonde you could take home to mother'.[80] While, after transmission ceased, a broadsheet reflected that 'Messalina lingers in the mind as being even rottener [than Agrippinilla], perhaps because her baby face was more innocent, until her top lip lifted at the scent of an orgy—a bared fang at the gang-bang's tang.'[81] But the newspaper's extraordinary, assonant description conjures up another

[79] On the criticism directed against *I, Claudius* by Mary Whitehouse, compare e.g. *The Times*, 7 December 1976; *Daily Express*, 8 December 1976.

[80] *The Sun*, 31 July 1976.

[81] *The Observer*, 12 December 1976.

popular cultural tradition for Messalina not addressed in this chapter, namely the *meretrix Augusta* as pornographic icon.[82] Perhaps it is that tradition on which the furniture company Cezar touches when it advertises on the web a two-seater sofa-bed as a 'Messalina'.[83]

[82] See, as just one of many examples, an advertisement for the 'big budget adult movie spectacular' *Messalina: The Virgin Empress* (dr. Joe d'Amato) at http://adult.salez.net/video/straight/messalina-f.htm, downloaded 25 January 2000.

[83] At http://www.cezar.limanowa.pl/eng/messalina-wymiary.htm, downloaded 25 January 2000.

# *Bibliography*

Quotations from Propertius, Tibullus, and Ovid follow the Oxford Classical Texts of E. A. Barber (1960)², J. P. Postgate (1915)², and E. J. Kenney respectively. Translations of both ancient and modern works are my own unless otherwise indicated.

Abbreviations for ancient works follow those of *The Oxford Classical Dictionary*.

Coin catalogues are abbreviated as follows:

| | |
|---|---|
| BMC 1 | *Coins of the Roman Empire*, i. *Augustus–Vitellius*, H. Mattingly (1923, London: British Museum Catalogue) |
| BMC Phoenicia | *Catalogue of the Greek Coins of Phoenicia*, G. F. Hill (1910, London: British Museum Catalogue) |
| BMC Ptolemies | *Catalogue of Greek Coins: The Ptolemies, Kings of Egypt*, R. S. Poole (1883, London: British Museum Catalogue) |
| BMCR 1–3 | *Coins of the Roman Republic*, 3 vols., H. A. Grueber (1970, London: British Museum Catalogue) |
| RRC 2 | *Roman Republican Coinage*, ii. M. H. Crawford (1974, Cambridge: Cambridge University Press) |

Abbrevations for classical journals are generally as in *L'Année Philologique*.

Adams, J. N. (1982). *The Latin Sexual Vocabulary*. London: Duckworth.

Ades, D., Benton, T., Elliott, D., and Whyte, I. B. (1995) (eds.). *Art and Power: Europe under the Dictators 1930–45*. Hayward Gallery Exhibition Catalogue. Manchester: Cornerhouse Publications.

Agan, P. (1979). *The Decline and Fall of the Love Goddesses*. Los Angeles: Pinnacle Books.

Alfonsi, L. (1979). *L'elegia di Properzio*. New York: Garland Publishing. Repr. of 1945 edn.

Allen, A. W. (1950*a*). '"Sincerity" and the Roman elegists'. *CP* 45: 145–60.

——(1950*b*). 'Elegy and the classical attitude toward love: Propertius 1.1'. *YCS* 11: 253–77.

Allen, J. (1980). 'The film viewer as consumer'. *Quarterly Review of Film Studies*, 5/4: 481–99.

Allison, J. W. (1980). 'Virgilian themes in Propertius 4.7 and 8'. *CP* 75: 332–8.

Alpers, J. (1912). *Hercules in Bivio*. Dissertatio Inauguralis, Göttingen.

Aly, A. A. (1992). 'Cleopatra and Caesar at Alexandria and Rome', in Carratelli *et al.*, 47–61.

Amengual, B. (1989). 'Maurice Tourneur, l'Américain'. *Positif*, 344: 42–5.

Ancona, R. (1989). 'The subterfuge of reason: Horace, *Odes* 1.23, and the construction of male desire'. *Helios*, 19: 49–55.

Anderson, W. S. (1964). 'Hercules exclusus: Propertius IV.9'. *AJP* 85: 1–12.

Arcari, P. (1899). *Di Pietro Cossa e del dramma in Italia*. Milan: Tipografia Artigianelli.

Archer, L. J., Fischler, S., and Wyke, M. (1994) (eds.), *Women in Ancient Societies: An Illusion of the Night*. Basingstoke: Macmillan Press.

Arthur, M. B. (1981). 'The divided world of *Iliad* VI', in Foley, 19–44.

Babington, B., and Evans, P. W. (1993). *Biblical Epics: Sacred Narrative in the Hollywood Cinema*. Manchester: Manchester University Press.

Badian, E. (1985). 'A phantom marriage law'. *Philologus*, 129: 82–98.

Baker, R. J. (1968). '*Miles annosus*: the military motif in Propertius'. *Latomus*, 27: 322–49.

Balio, T. (1993) (ed.). *Grand Design: Hollywood as a Modern Business Enterprise 1930–1939*. New York: Charles Scribner's Sons.

Ball, R. H. (1968). *Shakespeare on Silent Film: A Strange Eventful History*. London: George Allen and Unwin.

Balsdon, J. P. V. D. (1962). *Roman Women: Their History and Habits*. London: The Bodley Head.

——(1979). *Romans and Aliens*. London: Duckworth.

Barbiera, R. (1931). *Vite ardenti nel Teatro (1700–1900)*. Milan: Fratelli Treves Editori.

Barchiesi, A. (1997). *The Poet and the Prince: Ovid and Augustan Discourse*. Berkeley: University of California Press.

Barré, L. (1861). *Herculanum et Pompéi*, ii. Paris: Firmin Didot frères, fils et cie.

Barrett, A. A. (1996). *Agrippina: Mother of Nero*. London: B. T. Batsford.

Barsby, J. A. (1974). 'The composition and publication of the first three books of Propertius'. *G&R* 21: 128–37.

——(1979). *Ovid Amores 1*. Bristol: Bristol Classical Press. First pub. 1973.

Barthes, R. (1975). *S/Z*, trans. R. Miller. London: Jonathan Cape. First pub. 1970.

Bartman, E. (1999). *Portraits of Livia: Imaging the Imperial Women in Augustan Rome*. Cambridge: Cambridge University Press.

Bassett, E. L. (1966). 'Hercules and the hero of the *Punica*', in L. Wallach (ed.), *The Classical Tradition: Literary and Historical Studies in Honor of Harry Caplan*. Ithaca: Cornell University Press, 258–73.

Bauman, R. A. (1992). *Women and Politics in Ancient Rome*. London: Routledge.

Baxter, J. (1972). *Hollywood in the Sixties*. London: Tantivy Press.

Baxter, P. (1993). *Just Watch! Sternberg, Paramount and America*. London: British Film Institute.

Beard, M. (1980). 'The sexual status of virgins'. *JRS* 70: 12–27.

——North, J., and Price, S. (1998). *Religions of Rome*, i. *A History*. Cambridge: Cambridge University Press.

Becher, I. (1966). *Das Bild der Kleopatra in der griechischen und lateinischen Literatur*. Berlin: Deutsche Akademie der Wissenschaften zu Berlin, 51.

Becker, L. (1995). 'Black shirts and white telephones', in Ades *et al.*, 137–9.

Belton, J. (1992). *Widescreen Cinema*. Cambridge, Mass.: Harvard University Press.

Berger, J. (1972). *Ways of Seeing*. London: Penguin.

Berger, J. (1981). *A New Deal for the World: Eleanor Roosevelt and American Foreign Policy*. New York: Social Science Monographs (Columbia University Press).

Berman, K. E. (1975). 'Ovid, Propertius and the elegiac genre: some imitations in the *Amores*'. *Rivista di Studi Classici*, 23: 14–22.

Bernardini, A. (1985). 'Francesca Bertini', in Aldo Bernardini *et al.*, *Le dive*. Bari: Editori Laterza, 3–38.

——(1986). 'Le cinéma muet italien, étapes et tendances', in Bernardini and Gili, 33–45.

Bernardini, A. and Gili, J. A. (1986) (eds.). *Le cinéma italien: de La prise de Rome (1905) à Rome ville ouverte (1945)*. Paris: Centre Georges Pompidou.

——and Martinelli, V. (1979). *Il cinema italiano degli anni venti*. Rome: Quaderni di documentazione della Cineteca Nazionale, 11.

————(1996). *Il cinema muto italiano: i film dei primi anni, 1910*. Turin: Nuova ERI, Edizioni RAI.

Bernstein, M. (1994). *Walter Wanger: Hollywood Independent*. Berkeley: University of California Press.

——and Studlar, G. (1997) (eds.), *Visions of the East: Orientalism in Film*. New Brunswick: Rutgers University Press.

Bertellini, G. (1999). 'Italian imageries, historical feature films, and the fabrication of Italy's spectators in early 1900s New York', in M. Stokes and R. Maltby (eds.), *American Movie Audiences: From the Turn of the Century to the Early Sound Era*. London: BFI Publishing, 29–45.

Bertini, F. (1983). *Ovidio:Amori*. Milan: Garazanti.

Bertoni, A. (1987). 'Rétrocritic: A propos de la réédition de Cléopâtre'. *La Revue du Cinéma*, 423: 45–6.

Betensky, A. (1973). 'Forum'. *Arethusa*, 6: 267–9.

——(1974). 'A further reply'. *Arethusa*, 7: 211–17.

Beuselink, J. (1988). 'Mankiewicz's *Cleopatra*'. *Films in Review*, 39/1: 3–4.

Bianchi, P. (1969). *Francesca Bertini e le dive del cinema muto*. Turin: UTET.

Bianchi, R. S. (1988) (ed.). *Cleopatra's Egypt. Age of the Ptolemies*. The Brooklyn Museum Exhibition Catalogue.

Bielmeier, M. G. (2000). *Shakespeare, Kierkegaard, and Existential Tragedy*. Lewiston: Edwin Mellen Press.

Biskind, P. (1983). *Seeing is Believing: How Hollywood Taught Us to Stop Worrying and Love the Fifties*. London: Pluto Press.

Black, G. D. (1994). *Hollywood Censored: Morality Codes, Catholics and the Movies*. Cambridge: Cambridge University Press.

Blasetti, A. (1951). 'The historical film', in L. Malerba (ed.), *Italian Cinema 1945–1951*. Rome: Edizioni d'Arte, 55–6.

Bloom, H. (1990) (ed.), *Cleopatra*. New York: Chelsea House Publishers.

Bodeen, D. (1976). *From Hollywood: The Careers of 15 Great American Stars*. South Brunswick & New York: A. S. Barnes.

Bondanella, P. (1987). *The Eternal City: Roman Images in the Modern World*. Chapel Hill and London: University of North Carolina Press.

Bosworth, R. J. B. (1979). *Italy, the Least of the Great Powers: Italian Foreign Policy Before the First World War*. Cambridge: Cambridge University Press.
——(1996). *Italy and the Wider World 1860–1960*. London: Routledge.
Boucher, J.-P. (1965). *Études sur Properce: problèmes d'inspiration et d'art*. Paris: de Broccard.
Bowman, A. K. (1996). *Egypt after the Pharaohs: 332 BC–AD 642 from Alexander to the Arab Conquest*. London: British Museum Press. First edn. 1986.
Boyancé, P. (1956). *L'influence grecque sur la poésie latine de Catulle à Ovide*. Entretiens Hardt 2. Geneva: Foundation Hardt.
Boyd, B. W. (1984). 'Tarpeia's tomb: a note on Propertius 4.4'. *AJP* 105: 85–6.
——(1987). '*Virtus effeminata* and Sallust's Sempronia'. *TAPA* 117: 183–201.
——(1997). *Ovid's Literary Loves: Influence and Innovation in the* Amores. Ann Arbor: University of Michigan Press.
Brandt, P. (1963). *P. Ovidi Nasonis Amorum Libri Tres: Text und Kommentar*. Hildesheim: Georg Olms.
Brenk, F. E. (1979). 'Tarpeia among the Celts: watery romance, from Simylos to Propertius', in Deroux, 166–74.
——(1992). 'Antony-Osiris, Cleopatra-Isis: The end of Plutarch's *Antony*', in P. A. Stadter (ed.), *Plutarch and the Historical Tradition*. London: Routledge, 159–82.
Brett, A. B. (1937). 'A new Cleopatra Tetradrachm of Ascalon'. *AJA* 41: 452–63.
Bright, D. F. (1978). *Haec mihi fingebam: Tibullus in his World*. Leiden: Cincinnati Classical Studies, NS 3.
Brodsky, J., and Weiss, N. (1963). *The Cleopatra Papers: A Private Correspondence*. New York: Simon and Schuster.
Bruere, R. T. (1959). '*Color Ovidianus* in Silius *Punica* 8–17'. *CP* 54: 228–45.
Brunetta, G. P. (1982). *Storia del cinema italiano dal 1945 agli anni ottanta*. Rome: Editori Riuniti.
——(1986). 'L'évocation du passé: Les années d'or du film historique', in Bernardini and Gili, 55–60.
——(1991). *Cent'anni di cinema italiano*. Rome: Editori Laterza.
——(1993). *Storia del cinema italiano, i. Il cinema muto 1895–1929*. Rome: Editori Riuniti.

Brunetta, G. P., and Gili, J. A. (1990). *L'ora d'Africa del cinema italiano 1911–1989*. Trent: LaGrafica-Mori.
Bruno, G. (1993). *Streetwalking on a Ruined Map: Cultural Theory and the City Films of Elvira Notari*. Princeton: Princeton University Press.
Brunt, P. A. (1971). *Italian Manpower*. Oxford: Clarendon Press.
——and Moore, J. M. (1967). *Res Gestae Divi Augusti*. Oxford: Oxford University Press.
Bruzzi, S. (1997). *Undressing Cinema: Clothing and Identity in the Movies*. London: Routledge.
Burnett, A., Amandry, M., and Ripollès, P. P. (1990). *Roman Provincial Coinage*, i. *From the death of Caesar to Vitellius*. London: British Museum Publications.
Burton, P. (1995). 'The values of a classical education: satirical elements in Robert Graves's *Claudius* novels'. *Review of English Studies* NS 46, no. 182: 191–218.
Butler, H. E. (1976) (ed.). *Propertius*. Loeb Classical Library. Repr. of 1912 edn.
Butrica, J. (1982). 'Review article: the Latin love poets'. *EMC* NS 1: 82–95.
Byars, J. (1991). *All That Hollywood Allows: Rereading Gender in 1950s Melodrama*. London: Routledge.
Cagnetta, M. (1979). *Antichisti e impero fascista*. Bari: Dedalo Libri.
Caine, B. (1997). *English Feminism 1780–1980*. Oxford: Oxford University Press.
Cairns, F. (1972). *Generic Composition in Greek and Roman Poetry*. Edinburgh: Edinburgh University Press.
Calendoli, G. (1967). *Materiali per una storia del cinema italiano*. Parma: Edizioni Maccari.
Callow, S. (1987). *Charles Laughton: A Difficult Actor*. London: Methuen.
Cameron, A. (1968). 'The first edition of Ovid's *Amores*'. *CQ* NS 18: 320–33.
Camps, W. A. (1965). *Propertius: Elegies Book IV*. Cambridge: Cambridge University Press.
——(1967). *Propertius: Elegies Book II*. Cambridge: Cambridge University Press.
Cardillo, M. (1987). *Tra le quinte del cinematografo: cinema, cultura e società in Italia 1900–1937*. Bari: Edizioni Dedalo.
Carratelli, G. P., Del Re, G., Bonacasa, N., and Etman, A. (1992) (eds.),

*Roma e l'Egitto nell'antichità classica*. Atti del I Congresso Internazionale Italo-Egiziano. Rome: Istituto Poligrafico e Zecca dello Stato.

Carson, R. A. G., and Sutherland, C. H. V. (1956) (eds.), *Essays in Roman Coinage presented to Harold Mattingly*. Oxford: Oxford University Press.

Castillo, L. (1989). 'María Félix: No me llamen leyenda, que me suena a pasado'. *Cine Cubano*, no. 124: 68–74.

Caughie, J. (2000). *Television Drama: Realism, Modernism, and British Culture*. Oxford: Oxford University Press.

Chard, C. (1999). 'The road to ruin: memory, ghosts, moonlight and weeds', in Edwards, 125–39.

Charlesworth, M. P. (1933). 'Some fragments of the propaganda of Mark Antony'. *CQ* 27: 172–7.

Charnes, L. (1993). *Notorious Identity: Materializing the Subject in Shakespeare*. Cambridge, Mass.: Harvard University Press.

Childs, T. W. (1990). *Italo-Turkish Diplomacy and the War over Libya 1911–1912*. Leiden: E. J. Brill.

Christie, I. (1991). 'Cecil B. DeMille: Grand illusions'. *Sight and Sound* NS 1/8: 18–21.

Ciceroni, M. (1992). 'Introduzione ed evoluzione dei culti egizi a Roma in età repubblicana. La testimonianza delle fonte letterarie', in Carratelli *et al.*, 103–7.

Cieutat, M. (2000). 'Ben-Hur, une bible américaine'. *Positif*, 468: 91–6.

Clark, M. (1984). *Modern Italy 1871–1982*. London: Longman.

Clausen, W. (1976). 'Cynthius'. *AJP* 97: 245–7.

——(1987). *Virgil's 'Aeneid' and the Tradition of Hellenistic Poetry*. Berkeley: University of California Press.

Clayman, D. L. (1976). 'Callimachus' thirteenth iamb: the last word'. *Hermes*, 104: 29–35.

Coarelli, F. (1985). *Il Foro Romano: periodo repubblicano e augusteo*. Rome: Quasar.

Cohen, J. M. (1987). 'Autobiography, historical novels, and some poems', in H. Bloom (ed.), *Robert Graves*. New York: Chelsea House Publishers, 31–9. Extracted from J. M. Cohen, *Robert Graves* (Edinburgh: Oliver and Boyd, 1960).

Coleman, R. (1977). *Vergil: Eclogues*. Cambridge: Cambridge University Press.

Collins, J. J. (1983). 'Sibylline Oracles', in J. H. Charlesworth (ed.), *The*

*Old Testament Pseudepigrapha*, i. *Apocalyptic Literature and Testaments*. London: Darton, Longman, and Todd, 317–472.

——(1987). 'The Development of the Sibylline Tradition'. *ANRW* 2.20/1:421–59.

Commager, S. (1958). 'Horace, *Carmina* 1.37'. *The Phoenix*, 12:47–57.

*Commemorazione di Pietro Cossa*. (1881). Rome: Associazione della stampa periodica in Italia, Forzani e C.

Connolly, J. (2000). 'Asymptotes of pleasure: thoughts on the nature of Roman erotic elegy'. *Arethusa*, 33/1:71–98.

Consigliere, L. (1978). *'Slogans' Monetarii e poesia augustea*. Genoa: Istituto di Filologia Classica e Medievale, 56.

Conte, G. B. (1989). 'Love without elegy: the *remedia amoris* and the logic of a genre'. *Poetics Today*, 10: 441–69. Repr. 1994 in *Genres and Readers: Lucretius, Love Elegy, Pliny's Encyclopedia*, trans. by G. W. Most. Baltimore: Johns Hopkins University Press.

Cook, B. W. (1993). *Eleanor Roosevelt*. London: Bloomsbury.

Cooke, A. (1982). *Masterpieces: A Decade of Classics on British Television*. London: The Bodley Head.

Copley, F. O. (1947). 'Servitium amoris in the Roman elegists'. *TAPA* 78: 285–300.

Corbeill, A. (1996). *Controlling Laughter: Political Humor in the Late Republic*. Princeton: Princeton University Press.

Corner, J. (1999). *Critical Ideas in Television Studies*. Oxford: Clarendon Press.

Cosandey, R., and Albera, F. (1995). *Cinéma sans frontières 1896–1918/Images Across Borders*. Lausanne: Éditions Payot.

Costetti, G. (1978). *Il teatro italiano nel 1800*. Bologna: Arnaldo Forni Editore. First pub. 1901.

Courtney, E. (1969). 'Three poems of Propertius'. *BICS* 16: 80–7.

Croce, B. (1914). *La letteratura della nuova Italia*, ii. Bari: Laterzi.

Culham, P. (1986). 'Ten years after Pomeroy: studies of the image and reality of women in antiquity'. *Helios*, 13/2: 9–30.

——(1990). 'Decentering the text: the case of Ovid'. *Helios*, 17/2: 161–70.

Curl, J. S. (1994). *Egyptomania. The Egyptian Revival: A Recurring Theme in the History of Taste*. Manchester: Manchester University Press.

Curran, L. C. (1964). 'Greek words and myth in Propertius 1.20'. *GRBS* 5: 281–93.

——(1966). 'Vision and reality in Propertius i 3'. *YClS* 19: 187–207.

——(1968). 'Propertius 4.11: Greek heroines and death'. *CP* 63: 134–9.

——(1975). 'Nature to advantage dressed: Propertius 1.2'. *Ramus*, 4/1: 1–16.

Currie, H. MacL. (1973). 'Propertius IV.8—a reading'. *Latomus*, 32: 616–22.

dall'Asta, M. (1992). *Un cinéma musclé: Le surhomme dans le cinéma muet italien (1913–1926).* Translated from Italian by F. Arnò and C. Tatum Jr. Crisnée: Yellow Now.

Dalle Vacche, A. (1992). *The Body in the Mirror: Shapes of History in Italian Cinema*. Princeton: Princeton University Press.

Dalzell, A. (1980). 'Homeric themes in Propertius'. *Hermathena*, 129: 29–36.

D'Anna, G. (1981). 'Cornelio Gallo, Virgilio e Properzio'. *Athenaeum*, 59: 284–98.

David, R. (2000). *The Experience of Ancient Egypt*. London: Routledge.

Davis, J. T. (1981). 'Risit Amor: aspects of literary burlesque in Ovid's *Amores*'. *ANRW* 2.31/4: 2460–506.

Davis, N., and Kraay, C. M. (1973). *The Hellenistic Kingdoms: Portrait Coins and History*. London: Thames and Hudson.

Davis, P. J. (1999). 'Ovid's *Amores*: a political reading'. *CP* 94: 431–49.

Dawson, C. M. (1950). 'The iambi of Callimachus'. *YClS* 11: 1–168.

de Blasi, J. (1911). *Pietro Cossa e la tragedia italiana*. Florence: Tipografia Galileiana.

DeBrohun, J. B. (1994). 'Redressing elegy's *puella*: Propertius IV and the rhetoric of fashion'. *JRS* 84: 41–63.

de Cordova, R. (1990). *Picture Personalities: The Emergence of the Star System in America*. Urbana: University of Illinois Press.

Dee, J. H. (1974). 'Arethusa to Lycotas: Propertius 4.3'. *TAPA* 104: 81–96.

——(1978). 'Elegy 4.8: a Propertian comedy'. *TAPA* 108: 41–53.

DeForest, M. M. (1989). 'The central similes of Horace's Cleopatra Ode'. *CW* 82/3: 167–73.

——(1993) (ed.). *Woman's Power, Man's Game: Essays on Classical Antiquity in Honor of Joy K. King*. Wauconda, Ill.: Bolchazy-Carducci.

de Giorgio, M. (1992). *Le italiane dall'unità a oggi: modelli culturali e comportamenti sociali*. Rome: Editori Laterza.

de Grazia, V. (1992). *How Fascism Ruled Women: Italy, 1922–1945*. Berkeley: University of California Press.

De Lauretis, T. (1987). *Technologies of Gender: Essays on Theory, Film, and Fiction*. Bloomington, Ind.: Indiana University Press.

Del Boca, A. (1986). *Gli italiani in Libia: Tripoli bel suol d'amore 1860–1922*. Rome/Bari: Editori Laterza.

de Miro, E. C. (1978). 'Miti e riti del cinema: gli erotici fantasmi dell' immaginario'. *Nuovadwf (donnawomanfemme)* 8: 6–25.

Deroux, C. (1979) (ed.). *Studies in Latin Literature and Roman History*, i. Brussels: Collection Latomus, 164.

Desmond, M. (1993). 'When Dido reads Vergil: gender and intertextuality in Ovid's *Heroides*'. *Helios*, 20: 56–68.

Dever, S. (1992). 'Re-birth of a nation: On Mexican Movies, Museums, and María Félix'. *Spectator*, 13/2: 52–69.

de Vincenti, G. (1988). 'Il kolossal storico-romano nell'immaginario del primo Novecento'. *Bianco e Nero*, 49/1: 7–26.

Dijkstra, B. (1986). *Idols of Perversity: Fantasies of Feminine Evil in Fin-de-Siècle Culture*. New York: Oxford University Press.

Dixon, S. (1988). *The Roman Mother*. London: Croom Helm.

——(1992). *The Roman Family*. Baltimore: Johns Hopkins University Press.

——(2001). *Reading Roman Women: Sources, Genres and Real Life*. London: Duckworth.

Doane, M. A. (1989). 'The economy of desire: The commodity form in/of the cinema'. *Quarterly Review of Film and Video*, 11: 23–33.

duBois, P. (1982). *History, Rhetorical Description and the Epic: From Homer to Spenser*. Cambridge: D. S. Brewer.

Dupont, F. (1997). '*Recitatio* and the reorganization of the space of public discourse', in Habinek and Schiesaro, 44–59.

Du Quesnay, I. M. LeM. (1973). 'The *Amores*', in J. W. Binns (ed.), *Greek and Latin Studies, Classical Literature and Its Influence: Ovid*. London: Routledge and Kegan Paul, 1–48.

Dyer, R. (1987). *Heavenly Bodies: Film Stars and Society*. London: British Film Institute and Macmillan.

——(1998). *Stars*. London: BFI Publishing. First edn. 1979.

Earl, D. (1967). *The Moral and Political Tradition of Rome*. London: Thames and Hudson.

Eckert, C. (1978). 'The Carole Lombard in Macy's window'. *Quarterly Review of Film Studies*, 3/1: 1–21.

Edwards, C. (1993). *The Politics of Immorality in Ancient Rome*. Cambridge: Cambridge University Press.

——(1999) (ed.). *Roman Presences: Receptions of Rome in European Culture, 1789–1945*. Cambridge: Cambridge University Press.

Elley, D. (1984). *The Epic Film: Myth and History*. London: Routledge.

Ellis, J. (1982). *Visible Fictions: Cinema, Television, Video*. London: Routledge.

Elsner, J. (1996). 'Inventing imperium: Texts and the propaganda of monuments in Augustan Rome', in Elsner (ed.), *Art and Text in Roman Culture*. Cambridge: Cambridge University Press, 32–53.

*Enciclopedia dello spettacolo*, iii. (1956). Rome: Casa Editrice le Maschere.

Enk, P. J. (1962). *Sex. Prop. Elegiarum Liber Secundus*, i and ii. Leiden: A. W. Sijthoff.

Evans, S. (1971). 'Odyssean echoes in Propertius IV. 8'. *G&R* 18: 51–3.

Everson, W. K. (1976). *Claudette Colbert*. New York: Pyramid Publications.

Fairweather, J. (1974). 'Fiction in the biographies of ancient writers'. *Ancient Society*, 5: 231–75.

Fantham, E. (1986). 'Women in antiquity: a selective (and subjective) survey 1979–84'. *EMC* 5/1: 1–24.

——(1996). *Roman Literary Culture: From Cicero to Apuleius*. Baltimore: Johns Hopkins University Press.

——(1997). 'Images of the city: Propertius' new-old Rome', in Habinek and Schiesaro, 122–35.

Fau, G. (1978). *L'Emancipation féminine à Rome*. Paris: Les Belles Lettres.

Fear, T. (2000). 'The poet as pimp: elegiac seduction in the time of Augustus'. *Arethusa*, 33/2: 217–40.

Fedeli, P. (1965). *Properzio: Elegie Libro IV*. Bari: Adriatica Editrice.

——(1980). *Sesto Properzio: Il primo libro delle elegie*. Florence: Accademia Toscana Studi, 53.

——(1981). 'Elegy and literary polemic in Propertius' Monobiblos'. *Papers of the Liverpool Latin Seminar*, 3: 227–42.

——(1985). *Properzio: Il libro terzo delle elegie*. Bari: Adriatica Editrice.

Feeney, D. (1998). *Literature and Religion at Rome*. Cambridge: Cambridge University Press.

——(1992). '*Si licet et fas est*: Ovid's *Fasti* and the problem of free speech under the principate', in Powell, 1–25.

Ferguson, J. (1979) (ed.). *Juvenal: The Satires*. New York: St. Martin's Press.

Fineberg, B. H. (1993). 'From a sure foot to faltering meters: the dark ladies of Tibullan elegy', in DeForest, 249–56.

Finler, J. (2000). 'Une carrière hollywoodienne: De "Skippy" à "Cléopâtre", et au-delà'. *Positif*, 469: 78–82.

Fischler, S. (1994). 'Social stereotypes and historical analysis: the case of the imperial women at Rome', in Archer *et al.*, 115–33.

Fitzgerald, W. (1995). *Catullan Provocations*. Berkeley: University of California Press.

——(2000). *Slavery and the Roman Literary Imagination*. Cambridge: Cambridge University Press.

Flamarion, E. (1997). *Cleopatra: From History to Legend*. Eng. trans. by A. Bonfante-Warren. London: Thames and Hudson. French edn. 1993.

Flaschenriem, B. L. (1997). 'Loss, desire, and writing in Propertius 1.19 and 2.15'. *CA* 16/2: 259–77.

——(1998). 'Speaking of women: "female voice" in Propertius'. *Helios*, 25/1: 49–64.

——(1999). 'Sulpicia and the rhetoric of disclosure'. *CP* 94: 36–54.

Flory, M. B. (1993). 'Livia and the history of public honorific statues for women in Rome'. *TAPA* 123: 287–308.

Flynn, St J. E. (1997). 'The saint of the womanly body: Raimon de Cornet's fourteenth-century male poetics', in Gold *et al.*, 91–109.

Foley, H. P. (1981) (ed.). *Reflections of Women in Antiquity*. New York: Gordon and Breach.

Foreman, L. (1999). *Cleopatra's Palace: In Search of a Legend*. London: Discovery Books.

Forster, L. (1969). *The Icy Fire: Five Studies in European Petrarchism*. Cambridge: Cambridge University Press.

Foss, M. (1997). *The Search for Cleopatra*. London: Michael O'Mara Books (in association with BBC Timewatch).

Foucault, M. (1981). *The History of Sexuality*, i. *An Introduction*. Middlesex: Pelican Books. Repr. and trans. of original 1976 edn.

Fowler, D. (2000). *Roman Constructions: Readings in Postmodern Latin*. Oxford: Oxford University Press.

Fraenkel, E. (1957). *Horace*. Oxford: Clarendon Press.

Fraser, P. M. (1972). *Ptolemaic Alexandria*. 3 vols. Oxford: Clarendon Press.

Frayling, C. (1992). *The Face of Tutankhamun*. London: Faber and Faber.

Fredrick, D. (1995). 'Beyond the atrium to Ariadne: erotic painting and visual pleasure in the Roman house'. *CA* 14/2: 266–87.

——(1997). 'Reading broken skin: violence in Roman elegy', in Hallett and Skinner, 172–93.

French, B. (1978). *On the Verge of Revolt: Women in American Films of the Fifties*. New York: Frederick Ungar.

Gaines, J. (1989). 'The Queen Christina tie-ups: Convergence of show window and screen'. *Quarterly Review of Film and Video*, 11: 35–60.

——and Herzog, C. (1990) (eds.). *Fabrications: Costume and the Female Body*. New York: Routledge.

Gale, M. (1997). 'Propertius 2.7: Militia amoris and the ironies of elegy'. *JRS* 87: 77–91.

Galinsky, K. (1969). 'The triumph theme in the Augustan elegy'. *Wiener Studien* NF 3: 75–107.

——(1972). *The Herakles Theme: The Adaptation of the Hero in Literature from Homer to the Twentieth Century*. Oxford: Blackwell.

——(1996). *Augustan Culture: An Intrepretive Introduction*. Princeton: Princeton University Press.

Gamel, M.-K. (1989). '*Non sine caede*: abortion politics and poetics in Ovid's *Amores*'. *Helios*, 16: 183–206.

——(1998). 'Reading as a man: performance and gender in Roman elegy'. *Helios*, 25/1: 79–95.

Gardner, J. F. (1986). *Women in Roman Law and Society*. London: Croom Helm.

Geagley, B. (1984). 'Exhuming *Cleopatra*'. *American Film*, 9/5: 12.

Genini, R. (1996). *Theda Bara: A Biography of the Silent Screen Vamp*. Jefferson: McFarland.

Giangrande, G. (1981). 'Hellenistic topoi in Ovid's *Amores*'. *Museum Philol. Lond.* 4: 25–51.

Giannetti, R. (1989). *Rivoluzione, democrazia, legittimà nel pensiero politico di Guglielmo Ferrero*. Naples: Edizioni Scientifiche Italiane.

Gibson, R. K. (1998). 'Meretrix or matrona? Stereotypes in *Ars Amatoria* 3'. *PLLS* 10: 295–312.

Gigon, O. (1956). *Kommentar zum zweiten Buch von Xenophons Memorabilien*. Schweizerische Beiträge zur Altertumswissenschaft, Heft 7. Basle: Verlag Friedrich Reinhardt.

Gili, J. A. (1985). *L'Italie de Mussolini et son cinema*. Paris: Editions Henri Veyrier.

——(1990). 'I film dell'Impero fascista', in G. P. Brunetta and J. A. Gili, *L'ora d'Africa del cinema italiano 1911–1989*. Trent: LaGrafica-Mori, 39–112.

Gleason, M. W. (1995). *Making Men: Sophists and Self-Presentation in Ancient Rome*. Princeton: Princeton University Press.

Gledhill, C. (1991). *Stardom: Industry of Desire*. London: Routledge.

Gold, B. K. (1993*a*). '"But Ariadne was never there in the first place": finding the female in Roman poetry', in Rabinowitz and Richlin, 75–101.

——(1993*b*). '"The master mistress of my passion": the lady as patron in ancient and renaissance literature', in DeForest, 279–304.

——Miller, P. A., and Platter, C. (1997) (eds.). *Sex and Gender in Medieval and Renaissance Texts: The Latin Tradition*. Albany: State University of New York Press.

Golden, E. (1996). *Vamp: The Rise and Fall of Theda Bara*. New York: Emprise Publishing.

Goldhill, S. (1986). *Reading Greek Tragedy*. Cambridge: Cambridge University Press.

Gori, G. M. (1988). *Patria diva: la storia d'Italia nei film del ventennio*. Florence: La casa Usher.

Gorman, E. (2000). *Irony and Misreading in the Annals of Tacitus*. Cambridge: Cambridge University Press.

Gould, J. (1980). 'Law, custom, and myth: aspects of the social position of women in Classical Athens'. *JHS* 100: 38–59.

Gow, A. S. F. (1950). *Theocritus*, ii. Commentary. Cambridge: Cambridge University Press.

Grant, M. (1972). *Cleopatra*. London: Weidenfeld and Nicolson.

Graves, R. (1999). *The Claudius Novels*. London: Penguin Books. First pub. separately as *I, Claudius* (London: Arthur Barker, 1934) and *Claudius the God* (London: Arthur Barker, 1934).

——and Hodge, A. (1985). *The Long Weekend: A Social History of Great Britain 1918–1939*. London: Cardinal. First pub. 1940.

Graves, R. P. (1990). *Robert Graves: The Years with Laura (1926–1940)*. London: Weidenfeld & Nicolson.

Green, P. (1982). *Ovid. The Erotic Poems*. London: Penguin.

Greene, E. (1998). *The Erotics of Domination: Male Desire and the Mistress in Latin Love Poetry*. Baltimore: Johns Hopkins University Press.

——(1999). 'Travesties of love: violence and voyeurism in Ovid *Amores* 1.7'. *CW* 92/5: 409–18.

——(2000). 'Gender identity and the elegiac hero in Propertius 2.1'. *Arethusa*, 33/2: 241–61.

Greene, G., and Kahn, C. (1985) (eds.). *Making a Difference: Feminist Literary Criticism*. New Accents Series. London: Methuen.

Griffin, J. (1985). *Latin Poets and Roman Life*. London: Duckworth. Repr. Bristol Classical Press, 1994.

Griffin, M.T. (1984). *Nero: The End of a Dynasty*. London: B.T. Batsford.

Grignaffini, G. (1988). 'Female identity and Italian cinema of the 1950s', in G. Bruno and M. Nadotti (eds.). *Off Screen: Women and Film in Italy*. London: Routledge, 111–23.

Grimal, P. (1953). *Les intentions de Properce et la composition du livre IV des élégies*. Collection Latomus, 12. Brussels: Berchem.

——(1963). *L'Amour à Rome*. Paris: Hachette.

Gross, N. P. (1975–6). 'Ovid, *Amores* 3.11A and B: a literary mélange'. *CJ* 71: 152–60.

Gruen, E. S. (1984). *The Hellenistic World and the Coming of Rome*, ii. Berkeley: University of California Press.

Gurval, R. A. (1995). *Actium and Augustus*. Ann Arbor: University of Michigan Press.

——(forthcoming). 'Dying like a queen: the story of Cleopatra and the asp(s) in antiquity', in Miles.

Habinek, T. N. (1997). 'The invention of sexuality in the world-city of Rome', in Habinek and Schiesaro, 23–43.

——(1998). *The Politics of Latin Literature: Writing, Identity, and Empire in Ancient Rome*. Princeton: Princeton University Press.

——and Schiesaro, A. (1997) (eds.). *The Roman Cultural Revolution*. Cambridge: Cambridge University Press.

Hall, E. (1989). *Inventing the Barbarian: Greek Self-Definition through Tragedy*. Oxford: Clarendon Press.

Hallett, J. P. (1973). 'The role of women in Roman elegy: counter-cultural feminism'. *Arethusa*, 6: 103–24. Repr. in J. Peradotto and J. P. Sullivan (eds.) (1984), *Women in the Ancient World: The Arethusa Papers*. Albany: State University of New York Press, 241–62.

——(1974). 'Women in Roman elegy: a reply'. *Arethusa*, 7: 211–17.

——(1977). 'Perusinae Glandes and the changing image of Augustus'. *American Journal of Ancient History*, 2: 151–71.

Hallett, J. P. (1984). *Fathers and Daughters in Roman Society: Women and the Elite Family*. Princeton: Princeton University Press.

——(1989). 'Women as *same* and *other* in classical Roman elite'. *Helios*, 16/1: 59–78.

——(1990). 'Contextualising the text: the journey to Ovid'. *Helios*, 17/2: 187–95.

——(1993*a*). 'Feminist theory, historical periods, literary canons, and the study of Greco-Roman antiquity', in Rabinowitz and Richlin, 44–72.

——(1993*b*). 'Martial's Sulpicia and Propertius' Cynthia', in DeForest, 322–53.

——(1996). '*Nec castrare uelis meos libellos*: sexual and poetic *lusus* in Catullus, Martial and the Carmina Priapea', in C. Klodt (ed.), *Satura Lanx: Festschrift für Werner A. Krenkel*. Georg Olms Verlag: Hildesheim, 321–44.

——and Skinner, M. B. (1997) (eds.). *Roman Sexualities*. Princeton: Princeton University Press.

Hamel, R., and Méthé, P. (1990). *Dictionnaire Dumas*. Montreal: Guérin.

Hamer, M. (1993). *Signs of Cleopatra: Histories, Politics, Representation*. London: Routledge.

——(2001). 'The myth of Cleopatra since the Renaissance', in S. Walker and P. Higgs (eds.), *Cleopatra of Egypt: From History to Myth*. London: British Museum Press, 302–11.

Hannestad, N. (1988). *Roman Art and Imperial Policy*. Aarhus: University Press.

Hannsberry, K. B. (1998). *Femme Noir: Bad Girls of Film*. Jefferson, NC: McFarland and Co.

Hanslik, R. (1979). *Sex. Propertii Elegiarum Libri IV*. Leipzig: Teubner.

Hardie, P. (1986). *Virgil's Aeneid: Cosmos and Imperium*. Oxford: Clarendon Press.

Hark, I. R. (1993). 'Animals or Romans: looking at masculinity in *Spartacus*', in S. Cohan and I. R. Hark (eds.), *Screening the Male: Exploring Masculinities in Hollywood Cinema*. London: Routledge, 151–72.

Harrowitz, N. A. (1994). *Antisemitism, Misogyny and the Logic of Cultural Difference: Cesare Lombroso and Matilde Serao*. Lincoln: University of Nebraska Press.

Hartog, F. (1988). *The Mirror of Herodotus: The Representation of the Other in the Writing of History*. Trans. J. Lloyd. Berkeley: University of California Press.

Harvey, S. (1980). 'Woman's place: the absent family of film noir', in Kaplan, 22–34.

Hawkes, T. (1977). *Structuralism and Semiotics*. London: Methuen.

Hay, J. (1987). *Popular Film Culture in Fascist Italy: The Passing of the Rex*. Bloomington: Indiana University Press.

Helbig, W. (1868). *Wandgemälde der vom Vesuv verschütteten Städte Campaniens*. Leipzig.

Heller, A., and Rudnick, L. (1991) (eds.). *1915, The Cultural Moment: The New Politics, The New Woman, The New Psychology, The New Art and The New Theatre in America*. New Brunswick: Rutgers University Press.

Hemelrijk, E. A. (1998). Matrona Docta: *Educated Women in the Roman Élite from Cornelia to Julia Domna*. Doctoral thesis. Katholieke Universiteit Nijmegen. Pub. 1999 by Routledge, London.

Henderson, J. (1986). 'Becoming a heroine (1st): Penelope's Ovid'. *LCM* 11/1: 7–10; 11/2: 21–4; 11/3: 37–40.

——(1989). 'Satire writes "Woman": *Gendersong*'. *PCPS* 215 (NS 35): 50–80.

Hendry, M. (1993). 'Three problems in the Cleopatra Ode'. *CJ* 88/2: 137–46.

Herzog, C. C., and Gaines, J. M. (1991). '"Puffed sleeves before tea-time": Joan Crawford, Adrian and women audiences', in Gledhill, 74–91.

Herzog-Hauser, G., and Wotke, F. (1955). 'Valeria Messalina', in *Paulys Realencyclopädie der classischen Altertumswissenschaft*. Second Series 8A, cols. 246–58, no. 403.

Heyworth, S. J. (1986). 'Notes on Propertius, Books III and IV'. *CQ* NS 36: 199–211.

Higashi, S. (1978). *Virgins, Vamps, and Flappers: The American Silent Movie Heroine*. Montreal: Eden Press Women's Publications.

——(1994). *Cecil B. DeMille*. New York: Dell.

Higham, C. (1976). *Charles Laughton: An Intimate Biography*. London: W. H. Allen.

——and Moseley, R. (1983). *Merle: A Biography of Merle Oberon*. Sevenoaks: New English Library.

Hinds, S. (1987). 'The poetess and the reader: further steps towards Sulpicia'. *Hermathena*, 143: 29–46.

——(1998). *Allusion and Intertext: Dynamics of Appropriation in Roman Poetry*. Cambridge: Cambridge University Press.

Hirsch, F. (1973). *Elizabeth Taylor*. New York: Pyramid Publications.

——(1978). *The Hollywood Epic*. South Brunswick, NJ: A. S. Barnes.

Hoberman, R. (1997). *Gendering Classicism: The Ancient World in Twentieth-Century Women's Historical Fiction*. Albany: State University of New York.

Hobsbawm, E., and Ranger, T. (1983). *The Invention of Tradition*. Cambridge: Cambridge University Press.

Hodgdon, B. (1998). *The Shakespeare Trade: Performances and Appropriations*. Philadelphia: University of Pennsylvania Press.

Hollis, A. S. (1970). *Ovid: Metamorphoses Book VIII*. Oxford: Clarendon Press.

Holzberg, N. (1999). 'Four poets and a poetess or a portrait of the poet as a young man? Thoughts on book 3 of the *Corpus Tibullianum*'. *CJ* 94/2: 169–91.

Houston, P., and Gillett, J. (1963). 'The theory and practice of blockbusting'. *Sight and Sound*, 32: 68–72.

Hubbard, M. (1974). *Propertius*. London: Duckworth.

Hughes-Hallett, L. (1991). *Cleopatra: Histories, Dreams, and Distortions*. London: Vintage. First edn. pub. 1990.

Humbert, J.-H. (1994*a*). 'Denon and the discovery of Egypt', in Humbert *et al.*, 202–5.

——(1994*b*). 'Egyptomania: A current concept from the Renaissance to postmodernism', in Humbert *et al.*, 21–6.

——Pantazzi, M., and Ziegler, C. (1994). *Egyptomania: Egypt in Western Art 1730–1930*. Ottawa and Paris: National Gallery of Canada/Réunion des Museés Nationaux.

Hutchinson, G. O. (1984). 'Propertius and the unity of the book'. *JRS* 74: 99–106.

Innes, D. C. (1979). 'Gigantomachy and natural philosophy'. *CQ* 29: 165–71.

Ites, M. (1908). *De Propertii Elegiis inter se conexis*. Diss. Göttingen.

Izod, J. (1988). *Hollywood and the Box Office 1895–1986*. Basingstoke: Macmillan Press.

Jacobson, H. (1974). *Ovid's Heroides*. Princeton: Princeton University Press.

James, S. L. (1998). 'Introduction: constructions of gender and genre in Roman comedy and elegy'. *Helios*, 25/1: 3–16.

Janan, M. (1994). *'When the Lamp is Shattered': Desire and Narrative in Catullus*. Carbondale: Southern Illinois Press.

——(1998). 'Refashioning Hercules: Propertius 4.9'. *Helios* 25/1: 65–77.

——(2001). *The Politics of Desire: Propertius IV*. Berkeley: University of California Press.

Johnson, W. R. (1967). 'A Quean, a great queen? Cleopatra and the politics of misrepresentation'. *Arion*, 6: 387–402.

——(1973). 'The emotions of patriotism: Propertius 4.6'. *CSCA* 6: 151–80.

Joshel, S. R. (1995). 'Female desire and the discourse of empire: Tacitus' Messalina'. *Signs: Journal of Women in Culture and Society*, 21/1: 50–82. Repr. in Hallett and Skinner, 221–54.

——(2001). '*I, Claudius*: projection and imperial soap opera', in Joshel *et al*.

——Malamud, M., and Segal, D. (2001) (eds.). *Imperial Projections: Ancient Rome in Modern Popular Culture*. Baltimore: Johns Hopkins University Press.

Juhnke, H. (1971). 'Zum Aufbau des zweiten und dritten Buches des Properz'. *Hermes*, 99: 91–125.

Kahn, C. (1997). *Roman Shakespeare*. London: Routledge.

Kaplan, E. A. (1980) (ed.). *Women in Film Noir*. London: British Film Institute.

Keith, A. M. (1992). '*Amores* 1.1: Propertius and the Ovidian programme', in C. Deroux (ed.), *Studies in Latin Literature and Roman History*, vi. Brussels: Latomus, 327–44.

——(1994). '*Corpus eroticum*: elegiac poetics and elegiac *puellae* in Ovid's *Amores*'. *CW* 88/1: 27–40.

——(1997). '*Tandem uenit amor*: a Roman woman speaks of love', in Hallett and Skinner, 295–310.

——(1999). 'Slender verse: Roman elegy and ancient rhetorical theory'. *Mnemosyne*, 52/1: 41–62.

——(2000). *Engendering Rome: Women in Latin Epic*. Cambridge: Cambridge University Press.

Kellum, B. (1997). 'Concealing/revealing: Gender and the play of meaning in the monuments of Augustan Rome', in Habinek and Schiesaro, 158–81.

Kennedy, D. F. (1992). '"Augustan" and "Anti-Augustan": Reflections on terms of reference', in Powell, 26–58.

——(1993). *The Arts of Love: Five Studies in the Discourse of Roman Love Elegy.* Cambridge: Cambridge University Press.

Kenney, E. J. (1961) (ed.). *P. Ovidi Nasonis Amores, Medicamina Faciei Feminae, Ars Amatoria, Remedia Amoris.* Oxford Classical Text. Oxford: Clarendon Press.

Kent, J. P. C. (1978). *Roman Coins.* London: Thames and Hudson.

King, J. K. (1976). 'Sophistication vs. chastity in Propertius' Latin love elegy'. *Helios*, 4: 67–76.

——(1980). 'Propertius 2.1–12: his Callimachean second libellus'. *WJA* NF 6b: 61–84.

——(1981). 'Propertius 2.2: a Callimachean "multum in parvo"'. *WS* 15: 169–84.

Kleiner, D. E. E. (1992*a*). 'Politics and gender in the pictorial propaganda of Antony and Octavian'. *EMC* 36 (NS 11): 357–67.

——(1992*b*). *Roman Sculpture.* New Haven: Yale University Press.

Konstan, D. (1994). *Sexual Symmetry: Love in the Ancient Novel and Related Genres.* Princeton: Princeton University Press.

Kraggerud, E. (1998). 'Vergil announcing the *Aeneid*: On *Georgics* 3.1–48', in H.-P. Stahl (ed.), *Vergil's* Aeneid*: Augustan Epic and Political Context.* London: Duckworth (in association with the Classical Press of Wales), 1–20.

Kuntz, M. (1994). 'The Prodikean "Choice of Herakles". A reshaping of the myth'. *CJ* 89/2: 163–81.

Lachmann, K. (1816) (ed.). *Sex. Aurelii Propertii Carmina.* Leipzig.

Laguardia, R., and Arceri, G. (1985). *Red: The Tempestuous Life of Susan Hayward.* New York: Macmillan Press.

Lamb, M. (1980). *Antony and Cleopatra on the English Stage.* London: Associated University Presses.

Lampela, A. (1998). *Rome and the Ptolemies of Egypt: The Development of Their Political Relations 273–80 BC.* The Finnish Society of Sciences and Letters, *Commentationes Humanarum Litterarum*, 111.

Lange, D. K. (1979). 'Cynthia and Cornelia: two voices from the grave', in Deroux, 335–42.

Lant, A. (1992). 'The curse of the Pharaoh, or how the cinema contracted Egyptomania'. *October*, 59: 87–112.

——(1995). 'Egypt in early cinema', in Cosandey and Albera, 73–94.

La Penna, A. (1990). 'Pascoli, Giovenale e Pietro Cossa'. *Belfagor*, 45/2: 574–8.

Last, H. (1934). 'The social policy of Augustus', in *Cambridge Ancient History*, x. Cambridge: Cambridge University Press, 425–64.

Laurence, R. (1997). 'History and female power at Rome', in T. Cornell and K. Lomas (eds.), *Gender and Ethnicity in Ancient Italy*. London: Accordia Research Institute, 129–39.

Leach, W. (1993). *Land of Desire: Merchants, Power, and the Rise of a New American Culture*. New York: Pantheon Books.

Lee, G. (1962). 'Tenerorum lusor amorum', in J. P. Sullivan (ed.), *Critical Essays on Roman Literature: Elegy and Lyric*. London: Routledge and Kegan Paul, 149–79.

——(1968). *Ovid's Amores*. English trans. with Latin text. London: John Murray.

Lee-Stecum, P. (1998). *Powerplay in Tibullus: Reading* Elegies *Book One*. Cambridge: Cambridge University Press.

——(2000). 'Poet/Reader, authority deferred: re-reading Tibullan elegy'. *Arethusa*, 33/2: 177 215.

Lefkowitz, M. R. (1981). *Heroines and Hysterics*. London: Duckworth.

——and Fant, M. B. (1982). *Women's Life in Greece and Rome*. London: Duckworth.

Levick, B. (1990). *Claudius*. London: B.T. Batsford.

Lewis, J. (1984). *Women in England 1870–1950: Sexual Divisions and Social Change*. Brighton: Wheatsheaf Bks.

Lieberg, G. (1963). 'Die Muse des Properz und seine Dichterweihe'. *Philologus*, 107: 116–29 and 263–70.

Lilja, S. (1978). *The Roman Elegists' Attitude to Women*. New York: Garland. First pub. Helsinki 1965.

Lindheim, S. H. (1998*a*). 'Hercules cross-dressed, Hercules undressed: unmasking the construction of the Propertian *amator* in elegy 4.9'. *AJP* 119: 43–66.

——(1998*b*). 'I am dressed, therefore I am?: Vertumnus in Propertius 4.2 and in Metamorphoses 14.622–771'. *Ramus*, 27/1: 27–38.

Lindsay, J. (1971). *Cleopatra*. London: Constable.

Lipshitz, S. (1978) (ed.). *Tearing the Veil: Essays on Femininity*. London: Routledge and Kegan Paul.

Little, D. (1982). 'Politics in Augustan poetry'. *ANRW* 2. 30/1: 254–370.

Lopez-Celly, F. (1939). *Il romanzo storico in Italia: dai prescottiani alle odierne vite romanzate.* Bologna: Licinio Cappelli-Editore.

Lowe, N. J. (1988). 'Sulpicia's syntax'. *CQ* 38: 193–205.

Lowrie, M. (1997). *Horace's Narrative Odes.* Oxford: Clarendon Press.

Luard, E. (1989). *A History of the United Nations*, i. *The Years of Western Domination, 1945–1955.* London and Basingstoke: Macmillan Press.

Luck, G. (1964). *Properz und Tibull Liebeselegien, Lateinisch und Deutsch.* Zurich: Artemis.

——(1974). 'The woman's role in Latin love poetry'. In G. K. Galinsky (ed.), *Perspectives of Roman Poetry.* Austin: University of Texas Press, 15–31.

Lyne, R. O. A. M. (1979). 'Servitium amoris'. *CQ* 29: 117–30.

——(1980). *The Latin Love Poets: From Catullus to Horace.* Oxford: Clarendon Press.

——(1998). 'Propertius 2.10 and 11 and the structure of Books "2A" and "2B"'. *JRS* 88: 21–36.

McCarthy, K. (1998). '*Servitium amoris: amor servitii*', in S. R. Joshel and S. Murnaghan (eds.), *Women and Slaves in Greco-Roman Culture: Differential Equations.* London: Routledge, 174–92.

McClelland, D. (1975). *The Complete Life Story of Susan Hayward.* New York: Pinnacle Books.

McCoskey, D. E. (1999). 'Reading Cynthia and sexual difference in the poems of Propertius'. *Ramus*, 28/1: 16–39.

MacDonald, J. G. (1996). 'Sex, race, and empire in Shakespeare's *Antony and Cleopatra*'. *Literature & History*, 5/1: 60–77.

MacDonald, S. (1987*a*). 'Drawing the lines—gender, peace and war: An introduction', in Macdonald *et al.*, 1–26.

——(1987*b*). 'Boadicea: warrior, mother and myth', in MacDonald *et al.*, 40–61.

——Holden, P., and Ardener, S. (1987) (eds.). *Images of Women in Peace and War.* London: Macmillan Education.

McGinn, T. A. J. (1998). *Prostitution, Sexuality, and the Law in Ancient Rome.* New York: Oxford University Press.

MacKenzie, J. M. (1995). *Orientalism: History, Theory and the Arts.* Manchester: Manchester University Press.

McKeown, J. C. (1979). 'Augustan elegy and mime'. *PCPS* 205 (NS 25): 71–84.

——(1987). *Ovid: Amores*, i. *Text and Prolegomena*. Liverpool: Arca Classical and Medieval Texts, Papers and Monographs, 20.

Maclean, I. (1980). *The Renaissance Notion of Woman: A Study in the Fortunes of Scholasticism and Medical Science in European Intellectual Life*. Cambridge: Cambridge University Press.

Macleod, C. W. (1976). 'Propertius 4,1'. *PLLS* 1: 141–53.

McNamee, K. (1993). 'Propertius, poetry, and love', in DeForest, 215–48.

Macurdy, G. (1932). *Hellenistic Queens: A Study of Woman-power in Macedonia, Seleucid Syria and Ptolemaic Egypt*. Baltimore: Johns Hopkins University Studies in Archaeology, 14.

Madelaine, R. (1998) (ed.). *Antony and Cleopatra*. Shakespeare in production series. Cambridge: Cambridge University Press.

Mader, G. (1989). 'Heroism and hallucination: Cleopatra in Horace C. 1.37 and Propertius 3.11'. *Grazer Beiträge*, 16: 183–201.

Maehler, H. (1983). 'Egypt under the last Ptolemies'. *BICS* 30: 1–16.

Magill F. N. (1982) (ed.). *Magill's Survey of Cinema: Silent Films*, i. Englewood Cliffs, NJ: Salem Press.

Magli, P. (1989). 'The face and the soul', in M. Feher with R. Naddaff and N. Tazi (eds.), *Zone 4. Fragments for a History of the Human Body*, part 2, 87–127.

Malaise, M. (1972). *Les conditions de pénétration et de diffusion des cultes Egyptiens en Italie*, *EPRO* 28. Leiden: E. J. Brill.

Maltby, R. (1981). 'Love and marriage in Propertius 4,3'. *PLLS* 3: 243–7.

Maltby, R. (1993). 'The Production Code and the Hays Office', in Balio, 37–72.

Mandelbaum, A. (1981). *The Aeneid of Virgil. A Verse Translation*. Toronto: Bantam Books. First pub. 1961.

Marasco, G. (1995). 'Cleopatra e gli esperimenti su cavie umane'. *Historia*, 44/3: 317–25.

Marquis, E. C. (1974). 'Vertumnus in Propertius 4,2'. *Hermes*, 102: 491–500.

Marshall, E. (1998). 'Constructing the self and the other in Cyrenaica', in R. Laurence and J. Berry (eds.), *Cultural Identity in the Roman Empire*. London: Routledge, 49–63.

Martindale, C., and Martindale, M. (1990). *Shakespeare and the Uses of Antiquity: An Introductory Essay*. London: Routledge.

Martinelli, V. (1981). *Il cinema muto italiano 1923–31*. Rome: Bianco e Nero.

——(1993). *Il cinema muto italiano: 1913*. Rome: Bianco e Nero.

May, L. (1980). *Screening Out the Past: The Birth of Mass Culture and the Motion Picture Industry*. Chicago: University of Chicago Press.

Meskell, L. (1998). 'Consuming Bodies: Cultural Fantasies of Ancient Egypt'. *Body and Society* 4/1: 64–7.

Miles, G. (1996). *Shakespeare and the Constant Romans*. Oxford: Clarendon Press.

Miles, M. (forthcoming). *Cleopatra and Egyptomania*. Berkeley: University of California Press.

Millar, F. (1984). 'State and subject: The impact of monarchy', in Millar and Segal, 37–60.

——and Segal, E. (1984) (eds.). *Caesar Augustus. Seven Aspects*. Oxford: Clarendon Press.

Miller, J. F. (1982). 'Callimachus and the Augustan aetiological elegy'. *ANRW* 2.30/1: 371–417.

Miller, J. S. (2000). *Something Completely Different: British Television and American Culture*. Minneapolis: University of Minnesota Press.

Miller, P. A. (1994). *Lyric Texts and Lyric Consciousness: The Birth of a Genre from Archaic Greece to Augustan Rome*. London: Routledge.

——(1997). 'Laurel as the sign of sin: Laura's textual body in Petrarch's *Secretum*, in Gold *et al.*, 139–63.

——(2001). 'Why Propertius is a woman: French feminism and Augustan elegy'. *CP*, 96/2.

——and Platter, C. (1999*a*). 'Introduction' to special issue 'Power, politics, & discourse in Augustan elegy'. *CW* 92/5: 403–7.

————(1999*b*). 'Crux as symptom: Augustan elegy and beyond'. *CW* 92/5: 445–54.

Momigliano, A. (1960). *Storia della letteratura Italiana dalle origini ai nostri giorni*. [8th edn.]. Milan: Casa Editrice Giuseppe Principato.

Monaco, G. (1992). 'Connotazioni dell'Egitto negli autori latini', in Carratelli *et al.*, 261–4.

Montserrat, D. (2000). *Akhenaten: History, Fantasy and Ancient Egypt*. London: Routledge.

Moreno, E. (1979). *The Films of Susan Hayward*. New Jersey: Citadel Press.

Morgan, K. (1977). *Ovid's Art of Imitation: Propertius in the Amores*. Leiden: *Mnemosyne* Supp. 47.

Muecke, F. (1974). '*Nobilis historia*? Incongruity in Propertius 4.7'. *BICS* 21: 124–32.

Mulvey, L. (1975). 'Visual pleasure and narrative cinema'. *Screen*, 16/3: 6–18.

Murgatroyd, P. (1975). '*Militia amoris* and the Roman elegists'. *Latomus*, 34: 59–79.

Myers, K. S. (1996). 'The poet and the procuress: the *lena* in Latin love elegy'. *JRS* 86: 1–21.

Nadel, A. (1993). 'God's law and the widescreen: *The Ten Commandments* as Cold War "Epic"'. *Publications of the Modern Languages Association of America*, 108/3: 415–30.

Nash, E. (1961). *Pictorial Dictionary of Ancient Rome*, i. London: A. Zwemmer.

Neale, S. (1983). *Genre.* London: British Film Institute.

Nedergaard E. (1988). 'Nuove indagini sull'Arco di Augusto nel Foro Romano'. *Archeologia Laziale*, IX 16: 37–43.

Nethercut, W. R. (1968). 'Notes on the structure of Propertius Book 4'. *AJP* 89: 449–64.

——(1970). 'The ironic priest: Propertius' "Roman Elegies" iii, 1–5: imitations of Horace and Vergil'. *AJP* 91: 385–407.

——(1972). 'Propertius: Elegy 2.10'. *Symbolae Osloenses*, 47: 79–94.

——(1980). 'Propertius 2.18: "Kein einheitliches Gedicht . . ."'. *ICS* 5: 94–109.

——(1983). 'Recent scholarship on Propertius'. *ANRW* 2.30/3: 1813–57.

Newburn, T. (1992). *Permissiveness and Regulation: Law and Morals in Post-War Britain.* London: Routledge.

Newman, J. K. (1997). *Augustan Propertius: The Recapitulation of a Genre.* Hildesheim: Georg Olms Verlag.

Nisbet, R. G. M., and Hubbard, M. (1970). *Horace Odes 1.* Oxford: Oxford University Press.

Obeidat, M. M. (1998). *American Literature and Orientalism.* Berlin: Klaus Schwarz Verlag.

Ogilvie, R. M. (1965). *A Commentary on Livy Books 1–5.* Oxford: Clarendon Press.

O'Gorman, E. (2000). *Irony and Misreading in the Annals of Tacitus.* Cambridge: Cambridge University Press.

Oliensis, E. (1991). 'Canidia, Canicula and the decorum of Horace's *Epodes*'. *Arethusa*, 24/1: 107–38.

Oliensis, E. (1995). 'Life after publication: Horace *Epistles*, 1.20'. *Arethusa*, 28: 209–24.

——(1997). 'The erotics of *amicitia*: readings in Tibullus, Propertius, and Horace', in Hallett and Skinner, 151–71.

——(1998). *Horace and the Rhetoric of Authority.* Cambridge: Cambridge University Press.

O'Neill, K. (1995). 'Propertius 4.4: Tarpeia and the burden of aetiology'. *Hermathena*, 158: 53–60.

——(1998). 'Symbolism and sympathetic magic in Propertius 4.5'. *CJ* 94/1: 49–80.

——(1999). 'Ovid and Propertius: reflexive annotation in *Amores* 1.8'. *Mnemosyne*, 52/3: 286–307.

——(2000). 'Propertius 4.2: Slumming with Vertumnus?'. *AJP* 121/2: 259–77.

O'Prey, P. (1982) (ed.). *In Broken Images: Selected Letters of Robert Graves 1914–46.* London: Hutchinson.

Otis, B. (1938). 'Ovid and the Augustans'. *TAPA* 69: 188–229.

——(1968). 'A reading of the Cleopatra Ode'. *Arethusa*, 1: 48–61.

Paduano, G. (1968). 'Le reminiscenze dell'Alcesti nell'elegia IV.11 di Properzio'. *Maia*, 20: 21–8.

Panofsky, E. (1930). *Hercules am Scheidewege.* Leipzig: B. G. Teubner.

Pantazzi, M. (1994). 'Tutankhmun and Art Deco', in Humbert *et al.*, 508–14.

Papanghelis, T. (1987). *Propertius: A Hellenistic Poet on Love and Death.* Cambridge: Cambridge University Press.

Parish, J. R. (1971). *The Fox Girls.* New Rochelle, NY: Arlington House.

——(1972). *The Paramount Pretties.* New Rochelle, NY: Arlington House.

Parke, H. W. (1988). *Sibyls and Sibylline Prophecy in Classical Antiquity.* London and New York: Routledge.

Parker, H. N. (1994). 'Sulpicia, the *auctor de sulpicia*, and the authorship of 3.9 and 3.11 of the *Corpus Tibullianum*. *Helios*, 21/1: 39–62.

Parsons, P. (1977). 'Callimachus: Victoria Berenices'. *ZPE* 25: 1–50.

Paul, G. M. (1966). 'Sallust', in T. A. Dorey, *Latin Historians*. London: Routledge and Kegan Paul, 85–113.

——(1985). 'Sallust's Sempronia: The portrait of a lady'. *PLLS* 5: 9–22.

Pearson, R. A., and Uricchio, W. (1990). '"How many times shall Caesar bleed in sport?": Shakespeare and the cultural debate about moving pictures'. *Screen*, 31/3: 243–61.

Pelling, C. B. R. (1988). *Plutarch. Life of Antony.* Cambridge: Cambridge University Press.

—— (1996). 'The Triumviral Period', in A. K. Bowman, E. Champlin, and A. Lintott (eds.), *The Cambridge Ancient History* [2nd edn.], x. *The Augustan Empire, 43 BC–AD 69*. Cambridge, Cambridge University Press, 1–67.

Perkell, C. G. (1981). 'On Creusa, Dido, and the quality of victory in Virgil's *Aeneid*', in Foley, 355–77.

Pillinger, H. E. (1969). 'Some Callimachean influences on Propertius book 4'. *HSCP* 73: 171–99.

Pinotti, P. (1974). 'Sulle fonti e le intenzioni di Properzio IV 4'. *Giornale Italiano di Filologia*, NS 5: 18–32.

—— (1983). 'Properzio e Vertumno: anticonformismo e restaurazione Augustea'. *Colloquium Propertianum* III, Accademia Properziana del Subasio-Assisi, 75–96.

Platter, C. L. (1995). '*Officium* in Catullus and Propertius: a Foucauldian reading'. *CP* 90/3: 211–24.

Pomeroy, S. B. (1975). *Goddesses, Whores, Wives and Slaves.* New York: Schocken Books.

—— (1984). *Women in Hellenistic Egypt*. New York: Schocken Books.

Postle, M. (1995). *Sir Joshua Reynolds: The Subject Pictures.* Cambridge: Cambridge University Press.

Powell, A. (1992) (ed.). *Roman Poetry and Propaganda in the Age of Augustus.* Bristol: Bristol Classical Press.

Presley, J. W. (1999). '*Claudius*, the scripts'. *Literature/Film Quarterly*, 27/3: 167–72.

Prolo, M. A. (1951). *Storia del cinema muto italiano.* Milan: Poligono Società Editrice.

Pucci, P. (forthcoming). 'Every man's Cleopatra', in Miles.

Puccioni, G. (1979). 'L'elegia IV 5 di Properzio', in *Studi di poesia latina in onore di Antonio Traglia*, ii. Rome: Edizioni di storia e letteratura, 609–23.

Purcell, N. (1986). 'Livia and the womanhood of Rome'. *PCPS* 212 (NS 32): 78–105.

Putnam, M. C. J. (1970). *Virgil's Pastoral Art: Studies in the Eclogues.* Princeton: Princeton University Press.

Putnam, M. C. J. (1976). 'Propertius 1.22: a poet's self-definition'. *QUCC* 23: 93–123.

——(1980). 'Propertius' third book: patterns of cohesion'. *Arethusa*, 13: 97–113.

——(1998). *Virgil's Epic Designs: Ekphrasis in the Aeneid.* New Haven: Yale University Press.

Quadlbauer, F. (1968). 'Properz 3.1'. *Philologus*, 112: 83–118.

——(1970). 'Non humilem . . . poetam: zur literaturgeschichtlichen Stellung von Prop. 1,7,21'. *Hermes*, 98: 331–9.

Quaegebeur, J. (1988). 'Cleopatra VII and the Cults of the Ptolemaic Queens', in Bianchi *et al.*, 41–54.

Quartermaine, L. (1995). '"Slouching towards Rome": Mussolini's imperial vision', in T. J. Cornell and K. Lomas (eds.), *Urban Society in Roman Italy.* London: University College Press, 203–15.

Quinn, K. (1963). *Latin Explorations: Critical Studies in Roman Literature.* London: Routledge.

Quint, D. (1989). 'Epic and Empire'. *Comparative Literature*, 41: 1–32.

Rabinowitz, N. S., and Richlin, A. (1993) (eds.). *Feminist Theory and the Classics.* New York: Routledge.

Reinhold, M. (1981–2). 'The declaration of war against Cleopatra'. *CJ* 77: 97–103.

——(1984). *Classica Americana: The Greek and Roman Heritage in the United States.* Detroit: Wayne University Press.

——(1988). *From Republic to Principate: An Historical Commentary on Cassius Dio's Roman History*, vi. Books 49–52. Atlanta: Scholars Press.

Reitzenstein, E. (1935). 'Das neue Kunstwollen in den Amores Ovids'. *RM* 84: 62–88.

Renzi, L. (1991). 'Grandezza e morte della "femme fatale"', in R. Renzi (ed.). *Sperduto nel buio: il cinema muto italiano e il suo tempo (1905–1930).* Bologna: Cappelli Editore, 121–30.

Rice, E. E. (1999). *Cleopatra.* Stroud: Sutton Publishing.

Richard, C. J. (1994). *The Founders and the Classics: Greece, Rome, and the American Enlightenment.* Cambridge, Mass.: Harvard University Press.

Richardson, L. (1977). *Propertius Elegies I–IV.* Norman: University of Oklahoma Press.

Richlin, A. (1981). 'Approaches to the sources on adultery at Rome', in Foley, 379–404.

——(1983 and 1992[2]). *The Garden of Priapus: Sexuality and Aggression in Roman Humour.* New Haven: Yale University Press. Rev. edn. New York: Oxford University Press.

——(1984). 'Invective against women in Roman satire'. *Arethusa*, 17: 67–80.

——(1992*a*). 'Reading Ovid's Rapes, in Richlin (ed.), 158–79.

——(1992*b*). 'Sulpicia the satirist'. *CW* 86: 125–40.

——(1992*c*). 'Julia's Jokes, Galla Placidia, and the Roman use of women as political icons', in B. Garlick, S. Dixon, and P. Allen (eds.), *Stereotypes of Women in Power: Historical Perspectives and Revisionist Views.* New York: Greenwood Press, 65–91.

——(1992) (ed.). *Pornography and Representation in Greece and Rome.* New York: Oxford University Press.

——(1997). 'Gender and rhetoric: producing manhood in the schools', in W. J. Dominik (ed.), *Roman Eloquence: Rhetoric in Society and Literature.* London: Routledge, 90–110.

Robbins, R. (2000). *Literary Feminisms.* Basingstoke: Macmillan Press.

Roessel, D. (1990). 'The significance of the name *Cerinthus* in the poems of Sulpicia'. *TAPA* 120: 243–50.

Rognoni, L. (1952). *Cinema muto dalle origine al 1930.* Rome: Bianco e Nero Editore.

Rosivach, V. J. (1998). *When a Young Man Falls in Love: The Sexual Exploitation of Women in New Comedy.* London: Routledge.

Ross, D. (1975). *Backgrounds to Augustan Poetry: Gallus, Elegy and Rome.* Cambridge: Cambridge University Press.

Rothstein, M. (1966). *Propertius Sextus Elegien.* 2 vols. Zurich: Weidmann. Repr. of 1898 edn.

Rothwell, K. S. (1999). *A History of Shakespeare on Screen: A Century of Film and Television.* Cambridge: Cambridge University Press.

Rowlandson, J. (1998). *Women and Society in Greek and Roman Egypt. A Sourcebook.* Cambridge: Cambridge University Press.

Said, E. W. (1985). *Orientalism.* London: Peregrine Books. First edn. 1978.

——(1992). 'Egyptian Rites'. *Village Voice,* August 1983. Repr. in Frayling, 276–85.

Santirocco, M. S. (1979). 'Sulpicia reconsidered'. *CJ* 74: 229–39.

——(1986). *Unity and Design in Horace's Odes.* Chapel Hill and London: University of North Carolina Press.

Santoro L'Hoir, F. (1994). 'Tacitus and women's usurpation of power'. *CW* 88/1: 5–25.

Sarris, A. (1966). *The Films of Josef Von Sternberg.* New York: Museum of Modern Art.

Saunders, R.T. (1994). 'Note critiche e filologiche: Messalina as Augusta'. *La parola del passato: rivista di studi antichi*, 49: 356–63.

Schopp, C. (1985). *Alexandre Dumas: le génie de la vie.* Paris: Éditions Mazarine.

Schrijvers, P. H. (1976). 'O tragedia tu labor aeternus. Études sur l'élegie III, 1 des Amours d'Ovide', in J. M. Bremer, S. L. Radt, and C. J. Ruijgh (eds.), *Miscellanea tragica in honorem J. C. Kamerbeek.* Amsterdam: Hakkert, 405–24.

Scott, K. (1929). 'Octavian's propaganda and Antony's *De Sua Ebrietate*'. *CP* 24: 133–41.

——(1933). 'The political propaganda of 44–30 BC'. *Memoirs of the American Academy in Rome*, 11: 7–49.

Seymour, M. (1995). *Robert Graves: Life on the Edge.* London: Doubleday.

Seymour-Smith, M. (1995). *Robert Graves: His Life and Work.* London: Bloomsbury.

Sharrock, A. (1991*a*). 'Womanufacture'. *JRS* 81: 36–49.

——(1991*b*). 'The love of creation'. *Ramus* 20/2: 169–82.

——(1994). *Seduction and Repetition in Ovid's Ars Amatoria II.* Oxford: Clarendon Press.

——(1995). 'The drooping rose: elegiac failure in *Amores* 3.7'. *Ramus* 24/2: 152–80.

——(2000). 'Constructing characters in Propertius'. *Arethusa* 33/2: 263–84.

Shohat, E. (1991*a*). 'Gender and culture of empire: Towards a feminist ethnography of the cinema'. *Quarterly Review of Film and Video*, 13/1–3: 45–84.

——(1991*b*). 'Ethnicities-in-relation: Toward a multicultural reading of American cinema', in L. D. Friedman (ed.), *Unspeakable Images: Ethnicity and the American Cinema.* Urbana: University of Illinois Press.

Siclier, J. (1962). 'L'age du péplum'. *Cahiers du cinéma*, 22/131: 26–38.

Simon, E. (1986). *Augustus: Kunst und Leben in Rom um die Zeitenwende.* Munich: Hirmer.

Simon, R. (1987). *Libya between Ottomanism and Nationalism: The Ottoman Involvement in Libya during the War with Italy (1911–1919).* Berlin: Klaus Schwarz Verlag.

Skinner, M. (1983). 'Clodia Metelli'. *TAPA* 113: 273–87.

——(1986). 'Rescuing Creusa: new approaches to women in antiquity'. *Helios*, 13/2: 1–8.

——(1993*a*). '*Ego mulier*: the construction of male sexuality in Catullus'. *Helios*, 20/2: 107–30.

——(1993*b*). 'Catullus in performance'. *CJ* 89/1: 61–8.

——(1996). 'Zeus and Leda: the sexuality wars in contemporary classical scholarship'. *Thamyris*, 3/1: 103–23.

——(1997). 'Introduction: *Quod multo fit aliter in Graecia . . .*', in Hallett and Skinner, 3–25.

Skoie, M. (2000). '*Sulpicia Americana*: a reading of Sulpicia in the commentary by K. F. Smith (1913)'. *Arethusa*, 33/2: 285–11.

——(2002). *Reading Sulpicia: Commentaries 1475 to 1990.* Oxford: Oxford University Press. Based on 'The Hermeneutics of Commentating: A Case Study of Sulpicia in the History of Commentaries on Latin Literature'. University of Reading Ph.D., 1999.

Skutsch, O. (1975). 'The second book of Propertius'. *HSCP* 79: 229–33.

Smelik, K. A. D., and Hemelrijk, E. A. (1984). '"Who knows not what monsters demented Egypt worships?" Opinions on Egyptian animal worship in antiquity as part of the ancient conception of Egypt'. *ANRW* 2.17/4: 1852–2000.

Smith, B. G. (1989). *Changing Lives: Women in European History Since 1700.* Lexington, MA: D.C. Heath and Co.

Smith, G. (1991). *Epic Films: Casts, Credits and Commentary on over 250 Historical Spectacle Movies.* Jefferson, NC: McFarland and Co.

Smith, R. R. R. (1987). 'The Imperial reliefs from the Sebasteion at Aphrodisias'. *JRS* 77: 88–138.

——(1988*a*). 'Simulacra Gentium: The *Ethne* from the Sebasteion at Aphrodisias'. *JRS* 78: 50–77.

——(1988*b*). *Hellenistic Royal Portraits.* Oxford: Clarendon Press.

——(1991). *Hellenistic Sculpture.* London: Thames and Hudson.

Snipes, K. (1979). *Robert Graves.* New York: Frederick Ungar.

Sobchack, V. (1990). '"Surge and Splendour": A phenomenology of the Hollywood historical epic'. *Representations*, 29: 24–49.

Solmsen, F. (1948). 'Propertius and Horace'. *CP* 43: 105–9.

Solomon, J. (1978). *The Ancient World in the Cinema.* South Brunswick, NJ: A. S. Barnes.

Sorgi, G. (1983). *Potere tra paura e legittimà: Saggio su Guglielmo Ferrero.* Milan: Giuffrè Editore.

Sorlin, P. (1996). *Italian National Cinema 1896–1996.* London: Routledge.

Southern, P. (1999). *Cleopatra.* Stroud: Tempus.

Spangenburg, R., and Moser, D. K. (1997). *Eleanor Roosevelt: A Passion to Improve.* New York: Facts on File Inc.

Spentzou, E. (forthcoming). *Reading Characters Read: Transgressions of Gender and Genre in Ovid's Heroides.* Based on University of Oxford DPhil, 1997.

Spinazzola, V. (1985). *Cinema e pubblico: lo spettacolo filmico in Italia 1945–1965.* Rome: Bulzoni Editore.

Spivey, N. (1999). 'Introduction', in Robert Graves, *The Claudius Novels.* London: Penguin Books, pp. vii–xii.

Springer, C. (1987). *The Marble Wilderness: Ruins and Representation in Italian Romanticism, 1775–1850.* Cambridge: Cambridge University Press.

Stacey, J. (1991). 'Feminine fascinations: forms of identification in star-audience relations', in Gledhill, 141–63.

——(1994). *Star Gazing: Hollywood Cinema and Female Spectatorship.* London: Routledge.

Stahl, H.-P. (1985). *Propertius: 'Love' and 'War'. Individual and State under Augustus.* Berkeley: University of California Press.

Staiger, J. (1995). *Bad Women: Regulating Sexuality in Early American Cinema.* Minneapolis: University of Minnesota Press.

Stapleton, M. L. (1996). *Harmful Eloquence: Ovid's* Amores *from Antiquity to Shakespeare*. Ann Arbor: University of Michigan Press.

Stevens, M. A. (1984) (ed.). *The Orientalists: Delacroix to Matisse. European Painters in North Africa and the Near East.* London: Royal Academy of Arts and Weidenfeld and Nicolson.

Stokes, M. (1999). 'Female audiences of the 1920s and early 1930s', in M. Stokes, and R. Maltby (eds.), *Identifying Hollywood's Audience: Cultural Identity and the Movies.* London: British Film Institute, 42–60.

Stroh, W. (1971). *Die römische Liebeselegie als werbende Dichtung.* Amsterdam: Hakkert.

Studlar, G. (1996). 'The perils of pleasure? Fan magazine discourse as women's commodified culture in the 1920s', in R. Abel (ed.), *Silent Film*. New Brunswick, NJ: Rutgers University Press, 263–97.

——(1997). '"Out-Salomeing Salome": Dance, the New Woman, and Fan Magazine Orientalism'. In Bernstein and Studlar, 99–129.

Sullivan, J. (1961). 'Two problems in Roman love elegy'. *TAPA* 92: 522–36.

——(1976). *Propertius: A Critical Introduction.* Cambridge: Cambridge University Press.

Sutherland, C. H. V., and Carson, R. A. G. (1984). *The Roman Imperial Coinage*, i. *Augustus to Vitellius.* London: Spink. Rev. edn. of H. Mattingly and E. A. Sydenham, 1923.

Syme, R. (1978). *History in Ovid.* Oxford: Clarendon Press.

Takács, S. A. (1995). *Isis and Sarapis in the Roman World.* Leiden: E. J. Brill.

Tarn, W. W. (1931). 'The Battle of Actium'. *JRS* 21: 173–99.

——(1932). 'Alexander Helios and the Golden Age'. *JRS* 22: 135–60.

——(1936). 'The Bucheum Stelae: A Note'. *JRS* 26: 187–9.

——and Charlesworth, M. P. (1934). 'The triumvirs'; 'The war of the East against the West'; 'The triumph of Octavian', in S. A. Cook, F. E. Adcock, and M. P. Charlesworth (eds.). *The Cambridge Ancient History*, [1st edn.], x. *The Augustan Empire 44 BC–AD 70.* Cambridge: Cambridge University Press, 31–126.

Thomas, R. F. (1983). 'Callimachus, the Victoria Berenices, and Roman poetry'. *CQ* 33: 92–113.

Thomas, V. (1989). *Shakespeare's Roman Worlds.* London: Routledge.

Thompson, D. B. (1973). *Ptolemaic Oinochoai and Portraits in Faience: Aspects of the Ruler-Cult.* Oxford Monographs on Classical Archaeology: Clarendon Press.

——(1994). 'Egypt, 146–31 BC', in J. A. Crook, A. Lintott, and E. Rawson (eds.), *The Cambridge Ancient History* [2nd edn], ix. *The Last Age of the Roman Republic, 146–43 BC.* Cambridge: Cambridge University Press, 310–26.

Thumim, J. (1992). *Celluloid Sisters: Women and Popular Cinema.* Basingstoke: Macmillan.

Todd, J. (1988). *Feminist Literary History. A Defence.* Cambridge: Polity with Basil Blackwell.

Toynbee, J. M. C. (1934). *The Hadrianic School: A Chapter in the History of Greek Art*. Cambridge: Cambridge University Press.

Treggiari, S. (1991). *Roman Marriage.* Iusti Coniuges *From the Time of Cicero to the Time of Ulpian*. Oxford: Clarendon Press.

Trevisani, C. (1885). *Gli autori drammatici contemporanei*, i. *Pietro Cossa.* Rome: Casa Editrice Carlo Verdesi.

Tulloch, J. (1990). *Television Drama: Agency, Audience and Myth.* London: Routledge.

Turner, B. S. (2000). *Orientalism: Early Sources*, i. *Readings in Orientalism.* London: Routledge.

Turner, F. M. (1999). 'Christians and pagans in Victorian novels', in Edwards, 173–87.

Uricchio, W., and Pearson, R. (1995). 'Italian spectacle and the U.S. market', in Cosandey and Albera, 95–105.

Vance, E. (1973). 'Warfare and the structure of thought in Virgil's Aeneid'. *Quaderni Urbinati di Cultura Classica*, 15: 111–62.

Vance, N. (1997). *The Victorians and Ancient Rome.* Oxford: Blackwell Publishers.

Vance, W. L. (1989). *America's Rome*, i. *Classical Rome.* New Haven: Yale University Press.

Van Sickle, J. (1974). 'Propertius (*uates*): Augustan ideology, topography and poetics in elegy IV, 1'. *Dialoghi di Archeologia*, 8: 116–45.

Veyne, P. (1983). *L'Élégie érotique romaine: l'amour, la poésie et l'occident*. Paris: Éditions du Seuil. Repr. 1988 in English trans. by D. Pellauer as *Roman Erotic Elegy: Love, Poetry, and the West*. Chicago: University of Chicago Press.

Viviani, C. (1997). 'Claudette Colbert: Le profil dérobé'. *Positif*, 434: 95–8.

Volkmann, H. (1958). *Cleopatra: A Study in Politics and Propaganda.* Trans. T. J. Cadoux. London: Elek Books.

Von Sternberg, J. (1965). *Fun in a Chinese Laundry.* New York: The Macmillan Co.

Walker, A. (1966). *The Celluloid Sacrifice: Aspects of Sex in the Movies.* London: Michael Joseph.

——(1990). *Elizabeth.* London: Weidenfeld and Nicolson.

Wallace-Hadrill, A. (1985). 'Propaganda and dissent?' *Klio* 67: 180–4.

——(1986). 'Image and authority in the coinage of Augustus'. *JRS* 76: 66–89.

Wanger, W., and Hyams, J. (1963). *My Life with Cleopatra*. London: Transworld Publishers.

Warden, J. (1978). 'Another would-be Amazon: Propertius 4,4,71–72'. *Hermes*, 106: 177–87.

——(1980). *Fallax opus: Poet and Reader in the Elegies of Propertius*. Toronto: University of Toronto Press.

——(1982). 'Epic into elegy: Propertius 4.9.70f'. *Hermes*, 110: 228–47.

Warner, M. (1976). *Alone of all her Sex*. London: Weidenfeld and Nicolson.

——(1987). *Monuments and Maidens: The Allegory of the Female Form*. London: Picador.

Weigall, A. (1923). *The Life and Times of Cleopatra Queen of Egypt: A Study in the Origin of the Roman Empire*. London, Thornton Butterworth. First edn. 1914.

Welch, K. E. (1995). 'Antony, Fulvia, and the ghost of Clodius in 47 BC'. *G&R* 42/2: 182–201.

Wellesley, K. (1969). 'Propertius' Tarpeia poem (IV.4)'. *Acta Classica Univ. Scient. Debrecen*. 5: 93–103.

Wendorf, R. (1996). *Joshua Reynolds: The Painter in Society*. London: National Portrait Gallery.

West, D. A. (1975). '*Cernere erat*: The Shield of Aeneas'. *PVS* 15: 1–6.

——(1995). *Horace Odes I: Carpe Diem*. Oxford: Clarendon Press.

West, S. (1985). 'Venus observed? A note on Callimachus, Fr. 110'. *CQ* 35: 61–6.

Wheeler, A. L. (1910*a*). 'Erotic teaching in Roman elegy and the Greek sources. Part I'. *CP* 5: 440–50.

——(1910*b*). 'Propertius as *praeceptor amoris*'. *CP* 5: 28–40.

——(1911). 'Erotic teaching in Roman elegy and the Greek sources. Part 2'. *CP* 6: 56–77.

Whitaker, R. (1983). *Myth and Personal Experience in Roman Love-Elegy*. Göttingen: Vandenhoeck and Ruprecht.

White, P. (1993). *Promised Verse: Poets in the Society of Augustan Rome*. Cambridge, Mass.: Harvard University Press.

Whitfield, J. H. (1963). 'La belle Charite: the Italian pastoral and the French seventeenth century'. *Italian Studies*, 18: 33–53.

Whitfield, S. J. (1991). *The Culture of the Cold War*. Baltimore: Johns Hopkins University Press.

Whitehorne, J. (1994). *Cleopatras.* London: Routledge.

Wiggers, N. (1976–7). 'Reconsideration of Propertius II.1'. *CJ* 72: 334–41.

Wilders, J. (1995) (ed.). *Antony and Cleopatra.* London: Routledge.

Wilkinson, L. P. (1966). 'The continuity of Propertius ii.13'. *CR* 16: 141–4.

Williams, C. (1999). *Roman Homosexuality: Ideologies of Masculinity in Classical Antiquity.* New York: Oxford University Press.

Williams, G. (1958). 'Some aspects of marriage ceremonies and ideals'. *JRS* 48: 16–29.

——(1968). *Tradition and Originality in Roman Poetry.* Oxford: Clarendon Press.

——(1980). *Figures of Thought in Roman Poetry.* New Haven: Yale University Press.

Wimmel, W. (1960). *Kallimachos in Rom: Die Nachfolge seines apologetischen Dichtens in der Augusteerzeit.* Wiesbaden: *Hermes* Einzelschriften, 16.

Winkler, J. J. (1990). *The Constraints of Desire: The Anthropology of Sex and Gender in Ancient Greece.* New York: Routledge.

Winkler, M. (2001). 'The Roman empire in American cinema after 1945', in Joshel *et al.*

Wirszubski, C. (1960). Libertas *as a Political Idea at Rome during the late Republic and early Principate.* Cambridge: Cambridge University Press.

Wiseman, T. P. (1985). *Catullus and his World: A Reappraisal.* Cambridge: Cambridge University Press.

Witt, R. E. (1971). *Isis in the Graeco-Roman World.* London: Thames and Hudson.

Wollen, P. (1987). 'Fashion/Orientalism/The Body'. *New Formations* 1: 5–34.

Wood, M. (1975). *America in the Movies: Or 'Santa Maria, It had Slipped my Mind'.* London: Secker and Warburg.

Wood, N. (1996) (ed.). *Antony and Cleopatra.* Buckingham: Open University Press.

Wood, S. E. (1992). 'Messalina, wife of Claudius: propaganda successes and failures of his reign'. *Journal of Roman Archaeology*, 5: 219–34.

——(1999). *Imperial Women: A Study in Public Images, 40* BC–AD *68.* Leiden: E. J. Brill.

Woodman, A. J. (1983). *Velleius Paterculus: The Caesarian and Augustan Narrative (2.41–93).* Cambridge: Cambridge University Press.

Woodman, T., and Powell, J. (1992) (eds.). *Author and Audience in Latin Literature.* Cambridge: Cambridge University Press.

Wyke, M. (1984). 'The Elegiac Woman and her Male Creators: Propertius and the Written Cynthia'. University of Cambridge PhD.

——(1987*a*). 'Written women: Propertius' *scripta puella*'. *JRS* 77: 47–61.

——(1987*b*). 'The Elegiac Woman at Rome'. *PCPS* 213, (NS 33): 153–78.

——(1989*a*). 'Mistress and metaphor in Augustan elegy'. *Helios* 16/1: 25–47.

——(1989*b*). 'Reading female flesh: *Amores* 3.1', in Averil Cameron (ed.), *History as Text.* London: Duckworth, 111–43.

——(1989*c*). 'In pursuit of love, the poetic self and a process of reading: Augustan elegy in the 1980s'. *JRS* 79: 165–73.

——(1992). 'Augustan Cleopatras: female power and poetic authority', in Powell, 98–104.

——(1994*a*). 'Woman in the mirror: The rhetoric of adornment in the Roman world', in Archer *et al.*, 134–51.

——(1994*b*). 'Taking the woman's part: engendering Roman love elegy'. *Ramus*, 23: 110–28.

——(1997). *Projecting the Past: Ancient Rome, Cinema and History.* New York: Routledge.

——(1999). 'Screening ancient Rome in the new Italy', in Edwards, 188–204.

——and Montserrat, D. (forthcoming). 'Glamour Girls: Cleomania in Mass Culture', in Miles.

Yardley, J. C. (1987). 'Propertius 4.5, Ovid *Amores* 1.6 and Roman comedy'. *PCPS* 213 (NS 33): 179–89.

——(1991). 'The symposium in Roman elegy', in W. J. Slater (ed.), *Dining in a Classical Context.* Ann Arbor: University of Michigan Press, 149–55.

Yavetz, Z. (1984). 'The *Res Gestae* and Augustus' Public Image', in Millar and Segal, 1–36.

Yeğenoğlu, M. (1998). *Colonial Fantasies: Towards a Feminist Reading of Orientalism.* Cambridge: Cambridge University Press.

Zanker, P. (1988). *The Power of Images in the Age of Augustus.* Trans. A. Shapiro. Michigan: Michigan University Press.

Zeitlin, F. (1978). 'The dynamics of misogyny: myth and mythmaking in the *Oresteia*'. *Arethusa*, 11: 149–81.

—— (1990). 'Playing the Other: theater, theatricality, and the feminine in Greek drama', in J. J. Winkler and F. I. Zeitlin (eds.), *Nothing to do with Dionysos? Athenian Drama in its Social Context.* Princeton: Princeton University Press, 63–96.

Zeydel, E. H. (1944) (ed.). *The Ship of Fools by Sebastian Brant.* New York: Columbia University Press.

Ziegler, C. (1994). 'Cleopatra or the seductions of the East', in Humbert *et al.*, 552–61.

# Index of Classical Passages Cited

# *General Index*